Albert Moll

Hypnotism

Albert Moll

Hypnotism

ISBN/EAN: 9783742882493

Manufactured in Europe, USA, Canada, Australia, Japa

Cover: Foto ©Thomas Meinert / pixelio.de

Manufactured and distributed by brebook publishing software
(www.brebook.com)

Albert Moll

Hypnotism

THE CONTEMPORARY SCIENCE SERIES.

EDITED BY HAVELOCK ELLIS.

HYPNOTISM.

.

HYPNOTISM.

BY

ALBERT MOLL

FOURTH EDITION, REVISED AND ENLARGED.

LONDON:
WALTER SCOTT, LTD.,
PATERNOSTER SQUARE.
1897.

PREFACE

TO THE THIRD EDITION.

———•———

VARIOUS recent researches in the field of hypnotism
have rendered it necessary to remodel in part the
earlier edition of this work. I have brought the
history of hypnotism down to the present, and have
throughout, I trust, presented the subject in its
present state. In accordance with a wish which
has been expressed by many, I have especially
developed the chapter on "The Medical Aspects
of Hypnotism."

ALBERT MOLL.

PREFACE

TO THE SECOND EDITION.

———•———

I HAVE substantially enlarged the second edition of my book, and have completely remodelled several sections ; for example, the theoretical part. The appearance of some new works on hypnotism and some later experiments of my own made these alterations advisable.

I have willingly yielded to wishes expressed to me in numerous criticisms on the first edition. I cannot, however, yield to what several critics desired, namely, that I should write the book for physicians only, because I believe that hypnotism is a province of psychology, and is in consequence of as much interest to psychologists and lawyers as to doctors In order, however, not to weary the latter with explanations of medical expressions inserted in the text, I shall give these in the index which is to be found at the end of the book.

PREFACE.

It is a pleasant duty to offer my tribute of thanks to all those who have helped me with advice in the preparation of the second edition. I owe gratitude in particular to Prof. August Forel, of Zürich, and to Dr. Eduard Hartmann, of Gross-Lichterfeld, as well as to Drs. Max Dessoir and Arthur Sperling, of Berlin.

A. MOLL.

BERLIN, *January*, 1890.

PREFACE

TO THE FIRST EDITION.

————o————

IN writing this book I was guided by the wish to offer to the reader a survey of all that is most important in the whole province of hypnotism. While in the numerous and detailed works on this subject which have lately appeared, sometimes its therapeutics and sometimes its forensic significance have been exclusively brought forward, I, for my part, have endeavoured to treat hypnotism broadly and from various points of view, avoiding irrelevant matter ; and, being aided by my own experiments, I was in a position to add much that was new to what was already known.

I here express my hearty thanks to Prof. August Forel, Director of the Cantonal Lunatic Asylum in Zürich, who placed several of his most valuable experiments at my disposal for this book ; also to Dr. Max Dessoir, of Berlin, who has assisted me both with his wide acquaintance with the literature of hypnotism and with much good advice; finally, to all who have in other ways helped me in the work.

A. MOLL.

BERLIN, *April,* 1889.

CONTENTS.

———o———

CHAPTER III.

CHAPTER IV.

CHAPTER V.

CHAPTER VI.

CHAPTER VII.

CHAPTER VIII.

CONTENTS.

HYPNOTISM.

HYPNOTISM.

CHAPTER I.

THE HISTORY OF HYPNOTISM.

In order to understand the gradual development of modern hypnotism from animal magnetism, we must distinguish two points: firstly, that there are human beings who can exercise a personal influence over others, either by direct contact or even from a distance; and, secondly, the fact that particular psychical states can be induced in human beings by certain physical processes.

This second fact especially has long been known among the Oriental peoples, and was utilized by them for religious purposes. Kiesewetter attributes the early soothsaying by means of precious stones to hypnosis, which was induced by steadily gazing at the stones. This is also true of divination by looking into vessels and crystals, as the Egyptians have long been in the habit of doing, and as has often been done in Europe: by Cagliostro, for example. These hypnotic phenomena are also found to have existed several thousand years ago among the Persian magi

1

(Fischer), as well as up to the present day among
Indian yogis and fakirs, who throw themselves into
the hypnotic state by means of fixation of the gaze.
Relying on a statement of Stein's, Preyer believes that
the condition of a Japanese religious leader, who lived
long before Christ, was also an autohypnosis, and that
this kind of devotion came to Japan from India.
Preyer, to whom we owe various interesting historical
investigations in this field, also believes that the religious exercises of the Montanists, a Christian sect of
the second century, were of autohypnotic character;
he reached this conclusion on the strength of information given to him by Harnack. The Montanists were
sometimes called Taskodrugites, because they were
accustomed to hold the finger to the nose and mouth
during prayer. Brugsch Pasha also tells of genuine
hypnotic conditions which were produced in the
Egyptian Gnostic schools of the first century during
divine worship. At such times the eyes were closed
and various hallucinations appeared, especially apparitions of gods. The same thing has occurred since
the eleventh century in many convents of the Greek
Church (Fischer). Among the best known are the
Hesychasts, or Omphalopsychics, of Mount Athos,
who hypnotize themselves by gazing at the umbilicus.
The fact has often been verified in popular opinion,
apart from these religious customs, that it is possible
to induce sleep by looking fixedly at a certain point;
for example, at the tip of the nose. Hypnotic conditions appear often to occur among uncivilized
peoples, as is clearly to be gathered from the information of many travellers, and as Bastian, a chief
authority on ethnology, has particularly shown. He,
as well as Stoll, has pointed out the near relationship

of many phenomena among uncivilized populations to hypnotism. Bastian believes that a more exact study of hypnotism by individual travellers would be of great service to popular psychology; the phenomena which occur spontaneously among uncivilized populations could be more carefully examined and brought into closer relation to hypnotism.

The ethnologist Stoll also, in his laborious work, *Suggestion und Hypnosis in der Völkerpsychologie,* gives many facts concerning hypnotic conditions among various peoples and in various ages. He mentions such states among the ancient Persians and Jews; he investigates the manifestations of suggestion in Islam, among African races, and studies with special detail the different tribes of Central America and Australia. While some have asserted that auto-hypnotic states arise more frequently among the savage than among the civilised, Stoll is of opinion that no such distinction is possible, since even among civilized races the characteristics of savages still lie at the foundation. Nietzsche, also, expresses the opinion that certain dreamy conditions which among the civilized occur during sleep, among savages often occur in the waking condition. "We are all like savages in our dreams. The perfect clearness of dream ideas, which pre-supposes an unconditional faith in their reality, recalls conditions of primitive humanity when hallucinations were extraordinarily prevalent." In more recent times the facts communicated by Michaud concerning hypnotism as practised by the Annamites for religious purposes may be mentioned. Hypnosis is attained by the subject fixing his gaze on two burning sticks attached behind one ear of the magician, who turns his head.

Independently of this there has existed at all times in many quarters the belief that particular individuals could influence their fellows by the exercise of certain powers. This influence could be used as well for good as for evil. Of the first use we are reminded by the laying on of hands in benediction; also by the healing by touch which was obtained by the old Egyptians and other Oriental nations: numerous old monuments testify to this. If the meaning of many of them is not clear, in the case of others hardly a doubt exists as to the right interpretation. The Ebers Papyrus also, which represents the state of Egyptian medicine before the year 1552 B.C., contains a statement, according to which the laying of hands on the head of a patient plays a part in his treatment.[1] We see the same thing later in the cures which King Pyrrhus and the Emperor Vespasian are said to have effected.

It is known that Francis I. of France, and other French kings up to Charles X., healed by the imposition of hands. We see here already that this individual power took effect through contact; however, this appears not to have been always necessary, as is witnessed by the widespread and continued belief in sorcerers, who could bewitch other persons. The belief in sorcerers indicates that contact was by no means always necessary to produce an effect, which, it is pretended, could be induced even from a great distance.

This belief in the special powers of certain individuals still exists among uncivilized and even

[1] For the knowledge of this I have to thank a private communication from Dr. Heinrich Joachim, of Berlin, who has made a German translation of the Ebers Papyrus.

civilized peoples. Healing by breathing and by
contact, as Barrère described it in Guyana a century ago, as well as similar processes described by
Father Bryert in California, must here be reckoned.
Numerous facts of the same order may be found in
the writings of travellers, and especially in the works
of Bastian and Stoll. Among the Mohammedans also
there are persons who enjoy the reputation of pos-
sessing special powers of healing. Whoever has
seen the howling dervishes of the East will have
observed that the Sheik, in attempting to heal the
sick, especially children, breathes on them, or touches
them, and often treads with the foot.

The question here is only of solitary facts in
which no scientific system is discoverable. A system
presents itself to us only after the end of the Middle
Ages. It develops itself out of the doctrine of the
influence of the stars upon men which, as is known,
astrology puts forward. Even nowadays we find
remains of it, especially in the belief in the influence
which the moon is supposed to exercise. It is well
known that many people expect warts and so forth
to disappear as the moon wanes ; while more modern
doctors of mental diseases called in the influence of
the moon to explain special periodical mental disturbances.

At the end of the Middle Ages, Theophrastus
Paracelsus in particular (1530) came forward with
the theory of the effect of the heavenly bodies on
mankind, more especially on their diseases. Out
of this the belief gradually developed itself that not
only did the stars influence men, but that men also
mutually influenced each other—a belief which, as we
have already seen, had arisen sporadically.

Van Helmont taught with more precision that man possessed a power by means of which he could magnetically affect others, particularly the sick. Perhaps Helmont obtained the main features of his doctrine from Goclenius.

The Scotchman Maxwell maintained something of the same kind later (about 1600). He attributed to the human excreta, and also to mummies, an effect upon human beings ; they could be utilized for the curing of diseases (sympathetic cures); also men could cure themselves of diseases by transferring them to animals or plants. A remnant of this system developed by Maxwell still exists in country places, where people occasionally apply excreta to their wounds. Maxwell assumed in particular a vital spirit of the universe (*spiritus vitalis*), by means of which all bodies were related to each other. This vital spirit seems to be the same thing which Mesmer later called the universal fluid.

In the beginning of the eighteenth century we find Santanelli in Italy asserting a like proposition. Everything material possesses a radiating atmosphere which operates magnetically. Santanelli, however, recognized the great influence of the imagination (Avé Lallemant).

Although the foundation of the doctrine of animal magnetism was thus laid, universal attention was first drawn to it by Mesmer,[1] a Viennese doctor (1734-1815). He studied in his dissertation the influence of the planets upon human bodies. At the

[1] The name is often written "Messmer," instead of "Mesmer"; the latter spelling is, however, decidedly the correct one. At least it is so found in the book which Mesmer himself brought out—"General Explanations of Magnetism,"

beginning Mesmer made great use of the magnet in the treatment of diseases. In the year 1775 he sent out a circular-letter, particularly addressed to several academies. In this he maintained the existence of animal magnetism, by means of which persons could influence each other; he, however, distinguished animal magnetism completely from the magnetism of metals, which later he ceased to employ. The only academy which replied to him was that of Berlin, at Sulzer's instigation, and its reply was unfavourable. However, about this time Mesmer was nominated a member of the Academy of Bavaria.

Mesmer made much use of "animal magnetism" in the treatment of diseases. He cured at first by contact, but believed later that different objects of wood, glass, iron, and so forth, were also capable of receiving the magnetism. Consequently he made use of these as means for conveying his magnetism, especially later in Paris, where he went in 1778, chiefly in consequence of the enmities he had aroused in Vienna. In Paris Mesmer constructed the *baquet*, which was magnetized by him, and which was supposed to transmit the magnetism. Bailly represents it as a very complicated apparatus; an oak chest or tub, with appendages of iron, &c. Mesmer found many adherents in Paris—Dr. Deslon joined him first of all—but he also encountered many opponents. Several scientific Commissions which examined the question pronounced, in 1784, against the existence of animal magnetism, particularly the one to which

by Mesmer, Carlsruhe, 1815. Mesmer's friend, Wolfart, and his biographer, Justinus Kerner, write the name also with one *s*.

Bailly was reporter. One of the members of the Commission, Jussieu, made, however, a separate report, which was not considered decisive. No one, however, denied that far-reaching effects were produced by imagination; it was only denied that there was a physical force resembling true magnetism. In spite of all attacks, Mesmer made disciples. His pupils and successors are generally called mesmerists, and the doctrine of animal magnetism is also called mesmerism, vital magnetism, bio-magnetism, or zoo-magnetism.

I do not wish to join the contemptible group of Mesmer's professional slanderers. He is dead, and can no longer defend himself from those who disparage him without taking into consideration the circumstances or the time in which he lived. Against the universal opinion that he was avaricious, I remark that in Vienna, as well as later in Mörsburg and Paris, he always helped the poor without reward. I believe that he erred in his teaching, but think it is just to attack this only, and not his personal character. Mesmer was much slandered in his lifetime, and these attacks upon him have been continued till quite lately. Let us, however, consider more closely in what his alleged great crime consisted. He believed in the beginning that he could heal by means of a magnet, and later that he could do so by means of a personal indwelling force which he could transfer to the *baquet*. This was evidently his firm belief, and he never made a secret of it. Others believed either that the patient's mere imagination played a part, or that Mesmer produced his effects by some concealed means. Then, by degrees, arose the legend that Mesmer possessed some secret by means of which he was able to produce effects on people such as the cure of diseases, but that he would not reveal it. In reality the question was not at all of a secret purposely kept back by him, since he imagined, and always insisted, that he exercised some individual force. Finally, if he used this supposititious individual force for the purpose of earning money, he did nothing worse than do modern physicians and proprietors of institutions who likewise do not follow their calling from pure love of their neighbour, but seek to earn their own living by it, as they are quite justified in doing. Mesmer did not behave worse than those who nowadays discover a new drug, and regard the manufacture of it as a means of enriching themselves. Let us at last be just and cease to slander Mesmer, who did only what is done by the people just mentioned. That those who defame Mesmer know the least about his teaching, and have the least acquaintance with his works, is very clearly shown by a whole series of books about modern hypnotism.

A follower of Mesmer, Chastenet de Puységur, whose good faith cannot be doubted (Dechambre), discovered, in 1784, a state which was named artificial somnambulism. Apart from some falsely interpreted phenomena (thought-transference, clairvoyance, &c.), the chief characteristic of this state was a sleep, in which the ideas and actions of the magnetized person could be directed by the magnetizer. Whether Mesmer knew of this condition or not is uncertain, but it seems to me probable that he did. About the same time Pétetin, a doctor of Lyons, occupied himself with magnetism ; besides catalepsy Pétetin describes phenomena of sense transference (hearing with the stomach). The French Revolution and the wars repressed the investigation of magnetism in France till about the year 1813.

In Germany animal magnetism was recognized at the same time in two different places—on the Upper Rhine and in Bremen. In the year 1786 Lavater paid a visit to Bremen, and exhibited the magnetizing processes to several doctors, particularly to Wienholt, through whom Albers, Bicker, and later also Heineken, were likewise made acquainted with magnetism. Bremen was for a long time a focus of the new doctrine ; the town was often even brought into bad repute in the rest of Germany on account of the general dislike to animal magnetism. About the same time the doctrine of animal magnetism spread from Strassburg over the Rhine provinces; Böckmann, of Carlsruhe, and Gmelin, of Heilbronn, occupied themselves with it ; later they were joined by Pezold, of Dresden. Getting encouragement from Bremen, people began to make experiments in other parts of Germany. Selle, of Berlin, brought forward, in 1789, a series of experiments made at the Charité, by which he confirmed a part of the alleged phenomena, but excluded all that was super-normal (clairvoyance).

Notwithstanding the early dislike to it, magnetism finally gained ground in Germany. In particular, animal magnetism flourished much in Germany during the first twenty years of this century. In Austria only it met with ill-fortune; the exercise of magnetism was even forbidden in the whole of Austria in 1815. I do not enter more fully into the details of the teaching of different individuals, as they have no close connection with hypnotism. In the main two different tendencies can be distinguished—one critical and scientific, and the other mystical (Avé Lallemant). While the first had the preponderance in the beginning, later on the last came to the fore and led to the downfall of magnetism. Besides the scientific inquirers already mentioned I may name Treviranus, Schelling, Kieser, Passavant, Kluge ; also Pfaff, who attacked clairvoyance in particular; and further, Stieglitz and Hufeland. The last, who was at first a decided opponent, acknowledged certain facts later on, but excluded all the super-normal. He thus drew upon himself the hatred of the mystics. Even in the year 1834 Hufeland expressed himself as recognizing, to a certain extent, the existence of animal magnetism and its value in healing. Among the mystics I may mention Ziermann, Eschenmayer, Justinus Kerner, the well-known poet and editor of the " Seeress of Prevorst." Wolfart of Berlin must here be especially mentioned.

In the year 1812 the Prussian Government sent Wolfart to Mesmer at Frauenfeld, in order that he might there make himself acquainted with the subject. Wolfart came back a thorough adherent of Mesmer, introduced magnetism into the hospital treatment, and afterwards became a professor at the university. A prize which was offered by the Berlin Academy of Sciences, at the request of the Prussian Government, for an Essay on Animal Magnetism was, it appears, withdrawn. However, magnetism flourished so much at that time in Berlin that, as Wurm relates, the Berlin physicians placed a monument on the grave of Mesmer at Mörsburg, and theological candidates received instruction in physiology, pathology, and the treatment of sickness by vital magnetism. It was Mesmer's idea to teach it to the clergy. The well-known physician Koreff, also, whom Varnhagen von Ense mentions as one of the most gifted of men, and of whom Cuvier said that if he were not already in Paris he must be entreated to come there, interested himself much in magnetism, and often made use of it for healing purposes so long as he lived in Berlin.

In the rest of Germany also, many inquirers occupied themselves with animal magnetism ; in several universities a knowledge of the phenomena was spread by means of lectures — for example, by

Wolfart in Berlin, and by Bartels in Breslau.   As many authors inform us, a royal order in February, 1817, made magnetization in Prussia the privilege of physicians only; but in the official code of laws nothing is to be found on the subject.   At the same time such laws were enacted in other countries. Magnetism was introduced everywhere, especially in Russia and Denmark.   In Switzerland and Italy it was at first received with less sympathy.

After Mesmer had left France in the time of the Revolution, in order, after prolonged travels, to settle himself at his native place on the Bodensee, magnetism only regained its importance in France at the beginning of the present century.   In Germany there were more physicians who turned to the study of animal magnetism, which in France fell for the most part into the hands of laymen.   Among the most earnest inquirers Deleuze must here be mentioned. But the whole doctrine received a great impetus through the Abbé Faria, who came to Paris from India.   In 1814-15 he showed by experiments, whose results he published, that no unknown force was necessary for the production of the phenomena; the cause of the sleep, said he, was in the person who was to be sent to sleep; all was subjective.   This is the main principle of hypnotism and of suggestion, of which Faria even then made use in inducing sleep. Two other investigators in France must be mentioned, Bertrand and Noizet, who paved the way for the doctrine of suggestion, in spite of much inclination to animal magnetism.   In 1820 experiments were begun in the Paris hospitals, chiefly under the direction of Du Potet.   At the proposal of Foissac, and at the recommendation of Husson, the Paris

Academy of Medicine in 1826 appointed a Commission to examine the question of animal magnetism. The Commission worked for six years and pronounced a favourable opinion in 1831; but the Academy was evidently not convinced. In spite of several further experiments, for example those of Berna, no other result was obtained. Particularly because the chief emphasis was laid on the mystical side of the question the struggle was made substantially easier to the opponents of mesmerism, among whom Dubois was prominent.

The candidates for the Burdin prize for clairvoyance, Pigeaire, Hublier, and Teste, failed to obtain it; and in 1840 the Academy declined to discuss the question further.

Meanwhile, although in Germany another series of investigators were busying themselves with mesmerism, on the whole, after about 1820, the belief in magnetism declined more and more; the cognate phenomena also received hardly any attention. This retrogression was caused as much by the rise of the exact natural sciences as by the unscientific and uncritical hankering after mystical phenomena, which could not but revolt serious investigators. Mesmerism flourished relatively the longest in Bremen and in Hamburg, where Siemers was its advocate; also in Bavaria, where Hensler and Ennemoser, between the years 1830 and 1840, still represented it. In other towns we likewise still find a number of thoughtful inquirers, who allowed themselves to be influenced neither by the passion for the wonderful nor by the attacks of the principal opponents of magnetism, and who sought to defend their position in a thoroughly scientific manner; Most, Fr. Fischer, and Hirschel, may be mentioned. It may also be emphatically insisted that a series of philosophers have believed firmly and persistently in the reality of the phenomena, although not much regard has been paid to this fact. They have even founded scientific systems upon the phenomena : *i.e.,* Schopenhauer, Carus, Pfnor. Although magnetism lost many adherents in the scientific world, among the people the belief in the mysterious force continued prevalent. The more science drew back the more shameless became the cheating and fraud ; although in Germany there were fewer attempts to make money by it than in France. The abuse grew so strong that the Catholic Church several times came forward to interfere. But the more the extravagance and cheating increased the less inclined were serious-minded persons to interest themselves in these matters. In Germany, however, as well as in Austria, there were always a few scattered persons who used animal magnetism for healing purposes. In Hungary, Count Szapary became specially well known in this connection.

In England, in spite of the efforts of the London physicians Elliotson and Ashburner, magnetism could get no footing. A succession of investigators and writers, however, concerning whom Sinnett has furnished details, actively pursued the matter. Thus Townsend made experiments, while Scoresby occupied himself in writing about animal magnetism. Lee at the same time made experiments in clairvoyance. When the French magnetizer, La Fontaine, exhibited magnetic experiments in Manchester in 1841, Braid, a doctor of that place, interested himself in the question. He showed, like Faria, but with more method, that the phenomena were of subjective nature. By carefully fixing the eyes upon any object a state of sleep was induced, which Braid called " Hypnotism."[1]

In the foregoing sketch I have followed the history of animal magnetism down to the middle of the present century. The historical development begins with the popular opinion that, in the first place, there are certain men who can exercise a personal influence over others, and that, in the second place, by means of certain manipulations peculiar psychical conditions can be called forth. The scientific development of hypnotism now begins. In this we see, to a certain extent, a combination of the two processes just mentioned. That is to say, it is found that special manipulations can call forth a changed mental condition, hypnosis; it can, however, also be shown that when a man calls this out it is not by virtue of any peculiar and mysterious unknown power—animal magnetism—as was formerly supposed.[2]

At first Braid considered hypnotism to be identical with the mesmeric states, but he soon gave up this view; he was of opinion that the two conditions were only analogous, and he left mesmerism in an independent position by the side of hypnotism. Braid was acquainted with the cataleptic phenomena, and certain suggestions, and used hypnotism therapeutically; in particular he used it to perform painless surgical operations. Already, earlier, mesmerism had

---

[1] This name was not, however, altogether new, as already Hénin de Cuvillers had talked of "hypnoscope" and "hypnobat," with reference to magnetic states (Max Dessoir).

[2] Braid's later works, bearing on the significance of hypnotism, show great progress as compared with his earlier writings.

been several times made use of in surgical operations.
In the result we see mesmerism and Braidism, as the
state investigated by Braid is occasionally called, used
by different persons for the like purpose. Among
those who used animal magnetism or hypnotism in
surgery, the following deserve to be mentioned:
Loysel, Fontan, Topham, Joly, Ribaud, Kiaro (according to Max Dessoir), Varges, Herzog. Hypnotism, however, found no general acceptation, in spite
of the fact that a well-known physiologist, Carpenter,
as well as Laycock, James Simpson, Mayo, and
others, confirmed the facts.

In America, meanwhile, animal magnetism had
taken root; New Orleans was, for a long time, its
chief centre. A few years later than Braid, Grimes
appeared in the United States, and, independently of
Braid, obtained like results. His methods were not
essentially different from those of Braid; the states
produced by Grimes were called electro-biological.
Among his adherents Dods and Stone must be
mentioned. In 1850 Darling came from America
to England, where he exhibited the phenomena of
electro-biology; their identity with those of hypnotism was soon recognized. Durand de Gros,[1] a French
doctor who had lived in America, returned in 1853 to
Europe, and exhibited the phenomena of electro-
biology in several countries, but aroused little
interest.

Braid's discovery was first made known in Bordeaux
by Azam, in 1859. Encouraged by Bazin and mocked
by others, Azam made some hypnotic experiments;
he communicated the results to Broca in Paris. The
latter discussed hypnotism before the *Académie des*

[1] He wrote under the pseudonym of Philips.

Sciences. It was made use of several times to perform painless operations; Velpeau, Follin, and
Guérineau in particular made experiments. Other
physicians, Demarquay and Giraud-Teulon, as well
as Berend in Berlin, Pincus in Glogau, and Heyfelder
in St. Petersburg, showed the slight value of hypnotism for surgery. In consequence of this it found no
acceptance in medicine at that time. The experiments
of Lasègue in 1865, when he obtained cataleptic
phenomena by closing the eyes, aroused no particular
interest. We only find here and there, especially
in some English scientific works, brief 'notices of
hypnotism or mesmerism, as in Thomas Watson's
Lectures (1875), in Tanner's *Practice of Medicine*
(1875), and in Quain's *Dictionary of Medicine*, in
which Bastian urged the need for fresh investigation.

⟨Meanwhile, Liébeault, who later removed to Nancy,
had made himself familiar with the phenomena of
hypnotism and animal magnetism. The last he
endeavoured to refute, and he became the real
founder of the therapeutics of suggestion. His book,
published in 1866 (Du Sommeil, &c.), which is even
to-day very well worth reading, contains his ideas;
they remained little known, and the author was much
laughed at.

Suggestion had undoubtedly been applied before Liébeault's
time, in the waking as well as in the hypnotic condition. We
find even in the literature of mesmerism many indications that
the followers of animal magnetism frequently regarded speech
as the bearer of magnetism; for example, Ennemoser and
Szapery. In Braid's later writings there is also frequent reference to the great influence of verbal suggestion. It was, however, Liébeault who first fully and methodically recognized the
value of suggestion. It must not be forgotten also that it was

2

through Liébeault, as we shall see, that Bernheim was induced
to turn to the study of hypnosis, and that many other investigators
occupied themselves with the subject. Liébeault is, therefore,
of the first importance, since the later historical development
begins with him. That some earlier writers, however, knew
much that he more fully worked out, cannot be doubted.

Independently of Liébeault, Charles Richet came
forward in Paris in 1875 to contend for the real
existence of hypnotism, which he called "Somnambulisme provoqué." In the year 1878 Charcot began
his public classes, in which he directed attention to
the physical states of hystero-epileptics during
hypnosis; in 1881 Paul Richer published, in his
book on "La grande hystérie," many experiments
performed on the lines of Charcot. Among the later
pupils of Charcot I should name: Binet, Féré, Gilles
de la Tourette, Babinski, Barth, Bourneville, Regnard.

About 1880 many investigators in Germany, particularly Weinhold, Opitz, and Rühlmann in Chemnitz,
Heidenhain and Berger in Breslau, besides Möbius,
Benedikt, Eulenburg, Senator, Adamkiewicz, Börner,
Meyersohn, and Bäumler, occupied themselves with
the subject, incited thereto by the exhibitions of
Hansen. The investigations of hypnotism in animals,
published in 1872 by Czermak, and after him by
Preyer, aroused no lasting interest. The movement
of 1880 also soon ceased, although Preyer often
pointed out the importance of Braidism.

Many opinions of early investigators in the field of hypnotism
have been refuted by later writers. Of some authors scarcely
a single conclusion has been left standing. Even Charcot,
according to many, must be reckoned among these. Nevertheless, I consider that we owe thanks to all the serious early
investigators of hypnotism, on account of the attention they

drew to the matter, even if all their conclusions are refuted. It is much easier to push on a work which is already well advanced than to lay the first stones on which the structure must be erected. Among the investigators who, in my opinion, deserve enduring gratitude, even although a greater part or nearly all their results are surpassed by later workers, must be reckoned Charcot and Heidenhain. Others who in the early period occupied themselves with hypnosis have returned to it more recently, and with due reference to later investigations. I may here mention Preyer and Eulenburg, who in 1880 and earlier, as well as more recently, have done much to elucidate this subject. It is matter for regret that now and again one finds an investigator apparently viewing with disfavour new results which oppose his early views, and bitterly attacking them. A type of this kind, such as we fortunately seldom meet, is furnished by Benedikt.

The researches of Charcot likewise had little effect upon the further pursuit of the inquiry—as little as had the book of Prosper Despine on Somnambulism, which appeared in 1880. It is true that in some hospitals investigations were undertaken, particularly by Dumontpallier in Paris, by Pitres in Bordeaux, also by Ladame in Geneva, and later by Binswanger in Jena; these researches were, however, sporadic.

Only when a second medical school in France— that of Nancy — approached the subject, did the interest become more general. Professor Bernheim, of Nancy, who, incited by Dumont, had studied the question with Liébeault, and had accepted the latter's views, published a book, " De la Suggestion," &c., in 1884. He gave in it examples of the curative effects of hypnotism, the phenomena of which, he says, are entirely of a psychical nature. Besides this, in Nancy, Beaunis worked at the physiology of hypnotism, and Liégeois at the forensic side of the question Then followed in France the contest between the schools of

Charcot and of Nancy, in which the latter, however,
has gained ground more and more, even in Paris.

People began to busy themselves with hypnotism,
in other countries as well as France, chiefly on the
lines of the school of Nancy.   It is true that, as has
already been mentioned, the study of hypnotism had
been begun in various countries in connection with
the work of Charcot.   As, however, in consequence
of the rather one-sided standpoint of these investigations, the different inquirers failed to find any lasting
satisfaction, even the name of Charcot was powerless
to give a general extension to the study of hypnotism.
Only when the school of Nancy created a surer basis
for hypnotism by a profounder psychological conception could people elsewhere begin to devote themselves on a larger scale to the study of it.   In France
itself the importance of the Nancy investigators was
more and more recognized.   A. Voisin, Bérillon,
Déjerine, Luys, Cullerre, Nizet, Laloy, Regnoult, and
numerous other experimenters occupied themselves
with the subject, and even those who had at first considered the experiments of Charcot to be of higher
value turned in larg: numbers to the school of Nancy.
Hypnotism found an entrance to other countries, and
it appears that in the north of Europe a relatively
greater number of investigators interested themselves
in it than in France.   In Belgium the eminent psychologist Delbœuf, of Liège, smoothed the way for it.
Several lawyers, like Bonjean and Mallar, interested
themselves in the new science, especially in its
forensic aspects, and among physicians may be mentioned Van Velsen and Maes.   Numerous physicians—
Van Renterghem, Van Leden, De Jong, and others—
made use of hypnotism in Holland for curative pur-

poses. In Denmark, Sweden, and Norway we find also a series of inquirers—Johannessen, Sell, Fränkel, Carlsen, Schleisner, Velander, and most particularly Wetterstrand, of Stockholm, who uses hypnotism therapeutically to a very great extent; also in Russia, where Stembo, Tokarski, Becterew, Rossolimo, and Meyer should be named, although the Government have put many difficulties in the way of studying hypnotism. In Greece, Italy, and Spain, where Pulido used suggestion therapeutically many years before Bernheim, hypnotism is gaining in importance. Among Italian investigators may be mentioned Lombroso, Belfiore, Morselli, Tonoli, as well as Olinto del Torto, the editor of *Magnetismo e Ipnotismo*, Ellero, and Ehrenfreund.

In England there exists a society of private investigators—the Society for Psychical Research—which, besides examining certain mysterious phenomena, also studies hypnotism. Gurney and F. Myers must here be especially mentioned. Before this, in England, Hack Tuke had often called attention to hypnotism and its therapeutic value. He was, however, unable to excite any enduring interest in the matter, nor were Gamgee, who in 1878 reported on his observations of Charcot's hypnotic experiments, and Whitehead, who in 1885 wrote concerning some experiments at Manchester, more successful (Felkin). At the same time, as Felkin remarks, numerous works dealing with hypnotism appeared from time to time in England, as by Gasquet in 1887, by Karl Grossmann in 1888, by Foy, and especially by Preyer, who spoke concerning hypnotism at the British Medical Association Meeting in 1880. Among more recent investigators in England I may mention Lloyd

Tuckey, who has made many therapeutical applications of hypnosis, Felkin in Scotland, who has written a small but careful and interesting book on hypnotism, as well as Bramwell, Kingsbury, Hart, and Vincent. In spite of numerous opponents, among whom Norman Kerr and Burney may be named, hypnotism has thus won citizenship in England. At the Birmingham meeting of the British Medical Association in 1890, a committee of physicians was appointed to test hypnotism psychologically, physiologically, and therapeutically. This committee, which included among its members Hack Tuke, Langley, Needham, Broadbent, Kingsbury, and Clouston, presented its report in July 1892. In this report not only was the reality of hypnotism recognized, and its symptoms described, but hypnosis was warmly recommended for therapeutic purposes, especially for insomnia, pain, and numerous functional disorders. The results in dipsomania were mentioned as peculiarly encouraging.

In other quarters of the globe, especially in America, hypnotism had also awakened great interest. Beard had already long ago interested himself in the question. Unluckily his investigations are not known to the extent which they certainly merit. In 1881 Beard also attempted, in London, to interest European physicians in hypnotism. The results he attained were the opposite of those he desired, as may be seen from the writings of various eye-witnesses, Mortimer Granville, Donkin, and Crichton Browne, in the *British Medical Journal*, although the first-named, Granville, at the International Medical Congress in London in 1881, had himself referred to the possibility of hypnotizing the insane. Although Beard's exertions were at first fruitless, at a later period many in America occupied themselves with the problem of hypnosis. Among recent investigators may be named Hami'ton Osgood, Lee, Gerrish, Hulst, Vermeren, Axtell, Booth. In various univers'ties and colleges of the United States the study of hypnotism has been carried on; I may specially refer to Miss Whiton Calkins at Wellesley College. An American Society for Psychical Research, now affiliated to the English Society, has also been formed in the United States. In several of the South American States serious inquirers have turned to the study of hypnotic phenomena; for example, Octavio Maira and David Benavente in Chili. In Cuba, Villamonga and Diaz may be named.

Meanwhile, through Forel, hypnotism had gained ground, more particularly in Switzerland, and there is no doubt that the great movement spread to Germany from thence. Obersteiner of Vienna, Fränkel of Dessau, and Möbius, had already endeavoured to draw attention to hypnotism in Germany, by clear and impartial reports. Lesser experiments in therapeutics had also been made by Creutzfeldt, Wiebe, Fischer, and Berkhan. But a really stirring activity has only just lately set in; it began about eight years ago, and was the result of the publications of Forel, which appeared in the German periodicals. They demonstrate the great importance of hypnotism for therapeutics. The essential importance of suggestion had not hitherto had sufficient stress laid upon it, and in consequence many hypnotic experiments may have remained fruitless. Many other investigators, following the example of Forel, have made experiments in medical treatment by hypnotism in Germany lately; among them may be especially mentioned: Sperling, Nonne, Michael, Hess, Schrenck-Notzing (a pronounced advocate for the therapeutical application of hypnotism), Hösslin, Baierlacher (who became known by his discovery of reaction of degeneration, and who, unfortunately, died shortly after turning his attention to hypnotism), Corval, Schuster, Hirt, Ad. Barth, Brügelmann, Hecker, Hirsch, Scholz, Gerster, Tatzel, Placzek, Steiner, Schütze, Lowenfeld, Herzberg. We find likewise a number of physicians in Austria active in the same field; Krafft-Ebing, Freud, Frey, Schnitzler, Doneth, Mosing, and F. Müller may be named. Other men—for example, Ziemssen, Seeligmüller, Köberlin, Nothnagel, Richter, Schultze, Strümpell— set their faces most decidedly against the therapeutic use of hypnotism.

Although at first hypnosis was entirely thrown aside and suggestion ignored, it soon became quite otherwise. Hypnosis was indeed considered dangerous; but it was admitted that suggestion, in the waking state, might very well be applied in disease. Others placed less value in suggestion, but recognised the general significance of psychic treatment, although it was undoubtedly suggestion that first made this clear. Among those who have most ably written on this subject I may name Rosenbach, who at a much earlier date had often referred to the significance of mental influence in therapeutics, though almost standing alone, and more recently Fürstner. Other authors, again, worked at the particular subjects which have a relation to hypnotism without laying special stress on its therapeutic value; and here the works of Forel, Lilienthal, Rieger, and

Drucker must be named, which inquired into the legal side of the question. Krafft-Ebing published an extremely detailed experimental study of two cases; Max Dessoir compiled a valuable Bibliography of modern hypnotism; further, Bleuler, Hückel, Maack, Weiss, Sallis, Dreher, Binden, Obersteiner, Hebold, Moravcsik, Hitzig. A short but useful book was produced by Minde, who brought forward many little known facts from ancient and modern literature.

Putting aside the numerous works which deal exclusively with hypnotism, we find this subject and suggestion incidentally discussed in many books chiefly concerned with other themes. I may mention the various works on nervous diseases and on electrotherapeutics, especially that of Hirt, who is one of the most decided advocates of the medical use of suggestion. Möbius, also, in his small but able manual on nervous diseases, has devoted a valuable chapter to this subject. I may mention the comprehensive work of Gowers, who, however, only brings forward Charcot's stages, and Oppenheimer's book on nervous diseases. In Müller's *Handbuch der Neurasthenie* there is an extensive chapter by Schrenck-Notzing on psychic and especially suggestive therapeutics. Borel in his book, *Nervosisme ou Neurasthenie*, deals briefly with treatment by suggestion, which he conditionally allows; as also does Löwenfeld in his book on hysteria and neurasthenia.

In the works on psychiatry, also, the question of hypnotism has attracted attention, as in that of Krafft-Ebing, who had long since given attention to hypnosis on account of its psychological and therapeutical value. Kraepelin, also, in his book on mental diseases, speaks favourably regarding the limited use of hypnosis. In the same way, Sommer advocates hypnosis in certain cases when other methods fail; while Kirchhoff, in his *Psychiatrie*, deals with hypnotism more as a psychological phenomenon.

In many non-medical books hypnotism has become a subject of consideration. Thus Courmelles, in his book on mind in animals, deals fully with hypnotic conditions. Here, too, must be mentioned various works on psychology, that of James, for example, and that of Wundt on physiological psychology, in which hypnotism is also discussed.

In spite of the great importance of hypnotism to therapeutics, I think it a great mistake when some doctors fix the therapeutic value of hypnotism as the standard by which it is to be judged; and here another factor—the founding of an experimental psychology—may be well taken into consideration. As a matter of fact, a large number of investigators have recognized the great value of hypnotism, particularly in this direction—above all, Krafft-Ebing, Forel, Max Dessoir; and several scientific societies have been formed in Germany after the pattern of the above-mentioned English Society for Psychical Research, in the programme of which it is essentially the use of hypnotism in the carrying out of psychological experiments which plays the chief part. Such are the Psychological Society in Munich and the Society for Experimental Psychology in Berlin, to which we already owe a series of remarkable works by Max Dessoir, Bastian, Hellwald, and Bentivegni. By some psychologists —Wundt, for example—it is denied that hypnotism is of value in experimental psychology. At the same time Wundt admits that, like dreaming and insanity, hypnosis is a proper object for psychological observation ; but its value for the psychologist is not equal to its high value for the physician.

The theologians have not been altogether able to leave hypnotism alone, although they sometimes attribute it to the agency of the devil. Among the authors who have dealt with hypnotism from the standpoint of theology or of the church, I may name Franco, Méric, and Finlay.

The general significance of suggestion for social life, as well as for art and science, has been treated in *Der Psychologie der Suggestion* by Schmidkunz, assisted by Gerster, a physician. Although the book betrays mystical tendencies, I cannot agree with the unfavourable judgment which some have pronounced against it. I find in it a number of valuable ideas and interesting historical notices.

All · these works, and others that could be mentioned, show how actively this field of investigation is being worked at the present time.

In order to facilitate a general discussion of the most important questions in the domain of hypnotism, a congress met in Paris in August 1889, at which nearly all civilized nations were represented, and at which many important matters were cleared up. In general, it may be said that the views of the Nancy school carried the day. More recently, various congresses have occupied themselves with hypnotism. At the Olten meeting of the Swiss Medical Association, in 1888, Forel delivered an address on the therapeutics of suggestion. At the congress of Russian physicians in St. Petersburg, in 1889,

Tokarski and Danillo introduced an interesting
discussion in the Neurological section.   At the three
congresses of Experimental Psychology interesting
communications on hypnotism were brought forward ;
a section at the London congress in 1892 was devoted
to hypnotism, F. Myers being its secretary, and Van
Leden read a long paper on the principles of psycho-
therapeutics. In the same year at Brussels, and in 1896
at Geneva, hypnotism was discussed at Congresses of
Criminal Anthropology.   In 1894, at the International
Medical Congress in Rome, Hirt introduced the subject of hypnosis ; Sollier and Benedikt appeared as
opponents, and the chief advocates for the value of
hypnotic therapeutics, besides Hirt, were Hitzig and
Bérillon.

Various journals are now devoted to hypnotism.
While in France the *Revue de l'Hypnotisme* has now
been published for ten years, in Germany, three years
ago, Grossmann founded a *Zeitschrift für Hypnotismus*, and a succession of interesting articles has
already appeared in this periodical.   Another French
journal, the *Annales de Psychiatrie*, devotes substantial articles to hypnotism.   In Italy we find
Magnetismo e Ipnotismo, a journal, edited by Olinto
del Torto, which is at the same time the organ of an
Italian scientific society occupied with the questions
of animal magnetism and hypnosis.   The objection
to periodicals dealing exclusively with hypnotism
has been vigorously, but not altogether unreasonably,
brought forward by Sommer.   He especially refers to
the danger lest the connection between hypnosis and
psycho-pathology generally be lost sight of.   It is to
be hoped that this fear may prove unfounded.

Hypnotism has, moreover, made its entrance into

the lecture-rooms of several German universities ; lectures are delivered about it in Berlin, by the well-known physiologist, Preyer, and at one time at Frey-burg, by Münsterberg, a distinguished psychologist. In other countries also lectures on hypnotism have been given at universities, as at Zürich by Forel, who has thus done valuable scientific service. In Paris, Bérillon, the editor of the *Revue de l'Hypnotisme*, has delivered lectures on hypnotism, in common with Jennings. Lehmann, a distinguished psychologist at Copenhagen, has in his lectures there dealt thoroughly with the psychological significance of suggestion.

In any case hypnotism has for the time won great importance, as may be estimated from the fact that it influences even literary circles. As in former days animal magnetism provided Alexandre Dumas and Balzac with material for romances, so in later times several authors have chosen their themes out of the domain of hypnotism. Those who have become best known are Claretie, Belot, Meding, Epheyre, Maupassant.

In art, also, hypnotism has played a certain part. In this connection I may refer to the work of Charcot and Richer, *Les Démoniaques dans l'Art.* At the Paris Salon, not long since, a picture was exhibited by Brouillet with the title, " Une leçon clinique à la Salpêtrière."

Finally, it must be mentioned that animal mag-netism, out of which hypnotism has developed itself, has retained some adherents in the scientific world— F. Myers and Richet ; so that at present we can dis-tinguish three schools with many points of transition (Max Dessoir): (1) The school of Charcot, which now has but few followers, like Crocq, in Brussels, who

also recognizes the contentions of the Nancy school,
as indeed did Charcot at the end of his life (Dumontpallier); (2) the school of Nancy; (3) the school of
Mesmerists. Foveau de Courmelles reckons as a
fourth school that of Luys, which certainly admits
doctrines contested by the others; but in my opinion
this does not suffice to enable us to speak of a special
school.

CHAPTER II.

In order to give the reader an idea of the phenomena of hypnotism it will be best, first of all, to
describe a few experiments. The phenomena will in
this way be made more comprehensible than by
means of any number of definitions.

First Experiment. I begin the experiments
with a young man of twenty. I request him to
seat himself on a chair, and give him a button to
hold, telling him to look at it fixedly. After three
minutes his eyelids fall ; he tries in vain to open his
eyes, which are fast closed ; his hand, which until
now has grasped the button, drops upon his knee. I
assure him that it is impossible for him to open his
eyes. (He makes vain efforts to open them.) I now
say to him, "Your hands are stuck fast to your knee;
you cannot possibly raise them." (He raises his
hands, however.) I continue to converse with him ;
I find that he is perfectly conscious, and I can discover no essential change in him whatever. I raise
one of his arms ; directly I let go, he drops it as he
pleases. Upon which I blow upon his eyes, which
open at once, and he is in the same state as before
the experiment. The young man remembers all that
I have said to him. The only striking thing is, there

fore, that he could not open his eyes, and that he
feels a certain degree of fatigue.

Second Experiment. This is a woman of fifty-
three. When she has seated herself on a chair I
place myself before her ; I raise my hands, and move
them downwards, with the palms towards her, from
the top of the head to about the pit of the stomach.
I hold my hands so that they may not touch her, at
a distance of from two to four centimetres. As soon
as my hands come to the lowest part of the stroke
I carry them in a wide sweep with outspread arms up
over the subject's head. I then repeat exactly the
same movements ; that is, passes from above downwards, close to the body, and continue this for about
ten minutes. At the end of this time the subject
is sitting with closed eyes, breathing deeply and
peacefully. When I ask her to raise her arms, she
raises them only slightly ; they then fall down again
heavily. When I ask her how she feels, she explains that she is very tired. I forbid her to open
her eyes. (She makes useless attempts to open
them.) Now I lift up her right arm ; it remains in
the air, even after I have let go. I command her to
drop her arm. (She drops it.) I lift it again, and again
it remains in the air ; upon which I request her to
drop her arm, declaring at the same time that she cannot do it. (She now makes vain efforts to drop her arm,
but it remains in the air.) The same thing happens
with the other arm. When I forbid her she is unable
to drop it ; she cannot pronounce her own name
directly I have assured her that she is dumb. (She
only makes movements with her mouth, without producing any sound.) I tell her that now she can
speak. (She speaks at once.) I say to her : " You
hear music." (The woman shakes her head to show

that she hears no music.) I wake her by passes from below, upwards, over the surface of her body, turning the back of the hand towards her. (She now opens her eyes, and can control all her movements.)

We see here, then, that not only are the eyes closed during hypnosis, but that all sorts of different movements become impossible to the subject when I forbid them.

Third Experiment. This is with a boy of sixteen, whom I have hypnotized several times. I request him to look me straight in the eyes. After he has done this for some time I take him by the hand and draw him along with me. Then I let go, but our eyes remain fixed on each other's. Then I lift up my right arm. (The boy does the same.) I raise my left arm. (He does the same.) I make him understand by a gesture that he must kneel down. (He does so.) He tries to rise, but does not succeed so long as I look at him, and fix him to the floor by a movement of the hand. Finally I cease to look at him ; the charm is at once broken.

We see here, then, a young man whose movements take the character of imitation, and whose eyes at the same time are wide open and fixed upon mine.

Fourth Experiment. Mr. X., forty-one years old, seats himself on a chair. I tell him that he must try to sleep. " Think of nothing but that you are to go to sleep." After some seconds I continue : " Now your eyelids are beginning to close ; your eyes are growing more and more fatigued ; the lids quiver more and more. You feel tired all over ; your arms go to sleep ; your legs grow tired ; a feeling of heaviness and the desire for sleep take possession of your whole body. Your eyes close.; your head feels duller ; your thoughts grow more and more confused. Now you

3

can no longer resist ; now your eyelids are closed.
Sleep ! " After the eyelids have closed I ask him if
he can open them. (He tries to do so, but they are
too heavy.) I raise his left arm high in the air. (It
remains in the air, and cannot be brought down in
spite of all his efforts.) I ask him if he is asleep.
"Yes." "Fast asleep?" "Yes." "Do you hear the
canary singing?" "Yes." "Now you hear the
concert?" "Certainly." Upon this I take a black
cloth and put it into his hand. "You feel this dog
quite plainly?" "Quite plainly." "Now you can
open your eyes. You will see the dog clearly. Then
you will go to sleep again, and not wake till I tell
you." (He opens his eyes, looks at the imaginary
dog and strokes it.) I take the cloth out of his hand,
and lay it on the floor. (He stands up and reaches
out for it.) Although he is in my room, when I tell
him that he is in the Zoological Gardens he believes
it and sees trees, and so on.

In this case X. is thrown into the hypnotic state
by my arousing in his mind an image of the sleep.
This manner of hypnotizing is used by the Nancy
investigators, and may be called the method of Nancy.
The subject is completely without a will of his own. It
is not only possible in his case to prevent the most
various movements by a mere prohibition, but I can
also control his sense perceptions. On my assurance,
he thinks he hears a canary, or hears music. He
takes a black cloth for a dog, and believes himself
to be in the Zoological Gardens when he is in my
room. But the following phenomenon is still more
striking. X. hears all that I say to him, and allows
himself to be influenced by me in every way. Yet
two other men, A. and B., who are present, appear
not to be observed by the hypnotic at all. A. lifts

up the arm of the subject; the arm falls loosely down, and when A. desires the arm to remain in the air the subject takes no notice. He obeys my orders only, and is *en rapport* with me only. In order to wake him I now call to him: "Wake up!" He wakes at once, but only remembers going to sleep; of what happened during the sleep he knows nothing.

I interrupt here for a time the description of the experiments; I shall describe others in the course of this work, and shall occasionally return to those already depicted. I will merely remark that in all these experiments, however different they might be, the voluntary movements were always inhibited, that in one case hallucinations of the senses could be induced, and that it was possible for me in all cases to converse with the subject, and we could understand each other.

I wished to bring forward these examples in order that the reader might understand to a certain extent, in spite of the absence of living subjects, what different states are included in the idea of hypnosis, and how it is induced and terminated. The above experiments are typical, and every one who makes proper experiments can always repeat them.

At the conclusion of these experiments I add a short Terminology, which, however, is by no means complete, as some particular ideas can only be made clear in the further course of the work.

I mean by *hypnosis* the state into which the subjects were thrown during the experiments described above.

Hypnotism is not the name of the state itself, but of the whole science which deals with the phenomena of this state.

A person in the hypnotic state is called a *hypnotic*, or *subject*.

A *hypnotist* is a man who hypnotizes for scientific purposes. A *hypnotizer* is a man who makes hypnotism a profession.

The different commands which are given to the subjects in the experiments described, the prompting and persuasion, are called *suggestion*, a word to which I shall return, and which I shall define more exactly later on.

I shall use the phrase, "to suggest" for the giving of these hints or promptings.

If the suggestion takes effect it is said, from the point of view of hypnotism, that the subject is under the influence of suggestion.

There are several methods of inducing hypnosis, as can be gathered from the above examples.

In order to make a systematic survey, we divide these methods into two groups—the mental and the physical.

The mental methods induce hypnosis by giving a particular direction to the subject's imagination; this is done either by concentrating the attention upon an arbitrary point (Braid), or by raising an image of the hypnotic state in the subject's mind. The latter is most easily done by speech, as we have seen in the above four examples. Liébeault originated the process, which deserves particular attention, as by the use of it unpleasant accompanying phenomena are more surely avoided. As a matter of course, the methods are slightly modified to suit special cases, because individual character plays an incomparably larger part in mental states than in ordinary physiological investigations. Naturally, it is quite possible to call up the image of the hypnotic states by other means than speech, and thus to induce them, by the influence of imitation, for example. The hypnotic state is occasionally induced by the mere sight of others in that condition, as well as by speech. The recollection of earlier hypnoses has the same effect ; upon this fact depends the induction of hypnosis by means of letters, or of the telephone (Liégeois).

It is certain that these mental influences play a large part in hypnosigenesis,[1] that is, in the origination and production of hypnosis. It is equally sure that they suffice in many cases to induce hypnosis, particularly when the person concerned has already been hypnotized. Bernheim and Forel even consider the mental factor as indispensable to hypnosis ; they hold the opinion that all the other methods mentioned below only succeed when they are of a kind to call up the picture of hypnosis. As, under certain circumstances which we shall examine later, the hypnosis may be a momentary one (that is, may pass away quickly), and as further in certain circumstances it need only consist of one solitary recognizable symptom, the representation necessary for the purpose need not be a very complicated picture (v. Bentivegni). Under some circumstances the mere idea that an arm has lost the power of motion is enough to cause hypnosis, of which precisely this loss of motion is the only, or the most important, symptom.

[1] Although the terminology up to the present time is very deficient, I will not make use of new expressions. Only instead of " hypnogen " and " hypnogenesis " (= induction of sleep), I shall use " hypnosigen " and " hypnosigenesis " (= induction of hypnotic sleep). " Hypnogen " is derived from ὕπνος—sleep— and is often used for " sleep-producing." " Hypnosigen " is derived from hypnosis ; and its use will prevent confusion.

Here belongs also autohypnosis, or self-hypnosis. In this the idea of the hypnosis is not aroused by another person, but the subject generates the image himself. This can only happen by an act of will. Just as the will is otherwise able to produce particular thoughts, so it can allow the idea of hypnosis to become so powerful that finally hypnosis is induced; this is, however, rare. Autohypnosis generally takes place in consequence of some incident by means of which the idea of the hypnosis is produced; this often happens when the subject has been frequently hypnotized. It is possible that some states of sleep which are generally considered pathological, belong to autohypnosis.

Faria formerly made use of a mental method to obtain hypnosis. After he had strained the attention of the subject as much as possible, he called out suddenly, "Sleep!" Liébeault substantially developed and completed this process, Bernheim made it more universally known.

I will now speak of the physical methods, which for a long time were the only ones used. They consist of certain stimuli of sight, hearing, and touch. Taste and smell (Binet, Féré) have been rarely tried, and have generally given negative results. The best known is the so-called method of Braid. The hypnosis is caused by a fixed gaze at some object or other. It is of little consequence whether the object is bright or not. Later, Braid gave up placing the object so close as to cause a convergence of the eyes. It is considered advantageous to hold the object so much above the eyes that the eyelids are strained as much as possible in keeping the eyes open. Instead of a lifeless object, such as was used in the first experiment mentioned above, the experimenter can make use of his finger for the purpose, or, as the professional magnetizers prefer to do, of his eye (Du Potet). Luys has frequently used a rapidly revolving mirror, in order to produce speedy and extreme fatigue of the eye. Just the same effect can be produced by hearing as by sight ; for this the ticking of a watch is preferred (Weinhold, Heidenhain). Among uncivilized races particular instruments are used to produce analogous states ; for example, the sound of a magic drum among the Lapps ; among other races the monotony of uniform rhythm in song (Bastian). Instead of these continuous, monotonous, weak stimulations of the senses, we see also sudden and violent ones made use of, for example, in the Salpêtrière, the field of Charcot's work, the loud noise of a gong or a sudden ray of the Drummond light. However, it is more than doubtful whether these sudden strong physical stimuli, without any mental element, can induce true hypnosis. Perhaps we have to do here with states not far removed from paralysis from fright ; at least subjects thus hypnotized often wear an expression of fear (Richer). The effect can be also produced through the sense of touch, even by a gentle stroking of the skin, or by pressure upon it. Some have also sought to induce hypnosis by the stimulus of heat—*e.g.*, warm plates of metal (Berger). It is known that warmth easily brings on natural sleep, while cold, if it is not too great, keeps it off.

I here mention in particular the so-called mesmeric, mesmerizing, or magnetic passes, upon which Richet sets great value. I have already shown and described above, in the second experiment, how they are made ; I mention them here, though the question of how they act is not yet satisfactorily settled. It is not certain whether the stimulation of temperature, as Heidenhain and Berger suppose, or the slight motion of the air, or the mental influence, is the efficient agent in this case. I myself consider it most likely that the various agencies combine, but that the mental factor is the most important. It is not necessary to assume the existence of any peculiar force, such as the magnetic fluid of the mesmerist. An old hypothesis has been frequently revived, namely, that we have to do with an electrical action (Rostan, J. Wagner). Tarchanoff has shown that by means of gentle stimulations of the skin weak electric currents can be produced in it, but that these same can also be produced by strong concentration of the will, in consequence of which there is always muscular contraction. Now, as the mesmerists consider a strong effort of will necessary on the part of the operator, it is possible that a peripheral development of electricity takes place in him, which has an effect upon the mesmerized subject. This idea is, however, merely a supposition of individual investigators; we know nothing certain about it yet.

We should note that the method of so-called "mesmeric passes" was not used by Mesmer; it is true that he endeavoured to influence by touch, but these peculiar monotonous long-continued passes which I have described above, were unknown to him.

Pitres maintains that certain portions of the body are particularly sensitive to stimulation of the skin. The "*zones hypnogènes*" described by him sometimes exist on only one side of the body, and sometimes on both. Stimuli applied to them are said to produce hypnosis in certain persons, as is indeed maintained of other parts. Among these parts of the body the crown of the head, the root of the nose, &c., are named. Crocq is in agreement with Pitres. According to Chambard and Laborde a gentle scratching of the skin of the neck induces hypnosis. I myself have seen many persons who maintained that they became hypnotized only when I touched their foreheads. It is often stated that touches on the forehead induce a sleepy state in many persons (Purkinje, Spitta). An Englishman named Catlow magnetized by means of gentle stroking of the forehead (Bäumler). I also know some persons who, in order to go to sleep more easily, cause other parts of the body to be gently stimulated—the head, or soles of the feet, for example. Eulenburg maintains that pressure on the cervical· vertebræ induces hypnosis.

Finally, I mention the action of the electric battery, whose influence, according to Weinhold, has the same effect as mesmeric passes. Weinhold, however, writing in a critical spirit, does not consider that mental influences are in this case excluded. When Eulenburg obtained a lethargic condition, resembling hypnosis, by galvanizing the head, this experiment did not prove a true hypnosis, since the person experimented upon had already had attacks of lethargy. It is certain that in many cases where hypnosis is supposed to have been caused by the application of electricity to the head, the hypnosis has only come on because the subject believed that electricity induced hypnosis. Hirt often uses electricity in this way, but is at the same time perfectly clear that it is not the electricity but the subject's belief in its effect, that produces the hypnosis.

To conclude, I further mention stimulations of the muscular sense, such as the cradle rocking used to send little children to sleep; I leave on one side the question as to whether hypnosis can be attained by this means. Similar states are said to be produced among uncivilized peoples by violent whirling or dancing movements ; the movements are, however, accompanied by music and other mental excitations. The best known are the Aïssaouas, in Algiers (Figuier, Bert, Delphin). "They carry on their business chiefly in the Algerian town of Constantine. They are able by means of dancing and singing to throw themselves into a state of ecstasy difficult to describe, in which their bodies seem to be insensible even to severe wounds. They run pointed iron and sharp knives into their heads, eyes, necks, and breasts, without injuring themselves" (Hellwald). The same thing is related of the Buddhist convents in Tibet (Hellwald, Gabriel Huc), and Dr. Sperling has told me that he has himself seen dervishes in Constantinople, who, from the expression of their eyes and their whole appearance, as well as from the peculiar postures they maintained for a length of time, impressed him as being in a hypnotic state. The state may have been induced by monotonous singing and uniform whirling movements. I have, however, myself often watched the howling and dancing dervishes at Cairo and Constantinople, without being able to detect any indication of autohypnosis.

I have hitherto spoken only of sense-stimuli among the physical methods. But it must also be mentioned that the absence of these stimuli is likewise specified as an expedient for hypnosigenesis. Jendrássik, of Buda-Pesth, expresses the opinion that fixed attention is only effective because it causes fatigue of the nerves of sight, and consequently produces insensibility to stimulation. Perhaps the case related by Strümpell is of this class ; he observed a person who fell asleep immediately on the cessation of sense-stimulation.

This classification of hypnogenetic expedients is merely theoretical (Forel, Levillain) ; and that for two reasons. In the first place we cannot regard body and mind as two factors which are independent of one another. Sense-stimuli, which affect the body, nearly always exercise a certain effect on the mind ; the mind, on the other hand, can act upon nothing which has not previously entered it by means of the organs of sense. In the second place, in practice several hypnogenetic processes are habitually used at the same time. This will become perfectly clear if the hypnotized person is watched : let him be told that he must keep any particular idea well in mind, that he must concentrate his whole attention on the idea of sleep ; he will then, in order to obey the command, look steadily at some point, or at once shut his eyes, in order as much as possible to prevent distraction of thought.

Thus Bernheim occasionally uses fixed attention at the same time as the mental methods. Braid, again, who made use of fixation almost entirely, yet considered a particular mental activity also necessary. This is particularly to be noticed, because some people nowadays believe that they are using the method of Braid when they tell the subject to look steadily at something. In reality Braid considered a steady attention as well as a steady gaze indispensable if hypnosis were to be attained ; the subject must think steadily of the thing he was looking at, and must not allow himself to be diverted from it. According to Braid, one can hypnotize even in the dark.

But even theoretically we cannot always keep these things apart. Closing of the eyes, with slight pressure upon them, often leads, as Lasègue showed, to hypnotic states. How these come about, whether through the cessation of the sense stimulation, or through the idea of sleep, which the closing of the eyes certainly easily calls up, cannot be decided. After these details, the much discussed and disputed question must be answered, whether a person can be hypnotized without his knowledge; whether any one can be thrown into the hypnotic state merely by sense-stimuli, without these arousing an image of the hypnosis. I know of no well-authenticated case in which sense stimulation has produced hypnosis by a purely physiological action. Most people upon whom such experiments are made know that an attempt is being made to hypnotize them ; they have been already hypnotized, and the stimuli arouse conscious or unconscious mental images of the hypnosis ; or they have seen the same experiments with others, or have heard of them. Even when this is not the case, the objection of Bernheim and Forel remains to be considered, that the stimuli induce a feeling of fatigue, and through this induce the hypnosis.

Which of the above methods, or which combination of them is the best for practical use, is a question the answer to which is not so simple that every one who has made a dozen experiments is justified in trying to reply to it. When we find that Richet thinks he can throw nearly anybody into the hypnotic state by means of mesmeric passes, that Liébeault hypnotizes nearly all his patients by means of the Nancy process, that Braid hypnotized ten persons out of fourteen by means of fixed attention, we see that different methods bring about nearly identical results. I am decidedly of opinion that in each individual case that method should be selected by means of which the most vivid picture of the hypnosis, and the conviction that it will come on, can be produced in the subject. I lay stress on the fact that in individual cases persons appear refractory to one method while another succeeds. I have found persons insusceptible to the use of fixed attention, or to the method of Nancy, while I obtained results by mesmeric passes. Evidently this proves nothing against mental action, as many persons believe they can only be influenced by some particular process. On the other side I have seen that intense fixity of gaze sometimes induces hypnosis when other methods are useless, perhaps because the subjective expectation of the hypnosis is sooner aroused by the long, intense stare, than by verbal orders. Again, in some cases it is well to attain the aim quickly, by means of a sharp shock (Sperling, Forel, Van Eeden, Van Renterghem).

Chambard reckons chloroform, ether, &c., among hypnogenetic agents. In any case many phenomena analogous to those of hypnosis have been observed in the sleep induced by these agents (Spring, Rifat, Herrero, Roth). F. Myers, however, considers it better to distinguish the conditions thus produced from hypnosis. Attempts have been recently made from various sides, by Wetterstrand, Schrenck-Notzing, and others, to study these phenomena. They conclude that by chemical substances like chloroform, morphine, haschisch, hypnosis can be attained in persons who are insensitive to other methods. Whether hypnosis is thus produced only indirectly, the idea of sleep being aroused by these soporific substances, is for practical purposes of course immaterial. It would, however, be necessary to distinguish between cases in which deep sleep is first obtained by the drug, and hypnosis from this condition, as Coste advises, and those cases in which the hypnotic phenomena are primary. I have myself often produced hypnotic phenomena with post-hypnotic suggestions by the use of chloral hydrate.

I may mention here that, according to Landouzy, Proust,

Ballet, and Benedikt, the magnet also has a hypnotizing action, although my own numerous experiments have been unsuccessful. Many authors are in the habit of describing any new method by which it is possible to hypnotize. In many cases some advantageous artifice is brought forward ; in other cases some insignificant modifications of ordinary methods are described, modifications which are worthless, and which have often been already described in older literature, so that they are not even new. To this class belongs, for instance, the method of hypnotizing described by Montin, who seizes the finger of the subject seated opposite to him, then presses the knees close together, &c.

The waking from hypnosis (dehypnotization) can also occur in two ways—through immediate action on the imagination, or through sense stimulation, exactly as waking out of the natural sleep occurs sometimes from mental causes, for example, from habit, or from the resolution to awake at a certain hour ; and sometimes from stronger stimuli of the senses, for example, a loud noise. It is nearly always possible to put an end to the hypnosis by mental means, that is, by the command to wake up, or to wake up at a particular signal. It is hardly ever necessary to use other means, such as fanning, excitation by the faradism, sprinkling with water, loud calls, &c. I cannot confirm the statement of some, that cold has an arousing effect. Just as the mesmerizing passes induce hypnosis, so the demesmerizing passes—as I used them in the second experiment, above described —cause it to disappear. Whether the cool current of air, which is nearly always thereby generated, causes the awakening, or whether it is, as I think more probable, the belief of the subject that he must wake, remains undecided. Pitres and others think that there are parts of the body where stimulation produces awakening; they are called "*zones hypno-frénatrices.*"

Among them the ovarian regions are particularly notable. Finally, I mention the forcible opening of the eyes as a means of ending the hypnosis. Other processes which have been given, and which were supposed to induce awakening by physical means, such as bringing a coal near the patient, have only a mental effect, as they are understood as a command to awake. In rare cases these artificial means of awakening do not succeed quickly; a feeling of fatigue then continues. We feel the same thing occasionally when we wake out of natural sleep. After deep and long hypnosis a temporary state like extreme sleepiness follows, in which certain hypnotic phenomena continue.

If the awakening is not brought about by artificial means, persons in a light hypnotic state, such as is described in the first two experiments, habitually wake of their own accord after a few minutes or even seconds; this especially happens when the continuance of the state has not been expressly ordered. Some people wake at the exact moment when the experimenter leaves them, as they then no longer think themselves under his influence. Others awake of their own accord out of deep hypnosis if they hear an unexpected and loud noise, or have exciting dreams. Thus, I once saw a grown-up person wake herself by screaming, because in the hypnotic state she had believed herself to be a little child, and in that character had begun to cry. The awakening which comes about without any apparent cause is remarkable and unexplained (*mouvement psychique.*) The same thing is sometimes observed in natural sleep, especially at its beginning; O. Rosenbach traces it to increase of the reflexes. Generally, however, the deep hypnoses continue for some time when they are not artificially terminated. Sometimes many hours pass before the subject wakes.

The old mesmerists (Du Potet, Lafontaine) describe as a rare occurrence in hypnotic experiments a state of lethargy, in which artificial awakening was impossible. After some time there was a spontaneous awakening, and no evil consequences were to be observed. Guermonprez described lately how a person had remained three days in hypnosis, nobody being able to wake him. It appears that these incidents occur more often when sense stimulations are used—for example, the fixed gaze or the mesmeric passes. And again, this state has only been observed among hysterical subjects, so far as I am aware. Therefore I believe that this lethargy must be distinguished from hypnosis, the chief symptoms of which are wanting. We cannot identify this state with hypnosis, merely because it is a result of the same processes ; the identity could only be proved by a likeness of symptoms, not by a likeness in the manner of their production. When one person receives a blow on the ear and hæmorrhage under the skin follows, while another receives a like blow, and has the drum of the ear burst : these are two different injuries, and the fact that they have the same cause does not make them identical.

Who is hypnotizable? In order to settle this question without hypnotic experiments, Ochorowicz has invented a special instrument—the hypnoscope : it is an iron magnet in the form of a ring, which the person to be tested puts on his finger. Hypnotizable persons are supposed to experience certain sensations in the skin and twitchings of the muscles, while with the insusceptible nothing of the kind takes place. The researches of other investigators have not confirmed this (Obersteiner, Gessmann, Grasset, Bottey). Other signs which are supposed to indicate susceptibility to hypnotism I consider untrustworthy.

Neither neurasthenia nor pallor, neither hysteria nor general feebleness of health, produce a disposition to hypnosis. As far as hysteria is concerned, it is not in my experience peculiarly suited to hypnotism. Our ordinary hysteria with its variable characteristics of headache and the feeling of a lump in the throat (globus) combined with the general hysterical desire to be interesting and to exaggerate the sufferings endured, produces, according to my experience, very little disposition to hypnosis. The spirit of contradiction, very strongly developed in such patients, contributes not a little to this. The mistaken notion that hysterical or nervous patients are particularly susceptible to hypnotism results from the fact that most physicians have experimented with them only; besides which it is very easy to discover in all persons something which may be explained as a hysterical symptom, if only we try to do so. If, however, we consider every one who submits himself to a hypnotic experiment to be "nervous" (Morand), then, naturally, only nervous persons can be put into the hypnotic state; but this view cannot be taken seriously. In reality, if we are to take a pathological condition of the organism as a necessary condition for hypnosis, we shall be obliged to conclude that nearly everybody is not quite right in the head. For the rest, the old mesmerists in part (Wirth and others) maintained that hysteria only produced a disposition to the magnetic sleep.

Further, if general weakness is to be put forward as a predisposing factor, I, for my part, must emphasize the fact that I have hypnotized many very

muscular persons. It is known that Hansen, whose
practical experience is of some value, always preferred
muscular people for his experiments. The susceptibility of tuberculous patients is striking (Bernheim.)

With regard to mental aptitudes, Forel believes
that every mentally healthy human being is hypnotizable. In Liébeault's opinion heredity plays a great
part in the disposition to hypnosis. It is universally
agreed that the mentally unsound, particularly idiots,
even if not wholly insusceptible, are still very much
more difficult to hypnotize than the healthy. However, A. Voisin informs us that he has succeeded in
hypnotizing ten per cent. of the mentally unsound, by
exercising the necessary patience. With regard to
intelligence, intelligent persons are more easily
hypnotizable than the dull and stupid. Among the
lower classes the mentally superior are undoubtedly
easier to hypnotize than others. Mental excitement
easily prevents hypnosis. The numerous observations
made by Wetterstrand, Ringier, and others, that
certain individuals are occasionally refractory to
hypnosis, may be connected with this fact. I
could confirm this occasional disinclination to
hypnosis by a whole series of cases. I consider it a
complete mistake to say that the disposition to
hypnosis is a sign of weakness of will. Without
doubt the ability to maintain a passive state has a
predisposing effect. This is why soldiers are in
general easy to hypnotize. The ability to direct one's
thoughts in any particular direction is also very
favourable. As we habitually consider this power to
be a sign of strength of will, the disposition to
hypnosis would rather be a sign of strength than of
weakness of will. This ability to give the thoughts a
certain prescribed direction is partly natural capacity,

partly a matter of habit, and often an affair of will. Those, on the contrary, who can by no possibility fix their attention, who suffer from continual absence of mind, can hardly be hypnotized at all. It is specially among the nervous that a strikingly large number of this last class are to be found, who cannot hold fast to a thought, and in whom a perpetual wandering of the mind predominates. The disposition to hypnosis is also not specially common among those persons who are otherwise very impressible. It is well known that there are some who can be easily influenced in life, who believe all that they are told, upon whom the most unimportant trifles make an impression, nevertheless, when an effort is made to hypnotize them, they offer a lively resistance, and the typical symptoms of hypnosis cannot be induced in them.

Nationality (Ewald), or local surroundings (Brugia), have no influence upon susceptibility to hypnotism. Forel in Zürich, Renterghem in Amsterdam, and Wetterstrand in Stockholm, have shown that Teutonic peoples are as easy to hypnotize as Latin. Wetterstrand only failed to hypnotize eighteen people out of 718 in Stockholm. Besides, Braid's experiences in England show nearly the same thing. Recently it has been pointed out in many quarters that Russians are more easily hypnotized than any other people (Poirault and Drzewiecki). Ringier in Switzerland, and Terrien in La Vendée, have shown that rural populations are very easily hypnotizable. With regard to age, children under three years cannot be hypnotized at all, and even up to about eight years of age they can only be hypnotized with difficulty. Although children are otherwise easily influenced, their thoughts are so easily distracted that they cannot fix their minds on a prescribed picture, such as that of hypnosis. Old age is by no means refractory to hypnosis. According to the experiences of the school of Nancy, with which mine agree, older persons more often remember, after hypnosis, all that has happened than do younger ones. Sex has no particular influence ; it is a mistake to suppose that women are better adapted than men.

Besides this, individual observers (Brémaud, Maack) mention some points which are supposed to be favourable or unfavourable. Brémaud, for example, mentions alcohol as favourable, Maack as unfavourable. But universal conclusions should not be drawn from a few observations, as so doing will not contribute to any clear understanding. For the same reason I question the general accuracy of some of Ringier's statements, though the rest of his remarks have a great practical value. According to him, hypnotism is less easily practised in winter than in summer, because cold is supposed to be unfavourable ; thus persons who were easily hypnotized in summer become refractory in winter.

The frequency with which an attempt should be repeated on the same person is of more importance. While, according to Hähnle, only one person in ten proves susceptible on a first attempt, the proportion increases enormously with the frequency of the sittings. This is not to be wondered at, from the mental excitement shown by many people in the beginning. And as it is most important to hypnosis that the attention should not be distracted, many people are first of all obliged to learn to concentrate their thoughts. There are even experimenters who maintain that everybody is hypnotizable, if only the attempt is continued long enough. Without declaring this view to be false, I may remark that I have made forty or more attempts with some persons without obtaining hypnosis. Perhaps by even longer continued efforts a result would have been attained, as indeed has happened to me many times after forty vain attempts. In other cases the exact opposite happens, and the oftener the attempt is made, the less successful is it ; by a process of auto-suggestion the subject persuades himself that he is not hypnotizable.

Besides these subjective conditions there are some other objective ones. Thus, for example, disturbing noises at the first experiment have power to prevent the hypnosis ; they draw off the attention, and thus interfere with the mental state necessary for hypnosis. Later, when the subject has learnt to concentrate his thoughts, noises are less disturbing. But in hypnotic experiments the most absolute avoidance by those present of any sign of mistrust is necessary. The least word, a gesture, may thwart the attempt to hypnotize. As the mood of a large company is often distrustful, as a whole generation also is sometimes sceptical, the great variations in susceptibility to hypnosis which have shown themselves at different times and places are explicable. It is not surprising that on one occasion ten persons, one after the other, are hypnotized, while on another occasion ten other persons all prove refractory.

Experience and a knowledge of the mental conditions of mankind are indispensable for the hypnotizer. The first is absolutely necessary ; it is more important than a knowledge of anatomy and physiology. By experience one learns to discriminate and to enter into the particular character of the subject. Practice and a gift for observation enable the right stress to be laid at the right moment either on fixed attention or on the closing of the eyes. The experi-

enced experimenter knows how to judge whether it
is best in any particular case to attain his aim by
speaking or whether, as sometimes happens, speech
would be a hindrance, and the chief stress would be
best laid on fixed attention, &c. A person who is
easily hypnotized can be hypnotized by any one;
but one who is hypnotized with difficulty can only
be thrown into hypnosis by a good and experienced
experimenter. It is by no means a contradiction of
this that the personal impression made by the experimenter may be very important and have great
influence. In consequence of this it happens that a
certain person A. can be hypnotized by B., while
he remains refractory to the efforts of C. On the
other hand, it may happen that D. can be hypnotized by C. but not by B. This shows that the
influence of one person over another is dependent
on the individuality of both. We find the same in
life, in the relation of teacher to pupil, and of pupil
to teacher, in the reciprocal relations of friends, or
lovers. The influence of one person on another
always depends on the individuality of both.

That there exists an individual aptitude for hypnotization, and for making the suggestions—to which I
lay no claim—is certain. It is true that we must not
think of this ability as did the older mesmerists, who
supposed that certain persons exercised a peculiar
physical force upon others; we must represent this
natural ability to ourselves as we do many others,
when we have to do with particular mental aptitudes. Calm, presence of mind, and patience are
essential, and not every one can exercise these
qualities. To busy oneself with hypnotizing a
subject daily for hours at a time demands a per-
severance which everybody does not possess. Very

much more patience is necessary for this than for writing prescriptions, for example, several hundreds of which could be produced in the same length of time.

The question whether hypnosis can be induced against the wish of the subject is by no means unimportant. We must distinguish here whether the subject complies with the prescribed conditions or whether he does not. If he does; if, for example, he sufficiently concentrates his attention ; if he gazes at some object with the necessary attention, then hypnosis may be produced at the first attempt, even against the wish of the person experimented on. However, it must be remembered that a person who does not intend to allow himself to be hypnotized will hardly place himself in the necessary mental state. He will not generally fulfil the conditions ; he will fix his eyes, but will allow his attention to wander. However, I think I may assert that certain persons accustomed to obedience can be hypnotized at the first attempt even against their will, and without the ordinary necessary straining of the attention, if only they are told that hypnosis will occur. Notwithstanding, these cases appear to be rare. It is not to be doubted that many people who have been frequently hypnotized can be re-hypnotized against their will and without their intentional compliance with the ordinary conditions. The experiments of Heidenhain show that people can be hypnotized against their wish. He hypnotized soldiers in the presence of their officers, who had strictly forbidden them to sleep. Such a command would have as much effect on a soldier as the personal wish not to sleep. Post-hypnotic suggestion, of which I shall speak later, is also a means of sending persons to sleep against their wish. There is a third possibility, namely, that no wish should exist in either direction. The conditions necessary for hypnosis may occur occasionally by chance, without the subject being conscious of them (Max Dessoir). For example, some one over his work is obliged to look fixedly at a certain point ; this suffices to induce hypnosis (sometimes after earlier unfit experiments), without the person thinking of it. In this case the will is neither interested for it nor against it. The statement of Preyer, that persons being photographed sometimes remain sitting rigidly still after the taking of the photograph is finished, may be referred to a hitherto unsuspected hypnotic state, brought on by the fixed stare necessary to the process. It is known that some of the inmates of the Salpêtrière in Paris fall suddenly into catalepsy in consequence of some loud unexpected noise. There is an interesting case of a girl who had often been hypnotized by loud noises, and who went to a drawer to appropriate some photographs out of it. The casual beating of a gong threw her into a cataleptic state, so that she stood motionless in the act of carrying out her theft, and was discovered. Hack Tuke remarks that it is a pity all thieves cannot be taken as easily.

As Bertrand related, with certain persons natural sleep can be transformed into magnetic sleep. Many attempts have been made to do this in later times. Baillif, Gscheidlen, Berger, Bernheim, and Forel have even made these experiments on persons who had been refractory to hypnotism. I myself have been able to make some observations of this kind. One person concerned was a gentleman whom I had already frequently hypnotized, and whom I often threw into the hypnotic state while he was taking his afternoon sleep, without waking him. In another case I succeeded in producing various movements, as raising of the arms, through slight suggestions to a gentleman who was in his afternoon sleep. I was obliged to speak in a whisper to avoid waking him. It is doubtful whether such experiments would succeed with persons who had never heard of hypnotism. Schrenck-Notzing reports a case in which hypnosis was produced from post-epileptic coma. Cases in which conditions of hysterical sleep have been led on into hypnosis have been described by Löwenfeld and others. I may refer here to the question already raised, whether hypnotic states can be produced by chemical substances, such as chloroform.

In any case, however, previous consent is not absolutely necessary to the production of hypnosis, and, on the other hand, there are people who are refractory in spite of a decided wish to be hypnotized (Preyer, Forel). In general, however, the intentional resistance of the subject hinders hypnosis, simply because a person who is willing to be hypnotized complies more easily with the necessary conditions than another. Consequently it is not astonishing that patients who come to a doctor on purpose to be hypnotized, particularly when they come with full confidence, are more easy to hypnotize than others. These others often allow an attempt to be made with them, with the silent resolution to show that "they are not to be caught," or they submit themselves, as Nonne says, "only for fun," and yet many believe that susceptibility to hypnosis is a sign of defective will or intelligence!

As so many different circumstances influence the induction of hypnosis, it is not surprising that the proportion of hypnotizable persons should be differently stated. If Ewald in the Women's Hospital at Berlin can only hypnotize two persons, while Liébeault hypnotizes 92 per cent. of his patients, the reason of this enormous difference must lie in the different nature of the conditions. The insufficient mental preparation of Ewald's subjects is particularly to blame for his failure. Bottey gives 30 per cent. as susceptible, Otto Binswanger more than 50 per cent., Morselli 70 per cent., Delbœuf over 80 per cent. The latter's results appear to me of great value, having been evidently collected with critical care, as must be acknowledged by every un-prejudiced person who reads Delbœuf's works. He excludes simulators with the greatest care, and is, perhaps, in this respect more sceptical than the in-vestigators at Nancy. Bernheim refuses the right to judge of hypnotism to all hospital doctors who cannot hypnotize at least 80 per cent. of their patients ; Forel fully agrees with him.

An exact international investigation on aptitude for hypnosis has been made by Schrenck-Notzing, who applied to numerous investigators in various countries—England, Sweden, Germany, France, Algiers, Canada, Switzerland, &c. Among 8705 persons covered by the investigation, only 6 per cent. were completely refractory. The remaining 94 per cent. were divided by Schrenck-Notzing into three groups, according to Forel's classification, of which I shall soon have to speak : 29 per cent. attained to somnolence, 49 per cent. to hypotaxis, 15 per cent. to somnambulism.

The oftener hypnotic experiments are made the sooner hypnosis generally is induced. The first attempt often takes five minutes or more, although

on many occasions a few seconds suffice. When the
experiment has succeeded a few times, a few moments
are nearly always enough to attain the result. This
is because the remembrance of the earlier hypnosis
essentially favours its return. Besides this, the
strongest hindrance has been overcome by the earlier
hypnosis—which is the belief of the subject that he is
not hypnotizable, or that he can only be hypnotized by
certain persons ; this belief often prevents hypnosis.
The certainty with which well-known hypnotizers
hypnotize people, rests partly on the fact that these
subjects believe they can be hypnotized by one
celebrated hypnotizer and not by another. The
disposition to hypnosis may also disappear when
the experiments have been discontinued for a long
time. Thus I once saw a gentleman who was susceptible in a high degree become refractory again,
after no experiments had been made with him during
six months. I have observed the same thing in
several people, but the disposition to hypnosis can
generally be reproduced after a short time, if a few
attempts are made.

From the above examples it appears that the
various hypnotic states differ much from one another,
and that the depth of the hypnosis varies extraordinarily. This suggested that in order to obtain a
general survey an attempt at classification must be
made. A well-known classification is that of
Charcot, who supposes three stages—the cataleptic,
lethargic, and somnambulic. I shall go into more
detail as to these later, but will remark here that this
classification has no universal value. It cannot be
said that in its full extent this classification has
won a single new follower in recent years; among
the few who advocate it may be named Crocq, who,

however, only admits it for a small number of cases. The classification given by Pitres also need not be fully discussed here. He partly follows Charcot, but accepts so many different kinds of hypnotic states that a general view is rendered very difficult. The classification made by Gurney, containing two stages —alert and deep—is only accurate for a few cases. In the same way the three stages supposed by Richer, Fontan, and Ségard, are not sufficiently well marked for practical use. Nor does the classification of Del-bœuf seem to me entirely admissible. According to him there are two stages of hypnosis—a stage in which pain can be felt, and a stage in which it cannot (analgesia). As, however, complete insensibility to pain is very rare, and as the transitions are vague, insensibility to pain does not appear to me to be a suitable distinguishing characteristic. The classifications made by Liébeault, Bernheim, and Forel, have also become well known. As they agree in the main, only differing in the number of stages—according to Liébeault, 6; according to Bernheim, 5; according to Forel, 3,— I shall only cite that of Forel :—

Stage 1.   Drowsiness : the subject can resist suggestions only with great effort.

Stage 2.   Hypotaxy ("*charme*") : the eyes are fast closed and cannot be opened ; the subject is obliged to obey various suggestions.

Stage 3.   Somnambulism : it is characterized by loss of memory on waking—that is, the subject remembers nothing after waking that has passed during the hypnosis.

The classifications of Forel, Liébeault, and Bernheim, rest chiefly on loss of memory, as a particular group (Forel's 3rd stage) of hypnotic states with loss or memory is placed in contrast with the others

(Forel's 1st and 2nd stages), in which no loss of memory exists.

Those hypnotic states in which loss of memory exists, are called somnambulism by the authors above named. Wienholt also has already said that the magnetic states with ensuing loss of memory may be called somnambulism.

I think, however, it would be better not to make our estimate of the stages of hypnosis dependent on loss of memory, but on the phenomena which appear during the hypnosis itself. I shall show that memory after hypnosis is dependent on many other factors which have nothing to do with the depth of the hypnosis. A chance view of an external object will suffice to arouse a whole chain of mental images ; we shall see that memory is influenced by suggestion.

I should prefer on this account to judge of the depth of the hypnosis only from the phenomena of the hypnosis itself. Delbœuf, who often experimented with profound hypnoses, declares that the subjects after the awakening were nevertheless perfectly aware of all the hypnotic incidents.

The numerous sub-divisions given by Liébeault and Bernheim are not easy to utilize, because there exists no principle for such classification (Max Dessoir). For example, one stage is distinguished by the complete closing of the eyes, and a deeper stage by motor disturbances in the arms. As these last, however, can occur also when the eyes are open, they cannot be regarded as a sign of the deepening of the stage in which the eyes are closed ; for in the deepening all the phenomena of previous and lighter stages must also appear.

In order to avoid these difficulties, Max Dessoir has also published a classification of the hypnotic

states as simple as it is comprehensive and clear.
According to this the states fall into two large
groups, which are divided from each other by the
extent of the functional disturbances. In the first group
merely the voluntary movements show changes ; in
the second group abnormalities in the functions of
the sense organs are added.   In the first group, also,
only those functions are abnormal which we attribute
to the centrifugal nerves, while in the second group
the functions of the centripetal nerves are likewise
disturbed.   The principle of this classification was
already known to Kluge also.   The minority of subjects
belong to Group II. ;   if we take 75 per cent. to be
susceptible, then about 55 per cent. belong to Group I.,
and 20 per cent. to Group II.   According to Kron
this latter percentage is perhaps too high ;   in his
opinion a relatively smaller number of persons than
I give belong to Group II.   He conjectures that
through practice and other factors these figures might
vary considerably.   It will be understood that in
these two groups many stages and types can be
distinguished.   For example, we see that many a
hypnotic state belonging to Group I. is merely characterized by the closing of the eyes, which the subject
cannot voluntarily open, as in the first experiment
(p. 21).   As has been mentioned, this state used to
be considered as a particular stage of hypnosis, but
according to the explanation given above it takes its
place as merely a particular form of Group I.   It was
generally represented as a particular stage, because in
many cases hypnosis is ushered in by a closing of the
eyes, while other muscles are only affected later on.
However, this is really a pure accident (Max Dessoir);
we have accustomed ourselves more and more to
induce hypnosis by affecting the eyes, and to provoke

a closing of them as quickly as possible; but this is nothing but a habit, resulting from the identification of hypnosis with sleep. There are a large number of hypnotists who induce hypnosis when the eyes are wide open, as is the case in " fascination," which will be discussed later (*cf.* third experiment). I myself have met many people in whom it was impossible to bring about change of movement of the eye, while the other muscles were easily affected. For this reason I think the assertion of Michael that hypnosis can only be proved when the eyes are completely closed is mistaken. He is perfectly right, however, when he says that we should not ascribe to hypnosis the states of fatigue and giddiness which ensue after long attention, unless other phenomena typical of hypnosis also appear.

It is clear that the two groups cannot be sharply divided from one another. On the contrary, gradual transitions are everywhere to be found. Also the transition from a normal state to hypnosis is gradual, and certainly not so sudden as some think. We find many stages even before we arrive at the closing of the eyes, which certainly does not indicate a deep hypnosis; at first only heaviness of the eyelids, then the desire to close the eyes, then a difficulty in opening them, and finally a complete closing of them. All possible stages are displayed, and it would not be very difficult to describe a hundred different ones. Further, a deep hypnosis is not always attained at once; the light states are often passed through before the deepest appears. It is naturally difficult, through all these gradual transitions, to decide the exact moment of the appearance of hypnosis. A deep sigh, which is often heard at the beginning of hypnosis, is by many wrongly considered as diagnostic of the important moment, particularly as this symptom is easily spread by imitation (Delbœuf). The movements of swallowing which appear, especially after long fixation, have equally little significance.

As already shown, etymologically we can only understand by hypnosis a condition resembling sleep. In reality, however, the cases in the first group show no resemblance to sleep. On this account an attempt has been made of late to separate these conditions entirely from hypnosis; among others Max Hirsch has made such an attempt, and has proposed for such conditions the term Captivation. It must, however, be pointed out that it is quite usual to find that the etymological signification of a word no longer covers all the uses to which it was originally applied, or that in time it gains a much wider meaning. I may refer to the word electricity, which now scarcely reminds any one of electron, amber.

It has further been held by some, among others by Bernheim, that there is no such thing as hypnosis, but only suggestion. I cannot regard this somewhat oracular statement as altogether correct. We cannot class such conditions as are to be found in the four cases I have brought forward with ordinary suggestion in waking life. Pierre Janet has justly pointed out that because there are many transitions from the normal state to the hypnotic, we are not therefore entitled to say that there is no special condition of hypnosis. A condition which, on awaking, leaves no recollection behind, as in the fourth case, is a condition altogether distinct from our normal condition. It is quite in harmony with this position to admit that many suggestions may be carried out in the waking state.

CHAPTER III.

THE SYMPTOMS OF HYPNOSIS.

I COME now to the point which is most important and which requires the fullest consideration. In order to present as complete a survey as possible, I must make an arrangement under headings of Physiology and Psychology. It must not be thought, however, that we have to do with a real division ; of that there can be no question. For the bodily functions, of which I shall speak under the head of Physiology, show a deviation from the normal purely as a consequence of psychical states. Just as a man paralyzed by fright cannot move in consequence of a mental shock, and not in consequence of an injury to the muscles, so people in a state of religious excitement have visions, not because their eyes are abnormal in visual function, but because they are in an abnormal mental state ; thus in hypnosis the muscles, the organs of sense, &c., are abnormal in function only because the mental state is altered. Only from this point of view is the division made in what follows. It is doubtful whether there exist generally in hypnosis, besides the primary mental and secondary physical alterations, any primary bodily abnormalities. Descriptions have often been given of them, of which I shall speak later ; many such investigations, however, suffer from the fact that it is not

5

clear whether we are dealing with an effect of the
methods employed to induce hypnosis or with one of
its essential phenomena. In order to explain what is
meant by this I will suppose that a person looks for
a long time fixedly at a button. This will produce
watering of the eyes ; but this comes on in any case,
whether hypnosis is produced or not. Consequently
the watering of the eyes is not an essential phenomenon of hypnosis, but purely a consequence of the
means employed to engender it. In consequence of
the close tie which everywhere exists between the
mental · and bodily phenomena it will not be
surprising if in discussing the latter I am often
obliged to refer to the former, and *vice versâ ;* a
thorough separation is not possible. In order not
to destroy the inner unity for merely external con-
siderations, I shall occasionally deviate from the
purely tabular arrangement.

One peculiar quality of consciousness we shall very
often find in hypnosis : what is called suggestibility,
or, better, increased suggestibility. I shall so often
use this word, and words connected with it, that it will
be well to define exactly what is meant by it. For
this purpose I must make a little digression

Every concept in human beings has a particular
action, which is to be recognized by an external or
internal effect. For example, by the laws of association one concept calls up another. The· idea of
St. Helena awakes that of Napoleon I. This peculiar
arousing of ideas by other ideas was called the law of
suggestion by a great school of Scotch psychologists
(Thomas Brown and others), and Paul Janet thinks
that this expression induced Braid to introduce the
term "to suggest" for an analogous phenomenon—the
suggestion d'attitude—though Brandis used it earlier

of magnetism. A concept can, however, produce an
effect by arousing feeling; if any one thinks of a dead
relative, he feels grief, and the thought of a joyful event
awakens a feeling of happiness. Inclinations are called
up in the same way; the thought of an object for which
one has a great longing awakens the desire to possess
it. Sensations can be also produced in the same
manner. We have an example in the itching which
many persons feel directly fleas are talked of. These
ideas, feelings, sensations, and desires, aroused by
another idea, form internal processes, which we
recognize by internal experience. But an idea can
have an effect which displays itself externally—for
example, thoughts call up certain movements.

Let us here consider a proceeding which is called
thought-reading, which, as the "willing game," was
for a long time a favourite society game in England
in a somewhat modified form, and which became
popular in Germany through the exhibitions of
Cumberland. Most people have certainly seen it;
however, I will again describe the process. A person
A. is made to leave the room; among those who
remain, B. is chosen to think of some object present,
which A. is to find. A. comes back, takes B.'s hand
and demands that he shall think steadfastly of the
place of the chosen object; let us say it is the lamp.
B. thinks steadfastly of it, and it is seen that A. and B.
go together towards the lamp, till A., pointing to it,
says, "That was the object thought of." Simple as
this process—explained lately by Beard, Gley, Richet,
Obersteiner, Preyer, and known fifty years ago to
Chevreul—may be, it appeared enigmatical to many
at first. This is the explanation: B. thinks steadily
of the place of the lamp, and has at the same time
slight movements of the body, and particularly of

the muscles of the arm, in the direction of the lamp. A. feels these muscular movements and follows them, he permits himself to be directed by them, and finds in this way the object thought of. B. naturally did not make the movements intentionally, consequently they were involuntary and unconscious. All the same, the movements were strong enough to show A. the way. This example shows us the following; B. had a certain idea (namely, that of the place of the lamp) in his head, and this concept called up movements. The movement of the lips which occurs when one thinks intensely of a word, is of analogous character (Stricker).

We see, then, from the foregoing that ideas aroused in us have an effect which sometimes shows itself internally as other concepts, sensations, &c., and sometimes externally as movement; in many cases, perhaps in all, there is both an internal and an external effect. What effect appears, what idea, what feeling, what movement will be induced by the first concept, depends upon the individuality of the person, upon his mental imagery, upon his character, his habits, and upon the species of concept; but a certain effect always follows.

In many cases a person (A.) is able to attain some particular effect, which he intentionally aimed at, by rousing in B. a definite concept; and this effect is often attained independently of B.'s will, or even against it. We see an example of this in a juggler. He wants to take some object or other without being seen by the public: to attain this he looks at another point—for example, at his left hand. The eyes of the spectators involuntarily follow his. By glancing at his left hand the juggler has caused the spectators to look in the same direction. He has aroused, as quick as lightning, in the spectators the idea that something is going on at his left hand; and this idea has had the effect of making the spectators look at the left hand. A juggler is very often able to influence the spectators by some such proceeding. They are often thus induced to look in the direction desired by the juggler, in order that he may be able to change or hide some object unobserved. We see here, then, that he produces the effect he desires—namely, to make people look in another direction. But he takes great care not to tell the spectator to look in this direction. If he were to say this the spectator would discover his object, and certainly would not look at the spot which the juggler wishes, and he would not attain his end. On the other side there are also certain cases in which a desired effect is attained simply by directly assuring the person concerned that the effect will appear. He is certainly able in most cases to prevent arbitrarily the appearance of such an effect; but not always, however. An example which is brought forward by Bonniot should make this clear. One says to a person who is embarrassed, "You are getting red in the face now!" It is well known that many people really blush when the conviction that they are blushing is aroused in their minds. Now a proceeding of this nature, in which an effect is obtained simply by arousing in the person concerned a conviction of its appearance, is called a suggestion. We shall find it extremely often in hypnosis, and I have already given above a number of examples of such suggestions. The method of inducing hypnosis in use at Nancy is to be referred to this kind of process. By it an endeavour is made to create in the subject a conviction of the appearance of hypnosis, and through this to induce the hypnosis itself.

But there are also cases in which the idea of the appearance of an effect is not aroused by a second person, but generated by the subject himself. The corresponding effect very often appears, even against the subject's will. Under pathological conditions we find this process very common : a stammerer, for example, can often speak quite well, when he does not think about his stammering ; as soon as he thinks of it, and as soon as the conviction that he will not be able to speak without stammering takes possession of him, that moment he begins to stammer. Now, as the idea of stammering is here generated by the person himself, while the above-mentioned idea of blushing was generated by another person, the last process, in which an outsider induces the idea is called external suggestion, or hetero-suggestion, the first self-suggestion or auto-suggestion.

Such auto-suggestions are not very uncommon as pathological incidents. Dread of open spaces (agoraphobia) is nothing but an auto-suggestion. The patient in this case is possessed by the idea that he cannot step across some open space ; no reasoning is of avail here. The patient acknowledges its justice without permitting it to influence him, because his auto-suggestion is too powerful. As a rule, logic is for the most part powerless over these auto-suggestions. Many hysterical paralyses are likewise auto-suggestions ; thus a patient cannot move his legs because he is convinced that movement is impossible. If this conviction can be shaken, movement is at once practicable.

Auto-suggestion may be called up by some external cause ; this may affect the person from outside, and thus induce an auto-suggestion. Charcot referred some isolated traumatic paralyses to some such originating mechanism—though this point is still in debate. According to this view a violent blow on the arm, following on certain disturbances of sensibility, may produce in the person concerned a conviction that he cannot move his arm. As the conviction was called up by the blow, this case stands somewhere between external suggestion and auto-suggestion. We will call all cases in which the auto-suggestion did not arise spontaneously, but was the secondary result of something else, such as a blow, indirect suggestions; as opposed to direct suggestion, which arouses a certain idea immediately, of which I have already given several examples. It is, besides, not always necessary that there should be a conscious mental act in suggestion; individuality and habit sometimes replace this, and play a great part in the training of the subject, of which we have still to speak. For example, if some external sign, such as a blow on the arm, has several times, by means of a conscious mental act, produced the auto-suggestion that the arm is paralyzed, then the auto-suggestion may repeat itself later mechanically at every blow without any conscious thought about the effect of the blow.

A particular psychical state, disposing to suggestion, is a necessary condition of its appearance. The disposition to suggestion is called suggestibility; it must be present and must precede the suggestion if the latter is to succeed (Bentivegni). A person in such a state is said to be suggestible.

We shall now see that we can in this way obtain many effects during hypnosis. We shall also see that we can produce these effects not only during hypnosis (hypnotic or intra-hypnotic suggestion), but

that these extend to the time following. We call
this post-hypnotic suggestion. By means of this we
can tell the person in the hypnotic state that after his
awakening a particular result will follow. We can
also distinguish another kind of suggestion : something may be suggested to the subject before the
hypnosis, which is to follow in that state. This is
pre-hypnotic suggestion.

ⓘ *Physiology.*

We will now pass to a discussion of the functions
of the individual organs. The alterations which we
find in hypnosis affect the voluntary and involuntary
muscles as well as the organs of sense, common
sensation, the secretions, metabolism, and in rare
cases also the cell power of organization.

The voluntary muscles show the most frequent
abnormalities, and suggestion exercises a most
extraordinary influence over their functions during
hypnosis. We will ask, first of all, what is the state
of the functions of the voluntary muscles during
hypnosis, when no kind of external influence is
exercised. There are the greatest differences, according to the method of hypnotization selected, and
according to the character of the subject. Some are
able to move with perfect freedom during hypnosis
till the command of the experimenter inhibits some
particular movement ; many, on the contrary, look as
if they were asleep. In this case we see no movements, or very rare ones, which are slow and
laboured. When we discuss the phenomena of
suggestion we shall see that this incapacity for movement cannot in rare cases be removed by the command of the hypnotist. It is to be understood that

between complete freedom of movement and the incapacity to move at all there exist all sorts of transitional stages. It is all the same which of these characters has the preponderance ; muscular activity can nearly always be influenced in a high degree by suggestion.[1] By means of it we can make the exist-, ing movements impossible, or induce previously impossible ones.

I have shown (p. 32) with my second subject how easily I can make his arm powerless to move, simply by arousing in him the conviction that the arm is powerless. In just the same way the movements of the legs, trunk, larynx, and so on, escape the subject's control. "You cannot raise your arm ; cannot put out your tongue." This suffices to make the forbidden movement impossible. In some cases the inability to move arises because the subject cannot voluntarily contract his muscles ; while in other cases a contracture of the antagonistic muscles makes every attempt at voluntary movement useless (Bleuler). In the same manner the leg will lose the power of motion at command. We have seen (p. 32) in the second experiment how the power of speech can also be taken away. And it is even possible to allow the muscles to contract for one particular purpose only. If we say to a hypnotic subject, "You can only say your name ; for the rest you are absolutely dumb," the desired effect will most surely be produced. In the same way it is possible to prevent movements of the arms for one particular purpose. Thus we can make it impossible for a person to write, though he will be able to do any other kind of work. The subject can sew, play the piano, &c., but all efforts to write are vain. The movements only become possible at the moment when the experimenter gives permission. It is remarkable that in some persons one set of muscles is easier to influence by suggestion, and in others another set. For example, we can make a person dumb by suggestion, while all the other muscles obey his will in spite of suggestion. Another, again, loses the power of moving his arms at once, while his speech remains unaffected.

In just the same way as muscular movements are prevented by suggestion, so can movements be induced by it against, or without, the will of the subject. We have seen (p. 33) how the subject in the third experiment knelt down, followed me, and so forth. I say to another person, "You are lifting your right arm to lay it on your head." This happens at once. I would insist that it must be decided whether these movements take place without, or against, the will of the subject, as in the latter case an increase of sensibility is already demonstrated. I say, " Your left arm will now rise up in the air." And the arm rises as if drawn up by a string, although the subject makes no intentional movement ; but neither does it occur to him to resist. The movements without the subject's will can often be distinguished from those against it by a certain steady ease. These last are nearly always characterized by strong muscular contractions, and by trembling, which shows the intense effort not to obey the will of the hypnotist.

Just in the same way the hypnotic subject is obliged to cough, laugh, talk, jump, &c., at command. It is further possible to generate by suggestion the idea of a paralysis of one of the extremities. These isolated paralyses have a great resemblance to the psychical paralyses arising without hypnosis, such as Russell Reynolds described in 1869, as "paralysis dependent on idea"; and Erb, later on, as "paralysis by imagination." The pupils of Charcot have tried to find objective symptoms of these paralyses that depend on suggestion. It cannot be doubted that such objective changes *may* occur through a particular association of symptoms; this hypothesis is supported by Krafft-Ebing also. We must, however, recognize that this is not the rule. According to Lober, Gilles de la Tourette, and Richer, the clinical characteristics of these paralyses are marked by the absolute loss of motor power and sensation, increase of the tendon reflexes, ankle clonus, wrist clonus, complete loss of muscular sense, *i.e.*, of the ability to control perfectly the action of the muscles, and to be certain of the position of the limbs, changed electrical excitability, and vasomotor disturbances; these last are particularly said to show themselves by a bright flush of the skin on slight stimulation. These paralyses can be produced in both the hypnotic and post-hypnotic states. Besides these atonic paralyses, in which the muscles are completely relaxed, other paralyses, in which the muscles are persistently contracted, can also be produced by suggestion.

With these subjects who are deprived of will, besides the movements described above, complicated movements, or even performances (if I may be allowed the expression), also take place by suggestion. I say to the subject, "You will spin round three times." Or again, "You must lift that thing off the table; you must go and do it; you cannot help it." The subject performs the command.

The suggestion itself is made in different ways.
The main point, and all turns upon this, is that
the subject should thoroughly understand what the
experimenter wishes. Each of the organs of sense
is a door of entrance for suggestion. The most
common is naturally our habitual means of communication—speech (verbal suggestion)—by means
of which we *tell* the subject what we wish. But it is
very important, and much more effective than words
alone, that the experimenter should accompany his
words by a performance of the movement which the
subject is intended to execute. Consequently professional magnetizers habitually induce movements
by imitation. Heidenhain was at first by this led to
the false conclusion that all these movements of
hypnotics depended on imitation.

Imitation appears particularly in a hypnotic state,
which certain authors (Brémaud, Morselli, Tanzi)
have thoroughly studied, and which Descourtis calls
fascination. I have shown (p. 33) in the third
experiment a case of this kind. A professional
magnetizer, Donato, has demonstrated this state
completely ; and Morselli and others have on this
account called this form of hypnosis Donatism.

As I saw in Paris, Donato uses a particular process
to bring about this state. This process aims at a
primary forced contracture of all the muscles of the
body, in order, by this means, to limit the voluntary
movements as much as possible. In this case the
eyes of the hypnotist and the subject are firmly fixed
on one another. The subject finally follows every
movement of the experimenter. If he goes backward, the subject follows ; if he comes forward,
the subject does the same. In the same way the
latter imitates every movement of the experimenter,

only on the condition, however, that he knows he is
intended to do so.   We see here, as in the above third
experiment, that fascination may be a primary form of
hypnosis. But it can also be originated secondarily out
of the other hypnotic states; and this is more usual.
When the experimenter has hypnotized the subject in
some other way, and has made him open his eyes, he
can fix his own steadily on them, and thus induce the
same phenomena.   A variety of this fascination is to
fix the eyes of the subject on some other object—for
example, on the finger of the experimenter.   In this
case the fascinated person follows every movement
made by the finger.

But imitation plays an important *rôle* in hypnosis,
as well as fascination.   This results from the fact that
the sight of a movement arouses a much more vivid
mental picture of it in the hypnotized person than
does a mere command ; this last is, however, a necessary condition for the success of the suggestion.

Verbal suggestion is also made easier by other
gestures.   In order to compel some one to kneel
down, an energetic movement of the hand accompanying the verbal suggestion is very effective, as in the
third experiment.   With this fact is connected one of
the phenomena which magnetizers are fond of exhibit-
ing, namely, the drawing of the subject after the
experimenter, who makes movements with his hand
which show the subject that he is intended to
approach.

The experimenter can also repel the subject in the
same way.   This succeeds in particular by means of
movements of the hand, indicating that he is to go
away.   It is not at all necessary that the subject
should see the movements of the experimenter ; it is
sufficient that he should divine them either from a

noise or a slight current of air; thus the hypnotic
obeys the experimenter even when he has his back
turned towards him. Upon the same phenomenon
depend the attraction and repulsion of single limbs
of the subject, which happen in the same way, through
the hypnotic's perception of the experimenter's gestures. The experimenter can make the subject raise
and drop his hand, merely by gesticulating with his
own ; he can also obtain many effects by a glance
only.   It is not necessary to look steadily in the eyes
of the hypnotic, as in fascination. The operator looks
at the subject's leg—it at once becomes powerless to
move. The hypnotic is going away—the experimenter
looks at a spot on the floor and he stands chained to
the spot.   These phenomena vividly recall the " evil
eye," the fascinating gaze, and so on, by means of
which an evil influence was supposed to be exercised.

In Southern Europe, as well as among the Jews of Northern
Africa, the dread of the evil eye is strongly marked. Various
symbols here serve as a protection against it (Fitzner, Elworthy).
Among the Mohammedans and Christians in Palestine the belief
in the evil eye is still widely spread (Preyer, Einszler).   During
my residence in Palestine I have frequently been able to verify
this. Siegfried has brought together various passages in the
Bible and the Talmud which prove a belief in the evil eye.

I will mention here that not only speech but also
music has a suggestive effect. If dance music is
played the subject will dance, following the rhythm,
and when the dance is changed to another he alters
his step to correspond. The influence of music
upon human beings has long been known, and is
striking in hypnosis. By means of music during
hypnosis all sorts of different moods and feelings
can be aroused corresponding to the kind of music.
Naturally, the subject must have a taste for music,

otherwise—it—will—have no influence. Mesmer long
ago recognized this influence of music, and used a
then newly-invented instrument, the bell-harmonica,
to obtain the necessary effect. Before Mesmer, Kircher
had already referred to the effect of a similar instrument, the glass-harmonica (Ennemoser).

The muscular sense, which keeps us informed of the
position of our limbs, requires particular consideration
as a way of entrance for suggestion. It causes the
phenomenon which the school of Nancy calls "catalepsy by suggestion";[1] which is also to be found in
other states than hypnosis—for example, in some cases
of typhus fever (Bernheim). It is very common in
hypnosis, and is shown in the following example:
I lift the arm of a hypnotic, hold it in the air, and
then let go ; the arm remains as I placed it, although
I say nothing. Why does this happen? Because the
subject believes he must leave his arm thus, and
because this suggestion was conveyed to him by the
muscular sense. Another person lets his arm fall ; I
raise it again, and say at the same time, "The arm
keeps still ;" which happens ; but only because the
person now knows that this is intended, while he did
not understand the simple raising of the arm. Let us
return to the first subject. I raise the arm again, saying, "Now the arm falls down;" which, in fact, happens;
evidently only because the person believes that he is
to let it fall. The legs, head, trunk, and so forth, can
be put into the most different postures and maintained

[1] As the most different views exist as to what "Catalepsy"
means, I remark here that, for the sake of brevity, I shall so
name any state in which voluntary movements disappear
and the limbs remain as they are placed by the experimenter
—without having regard to the length of time which elapses
before the limbs move freely again, or fall from their own
weight.

there in exactly the same way; the muscular sense
here is the only transmitter of the suggestion. The
inclination of the subject to maintain cataleptic
positions is so great that Heidenhain considered the
hypnotic state to be a catalepsy artificially produced.
Catalepsy by suggestion has nothing whatever to do
with physical alterations of the muscles.

The main point for the attainment of catalepsy is
that the subject should accept the idea of the corresponding attitude. Consequently the idea must take
root before the desired result can be attained. For
this purpose some means or other must be employed
to allow it to operate during a certain period. Words
answer the purpose as well as other signs; many persons can only be thrown into catalepsy from suggestion
when the attitude required is maintained for some
time.

The mesmeric passes (p. 32), which I have mentioned
as a method of hypnotizing, here deserve especial mention. These mesmeric passes can be used locally in
hypnosis—for example, over an arm, in order to make
it cataleptic. Cataleptic attitudes which cannot be
produced by verbal suggestion may often be obtained
in this way. As far as I have been able to study
these phenomena,[1] it is unnecessary in their case
to imagine any special force as an explanation.
According to my view the efficiency of the mesmeric
passes results from the fact that by means of them
the whole attention of the subject is directed to his
arm for a long time. By this means the idea has
time to take root. Let any one allow his arm or
leg to be mesmerized in this fashion and he will find

[1] In a monograph, *Der Rapport in der Hypnosis* (Am-
brosius Abel, Leipzig, 1892), I have published many experiments bearing on this point.

that his whole attention is directed to this part of his
body, and much more strongly directed than if the
attention was concentrated on the limb in another
manner. From this it follows also that contractures
often only appear when the mesmeric passes have
drawn the attention for some time to the part of the
body concerned. The passes with contact act in
exactly the same way as the passes without contact.
In any case—and this is important—the effect only
appears when the individual has an idea of what
is intended to follow. That centrifugal passes call up
contractions and centripetal ones dissipate them, is a
phenomenon frequently mentioned ; but we appear to
have to do here with unintentional suggestions. Besides, I have been as often able to do the same thing
with centripetal passes as with centrifugal.

We thus see in what manner suggestion affects the
movements. A particular attitude is adopted by the
subject because the corresponding idea has been implanted in him by the operator.
Such an implanted idea has yet another particular
effect in hypnosis. It has often a tendency to fix
itself firmly in the mind and consequently to exercise
a longer continued effect. This continuation of the
effect may express itself in three ways : firstly, by
the fact that a certain state of contraction is continued
for a long period—there is, in fact, a contracture ;
secondly, by a particular long-continued movement ;
thirdly, by the fact that when the muscles are relaxed
a contraction of them can only be obtained with difficulty or not at all. I am decidedly of opinion that
these phenomena of the muscles must be distinguished
from suggestion ; they certainly produce a particular
function, but do not explain its long duration. Some-

times it is not even possible to counteract the effect of
the first suggested by a second.

These cases, in which the action of the original suggestion
cannot be easily inhibited, recall certain forms of insanity, such
as melancholia cum stupore. Bancroft has lately shown that
the disturbances of movement in this and other insanities can
be produced by a primary psychic process, even by a delusion,
but that when the cause has passed, the disturbance of movement still persists.

Vincent denies that there is any tendency for the suggestion
to become fixed in hypnosis, he has always been able to remove the suggestion at once. At the same time he remarks
that he has sometimes found opposition during several seconds,
but that this is only to be regarded as an autohypnosis. Whether
this tendency to retain the suggestion, which may be found in
many hypnotic subjects, is to be referred to auto-suggestion or
not, seems to me a matter of indifference. The phenomenon is
found in a certain group of cases, and nothing is gained in the
symptomatology of hypnosis by applying the same label—such
as suggestion—to all phenomena. The symptoms must be
described as they are observed. And it must further be remembered that explanation is not the same thing as description.

I order a person to stretch out his right arm stiffly.
The arm is stretched out, and the subject is unable to
bend it of his own accord ; that is, the muscles are
in a state of contracture. In most cases, directly I
command the arm to be bent it can be done. But
there are some cases in which the experimenter is
unable to put an end to the contracture at once
because the effect of the earlier idea continues. The
stronger was the contraction of the muscles the more
difficult it is to put an end at once to the state of
contracture. A particular movement can also be
continued for a long time in the same way. The so-
called automatic movements (Liébeault, Bernheim),
or continued movements, as Max Dessoir calls them,
belong to the same category. If we turn the arms of

a hypnotic round and round each other, he has a tendency to continue the movement after the operator has ceased to compel it. This <u>happens because the subject believes that he has been ordered to go on.</u> In some cases he continues turning his arms passively, while on other occasions he makes the strongest possible effort to keep them still, particularly when requested to do so. This resistance is useless, however; in spite of all exertion of the will the movement is continued. A new suggestion of the experimenter, that the arms shall stop, is enough in most cases to arrest the movements. Sometimes the idea has taken root so strongly that the experimenter finds it impossible to obtain an arrest at once by a counter-command. I have often observed that a movement has continued for some time in spite of my order. The most varied movements are continued in this manner after they have once begun. I lift up an arm and bend it gently at the elbow joint; directly I let go it repeats the movement. If it is desired that the hypnotic shall walk, and he does not obey the command, let him be pulled forward a little; he will then, when left to himself, continue to walk (Heidenhain). The involuntary laughter, which I have often heard, is connected with this; it begins at command, or on a slight provocation. It can be put an end to neither by the order of the experimenter nor by the will of the hypnotic. There are also pathological cases of uncontrollable laughter showing a decided resemblance to these cases of hypnosis; Feodorot, who has published several observations, refers it to a weakening of the will, and also to a similar condition to that found in hypnosis. This laughter in hypnosis also resembles the cheerfulness produced by haschisch; under the influence of

this drug, expressions which are quite insignificant,
excite involuntary laughter (Moleschott). Obersteiner,
who first began the scientific study of hypnotism in
Austria, has observed the automatic laugh in his own
case, and has described it. We can also induce
alternate movements of drawing up and stretching
out in the arm or leg, and nodding or shaking of the
head, &c.

In some cases the passivity of the subject is so
great that the idea of a movement will not take root
at all. In this case the suggestion of the experimenter is unable to overcome the muscular relaxation. Subjects of this kind let their arms drop after
they have been raised, in spite of all suggestions.
Questions are not answered, or only slight movements
of the lips show that they have been heard at all.
Two different types of hypnosis, which are called
active and passive, may be distinguished by the
presence or absence of this muscular relaxation.
The passive form has a greater external likeness to
natural sleep, while the active might be taken for a
waking state on superficial observation. Passive
hypnosis is not regarded by some authors (Braid) as
a form of hypnosis, but is considered to be a sleep,
because the especial symptom is wanting which every
investigator regards as the necessary characteristic of
hypnosis, namely, catalepsy. This does not appear
to me absolutely necessary in order to show
hypnosis. Hypnosis often shows itself as passive
at the beginning ; as soon as the eyes are closed the
head drops forward, or backward, while the supporting muscles of the neck are relaxed. There are
many transitional states between active and passive
hypnosis, and one often passes into the other.

The motor disturbances which appear in the eye

must here be particularly discussed. We have
already seen that many hypnoses are characterized
only by the closing of the eyes, while in many cases
this is added to other symptoms. But the closing of
the eyes can also be influenced by suggestion, and an
order of the experimenter is enough in most cases to
cause their instantaneous opening. Closing of the
eyes greatly favours the appearance of other hypnotic
phenomena, but is not absolutely indispensable.
There are persons who can be thrown into the
deepest stage of hypnosis by a fixed gaze, without
closing the eyes at all (Gurney).

It must be mentioned that Heidenhain already knew and recognized the closing of the eyes as the only symptom of hypnosis.
It is so much the more astonishing that the knowledge of
this light hypnotic state was afterwards completely lost. Some
years ago, when I threw a person in the Women's Hospital at
Berlin into this hypnotic state by means of the Nancy process,
Professor Ewald, who had made earlier fruitless attempts with
the same person by means of fixing the eyes, believed that the
closing of the eyes was simulated. These light states were
then very little known.

Although, then, as we say, closing of the eyes is not
a necessary preface to hypnosis, yet the eyes are in
most cases closed, and it is often impossible to permit
them to open without ending the hypnosis at once.
Even when the eyes open during a long hypnosis,
there is in many cases a certain heaviness in the lids
and a desire to close them. Much depends, however,
upon the method employed; and primary fascination
in particular always occurs while the eyes are wide
open. The closing of the eyes is sometimes very
gentle, and not spasmodic; though I have seen the
muscles which close the eye contract spasmodically
in a large number of cases. Braid and Heidenhain

already pointed out that when the lids close, even in the deepest hypnosis, the closing is not complete. There is often a slight chink of opening, and this is not unimportant, because many experiments in clairvoyance, and also pretended reading with the pit of of the stomach, may be explained by the ability to see through this small opening. In any case the closing of the eyes is a common occurrence in hypnosis, especially when the Nancy method is used. Everybody will remember that a heaviness of the eyelids and a feeling of fatigue about the eyes is one of the first symptoms of natural sleep.

While the eyes are closed the lids not unseldom have a vibratory, trembling movement; but this symptom is of no real importance for diagnosis, as on the one hand it is sometimes wanting and on the other hand often appears without hypnosis. We often see the eyeballs roll upwards as the eyes are closing. While in some cases this position of the eyeball is maintained, in other cases the eyeball resumes its natural position directly the eyes are closed. If this does not take place, the white sclerotic only is visible when the lids are artificially raised.

I have only been able to find the convergence of the pupils described by some observers in one case of hystero-epilepsy. Borel affirms that this convergence can occasionally be obtained by suggestion. If the eyes are open, a slight state of exophthalmos is said to be observed; however, this symptom appears only to occur when the method of fixed attention is used.

As we have seen, the voluntary muscles are entirely under the influence of external suggestion during hypnosis. A further peculiarity is, that a particular movement or state of contraction of the muscles cannot always be controlled at once; and finally, we have seen that in some cases muscular contraction can only be brought about with difficulty or not at all. *One of these two functional abnormalities of the muscles exists in all hypnotic states.* Though it is occasionally confined to an inability to open the eyes, in other hypnotic states the functions of other muscles of the body are affected. The different phases result, then, from various combinations of the above-mentioned abnormalities, and from their different localization in the muscles. The various kinds of catalepsy arise in this manner. Bernheim distinguishes several forms of this catalepsy, according to the facility with which the cataleptic position can be changed. Sometimes this is very easily done, sometimes with more difficulty, as in tonic contracture; the *flexibilitas cerea* forms an intermediate stage. These different kinds of catalepsy are affairs of hypnotic training and suggestion (Berger). I have never clearly seen a typical *flexibilitas cerea* in hypnosis, except when the training of the subject had been directed to that point. It appears from a remark of Nonne concerning the *flexibilitas cerea*, that he has collected other experiences regarding it. On that account I would say emphatically that I mean here the typical *flexibilitas cerea*, in which the feeling of resistance is the same as if we were bending limbs of wax; this feeling of resistance must further be uniform, it must not be stronger at one moment than at another. According to my experience a *flexibilitas cerea* taken in this sense is only to be obtained in hypnosis by training. In any case all these phenomena are of a purely psychical nature.

One of the best known features in hypnosis is the rigidity of the whole body. There is sometimes a complete tonic contracture of nearly all the voluntary muscles, through which the head, neck, trunk, and legs become as stiff as a board. A well-known experiment can be carried out in this state: the head can be placed on one chair and the feet on another, and the body will not double up. A heavy weight, that of a man, for example, may even be placed upon the body without bending it. It is not astonishing, after what I have said of the effect of the mesmeric passes, that this stiffening should be more easily induced by their means; it cannot always be induced by mere verbal suggestion. A command or sign of the experimenter generally suffices to put an end to the rigidity.

We must now ask whether any further abnormalities appear in the voluntary muscles during hypnosis. Changes which are supposed not to be of psychical nature have often been assumed. It is frequently maintained that reflex action is altered in hypnosis, that reflexes appear which do not appear in normal conditions. Heidenhain, Obersteiner, and Charcot are to be mentioned among those who have expressed this view. Charcot based his classification of the hypnotic states upon the alteration of the reflexes; so I will here briefly give the chief characteristics of his three stages.

Charcot distinguished a *grand hypnotisme* and a *petit hypnotisme.* The last he does not describe in detail; in the first, which is found in hystero-epileptics, he distinguishes three stages:—I. The cataleptic stage, which is produced by a sudden loud noise, or results from the opening of the subject's eyes while he is in the lethargic stage; in this stage the position of the limbs is easily changed while the hypnotic's eyes are open. Every position which is given to the limbs is maintained for some time, but is also easily changed by the experimenter without resistance on the part of the subject; there is also no wax-like flexibility (*flexibilitas cerea*). No tendon reflex, no increase of muscular irritability. There is analgesia, but it is possible to exercise a certain influence over the subject through sight, hearing, and the muscular sense. 2. The lethargic stage. It can be induced primarily by fixed attention, or secondarily out of the cataleptic stage by closing the eyes. The subject is unconscious and not accessible to external influences, and there is analgesia. The limbs are relaxed and fall by their own weight; the eyes are closed, the tendon reflexes increased. There is increased excitability of the muscles, the so-called neuro-muscular hyper-excitability. These increases are demonstrated by mechanical stimulation of the muscles, nerves, or tendons. For example, if the ulnar nerve is pressed a contraction of all the muscles which it supplies follows, so that a characteristic posture of the fingers results; if a muscle is stimulated, it alone contracts. The same thing is attained by this as by local faradization in normal states, which was shown by Duchenne. While at the extremities the contraction passes into contracture—that is, becomes permanent—a stimulation of the facial nerve only causes a simple contraction in the face, which soon ceases. The resolution of the resulting contracture is produced by exciting the antagonistic muscles; thus, for example, a contracture of the wrist is put an end to by excitation of the extensors, and the contracture of one sterno-mastoid by stimulation of the other. It is striking that, according to Charcot, the motor parts of the cerebral cortex, can be stimulated through the cranium by means of the galvanic current, so that the muscles in connection with them contract. 3. The somnambulic stage. In some persons it arises primarily by means of fixed attention; it can be induced in all by friction on the crown of the head during the lethargic or cataleptic stages. The eyes are closed or half-closed. By means of gentle stimulation of the skin the underlying muscles can be put into rigid contraction, but not, however, by stimulation of the muscles, nerves, or tendons, as in the lethargic stage. Also the contracture does not disappear on stimulation of the antagonistic muscles as in that stage. The posture of the limbs produced by contracture in somnambulism cannot also be so easily altered as in catalepsy ; a certain resistance appears, as in *flexibilitas cerea ;* Charcot calls it the cataleptoid state. The same stimulation of the skin which induced the contractures also resolves them. In somnambulism many external influences are possible by means of suggestion, of which I will speak later in their proper connection.

With regard to these stages of Charcot, most investigators doubt if they really exist, and think that they are only an artificial product, the result of an unintentional training process. It is certainly striking that since the school of Nancy pointed this out, and since it has shown the many sources of error that should be avoided, the stages of Charcot are less and less frequently observed. Wetterstrand never found them at all among 3,589 different persons (Pauly) ; experimenters who have occasionally observed them, themselves remark that they only appear in certain persons after numerous experiments (Stembo). I have been as little able as have many others to observe the stages of Charcot in my experiments ;

though even a thousand negative results would not
be able to overthrow one positive result of Charcot's. ✝
I have besides often experimented on several hystero-
epileptics, but have failed to observe the stages, in
spite of Richer's opinion that every one who experiments on such persons will obtain the same results as
the school of Charcot. However, I think it possible
that in some few cases of hystero-epilepsy the stages
do exist. But let us confine ourselves to these few
cases ; let us give them no greater importance than
did Charcot himself, who by no means insisted that
these three stages are always to be found. Even those
authors who on the whole accept Charcot's stages
agree that there are many exceptions.

Charcot himself lays the chief stress on the variations of muscular excitability in the different stages.
Dumontpallier and Magnin, however, maintain that
the increase of neuro-muscular excitability is by no
means confined to the lethargic stage, but appears in
all of them. They have likewise pointed out that
there are numerous mixed states (*états mixtes*) in
which the symptoms, partly of the lethargic and partly
of the cataleptic stages, show themselves. Richer
finds single cases in which the catalepsy is signalized
by greater rigidity and disposition to contracture.
Tamburini and Seppilli find a lethargy with hyperæsthesia of the ovaries. Jules Janet again has produced
a fourth stage in Wit.,—one of the best-known of
Charcot's subjects—which is distinguished from the
three others, both physically and mentally. Besides
which, many deviations from the types of the three
stages are to be found in the writings of Charcot's
pupils. Thus Richer describes forms of lethargy, in
which the subject performs movements at command,
and Gilles de la Tourette describes a lucid lethargy,

in which there was no loss of consciousness. In any case the idea of the stages has become somewhat confused, as an attempt has been made to include everything possible under them. Every one looked for the stages ; when he could not find them, as was usually the case, he believed himself obliged to add certain new characteristics to them.

The methods used to induce the different stages have a very doubtful value. Magnin maintains that all the stages can be brought on by one particular stimulation—for example, by pressure on the crown of the head. Which stage appears, depends, he says, upon the duration of the stimulation. Dumontpallier and Magnin have besides asserted that the same method which induces a stage will also cause it to disappear (*l'agent qui fait défait*); for example, if catalepsy is caused by a dazzling ray of light it disappears when a new ray of light falls on the eye. Braid formerly maintained something of the same kind (Max Dessoir).

The main point, however, is that Charcot and his pupils describe specific muscular phenomena, which are supposed to appear without a psychical cause. Thus, as we have seen, contractions of the muscles are said to arise during the lethargic stage by means of pressure on the nerves ; muscles are contracted by stimulation of the skin without any mental act taking place ; that is, without the subject's knowing that a muscle is to contract, or which muscle it will be. Heidenhain stated exactly the same thing, except that he found no contractures from pressure on the nerves, but only from stimulation of the skin. Heidenhain also believes that these contractures occur without any participation of the consciousness, and that they are reflexes, which are set going by stimu-

lation of the skin. According to Heidenhain's view
only the underlying muscles contract through gentle
stimulation ; by means of stronger stimulation neighbouring ones also contract, and the consequent
contracture spreads, in proportion to the strength of
the stimulation. In this manner Heidenhain considers
the tonic spasm or rigidity, which is seen in hypnosis,
to be a reflex. Heidenhain tried to find new reflexes.
By means of stimulation of certain tracts of the skin
particular movements were supposed by him to be
induced ; thus stimulation of the neck produced vocal
sound—as in Goltz's experiments. Born also believed he had discovered a series of new reflexes,
which might be seen after stroking certain portions of
the skin.

The much-discussed question, whether in the experiments of Heidenhain and Charcot we have really
to do with reflexes or not, is not easy to answer,
because many physiologists do not distinguish with
sufficient clearness between two sorts of reflexes—the
physical and the mental. In order to render this
clear I must make a short digression and say something about reflex action. We understand by reflex
action of the muscles that particular action which is
induced by excitation of a sensory nerve, without the
co-operation of the will. When, for example, an
insect flies into the eye it closes ; this closing is
reflex, because it is involuntary. When on another
occasion the eye is voluntarily closed, this is no reflex,
but a voluntary movement, so that the same movement
may be performed either voluntarily or by reflex
action. Let us take the following case : I touch the
eye of a person (A.) ; the eye closes in consequence by
reflex action, that is, without the participation of A.'s
will. I bring my hand near to the eye of another

person (B.); long before it is touched it closes, not only
without, but also against, B.'s will. The closing of
B.'s eye is also reflex action; the stimulation here
affects the nerves of sight. And yet there is a great
difference between the closing of A.'s eye and the
closing of B.'s. While in the case of A. no mental
action is necessary to produce the reflex, in the case
of B. it is otherwise. He shuts his eye because he
imagines that it will be touched—at least, this is the
general opinion. If B. puts his own finger near his
eye it does not close, because this idea does not then
arise. In any case a decided mental action takes
place in B. and not in A. On this account we call
the closing of B.'s eye a mental reflex, and A.'s a
physical one. The mental reflexes are extremely
common; stooping at the whistling of a bullet,
laughing at sight of a clown, sickness produced by a
disgusting smell, are mental reflexes. The involuntary muscular action is caused by a stimulation of the
eye, ear, or sense of smell, after the stimulation has
been interpreted in a particular way by the consciousness.

The classification of the reflexes into physical and
mental is not valueless for us; I think it better at
present to keep to this classification, although it
is only schematic, and although an authority as
high as Lewes supposes a mental action in all
reflexes. Gurney, Max Dessoir, and Hückel, have
directed attention to the importance of mental
reflexes for hypnosis. Heidenhain and Charcot denied any mental action in the contractures which
they induced; the Nancy school, on the contrary,
believes that it occurs, that the subject knows what
is intended to result, but that his will is unable to
prevent the contracture; this is called a suggestion,

and is only a kind of mental reflex. Consequently the question put forward above, whether Heidenhain's and Charcot's contractures are reflexes, may be thus modified : Have we to do as these authors suppose, with physical reflexes, or with mental ones ?

Without wishing to maintain *a priori* that the views of Heidenhain and Charcot are mistaken, I should say that they would at least require careful examination before they could be accepted. Nowadays, when we know from Bernheim, Forel, Delbœuf, and others, that these things can all, or almost all, be brought about by suggestion—that is, by means of the hypnotic's belief in their appearance—we are obliged to suppose that this is actually the case whenever suggestion is not rigidly excluded in experiment. Heidenhain's experiments offer no guarantee on this point. As the influence of suggestion was then unknown, it was naturally not excluded, and it even appears, from Heidenhain's publications, that the experiments proposed were discussed before the subject. When, then, Heidenhain maintains that the contractures spread according to rule, and even according to the laws for physical reflexes laid down by Pflüger, my own experiments oblige me to doubt it ; according to these the contractures progress in proportion to the hypnotic's comprehension of the experimenter's wish or command ; so that there can be no question of an adherence to rule.

With regard to Charcot's propositions I will discuss later some particular points—for example, the loss of consciousness in lethargy. I will only remark here that most of the phenomena can be explained by suggestion. In the contractures of somnambulism the thing is clear. Nothing is easier than to cause such contractures by suggestion. If it is to be proved

that these really occur without suggestion, suggestion
must first be excluded. Only the publication of more
exact and detailed accounts of the first experiments
made with these subjects would convince us that it
was excluded. Unconscious and unintentional suggestion is the greatest source of error in hypnotic
investigation. I should conjecture that the contractures of somnambulism are only brought about by
mental action. This is also to be concluded from
another phenomenon. We have seen above, in the
fourth experiment, that only one person, the experimenter, can influence the subject, is in _rapport_ with
him, as the technical term goes. Only the experimenter can induce contraction of the muscles ;
stimulation by other persons has no effect. If the
contractions were produced without participation of
the consciousness, this would be incomprehensible.
Charcot's pupils also speak of this phenomenon ;
they assert that in somnambulism certain persons
only can influence the muscular action of the hypnotics
by stimulation of the skin ; those persons, that is,
who are in _rapport_ with the subject. This decidedly
favours the view that the contractures are caused by
an act of consciousness ; though Charcot's pupils have
not drawn this evident conclusion.

In the case of contractures in lethargy the question
is rather more complicated, particularly in those
where a certain group of muscles—for example, those
of the ulnar nerve—are acted upon, or those in which
an isolated muscle is excited. It would be well here,
also, if more exact accounts of the first experiments
were published. For it can hardly be avoided, that
when the same experiments are repeated certain
indications should be given, from which the subject
draws conclusions as to what he is expected to do.

I have no doubt that by means of such indications even tolerably complicated movements, such as an isolated contracture of the muscles supplied by the ulnar nerve, can be induced ; that is, purely by suggestion. With the quick perceptions which hypnotics possess, they could easily be brought to this point. I do not think it at all impossible to induce by suggestion the few movements which Charcot showed in his public classes. I also should note particularly that Jendrássik, an adherent of Charcot, who accepts his classification of the stages of hypnosis, thinks that the contracture of lethargy is brought about by suggestion only.

It must be admitted that Richer emphatically asserts that in these experiments, which were varied a thousandfold, the results were always identical, that imitation was excluded, and that the stimulation of muscles and nerves at once caused the corresponding contractures which very few physicans would be able intentionally to induce. But it may be concluded from the statement of Vigouroux that the thing is not so plain. He excepts the deltoid muscle from the rule. Gilles de la Tourette also says that the results were only attained after long previous experiment.

Although we are justified in refusing to recognize Charcot's three stages as a general principle of classification, there still remains the question whether in hypnosis there are reflexes such as Heidenhain and Charcot have described. Although there has been little tendency lately to accept them, they have yet found some defenders. Among these we must especially reckon Obersteiner, whose experiments are the more valuable since he had them made on himself while in the hypnotic condition. Obersteiner asserts that in hypnosis there is an action on nerve and muscle which has nothing to do with suggestion. He describes the following experiment on himself: "When I was in light hypnosis and the skin of my hand on the ulnar

7

side was stroked, I expected that the little finger would be bent; instead of that, to my surprise, it was abducted. As a matter of fact, beneath the irritated portion of skin lay not the flexor but the abductor minimi digiti, of which, in my half-sleeping state, I had not thought." However exact this statement may be, I would not accept it as an argument against the suggestive origin of contractures. That Obersteiner, after hypnosis was over, believed he had not thought of the abductor shows nothing, for there might very well have been a deception of memory. It is certain that Obersteiner knew previously what muscle lay beneath the spot in question. Even if we admit that the fact never came into consciousness during hypnosis, the knowledge was certainly not new to him. I may here refer to the sub-consciousness which I shall have to speak of later. We shall then find that experiences that we have once gone through, but which have momentarily become unconscious, may still influence our action. F. Myers has shown this very thoroughly in his work on *The Subliminal Consciousness*. For this reason, Obersteiner's experiment, interesting and valuable as it is, does not prove his view.

Interesting experiments on contractures have also been made by Schaffer. He was able to produce them by various sensory stimuli, by stimulation not only of touch but of the ear, and especially of the retina. In one-sided stimulation the contractures always appeared on the stimulated side. Schaffer believes that he has excluded suggestion. In two-sided stimulation the contraction appeared on both sides. When one side was made anasthetic, all sensory stimuli on that side were inoperative. On the other hand, Schaffer could also produce contractions by suggesting any sensory impression. The same thing then happened as if the stimulus had really been applied. On the ground of this observation, Schaffer naturally concluded that the reflex path is through the cerebral cortex; yet he does not admit pure suggestion.

The phenomena of imitative speech (*echolalie*), observed by Heidenhain and Berger belong to this section. Berger says that hypnotics will repeat everything that is said before them, like phonographs; even what is said in foreign languages is repeated with some exactness. The notion that only certain tracts of the bodily surface must be stimulated in order to produce this repetition (Heidenhain, Berger) may be considered a mistake, the result of insufficient acquaintance with suggestion on the part of the Breslau investigators. I believe that the hypnotic echoes what he believes he is intended to echo. It is certain that some persons are able to perform great feats in this way, imitating a hitherto unknown language quickly and correctly, particularly after the necessary practice. It is perfectly indifferent whether the speech be addressed to the stomach, or the neck—this was supposed to be the sensitive region—or to any other part of the body. The main point is that the hypnotic should know he is intended to repeat the sounds. Certain reflexes, which are supposed to be induced by touching the head, the appearance of aphasia, or of twitchings or contractures in the arm or leg on touching certain parts of the cranium, should be understood in the same way ; statements of this kind were made by Heidenhain, and have been repeated lately by Silva, Binet, and Féré. These last even believe that they can place single limbs in the somnambulic state by stimulating the parts of the head which correspond to the motor centres of the limbs concerned. The experiments have not been carried out with sufficient caution. It is inexplicable that the result should be attained by pressure on the head, and the reference of these authors to the phrenology of Gall explains nothing. Chalande even wishes to study the physiology of the brain in this way (Delbœuf). What would our physiologists say if, in order to stimulate some portion of the brain, it were only necessary to rub the cranium on the corresponding spot during hypnosis? The method would · certainly be practicable on account of its simplicity.

but unfortunately it is founded on inexact observations, and is perfectly useless.   Braid described
similar phenomena, which he called phreno-hypnotic.
He invented explanations, which were themselves in
need of explanation.   One of Braid's suppositions
was that there was a kind of reflex stimulus.   By
pressure on a portion of the skull a nerve was stimulated which by reflex action excited a part of the
brain, and by this means excited feelings of benevo-
lence, for example ; by stimulating another spot,
another nerve was excited, which by reflex action
produced an expression of piety, &c.   Braid appears
to have given up phreno-hypnotism later (Preyer).

Let me here point out that it is possible to induce
hemi-hypnosis, or hypnosis of one side, by suggestion,
or to influence each half of the body in a different
way.   It was known even to Braid that by blowing on
one eye the corresponding side could be awakened.
Descourtis, Charcot, Dumontpallier, Bérillon, Lepine
Strohl, as well as Grützner, Heidenhain, and Berger,
who were under Kayser's influence, carried on these
experiments in various modified forms ; Berger later
on changed his views.   Though these authors regard
hemi-hypnosis as a physiological condition induced
by the closing of one eye or by friction of one-half of
the crown of the head, their statements do not now
prove their point.   We know by this time that we can
produce all these states by mental influence, and
suggestion must be excluded before the experiments
can be considered conclusive.   It appears very
probable, from Heidenhain's publications, that the
expected results were discussed in the presence of the
subject, who only needed to divine the expected
result to act accordingly.   Sometimes stroking the
left side of the head was supposed to make the left

half of the body hypnotic; sometimes the result
followed on the right side. The rules which Heidenhain laid down on this question are not tenable. The
main point still is that the subject shall know what
is intended to happen to him, and what effect is
expected from the processes.

As is evident from what has been said, I regard the
functional changes which the voluntary muscles show
in hypnosis as dependent on central conditions; a
suggested idea can cause either paralysis or movement of the limbs. The question must now be
discussed whether, in consequence of this suggestive
central action, alterations in the functions of the
muscles may appear which are not normally to be
found, that is, whether the action causes objective
abnormalities which could not be induced by the will
of the hypnotic.

A priori, I think the probability that there are such
changes is not great, for it cannot be supposed that
an idea which I implant in the subject should have
more effect than the idea he himself originates. If,
then, there are some symptoms which are characteristic, this proves that the idea called up by external
suggestion, and the self-suggested idea, have different
effects on the functions; or else that the muscles are
influenced in hypnosis by something besides suggestion, *i.e.,* the propensity to contracture, of which I
have spoken above. We must understand the objective phenomena in one way or the other. I have
already spoken of the physical symptoms of suggested
paralyses. I will here mention a few other cases in
which suggestion heightened the normal muscular
powers.

The cataleptic posture of the limbs is sometimes

maintained for a very long time, even for several hours. One person remained for seventeen hours in a cataleptic posture. Berger mentions the case of a young girl who maintained this condition without perceptible change for seven hours, during which she was continually watched. In these cases the fatigue and pain which ordinarily follow on great muscular exertion do not ensue. Great fatigue rarely results even when the same position is maintained for as long as an hour. Some distinctly marked cases of imitative speech (*echolalie*) must be mentioned here. Braid relates that a hypnotized girl once imitated some of the songs of the famous Jenny Lind perfectly, which she was quite incapable of doing in the waking state. Braid attributes this feat to the delicacy of hearing and of the muscular sense in hypnosis.

However, we find in hypnosis frequent connecting links with the normal life. We see that in hypnosis an arm remains longer in the position commanded than a leg, for example. This is because the muscles of the leg are more difficult to fix in any desired posture than those of the arm ; the leg falls more quickly by its own weight.

Dynamometric investigations, that is, measurements of the muscular force, have often been undertaken during hypnosis. I myself have made a number of such investigations, which for the most part agreed with the results of Beaunis. The most important point appears to me to be that in most cases the muscular force is lessened in hypnosis. I have seldom found it increased. I have made these investigations during the different hypnotic states, but have hardly ever found an increase. However, there are variations, and I have occasionally seen the strength of one hand

THE SYMPTOMS OF HYPNOSIS.

increase while that of the other diminished. I have also obtained different results at different times with the same person. When there were such variations they were always of small amount, and they are the less important that all dynamometric investigations suffer from certain sources of error.

We may here consider the electric excitability of the nerves and muscles, to which little attention has hitherto been paid. Moriz Rosenthal finds an increase of electric sensibility in hypnosis. Tereg also found changes in one case, which, however, was investigated without the galvanometer; and Marina has done the same in the case of a person in the waking state who, however, had often been hypnotized. I, for my part, like Heidenhain, Berger, and Rieger, have been unable to discover anything of importance in this direction. I have tried more than a hundred different experiments without finding a perceptible difference on this point between the hypnotic and waking states. I made my experiments with the galvanic and faradic current; I always used Hirschmann's galvanometer, and made most of the experiments on the ulnar nerve just above the elbow. I have already said that the electric susceptibility is decreased in suggested paralyses; it appears that electric susceptibility undergoes changes in certain cases from a mental cause; a further investigation of this would be very interesting. I do not at all believe that we have to do with primary changes in the muscles or nerves. I may just mention that according to Morselli and Mendelsohn the muscles contract more quickly from stimulation in hypnosis than in the waking state.

I have discussed above a whole series of pheno-mena, which I, in common with the school of Nancy,

consider to be produced by suggestion, but which
Heidenhain and Charcot, among others, regard as
ordinary reflexes, having no mental cause. I have
shown that imitative speech (*echolalie*), many contractures, and the newly discovered reflexes of Born
and Heidenhain, are probably phenomena of suggestion. There appear to be no new reflexes in hypnosis
independent of suggestion ; no sure proof has yet
been offered, at least. We must now examine the
ordinary reflexes of hypnosis.

I have spoken occasionally of the tendon reflexes,
whose increase we observed in the lethargic stage of
Charcot, and in certain paralyses by suggestion.
Berger has also observed an increase of the patellar
reflex. But, as I have often noticed, the increase
seems to depend upon the kind of suggestion. I
have several times found increases when the muscles
were completely relaxed ; on the other hand, I have
found decrease of the reflexes in cataleptic postures.
This is easily explained ; it has an analogy in waking
states, and must not be too easily regarded as a
phenomenon peculiar to hypnosis, since apart from
hypnosis the tendon reflexes are more perceptible
when the muscles are relaxed than when they are
contracted.

With regard to the pupil of the eye, Braid has
already mentioned a difference between its states in
hypnosis and in sleep. In sleep there is a contraction
of the pupil ; but Braid found that it often dilated in
hypnosis. This is confirmed by Heidenhain. I have
never observed this dilatation except when I have
employed the method of fixed attention ; at other
times I have more often found contraction of the
pupil. I can confirm Braid's assertion that oscilla-
tions of the pupil appear not seldom in fixation ;
contraction and dilatation alternate rapidly.

Spasm of accommodation is also often mentioned (Heidenhain, Cohn, Rumpf). The assertion that the pupil reflexes are abnormal in hypnosis is often met with (Luys, Bacchi). It is said that a ray of light does not cause a reflex contraction of the pupil during hypnosis. I have never observed a complete absence of the reflex, but I have often remarked very slight reaction when I have used the method of fixed attention to induce hypnosis. I do not know whether this was an effect of the method or of the hypnosis, but am inclined to consider the method as the cause. Sgrosso noticed dilatation of the pupils in his two subjects on the appearance of hypnosis, followed by contraction during the state.

Up to this point we have only studied those changes which appear in the voluntary motor system during hypnosis. The hypnoses belonging to the first group (p. 62) are characterized by various combinations of these changes, which are, notwithstanding, also found in the second group. The hypnotic states belonging to this group are, however, distinguished by an increase of susceptibility to suggestion. The functions of the organs of sense, in particular, are influenced by it. How these act in hypnosis without suggestion it is difficult to say decidedly ; the statements of different authors are very contradictory. There is no essential change in the functions of the organs of sense in the light stages of hypnosis ; the subject sees, hears, smells, &c., normally. According to Liébeault, the senses of sight and taste decrease first, then the sense of smell, then hearing and feeling disappear in turn. But when the method of fixed attention is used, sight is the last to go. According to my experience these statements are not quite exact ; if we compare them with those of other authors we find many contradictions. I think that these contradictions occur because the condition of the hypnotic in relation to various objects and persons is not enough considered. For example, he hears the person who is hypnotizing him, and not others ; he feels this man's touch, and not another's. For this reason I believe that we must regard the whole state from the beginning as a purely psychical one. Braid distinguishes two grades, according to the functions of the sense organs ; in one an increased activity of sense is shown, and in the other a diminution of it. My observations have not confirmed this.

It is possible to induce all kinds of sense hallucinations in hypnosis. The images produced are so changing that any one who sees them for the first time is justified in doubting whether the phenomena are real or not. We have accustomed ourselves to depend so completely on the perceptions of our senses, to think them such trustworthy witnesses in all cases, that we are indeed astonished when we find that a word suffices to place a hypnotic among utterly different surroundings.

Sense delusions are divided into Hallucinations and Illusions. The first is the perception of an object where in reality there is nothing ; the second is the false interpretation of an existing external object. If, for example, a book is taken for a cat, or a blow on the table for the firing of a cannon, we talk of an illusion ; but if a cat is seen where there is nothing, we call it a hallucination. We have thus to do with a hallucination when an external object causes a perception by means of association. A chair on which a particular person has often sat, may by association call up an image of that person ; this is a hallucination called up by an external object.

We observe numerous hallucinations and illusions in hypnosis. We have seen in Case IV. that it suffices to assert that a dog is present, and a dog will apparently be seen. A handkerchief was in this case taken for a dog, consequently this was an illusion. An illusion is more easily induced than a hallucination ; in the absence of an external object, such as the handkerchief, the suggestion very often fails. When I do not offer some such object the hypnotic often finds it for himself. Hallucinations of sight are more easily caused when the eyes are closed ; the subjects then see objects and persons with their eyes shut, as in dreams. They think, at the same time, that their eyes are open, just as we are unaware in dreams that our eyes are shut. If we wish to cause a delusion of the sense of sight at the moment of opening the eyes, it is necessary to make the suggestion quickly, lest the act of opening the eyes should awaken the subject. I advise the use of fixed attention while the suggestion is being made (*cf.* Experiment IV.), so that the subject may not awaken himself by looking about. The other organs of sense may also be deluded. I knock on the table and give the idea that cannon are being fired, I blow with the bellows and make the suggestion that an engine is steaming up. A hallucination of hearing something, *e.g.*, the piano, is induced without the aid of any external stimulus. In the same way smell, taste, and touch may be the senses deceived. It is well known that hypnotics will drink water or even ink for wine, will eat onions for pears, will smell ammonia for Eau de Cologne, &c. In these cases the expression of face induced by the suggested perception corresponds so perfectly to it that a better effect would scarcely be produced if the real article were used. Tell the subject he has taken snuff, he sneezes. All varieties of the senses of touch, of pressure, of temperature, of pain, can be influenced. I tell a person that he is standing on ice. He feels cold at once. He trembles, his teeth chatter, he wraps himself in his coat. "Goose-skin" can be produced by the suggestion of a cold bath (Krafft-Ebing). In like manner itching and so forth can be induced. I say to a gentleman, "To-morrow at three o'clock your forehead will itch." The post-hypnotic suggestion proves true; the fore-head itches so much that the subject rubs it con-tinually. It appears to me that the senses of touch and taste are the most easily and frequently in-fluenced. For example, the suggestion of a bitter taste takes effect much sooner than the suggestion of a delusion of sight or hearing. It is true that the subjects often account to themselves for the delusion; they taste the bitterness, but say at the same time that it must be a subjective sensation, since they have nothing bitter in their mouths.

Sense delusions can be suggested in any way. We can tell the subject that he sees a bird. We can suggest the same thing by gesture—for example, by pretending to hold a bird in the hand—particularly after the subject has received some hypnotic training. The chief point is that the subject should understand what is intended by the gesture.

Naturally, several organs of sense can be influenced by suggestion at the same time. I tell some one, "Here is a rose;" he not only sees, but smells and feels the rose. I pretend to give another subject a dozen oysters; he eats them at once, without further suggestion. The suggestion here affects sight, feeling, and taste at the same time. In many cases the

muscular sense is influenced in a striking manner by
such suggestions. I give a subject a glass of wine to
drink; he lifts the pretended glass to his lips, and
leaves a space between hand and mouth as he would
if he held a real glass. I am not obliged to define
the delusion for each separate sense; the subject does
this spontaneously for himself. The subject in this
way completes most suggestions by a process resembling the indirect suggestion described on page
71. The external suggestion does not remain an
isolated phenomenon, but causes a series of other
mental processes, according to the character of the
subject and to the hypnotic training he has received.
I say to the subject, " Here, take this bottle of Eau
de Cologne!" He believes that he feels the bottle in
his hand, which in reality is empty; besides which he
believes he sees the bottle and smells it, although I
add nothing to my original suggestion. In short, he
completes it independently. This is a very common
occurrence.

Besides which the deception, if it is thorough, is
clearly reflected in the subject's expression and
gestures. No gourmand could wear a more delighted
expression over some favourite dish than does a
subject over a suggested delicacy. Very few people
would be able to imitate by art the expression of
fear on the face of a subject when he believes that a
tiger is about to attack him. A subject will drink
several glasses of wine by suggestion, will become red
in the face, and will then complain of his head. I
give a piece of cork to a subject for an onion; he
smells it and his eyes fill with tears. We can in this
manner place a subject in any situation we please,
and from his behaviour under the circumstances draw
conclusions as to his character (Morselli). But it

would be necessary to exercise caution in such a
case, since the subject nearly always has some dim
consciousness of his real surroundings, however completely he may seem to be transported into the
imaginary ones. I shall return later and more fully
to these incomplete sense delusions.

Some authors (Dumontpallier, Bérillon) have particularly
directed attention to the suggestions which take effect on one
side of the body only. For example, we can cause a dog to be
seen on the right side, and a bird on the left, and so forth; this
appears to be only an affair of training and suggestion. It is
useless to draw conclusions from this about the independent
functions of the two hemispheres of the brain. The case
mentioned by Magnin is connected with this; a person
affected by weak sight of the left eye, of hysterical origin, believed in the hypnotic state that he saw with the right eye things
which he really saw with the left, and so thought they were
on his right side when they were really on his left (allochiria).

In contrast with the delusions of sense hitherto
described, which are sometimes called positive, there
are also negative hallucinations, or negative delusions
of sense. The older mesmerists (Deleuze, Bertrand,
Charpignon) published many observations of them.
This kind of suggestion, which at first seemed more
incredible than the positive, nevertheless has analogies
in the normal state, like all the hypnotic phenomena.
Consider the juggler, who knows how to use the most
important psychological laws for practical purposes.
Let us watch him carefully, and we shall see how he
hides things, how he makes a change, how he sub-
stitutes one card for another under the very eyes of
the spectators. But he knows how to draw off their
attention by clever talk, so that even those who have
watched him are unable to give an account to themselves of his proceedings. For example, the cards
are changed in the spectator's field of view; the

sense stimulation takes place, but does not penetrate to the consciousness. We find analogous
occurrences in ordinary life. It has happened to
everybody to look for something which is before his
eyes. In this case also the thing is not perceived,
although it is in the seeker's field of view and he is
actually thinking about it. It is no longer incredible,
then, that we should find analogous processes in
hypnosis. If we can make the hypnotic see what
does not exist, after the above explanation it is on
longer surprising that we can prevent his seeing what
does exist.

Let us examine such a case. Mr. X. is in hypnosis.
Two persons are present besides myself. I tell him,
" From this moment you will only be able to see
me ; you can no longer see the other men, though
they are still here." X. then replies to every question addressed to him by these gentlemen, and can
feel them, but he cannot see them. This is a negative
hallucination of sight only. But a negative hallucination of several senses can be induced as readily as a
positive one. I say to X., " The two men have gone
away ; you and I are alone. From this moment X.
neither sees nor hears them, nor perceives them by
means of any sense. When I ask who is in the room
he replies, " Only you and I." Part of an object
or person can be made invisible in the same way.
We can cause people to appear headless and arm-
less, or make them disappear altogether by putting
on a particular hat, as in the story of the Magic
Cap. The situation may be varied in any way we
please.

Forel has lately pointed out that the insane often
have these negative hallucinations. He has also
pointed out that hypnotics complete the hallucination

at their pleasure. Thus I say to X., while A. is sitting on a chair, " A. has gone away ; there is nobody on that chair." X. examines the chair, and as he feels something there he imagines that a plaid is lying on it. We see here how a suggested negative hallucination passes into an illusion through the auto-suggestion of the hypnotic ; this is very common. To be exact, we can regard every illusion as the sum of a. positive and a negative hallucination, as in each illusion something present is not perceived and something not present is perceived.

Further, it is possible to prevent recognition of certain colours, and to induce colour-blindness by suggestion. But we have here only to do with a defective perception of colours, and not with an alteration of the stimulus affecting the eye ; the disturbance is purely mental (Schirmer). Cohn's assertion that, on the other hand, colour-blindness sometimes disappears in hypnosis, has been justly contested by Königshöfer ; at the most this could only be a hysterical disturbance of the sense of colour, temporarily removed by hypnosis, and not a disturbance founded on peripheral alterations.

An entire cessation of the functions of any sense organ can be induced in the same way as a negative hallucination. "You can no longer hear"; "you are deaf," or "you are blind." These words suffice to deprive the hypnotic of the corresponding sense perceptions. Not only does he cease to recognize any particular object, but the sense organ is insusceptible to anything. A command suffices to restore the functions. It is certain that blindness, deafness, &c., can be induced in this way ; but the effect is a mental one. Exactly speaking, the corresponding organ of sense performs its functions, but the central

process does not reach the consciousness. In the
same way the sight of one eye can be prevented
though the other can see as usual ; a one-sided
amaurosis can be created (Borel). Even hemianopia
has been observed in hypnosis (Willy).

To this category belongs anæsthesia of feeling. The
mucous membranes can be made anæsthetic by suggestion. The fumes of ammonia in the nose, and tickling
of the throat are not felt ; the conjunctiva can be
touched without producing the corresponding reflex,
and even the cornea may become insensitive either
spontaneously or by suggestion. Preyer quotes a
cynical experiment of the American physician, Dr.
Little, who thrust a needle through the cornea of a
subject whom he suspected of simulation, in order to
test its insensibility. But in my experience these
last-mentioned phenomena are uncommon. When
this anæsthesia of the conjunctiva and cornea exists,
the eye no longer closes on reflex stimulus ; but this
is a consequence of the anæsthesia, and not an
independent phenomenon (Gurney).

After what precedes, it is hardly necessary to
mention that the muscular sense can also be inhibited
by suggestion. The frequently observed absence of
the muscular sense in a completely anæsthetic arm,
of which the subject still retains complete control, is
interesting. The state is like that of persons suffering
from locomotor ataxy. Such people are able to
write correctly, or do anything else with their eyes
open, while they do it very badly with their eyes
closed (William James, Carnochan).

I have shown above that perceptions of each sense
by itself can be prevented by suggestion ; but very
important hyperæsthesia of the organs of sense

8

likewise exist in hypnosis. It is indifferent whether
these come on from external suggestion or in other
ways, and is besides not always exactly to be
distinguished ; the main fact is, that they do exist.
Although they are not on the whole very common,
I shall here add some of these remarkable cases.
It is exactly these rarer cases which deserve the most
careful consideration, since they often offer us a key
to a natural explanation of apparently supernatural
phenomena, such as transposition of the senses, of
clairvoyance.

An increased sensitiveness to touch has been often
observed. The two points of a compass are used
for examining the least distance of space that can
be felt. We try to find out what distance must
separate them in order that they may be felt as
two separate points. In this way an increase of
sensitiveness is found in hypnosis, as the points can
be distinguished at a less distance than in the
normal state (Berger). I have made a series of
experiments on this point, and can confirm Berger's
statements. I have found the same thing under
pathological conditions. In cases of locomotor ataxy,
with profound anæsthesia, increase of sensitiveness
has also been found when the patients were under
the influence of suggestion ; the state may continue
post-hypnotically. In one case of locomotor ataxy,
I found that on the right fore-arm the two points
were distinguished at 6·1 centimetres distance.
During hypnosis the separate points were perceived
at 4·9 centimetres distance, and after waking even at
4·1 centimetres.

The senses of pressure and temperature become
sometimes much more delicate. The hypnotic recognizes things half an inch distant from the skin, and

this simply by the increase and decrease of temperature (Braid). He walks about a room with bandaged eyes or in absolute darkness without striking against anything, becauses he recognizes objects by the resistance of the air, and by the alteration of temperature (Braid, Poirault, Drzewiecki). D'Abundo produced enlargement of the field of vision by suggestion.

Bergson has described one of the most remarkable cases of increased power of vision. This particular case has been cited as a proof of supersensual thought-transference ; but Bergson ascribes the result to hyperæsthesia of the eye. In this case the hypnotic was able to read letters in a book which were 3 mm. high ; the reading was made possible by a reflected image of these letters in the eye of the experimenter. According to calculation the reflected image could only have been 0·1 mm. ($=\frac{1}{250}$ inch) high. The same person was able, without using the microscope, to see and draw the cells in a microscopical specimen, which were only 0·06 mm. in diameter. Sauvaire, after some not quite irreproachable experiments, supposed the existence of such a hyperæsthesia of sight, that a hypnotic recognized non-transparent playing cards by the rays of light passing through them. A case of Taguet's, in which an ordinary piece of cardboard was used as a mirror, is said to have proved quite as strong a hyperæsthesia. All objects which were held so that the reflected rays from the card fell upon the subject's eye, were clearly recognized. The same thing is shown by a great increase of the sense of smell. A visiting card is torn into a number of pieces, which pieces are professedly found purely by the sense of smell ; pieces belonging to another card are rejected The subject gives gloves, keys, and pieces of money to the persons to whom they belong, guided only by smell. Hyperæsthesia of smell has often been noticed in other cases. Carpenter says that a hypnotic found the owner of a particular glove among sixty other persons. Sauvaire relates another such case, in which a hypnotic, after smelling the hands of eight persons, gave to each his own handkerchief although every effort was made to lead him astray. Braid and the older mesmerists relate many such phenomena. Braid describes one case in which the subject on each occasion found the owner of some gloves among a number of other people ; when his nose was stopped up the experiments failed. This delicacy of certain organs of sense, particularly of the sense of smell, is well known to be normal in many animals ; in dogs, for example, which recognize their masters by scent. Hypnotic experiments teach us that this keenness of scent can be attained by human beings in some circumstances.

The muscular sense again requires a few words. This sense informs us of the position of our limbs at a given moment. The great dexterity of movement, which is sometimes found in deep hypnosis, must be ascribed to an increased acuteness of this sense. Braid believes that imitative sounds (*echolalie*) must be referred to this, as has been already mentioned.

With reference to this hyperæsthesia of the sense organs, I will quote an experiment which is often repeated, and is wrongly considered as a proof of increased keenness of the senses. Let us take a pack of cards, which naturally must have backs of the same pattern, so that to all appearance one cannot be distinguished from the other ; let us choose any card—the ace of hearts, for example—hold it with its back to the subject, and arouse by suggestion the idea of a particular photograph on it—his own, let us say. Let us then mix the cards, and request the hypnotic to find the photograph, of course without having allowed him to see the face of the card. He will often find the right one, although the backs are all alike. The experiment can be repeated with visiting cards or sheets of paper, if the selected one is marked, unknown to the hypnotic. This experiment makes a greater impression on inexperienced people than it need do. For most people are able to repeat the experiment without hypnosis; I do not think hyperæsthesia is generally a condition for its success. If the backs of these cards and papers are carefully examined, minute differences (*points de repère.*—Binet) will be discovered. I have myself often made the experiment with good results, without hypnosis. There can be no question of simulation here. Naturally, I do not contend that a hypnotic cannot find a paper in such a case better than a waking man; the hyperæsthesia is a fact. I only wish to point out that hyperæsthesia is not absolutely necessary, though this experiment is often used to demonstrate its presence. I have seen men of science of the first rank show astonishment when a hypnotic distinguished apparently identical sheets of paper. They did not consider that there are essential differences in the sheets, which suffice for distinguishing them even without hypnosis. Yung justly says, "It is surprising to see that even scientific people sometimes allow themselves to be confounded by apparently marvellous phenomena." The experiment is to be explained thus: the *point de repère* presented to the hypnotic at the moment when the idea of the photograph was suggested to him, recalls the suggested image directly he sees it again. The point is associated with the image, so that one calls up the other. Binet and Féré have rightly pointed out that the image only recurs when the *point de repère* is recalled to the memory ; it must first be seen. Consequently, if the paper is held at a distance from the subject's eyes, the image will not be recognized, for the *points de repère* are not visible. Binet and Féré have made some interesting experiments. They have caused photographic impressions to be made of white papers on which a portrait had been created by means of suggestion. It was shown that the hypnotic always took the copies for the original, because the photographed *point de repère* aroused the same image in his imagination. Jendrássik has observed the same sort of thing : if a " d " is drawn with the finger on a sheet of white paper, and it is suggested that the " d " is real, the subject sees the " d." If the paper is turned upside down he sees " p," and in the looking-glass "q." This is because the " d " was attached to certain points on the paper, which were what the subject remembered, and when the paper was placed in different positions the points appeared in different positions also.

Suggestion influences common sensation in the same way as the functions of the organs of sense. Nothing worthy of remark takes place in hypnosis with regard to this, unless suggestion is called into play. I may, however, mention the feeling of fatigue which many hypnotics experience ; it sometimes appears in the lightest hypnosis, and may also exist in the deeper stages. We can influence common sensation very materially by suggestion in hypnosis. This is not surprising when we consider that it is exactly the common sensations which are most under the influence of mental processes. Just as looking down from a tower causes giddiness, as the thought of repugnant food produces disgust, so we can call up these, and related phenomena, or cause them to disappear, by suggestion. It is in this direction that suggestion has to record its most striking successes, since the common sensations, of which pain is one, are the cause of most of the complaints we hear. As pain, &c., can be induced by suggestion, so by suggestion it can often be banished. I say to a subject who complains of want of appetite, "The loss of appetite has disappeared ; you are hungry." I can cause another to feel thirst. Feelings of pleasure can likewise be excited. Debove, on the other hand, has induced loss of appetite by suggestion to such an extent and for so long a time that the person concerned took no regular meal for fourteen days. Further, it is possible up to a certain point to satisfy the hunger and thirst of subjects in deep hypnosis by merely suggested food and drink, as Fillassier informs us. It is a pity, however, that this result can only be obtained with a few persons, and in a certain measure; for otherwise our politicians would no longer need to puzzle their heads over social questions and the feeding of the masses. Sexual feeling can also be produced by suggestion. Leopold Casper tells of a case in which Tissié hypnotized a patient, and suggested to him that the right ring-finger should indicate sexual desire and the left abstinence. When the patient awoke, contact with the right ring-finger caused sexual excitement, contact with the left subdued it. Once Tissié forgot to remove the suggestion, and the consequence was that for twenty-four hours the patient was unable to refrain from coitus and masturbation, as well as spontaneous emissions.

I shall here particularly discuss the feelings of

pain. What effect has hypnosis upon them, with and without suggestion? Apart from some particular hypnotic states, in which Berger finds increased sensitiveness to pain, we occasionally find analgesia in hypnosis. Sometimes this exists to such a degree that the severest surgical operations can be performed during the state. It is also known that needles may be run into some persons during hypnosis without their feeling pain, though they feel the touch. And yet a complete analgesia is extremely rare in hypnosis, although authors, copying from one another, assert that it is common. There is an immense difference between pricking the subject with a needle and using the faradic brush. The pain caused by the use of the latter is so great, especially when a considerable electric force is employed, that very few persons in hypnosis can endure it, even when they show no pain on being pricked with a needle. In some cases, where analgesia does not appear spontaneously, it can be produced by suggestion. But suggestion more easily produces a certain decrease of sensitiveness to pain. Complete analgesia is seldom attained. Many cases described as completely analgesic—for example, those of Tamburini and Seppilli—proved on a closer examination not to be so, as a strong faradic current finally produced pain. I will just remark that all kinds of pain can be induced by suggestion; the pain caused by a needle as well as that caused by a knife or a burn. The face of the subject expresses pain in such a manner, that an impartial person can hardly decide whether the pain is real or suggested.

The state of mind which is intimately connected with common sensations can also be influenced by suggestion. It is consequently easy to induce either sadness or cheerfulness in hypnosis. We often find the view promulgated that the hypnotic is strikingly grave. My experience obliges me to dispute this; most people, on the contrary, seem particularly comfortable in hypnosis (Richet). The method of hypnotization has some influence here. The desires and affections can be controlled in hypnosis as well as the moods. Love and hate, anxiety, anger, and fear can be easily called up, and produce corresponding expressions and postures in the hypnotic.

Recent observations in the field of sexual perversions (Krafft-Ebing, Schrenck-Notzing, Wetterstrand, Renterghem, Naret) show that suggestion has great power over the impulses, for there can be no doubt that it is possible to combat general morbid changes in the sexual impulse, as well as special inclinations, by means of suggestion.

Abnormalities of voluntary movement apart, nearly all the phenomena of suggestion hitherto described are the exclusive privilege of the second group of hypnotic states. I come now to some other physical functions which require a deep hypnotic state if they are to be influenced. I mention, first of all, the phenomena of that part of the muscular system which is normally independent of the will.

We will here particularly consider the circulation of the blood, and the respiration, as these are essentially results of involuntary muscular action. A large number of physiological observations have been made in this field during hypnosis, in order to decide what is the state of the pulse and respiration without suggestion. Of course the pulse has been often examined, since this is a simple thing to do, and yet the statements about it are so contradictory that we only dare to receive them with caution. Although some have believed they had discovered objective symptoms in changes of the action of the heart and the respiration, we cannot doubt that there has been considerable exaggeration. A great acceleration of the pulse and of the respiration has been often observed when the method of Braid, or fascination (Brémaud), or mesmeric passes (Ochorowicz) were employed. The respiration, which was normally 18 per minute has risen to 50, or even more. I have myself made a number of experiments on this point, and fully agree with Bernheim and Preyer that these changes are not so much an effect of the hypnosis as of the fixed attention. I believe that it is only the effort made which causes these abnormalities; the irregularities in the respiration should probably likewise be ascribed to mental excitement and effort. Preyer mentions that the respiration of a person looking at a microscopic object often changes; in the same way it displays abnormalities when a person believes himself watched. An experienced doctor, therefore, prefers to examine the respiration unobserved by his patient. In any case I have seen a material acceleration of the pulse and respiration set in after long strain of attention without a trace of hypnosis; the respiration also became irregular. If there is hypnosis, in a little while the irregularity and acceleration cease. I have only seen a few cases in which they persisted, but am by no means inclined to think this a sign of hypnosis, as some persons show an acceleration of pulse and breathing on the smallest provocation. Even a conversation is enough to induce acceleration. I have also seen persons in whom an uncomfortable sitting posture induced changes of pulse and respiration. Besides which it must be added that in many people there is an important acceleration of pulse and respiration in the strong muscular contractions of the cataleptic phenomena (Braid), and also in tonic contracture (Rumpf). If I made such persons lie quietly down, and avoided conversation, physical effort, and mental excitement, I never observed any lasting acceleration. On the other hand, I have often found a deepened and somewhat long-drawn respiration, and also a slight slowing of pulse, in hypnosis. These were the cases which bore a greater external resemblance to sleep, and in which, as I have several times mentioned above, there was no important spontaneous movement. It was also more difficult to induce movements by suggestion in these cases. Beaunis occasionally finds an increased blood pressure in the pulse, which he does not, however, think of much importance. Horsley finds no alteration in the curve of the pulse tracing.

Of any further unsuggested abnormalities of the involuntary muscles there is little to be said. Moriz Rosenthal has observed vomiting, which he ascribes to stimulation of the cerebral cortex. Nausea is occasionally observed in frightened or excited persons (Friedemann).

Let us now ask, To what extent can the involuntary muscular system be influenced by suggestion? The peristaltic motion is relatively easy to affect. I have had several experiences of the facility with which the bowels of some hypnotics are affected by suggestion. I say to one of them, " In half an hour after awakening your bowels will act." This is certain to happen. " To-morrow morning at eight your bowels will act." The effect follows. " To-morrow between eight and nine your bowels will act three times." Exactly the

same result, though the subject remembers nothing of
the suggestion on awaking.   It is interesting to note
that the action of aperients can be checked by suggestion, though this does not often happen.   A patient
takes a dose of castor-oil which is sufficient to procure
copious action of the bowels.   He is told in hypnosis
that the medicine will only take effect in forty-eight
hours.   The suggestion is effectual, although with this
person the dose habitually acts quickly and abun-
dantly (v. Krafft-Ebing).   Or let a few drops of water
be given to the hypnotic with the assertion that it is
a strong purge ; motion of the bowels follows.   Suggested emetics act in the same way.   This is not
very surprising, as we know that these and other
functions, even though they are independent of our
will, are yet under the influence of the mind.   Vomiting
at the sight of disgusting things, and the celebrated
mica panis pills administered as aperients prove this
well enough.

In some persons the vessels and the heart can be
influenced in the same way, as several experiments
have proved.   Dumontpallier has made some, which
should here be mentioned.   He induced by suggestion a local increase of temperature of as much as
3° C.   Forel, Beaunis, and F. Myers have also observed local reddening by suggestion.   Even this
phenomenon should not surprise us too much, since we
observe the same sort of vaso-motor disturbance to
result from mental condition.   I have spoken above
(p. 69) of the blushing which occurs when any one
is confused.   I will here mention the contrary of
this—the paleness which often follows fright. And as
a curiosity I will mention the local reddening of the
skin which has often been observed in spirit mediums
(Carpenter, Carl du Prel), and which has been explained

as a supernatural phenomenon. As these mediums are often at these times in a state of trance—that is, in a state resembling hypnosis, and perhaps identical with it—this phenomenon admits of a perfectly natural explanation.

Some observations have also been made upon the influence of suggestion on the action of the heart. I myself have often been able to produce a slowing of a normal or rapid pulse. However, we should be cautious how we draw the conclusion that the suggestion has affected the nerves of the heart directly; the effect is an indirect one, rather. For, independent of the fact that the action of the heart is to a certain degree dependent on the respiration, it is likewise under the influence of ideas, which affect the emotions. Such ideas have the power of quickening or slowing the heart's action; it is possible that the suggestion which retards a quick pulse only produces this result indirectly by a removal of the mental exciting cause, or, *vice versâ*, quickens the pulse by excitement. My observations of the quickening and slowing of the heart's action by suggestion leads me to take this view rather than that of a direct influence of suggestion on the nerves and nerve centres of the heart. In any case it would be difficult to exclude this indirect action, especially as its effects are rapid. However, the method is of no consequence. Beaunis has seen a momentary effect of suggestion in several people without change of respiration from suggestion. He has seen the pulse fall in consequence of suggestion from 98 beats to 92, and then rise to 115 beats. He infers a direct action of suggestion upon the inhibitory centre of the heart, and thinks himself also obliged to exclude ideas which affect the mental state, such as

are mentioned above, since the effect of the suggestion was always momentary. But his reasoning on
this point is not conclusive.

Respiration, which holds a middle position between
the voluntary and involuntary movements,[1] can also
be influenced by suggestion. From motives of pru-
dence I have never continued such experiments for
longer than half a minute. I suggested to the subject
that he could not breathe ; an apparently complete
pause in respiration followed. Jendrássik relates a
case in which he inhibited respiration for three minutes,
simply by assuring the subject that he could not
breathe. In 1853, Beesel reported a case of the magnetic state in which the subject lay from six to eight
minutes without apparent respiration, and was thought
to be dead. But shallow respirations are easily overlooked.

We find but scanty accounts of physiological researches into the processes of secretion during hypnosis.
Perspiration has often been observed (G. Barth,
Demarquay, Giraud-Teulon, Heidenhain, Preyer). I
doubt if the secretion of sweat depends on the hypnosis ; I believe that it is rather a result of the
straining and excitement of fixed attention. We
know a little more about the influences of suggestion. Burot shows that secretion of saliva can be
induced by suggestion, and Bottey demonstrates the
same thing of perspiration. Charles Richet shows
that erection and emission of semen can be effected
by it, so as to produce on the subject an impres-

---

[1] That is, it is generally involuntary, but up to a certain point
it is under the influence of the will, and can be accelerated or
retarded.

sion of sexual intercourse. I have mentioned above that I have myself seen a hypnotic's eyes water when it was suggested to him that he was smelling an onion. By producing emotion it is possible to influence the secretion of tears. A gentleman who believed he was a child again, imagined he had just been disobedient to his parents, and as he asked forgiveness in the hypnotic condition he shed many tears. In a case of increased secretion of gastric juice through hypnotic suggestion, Bergmann believes that he has exerted therapeutic influence and rendered the gastric juice normal; but the evidence is not sufficiently exact to be conclusive.

The secretion of milk is also under the influence of suggestion. A case, which only shows, however, the indirect influence of suggestion, has been reported by Hassenstein. In a wet nurse in whom the secretion had ceased, it again flowed copiously by suggestion. It had ceased, however, owing to excitement over the child's condition, and was renewed by suggesting away the excitement. Grossmann reports a case in which the secretion of milk was produced by direct suggestion.

Heidenhain induced discharge of urine by tickling the perinæum. I do not think this phenomenon should be regarded as a physical reflex ; I believe that the patient emptied the bladder because he believed that , he was . intended to do so. Preyer mentions this as an example of secretion ; I hold a different opinion ; I believe that the patient did not *secrete* the urine in consequence of the external stimulus or command, but merely passed it. This is, then, a motor suggestion. I have often been able to produce the same effect : " After waking you must make water five times." The patient is surprised after the hypnosis that he wishes to make water so often, but obeys. Few investigations have been made as to whether the kidney secretions can be influenced by suggestion However, Wetterstrand mentions results produced in diseases of the kidneys which almost justify the conclusion that in certain persons it is possible to influence the kidney secretions by suggestion. This is not so strange when we reflect that many diseases in which there is increased secretion of urine are of nervous origin, and that anxiety and fear also appear to influence it.

Krafft-Ebing draws conclusions as to the increase of intestinal secretions from one experiment. He suggested to his subject a profuse watery evacuation of the bowels, which followed. As the bladder had been emptied shortly before, and only a small quantity of urates had been found in the urine, Krafft-Ebing thinks himself obliged to consider the fluid as an increase of the intestinal secretions.

Some special investigations have been made of the organic changes during hypnosis, but no sort of conclusion can be drawn from them in any case. Brock finds that in a short hypnosis of twenty minutes' duration, with partial catalepsy, the sum of the solid constituents and the phosphoric acid decreases; as Strübing has described in catalepsy. But as Brock forgot to examine his patients under analogous circumstances, sitting quietly without hypnosis (Preyer), his experiments are not conclusive. In any case no conclusion as to the action of the brain must be drawn from them. Brock concludes that the activity of the brain is lessened, because the quantity of phosphoric acid is decreased. Gürtler is much more cautious in his conclusions. He also finds a

difference in the phosphoric acid; it is true that he
has not made a sufficient number of comparative
experiments with the same subject in analogous
circumstances, without hypnosis. He refrains from
drawing final conclusions, because to justify these the
evacuations of the bowels and the respiration must be
investigated also. A. Voisin and Haraut conclude
from their investigation of the urine of hypnotic
subjects that assimilation is carried on better during
hypnosis than in the waking condition, and that
hypnosis is not a pathological condition.

The experiments of some investigators who produced a change in the bodily temperature must be
reckoned to belong to this section. Krafft-Ebing's
experiments are particularly surprising. He succeeded
in producing any temperature he pleased in his subject.
The most enigmatical point with regard to this appears
to me to be that the subject showed the exact degree
of temperature commanded—namely, 36° C.—when
examined by the thermometer. As it is evidently
utterly out of the patient's power to influence this
instrument mentally, we must assume an astonishing
capacity for regulating the temperature of the body.
The experiments carried out by Marès and Hellich are
very interesting. They often succeeded in lowering
the temperature of a hypnotic from 37° C. to 34·5° C.,
in twenty-four hours. This result was not produced
by immediate suggestion, but rather by suggestive
influence on the feelings of cold and warmth. I may
here refer to the experiments of Lehmann, who in
himself and in another person found that when the
subject vividly imagined to himself a rise of temperature and feeling of warmth in the hand, there was an
actual rise of 0.06' C. and 0.02' C.

9

I now come to some phenomena which, for the most part, will awaken distrust. I mean the anatomical changes effected by suggestion during hypnosis. But however enigmatical this may appear, we have only to do with quantitative differences in phenomena, which we have observed elsewhere. The physiognomy of certain professions—for example, the type of the clergy shows how mental processes gradually exercise an influence on organic construction. The mental moods and occupation impress their stamp by degrees upon the physiognomy.

The most general and frequently repeated experiment carried out in hypnosis, is to induce the subject to believe that a blister has been applied to him, and thus to obtain real blisters. The whole collection of observations on this point are not free from objection. Even when exact accounts of the experiments are published, the sceptic has sufficient cause for hesitation. But every man of science should be sceptical, not of these statements in particular, but of all statements. The reason for hesitation with regard to the above experiments is, as a rule, the insufficient watching of the subject. But if the published experiments are not convincing they are at least worthy of consideration. It is a fundamentally false principle to dispute such things *a priori*, either because we have not ourselves seen them or because they are rare. This false principle is far too much acted on, according to my view. For there are certain things which are rare ; for example, some monsters, and triplets, and also millionaires, and yet they are none the less to be seen sometimes. Every one believes in their existence without having seen them. Consequently, neither rarity nor the fact that we have not seen a thing ourselves precludes its existence. For this reason the rare observations of others are of importance.

Among the experiments in this direction I will first of all mention the cases in which menorrhagia is induced or arrested by suggestion. It is not to be doubted that this is practicable in the case of certain persons. Forel has made a whole series of experiments on this point, and has also partly confirmed the accuracy and the effect of suggestion by personal investigation. Many other experimenters have also been able to confirm the effect of suggestion on menstruation (Sperling, A. Voisin, Gascard, Briand). Liébeault's statement that he was never able to cause abortion by suggestion is curious. The influence of suggestion in menorrhagia seems less wonderful and striking when we reflect how very much psychical influences otherwise affect it. It is known, for example, that the periods often become irregular in women who are about to undergo a surgical operation.

I have mentioned the influence of suggestion in this place in spite of the fact that these experiments do not, properly speaking, demonstrate an organic influence. We may be concerned here with a vasomotor disturbance, which secondarily induces the organic changes. This appears to me probable.

Jendrássik and Krafft-Ebing obtained marks like burns on their subjects by means of suggestion. If some object, such as a match-box, a pair of scissors, a snuff-box, a linen-stamp, &c., was pressed upon the skin, and the subject was at the same time told that the skin was being burned, a blister in the form of the object resulted. The marks remained a long time visible. If the object was pressed upon the left side of a hysterical patient anæsthetic on the right, the burn appeared symmetrically on the right as it would if reflected in a glass, as could be especially seen when

letters were used. Jendrássik maintains that deception
was absolutely excluded in these cases of suggested
burns. Besides this, a dermatologist, Lipp, at one
of the experiments, declared that it would be impossible to cause the suggested lesion mechanically or
chemically. Burns caused by suggestion have often
been observed in the Salpêtrière. The same may be
said of the experiments of Bourru, Burot, and Berjon,
who induced bleeding by suggestion in the same
subject as Mabille, Ramadier, and Jules Voisin.
Puységur had witnessed the same thing. Bleeding of
the nose appeared at command in the above-mentioned
subject, and later on bleeding from the skin at a time
decided on beforehand. When the skin had been
rubbed with a blunt instrument in order to give point
to the suggestion, bleeding of the skin is said to have
appeared at command, the traces of which were visible
three months later. It is interesting that in the case
of this person, who was hemiplegic and anæsthetic on
the right side, the suggestion would not take effect on
that side. Mabille's observations of this subject are
particularly interesting, because they show that a
person in hypnosis can cause these bleedings by auto-
suggestion. Unfortunately the accounts we possess
of such cases do not enable us to draw a definite
conclusion as to whether contact will induce bleeding
under other circumstances (F. Myers). Meanwhile
we must remember that the bleeding did not follow
closely on the contact, which would have been the
case if the effect were mechanical. Berjon reminds
us, also, that precautionary measures were taken to
prevent the subject from touching his own arm, and
thereby causing a wound. Artigalas and Rémond
have published the case of a woman of twenty-two in
whom tears of blood appeared. By suggestion it was

also possible to call out bloody sweat on her hand. In
the abbreviated report, which alone I have seen, it is
not stated whether the sweat was subjected to a
microscopical and chemical analysis.

Everybody will here remember the stigmatics of the Roman
Catholic Church. Bleeding of the skin is said to appear in
them, generally in spots which correspond to the wounds of
Christ. It was first observed in Francis of Assisi, on whom
Bournet has lately written at length. Bournet asserts that the
opinion of the phenomenon as not a matter of deception or of
miracle, but as the result of heightened imaginative power, is by
no means new; even in the thirteenth century Jacobus de Vora-
gine so regarded it. The best known is Louise Lateau, of Bois
d'Haine, near Mons, who was much talked of in 1868. It appears
from the literature concerning her, that the anatomical process
was rather a complicated one in her case (Virchow, Lefebvre).
Blisters first appeared, and after they burst there was bleeding
from the true skin (*corium*), without any visible injury. I will
not enter into the question of simulation, which a Belgian doctor,
Warlomont, decided was impossible, after personal investigation.
Delbœuf and others believe that the phenomena were caused
by auto-suggestion. Lateau directed her own attention continually to those parts of her body which she knew corresponded
to the wounds of Christ, and the anatomical lesions resulted
from this strain of attention, as in other cases from external
suggestion. Virchow, as is known, thought that fraud or miracle
were the only alternatives. In the well-known case of Catherine
Emmerich the bleedings are said to have appeared while she
was looking at the crucifix. Without deciding as to the reality
of these phenomena, since no scientific investigation was undertaken, or was even possible, I will remark that at present a
natural explanation of the facts is possible, because such things
can be induced by suggestion in a suitable mental state. The
conditions resemble each other; the ecstasy of Lateau has a
great likeness to the hypnotic state. Ecstasy and hypnosis
have many points in common, and are, perhaps, identical conditions (Mantegazza).

The Catholic clergy, many of whom, as Sancha Hervas,
condemn hypnotism altogether, object to the identification of
stigmatization with suggested bleeding. Méric denies the

possibility of a comparison. But Méric does not reflect that an auto-suggestion in ecstasy may have exactly the same effect as an external suggestion. Méric maintains that stigmatics are certainly not in an abnormal condition, but quite awake. But as far as Lateau is concerned, she was evidently not awake ; that is, if we take it for granted there was no fraud in the case. Lateau spoke to certain persons only ; consequently some *rapport* existed as in hypnosis.

The experiments of Delbœuf also belong to the class of organic lesions. He experimented, in common with Winiwarter and Henrijean, and he produced symmetrical burns, and made one of the wounds painless by suggestion. It was observed in this case that the painless wound showed a much greater tendency to heal, and, in particular, that the inflammation showed no tendency to spread. As, however, there are some slight anomalies, the experiments are not fully convincing.

I now come to some experiments in which the hypnotic was told that a blister had been applied to him, which blister was really only an ordinary piece of paper. As Binet and Féré inform us, this experiment was first made as long ago as 1840, by the Italian doctor, Préjalmini, and Du Prel tells us that in 1819 a sloughing of the skin was obtained on a hypnotized somnambule of Celicurre de l'Aupépin, by means of a piece of linen, although the linen had been applied like a simple plaster. Focachon, an apothecary of Charmes, has recently repeated the experiment. Sometimes alone, and sometimes in company with the Nancy investigators, he has applied pieces of paper, suggesting that they were blisters. He is said to have often produced blistering. Beaunis has published an exact report of some experiments of this kind. After the suggestion had lasted twenty-one hours the paper was taken off, and it was found that the skin was thickened, dead, and of a yellowish tint; later, perhaps as a result of the pressure or the clothes, several small blisters appeared. The reverse experiment has also been successfully made by the Nancy investigators; the effect of a real blister has been counteracted by suggestion. Meunier has published an account of such an experiment made at Nancy. Forel, of Zürich, who has done so much for the development of hypnotism in Switzerland and Germany, has often tried to produce organic changes by means of suggestion. Thus, after an endeavour to produce blisters by suggestion little pustules of acne appeared. Besides this, Prof. Forel has made some other experiments, the results of which he has kindly allowed me to publish.

The experiments were made on a nurse, twenty-three years old, who is not at all hysterical. She is the daughter of plain country people, and has been for a long time an attendant in the Zürich Lunatic Asylum, which Forel directs. He thinks her a capable, honest person, in no way inclined to deceit. The experiments were as follows : A gummed label was fixed upon her chest above each breast; the paper was square. In no case was an irritating gum used. At midday Forel suggested that a blister had been put on the left side; and at six o'clock in the evening a moist spot had appeared in this place; the skin was swollen and reddened around it, and a little inflammation had appeared also on the right side, but much less. Forel then did away with the suggestion. On the next day there was a scab on the left side. Forel had not watched the nurse between noon and six o'clock, but had suggested that she could not scratch herself. The other nurses said that the sub-

ject could not raise her hand to her chest, and made
vain attempts to scratch. Forel repeated the experiment later ; he put on the paper at 11.45 a.m., and
ordered the formation of blisters in two and a half
hours. Little pain was suggested, and the nurse
therefore complained but little. At two o'clock Forel
looked at the paper on the left side, for which the
suggestion had been made, and saw around it a large
swelling and reddening of the skin. The paper could
be with difficulty removed. A moist surface of the
epidermis was then visible, exactly square like the
paper. Nothing particular appeared under the paper
on the right side. Forel then suggested the dis-

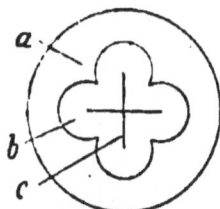

Fig. I

Fig. II

appearance of the pain, inflammation, &c. In spite
of this the place suppurated, and was discharging for
eight days, and the scab lasted for some time. Even
when Prof. Forel related this to me, seven weeks later,
the place was still brownish. The nurse was a little
annoyed and uneasy about the experiment, and she
was not strictly watched while it lasted.

A few days after this experiment Forel drew two
light crosses with the point of a blunt knife on the
same person. They did not bleed. Another cross
(shown in Fig. 1) was made on the inner side of each
fore-arm. Several doctors were present. Forel suggested the appearance of blisters on the right side.

Even at the end of five minutes, during which Forel watched the subject, so that fraud was out of the question, a considerable reddish swelling of the skin had appeared (Fig. 2, *a*). A wheal, *b*, looking like nettle-rash, had formed itself round the cross, *c*, somewhat in the shape of a cross. On the left side nothing was to be seen but the cross that had been drawn, unaltered, as in Fig. 1.

The wheal on the right side resembled a vaccination pustule, in the form of a cross ; but it was simply a papular swelling, as in nettle-rash. Forel then suggested the disappearance of the swelling and the wheal, and, further, the appearance of a drop of blood at the end of an hour. At the end of this time a very small drop was to be seen ; but the wheal, redness, and swelling had disappeared. But as Forel had not watched the subject during this hour, he attached no importance to the drop of blood, which might have been caused by a prick.

Forel wished later to watch this experiment in vesication from beginning to end. But the subject was made very angry and excited by the words and gestures which showed her that she was mistrusted. In Forel's opinion this caused the non-success of the experiment. After this no more vesication appeared, either with or without watching ; a slight reddening of the skin was all that was obtained. Forel holds the very plausible view that the subject's mental excitement was prejudicial to her later suggestibility. Among the above-mentioned experiments he only considers the one in which the papular swelling was produced to be proved ; as concerns the others he reserves his opinion, since no strict watch was kept.

Stress must be laid on the fact that Forel only made a gentle scratch to give point to the suggestion.

The injury, such as it was, did not cause the wheal; for if it had, the same thing would have appeared on the other side of the subject. It may be objected that the same force may not have been used to make the mark on both sides. However, it should be said that the nurse was not one of those persons who get a wheal whenever their skin is slightly stimulated. This seems conclusive to me. She showed wheals, only when bitten by gnats. When her skin was scraped it showed a disposition to redden, but wheals never formed. She had, besides, often been scratched by insane patients, but no remarkable result had ever been observed.

It should be added that there are people who develop wheals under mental excitement without hypnosis. A very trustworthy observer told me of the case of a person who had once been much frightened by a thunderstorm, and who showed afterwards wheals with a red border whenever a storm was approaching.

It is to be understood that great caution is necessary in dealing with experiments in which anatomical injury is caused by suggestion. This is all the more necessary because by certain spiritualists these experiments are regarded as proving that the soul is an organising as well as a thinking power. Apart from this, as already mentioned, it sometimes happens that no sufficient precautions against deception are adopted, so that many experiments lose in significance. This is unfortunately the case with Hebold's successful removal of a wart by suggestion in a hysterical subject.

(2) *Psychology.*

In the foregoing sections we have studied the physical changes of hypnosis. We have seen how strikingly suggestion modifies the different functions. I have already had occasion to touch upon some psychical phenomena, closely connected with the physical. In what follows I shall frequently be obliged to refer to the physical phenomena, the variations in which, during hypnosis, are purely the result of changed central processes. Our conclusions as to these central processes must be drawn, then, from the physical functions.

We shall now study the changes which the mental functions undergo during hypnosis. As a matter of course, I shall not note each individual mental action ; I shall only discuss such as are characteristic from our present point of view.

For practical reasons I must first speak of the memory, because it determines the other psychical activities. Without memory no action of the understanding is possible. Memory during and after hypnosis has been specially studied by Richet, Delbœuf, Dichas, Beaunis, and Pitres.

Memory, in its broadest sense, consists of three parts : firstly, of the power of retaining ideas ; secondly, of the power of reproducing these ideas ; thirdly, of the power of recognizing the ideas and of localizing them correctly in the past. To make this clear, let us take any event which we remember—for example, a severe scolding given to us by a teacher. The memory in this case acts in three ways : in the first place, what is said is received and retained in it ; in the second place, the memory can reproduce the lecture ; and in the third place, we can place it in its correct position in time, by recalling its relation to other events, &c. It will be made clear in what follows that under certain circumstances these different processes of the memory show abnormalities in hypnosis.

The retention of ideas in hypnosis has been little investigated. Beaunis has found no essential difference in this respect between hypnosis and waking life. Max Dessoir has also made experiments, whose results he has communicated to me. From these it appears the memory is weakened in hypnosis, when this is not prevented by suggestion. Dessoir repeated a number of syllables which the hypnotic was to try to remember; a suggestion of improved memory was carefully avoided. Under these circumstances the hypnotized subject remembered fewer syllables than did the same person awake. The older mesmerists, on the contrary, believed that the memory was intensified in the magnetic sleep; poems could be learnt by heart in a much shorter time than in the normal state. However, these investigators did not avoid suggestion.

Is the chain of memory in ordinary life broken by the hypnosis or not? It was formerly supposed that a break in the memory occurred, because the subject always forgot on awaking what had taken place during hypnosis. But this view has not proved correct.

In the lighter hypnotic stages, specially in the first group, no abnormality of memory is found; the subject remembers everything in the hypnosis which concerns his normal life, and after the hypnosis remembers all that has occurred. In the deeper hypnoses it is very different; they belong for the most part to the second group, and there is loss of memory after the hypnosis. The subject is much astonished when he hears what he has done during the hypnosis—

that he has been running about, that he has had
hallucinations, &c. Often, however, a dim memory
persists, like the memory of a dream. I suggest to
some one the hallucination of a bird flying about the
room ; the hypnotic tries to catch it, amuses himself
for a long time with it, gives it sugar, puts it in an
imaginary cage, and so on ; after waking he dimly
remembers that he has seen a bird, but that is all ; he
certainly does not believe that he has left his seat.
However, there are certain people who recall everything after being told what they have done.

In other cases, associations of ideas will call up
memory. A hint is given to the hypnotic after the
awakening and everything recurs to him (Heidenhain).
There is something of this sort in dreams ; we very
often remember a whole dream when we see some
object that is in any way connected with it (Delbœuf). The same thing happens when a person is
able to repeat a quotation or a poem directly he has
heard the first words. Let us consider an example in
hypnosis. I suggest a great concert to a subject ; he
hears various pieces, and among them the overture to
" Martha " ; meanwhile he eats his supper at the concert, drinks his beer, and talks to imaginary people.
After the awakening there is no trace of memory. I
ask him then if he knows the opera of " Martha " ;
this suffices to recall nearly all the events of the
hypnosis. Sometimes memory is aroused in the same
way by pure chance, after a longer or shorter interval.
X. believes in hypnosis that he sees a number of
persons at my house whose presence I have suggested
to him. X. goes through several scenes with them,
but remembers nothing on awaking. Only when he
meets one of these people several days later does the
whole thing recur to him. Delbœuf draws attention

to one method of making the memory last ; he thinks
that subjects remember any hypnotic event if they
are awakened in the middle of it ; but this is certainly
not universally true (Gurney).   It sometimes happens
that the first or last occurrences are remembered,
while all the others are forgotten.   It has often been
observed that memory after awakening can be produced by a special effort of the hypnotist (Bleuler,
Pierre Janet).   Some persons remember all the hypnotic proceedings during their nightly sleep ; it is not
rare for the hypnotic dream to be repeated in natural
sleep.

However, in some cases, chiefly in the deepest hypnoses, memory cannot be recalled by any of the above-
named expedients, though some think that a carefully
directed conversation will always re-constitute it
through the association of ideas.   In such cases there
is complete loss of memory in the waking state.   Such
a person does not even generally know how long he
was in the hypnotic state.   On the other hand the
subject remembers in hypnosis all that has happened
in previous hypnoses.   Things that happened in hypnoses dating many years back, even as many as ten,
may be recalled, although they are completely forgotten in the waking state.   Wolfart relates the case
of a woman who remembered in the magnetic sleep
all that had taken place in a magnetic sleep thirteen
years before, although in the meantime she had never
recollected it.

Events of the normal life can also be remembered
in hypnosis, even when they have apparently been long
forgotten.   This increased power of memory is called
hypermnesia.   Benedikt relates a case of it.   An
English officer in Africa was hypnotized by Hansen,
and suddenly began to speak a strange language.

This turned out to be Welsh, which he had learnt as a child, but had forgotten. Breuer and Freud point out that many cases of hysteria are called forth by some psychic moment that the patient cannot recall in the waking condition, though hypnosis may again bring it back to memory.

Such cases as these recall others which are mentioned in the literature of hypnotism ; for example, the famous one of the servant who suddenly spoke Hebrew. She also, in an abnormal state of consciousness, spoke a language which she did not know, but which she had often heard when young in the house of a clergyman. We hear of like cases of hypermnesia in dreams. Maury, whose investigations on the subject of dreams are classic, relates a number of things which returned to his memory in dreams, although when awake he knew nothing about them. The heightened faculties of hypnotic subjects of which we so often hear, and which we can observe in auto-hypnosis also, are a result of this increased power of recollection. Many apparently supernatural facts may be explained in this way. Among these I may mention the carefully constructed religious addresses, sometimes supposed to be inspired, which are delivered by pious but uneducated fanatics in a peculiar psychical state of ecstasy ; and the eloquence occasionally displayed by some spiritualistic mediums in trance belongs to the same category. Bastian also describes such increase of natural powers in hypnosis among savage populations. In many cases other factors may be at work besides the improvement of memory, such as hyperæsthesia of the organs of sense, &c. A characteristic example is furnished by the journeyman-smith, Köhn, at a place near Danzig. The report furnished by Beesel in 1853 shows that insufficient criticism was exerted. This author recognizes Köhn's ability to repeat passages from the Bible with literal accuracy when in the magnetic state, but he relies on the subject's assertion that he had not previously read the Bible. Peesel thinks that Köhn was not drawing on his memory, since he himself denied this, but that some supernatural influence had given him this power.

Dreams, also, which have occurred in natural sleep are sometimes reproduced in hypnosis, although they may have been forgotten on waking. It is naturally very difficult to judge of the accuracy with which dreams are reported. But as dreams sometimes lead to talking in sleep, it is then possible to make observations. I know of a case in which a person betrayed his dreams by talking in his sleep ; the loss of memory which followed on waking disappeared in hypnosis, and the dream was remembered. A bedfellow was able to confirm the accuracy of the recollection.

But, apart from these cases of hypermnesia it is characteristic that in the deeper hypnotic states not only the events that have taken place in earlier hypnoses are remembered, but also the events of waking life. On the other hand, in the waking state the events of that state alone are remembered. This state of things is named "double consciousness (*double conscience* in the broad sense of the term). It was evidently well known to the old mesmerists—Kluge and Deleuze, for example—and was later observed by Braid, though not in the early part of his experience.

The state of double consciousness is also found under pathological conditions. One of the best-known cases was published by Azam. The life of the patient for nearly thirty years was divided into certain periods—a, b, c, d, e, f. In the periods a, c, e (normal condition) she remembered only what had happened in them ; in the periods b. d, f (second condition) she remembered what had occurred in these periods, as well as what had happened in the periods a, c, e. The normal state was a, c, e, while the pathological one was b, d, f. Max Dessoir's thoughtful work on the " Doppel-Ich " contributes much to the elucidation of this question of double consciousness ; he shows that indications of such a splitting of the consciousness are much more common than has hitherto been believed ; he refers us to examples in dream-life and in pathological states. But it appears to me that Max Dessoir, perhaps, supposes a greater extension of these phenomena than is really the case ; Bentivegni makes the same reservation. I shall return to the double consciousness with more detail in the theoretical part of the book.

One phenomenon which I have often observed depends on memory in the later hypnoses. If a whole series of scenes is suggested to a subject in hypnosis a very slight impulse suffices to cause the whole panorama to pass before him again in a later hypnosis. A hypnotic imagines himself hunting a lion ; he kills the lion and cuts it to pieces ; and then by suggestion he is turned into a general, and then into a child. In a later hypnosis he hears an unexpected noise, which he immediately believes to be the roaring of a lion. In consequence he goes through all the scenes again, without omitting the smallest detail. This incident may be counted among the indirect suggestions, since the auto-suggestion was aroused by an accidental circumstance. The case observed and quoted above by Mabille, in which a person induced hæmorrhage by auto-suggestion, after it had once been induced by external suggestion, belongs to the same category. The subject separated herself, so to speak, into two persons, one of whom made the suggestion to the other, as is proved by the conversation she carried on with herself. The subject's recollection of all that he has experienced in earlier hypnoses is most important. The possibility of hypnotic training depends upon this, and it is also a frequent cause of error in new experiments, since they are easily spoiled by memory of the earlier ones. I say to the hypnotic (X.), " You will now raise your left leg." X. does so. While I make the suggestion I unintentionally take hold of his right hand. When, in a later hypnosis, I take hold of his right hand, he again raises his left leg. Evidently he remembers the first event, and regards the taking of his hand as an order to lift his leg. It is probable that the new reflexes which Born thought he had discovered, and which I have mentioned before, came about in this manner.

I have hitherto described the state of things when suggestion is not called into play. Suggestion exercises a most active influence. In the first place, hypermnesia can be increased by suggestion ; though as far as I know no careful investigations have yet been made on this point. But we possess many accounts of careful investigations into the possibility of inducing errors of memory (paramnesia), or failures of memory (amnesia) ; Bertrand collected many observations on these points. These memories may consist of former perceptions ; the suggestive influence of these former perceptions has often been observed ; by means of them the subject may be completely deluded about his former experiences. As these suggestions have a certain retroactive force, they are called retroactive suggestions ; or, as they are concerned with sense perceptions altered by suggestion into sense delusions, they are sometimes called retroactive hallucinations. They are positive or negative, according as a new erroneous memory is created or an old one annulled. I say to a subject, "You remember that we went to Potsdam yesterday, and took a drive on the Havel?" The suggestion takes effect, and the gentleman at once begins to relate his experiences in Potsdam. This is a retroactive positive hallucination. Again, "You have just been running extremely fast ; you ran half a mile as hard as you could go." In this case the delusion of memory is so great that palpitation and gasping for breath follow, in consequence of the imaginary race (Delbœuf). These are positive retroactive hallucinations, because the hypnotic believes he has experienced something which did not really happen. The following would be a retroactive negative hallucination, as the hypnotic here forgets something which did happen : I say to him, "You have not had any dinner ; you have not had any breakfast." Upon which he immediately feels hungry, as he thinks he has had nothing to eat since he got up.

Many motor disturbances of which I have before spoken may be reckoned as related to amnesia, or loss of memory. For example, when I tell somebody that he cannot lift his arm, or that he cannot speak, I am sometimes dealing with loss of memory, because a movement is made impossible if the memory of it cannot first be called up. This is the case in those paralyses which some French authors (Binet, Féré) call *paralysies systématiques*—a paralysis for a special act. Such a paralysis is not followed by total functional incapacity of a whole group of muscles ; the function is rather interfered with for one particular use only. The incapacity to say *a*, or to sew, for example, would be a paralysis for a special act ; if the person could not speak or move his arm at all, this would be a total paralysis. It is possible in this way to deprive the subject of all memory of the letter *a*, so that he can neither speak nor write it. These forms of loss of memory become very clear when we consider the disturbances which may be produced by suggestion in the signs we use for mutual comprehension ; that is, in vocal sounds, gestures, and writing. It is possible to produce almost all kinds of aphasia experimentally, as Kussmaul, Arndt, and others have clearly demonstrated. We can cause any one to forget a language he has learnt—French, for example (Forel, Frank) ; we can make writing impossible (agraphia). By a suitable suggestion a hypnotic can be deprived of the power of making himself understood by facial expression (amimia). Drawing, sewing, every form of activity in fact, can be prevented by suggestion.

It is known that there is a particular group of disturbances of speech in which the perception of words is wanting ; this is called sensory or amnesic aphasia. The patient still attaches ideas to words. But it is possible by means of suggestion to deprive him not only of the perception of a word or letter (*e.g.*, the letter *a*), and of the consequent power to write and speak it ; he can also be deprived of the idea which he attaches to such a word or letter. This difference will become clear if we observe the behaviour of a person under the different circumstances. If he retains the idea of the letter he is conscious of his inability to utter or write it ; he is aware that he is writing or speaking nonsense, and even tries to avoid using words in which the letter *a* appears (Max Dessoir). But if he is deprived of the conception or idea of the letter, he is no longer surprised that he cannot write or speak it. This becomes still more interesting in post-hypnotic suggestion. It is possible to cause a post-hypnotic loss of memory, and to make the subject invariably replace one letter by another. I told a hypnotic that after he was awakened he would always say *e* instead of *a*. I woke him, and asked, "Are you awake?" "Je" (Ja), he replied. "What have you been doing?" "Ich heb geschlefen" (ich habe geschlafen). The subject laughed, but was at the same time slightly annoyed, and was perfectly aware that he was talking nonsense. But if the *idea a* were also missing, the subject would say *e* instead of *a* without observing it.

I have shown above that subjects may be made to forget certain of their experiences (negative retro-active hallucinations).

In the same way whole periods can be made to vanish from the subject's consciousness. Mr. X., who is forty-three years old, was told, "You no longer remember anything that has happened to you since you were thirty!" This sufficed to cause a blank in X.'s consciousness. He was unable to answer any questions about this period; he did not know how he made my acquaintance, nor how he got into my room; when such questions were put to him he shrugged his shoulders and answered, "I don't know."

It is possible to carry this still further, and trans-port the subject back to an earlier period of his life. In this case the subject finds no gaps in his memory; he believes that he is living in this earlier time, and brings his present surroundings into relation with it. Here is a man who fought at St. Privat in the French war. His age was forty-one; I suggested to him that he was nineteen years younger, and in the battle. He stood up at once, gave military orders, and commanded the artillery to fire. When I asked him if he knew Dr. Moll, he said, " No ; my doctor's name is R. I do not know Dr. Moll." He knew nothing that had happened since the battle ; he was unaware of the rheumatism for which I was treating him ; he said he was quite well. When I asked him who I was, he replied that he did not know. It was interesting that he could not be induced to retreat ; I tried to make him take a few steps backward, but he replied, " I will not retreat one step without orders." I suggested that the enemy was still approaching, but nothing would induce him to retreat. When I drew his attention more and more upon myself, and told him that he must know who I was, the situation suddenly altered. He recognized me, and knew his real age, but had no idea of what had just passed.

I caused a lady, æt. 34, to believe that she was eight years old again. She spoke to her doll in a childish voice, cried when she thought I was about to take it away, and called for her mamma.

Finally, it is possible to make a person believe that he has never been born. Even this suggestion will be accepted, and the consciousness will be an absolute blank.

In recent times Krafft-Ebing's attempts have attracted attention. He endeavoured to obtain an experimental solution of the question (to which I have already referred) as to whether events which have disappeared from consciousness can be brought back during hypnosis. The method employed by Krafft-Ebing was different from that previously mentioned. He tried to solve the question by placing the subject back in some earlier period of life, and endeavouring to discover if forgotten events of childhood were recalled. He considers that his experiments settle this question in the affirmative.

New memories can be created at the time the old X ones are cancelled. This is the case with the phenomenon which Charles Richet describes as *objectivation des types*. In this case the subject believes himself another personality, another being; not only do many memories connected with his own *ego* disappear, but he also endeavours to connect the remaining memories with his suggested personality. Durand de Gros was acquainted with these phenomena; he appears to have studied them in America, where they were already observed in 1840.

I told a certain Mr. X. that he was Dr. Moll, and that I was Mr. X.; upon which he asked me to take a seat, that he might hypnotize me. He did hypnotize me; that is, he went carefully through the process which I go through with him, and did not forget to make several pleasant suggestions.

I experimented with another man, in whom these phenomena are very easily produced. He would represent with dramatic vividness any character which was within the grasp of his ideas. I told him, "You are Napoleon I.," upon which he assumed the famous posture of Napoleon after the battle of Waterloo, but spoke German, as he did not know French. As Frederick the Great, he walked with a crutch in the well-known gait, and knew nothing about railroads. Subjects can be made to believe they are animals; they will bark like dogs, or croak like frogs. They can even be changed by suggestion into inanimate objects, such as stoves, chairs, tables. When X. thinks himself a chair he crouches down on both legs; when it is

suggested that the chair has a broken leg, he sinks
his knee to the ground and rests on one leg; when
he is a carpet he lies flat and motionless. These
experiments in suggestion may be carried still further.
"You are made of glass," I say to a subject; he
stands perfectly still. When I tell another that he
is made of marble, he stands stiffly and cannot be
moved; but directly he believes himself to be made
of wax he becomes plastic and allows himself to be
placed in any attitude.

Baret reports that in a certain form of insanity
often occurring in Japan, the subject believes that he
has been changed into a fox, and speaks in a strange
voice It is popularly believed that such a person
is possessed by a fox, and the condition is called
Kitsune-tsuki. The transformation of a hypnotized
person into an animal is certainly allied to this
phenomenon.

It should be remarked that the subject always
obeys, even when he believes himself an inanimate
object. Moreover, hypnotized subjects are by no
means always consistent; they often forget their part,
though this may be generally prevented by training.
For example, another person, whom I had changed
into Frederick the Great, travelled contentedly in a
railway carriage, evidently not reflecting that there
were no railways in those days. Another, whom I
had carried back into the year 1864, spoke of the new
German Empire, of the Emperor William, and so on.
In spite of such inconsistencies, the mental images
are much more consistent with hypnotics than with
many lunatics who believe themselves to be kings
and prophets. The inconsistencies of lunatics are
much greater, and hypnotics sooner get rid of them.
Besides this, when they represent a new personality,

memories of former experiences disappear more completely than is the case with lunatics (Cullerre).

The change of personality in hypnotic subjects has often-been
compared with the performances of actors. It is a fact that the
actor who himself creates the idea of his part, and allows himself to be governed by it, will play his part the best. This is
the opinion of Dumesnil ; others—for example, the famous
Clairon—held a different opinion on this point. In any case
few actors are able to accommodate and assimilate themselves
to their own idea of a character, *e.g.*, that of Julius Cæsar, as
thoroughly as a hypnotic subject can do. The subject is not
distracted by sense perceptions, while the most accomplished
actor cannot always avoid being affected by his surroundings.
Some actors, in order to play their parts as naturally as possible,
call up imaginary objects by force of imagination, so as to
place themselves amongst suitable surroundings.

These changes of personality, and the changing of hypnotic
subjects into animals, remind us forcibly of the stories of
changing men into animals (zoanthropia), which was occasionally epidemic in the Middle Ages and later. People believed
themselves changed into animals—usually into wolves. Such
persons attacked and tore others, and displayed the fierce-
ness and the instincts of wild beasts. This phenomenon was
supposed to be the work of the devil ; Johann Wier tells us
many strange things about it. Herodotus and Pliny mention
like phenomena.

Graphological investigations have been undertaken
in several quarters in order to decide whether the
handwriting of the hypnotized subject changes with
the personality, and if the change bears any relation
to the suggested personality. Changes have been
observed (Lombroso, Ferrari, Héricourt, Richet
Varinard, Mayeras). The expert Hoctès, however,
thinks that the subjects' writing is never altered to
such a degree as not to be recognizable. I have
never seen changes of handwriting follow on changes
of personality ; only when I placed the subjects in

different periods of life has the handwriting altered.
As children they wrote awkwardly and made faults
of spelling ; as old people they wrote shakily.
The trials made with Krafft-Ebing's patient, who
wrote different hands, corresponding to the different
earlier periods of her life, are very interesting ; but,
unluckily, the writing could not be compared with the
true normal writing of the subject at those periods.
Nuel's statement that in hypnosis the writing always
differs from the subject's normal hand, and that consequently hypnotic signatures may always be distinguished from others, seems to me too general. He is
probably right when he says that in many cases the
writing of hypnotic subjects is irregular and spasmodic.

I will here remark that all the above-mentioned
suggestions influencing the memory can also be made
post-hypnotic, and in all hypnoses it is only necessary to tell the subjects before awakening them that
they will remember everything, and they will do so.
Also, in some of the hypnotic states, memory may be
prevented by command. We can also cause loss of
memory of particular events or things ; for example,
we can prevent the recollection of certain letters, as
we have seen before. Retroactive hallucinations can
be transferred to waking life in the same way. I say
to a subject in my house, " You know that we drank
two bottles of wine just now, and that we had roast
goose for supper." When he answers, " Yes," I
further tell him that after he wakes he will remember
all about it. He wakes and relates it all ; he declares
he has eaten too much, and that the wine has made
his head heavy ; he even thinks himself slightly
intoxicated. This is a purely imaginary intoxication
produced by suggestion. Hytten relates an even

more interesting case ; he says he has cured real
intoxication by suggestion.

These delusions of memory may last for weeks and
months. However, I have seen them disappear a
short time after waking. A man, who directly after
waking believed he had seen his mother at my house
before the hypnosis, forgot all about it after a few
minutes. We had spoken of other things in the
meantime, and this probably caused the rapid
oblivion. Bernheim has lately shown that in some
cases the subject forgets not only what has taken
place during the hypnosis, but also what immediately
preceded it, and this without any kind of suggestion
having been made.

I shall speak of these delusions of memory transferred
to waking life when I discuss the legal side of the question.
Bernheim first pointed out their great importance, and rightly
called attention to analogous occurrences in waking life. For
example, there are people who will repeat a lie so often that at
last they no longer know whether they are lying or not. The
mental image is called up again and again as they talk, and
each time becomes more vivid. Bernheim also shows that
complete delusions of memory can be induced in certain people
without their ever having been hypnotized. It is only necessary
to repeat to them confidently that such and such a thing has
happened, and they become unable to distinguish fact from
fiction.

I have already mentioned several cases in which
changes of memory in the waking state have been
caused by post-hypnotic suggestion. The memory
in later hypnoses can be influenced in the same way.
For instance, we can make the loss of memory, or
the paramnesia above mentioned, continue in later
hypnoses. And the subject may be made to forget
in later hypnoses what happened in the earlier ones,
just as he may be made to forget in the waking state

what has happened in hypnosis. It suffices to tell
him that in later hypnoses he will not remember this
or that.

I have said above that hypnotic subjects remember
the events of earlier hypnoses in later ones. But this
statement needs some limitation, apart from what has
just been said. In the first place, we see that when
there is a change of personality, there is generally
loss of memory also; a subject as Napoleon does
not remember what he did as Frederick the Great.
I further mention some little unconscious actions,
which cannot be recalled to the subject's memory; I
say, for example, "In five minutes you will say,
'Ha!' three times." The subject obeys, but remembers
nothing about it later. In the same way certain
post-hypnotic suggestions may be obeyed in a new
hypnosis, and the subject may be unconscious that
they were suggested in an earlier one.

Finally, Gurney supposes two stages of hypnosis,
distinguished from each other by completely different
memories. The old magnetizers described such stages.
I have been unable to convince myself of their existence, and think them a result of hypnotic training.
Gurney distinguishes two stages, *a* and *b*. In stage
a the subject knows nothing of stage *b;* and in *b*
nothing of *a*. I do not dispute that in some persons
several sharply divided states of consciousness may
exist, apart from the waking consciousness; this is
also affirmed by Krafft-Ebing and Pierre Janet; I
only object to speaking of it as universal.

I have spoken several times of post-hypnotic suggestion. This is a point of such importance in
medicine and psychology that it must be examined
in detail. No serious observer can doubt the reality

of post-hypnotic suggestion The old mesmerists observed some cases of it. In 1787 Mouillesaux ordered a lady in the hypnotic state to pay a visit to a certain person the next day; the command was exactly obeyed (Du Prel); Kluge, Schopenhauer, and Noizet mention other cases. Liébeault, Richet, Bernheim, and Delbœuf have lately studied post-hypnotic suggestion; Gurney and Forel in particular have done so in various ways. It is certain that many suggestions are obeyed post-hypnotically. Jendrássik has seen a paralysis last several days in consequence of hypnotic suggestion; Krafft-Ebing successfully suggested to one of his patients to maintain a definite bodily temperature for a fixed time. Reddening of the skin has also been induced by post-hypnotic suggestion. Any suggestion that takes effect in hypnosis will also take effect post-hypnotically; movements and delusions of the senses, itching, pain, action of the bowels, hunger, thirst, &c., can be induced. Dreams can be influenced. "To-day you will dream that you are at Swinemünde; you will go on the Ostsee in a boat with six people; the boat will be upset, and you will fall into the water and wake." The subject dreams this in detail. Dreamless sleep can be induced in the same way; or at least the subjects do not remember if they have dreamt.

It is possible to carry on suggestions from hypnosis into waking life; they are then called continuative suggestions. I suggest that my photograph is on a visiting card, and say that the subject will continue to see it after awakening. The subject is firmly convinced that the photograph is there. According to Londe an illusion of this kind has lasted for two years. This carrying on of the suggestion into normal life happens sometimes by chance, when the suggestion has not been cancelled before the awaken-ing. One of my subjects drinks what has been sug-gested to her as peppermint water; I awake her, and she says for an hour after that she has a taste of pep-permint in her mouth. The following often-repeated experiment belongs to the continuative suggestions: I say to the subject, "Count up to ten, and wake when you get to three." He counts up to ten, but is awake while counting from four to six.

In other cases the suggestion only takes effect after waking. I say to the subject, "You will not be able to move your right arm after you wake." He wakes, and is unable to move it, though otherwise in a normal state. Exactly the same effects may be produced after an interval of hours, days, weeks, and months. I say to a subject, "When you come to see me in a week you will not be able to speak when you come into the room." He comes to see me in a week, and is fully awake when he enters the room; I ask him his name, but he is unable to say it, or anything else. Here we have an example of fulfilment of suggestion after an interval, or *suggestion à échéance,* deferred suggestion.

It is remarkable that these deferred suggestions should have at first aroused so much incredulity, since analogies are certainly to be found for them in normal life. Post-hypnotic suggestions may be divided into two groups; but I make this division merely for practical convenience in considering them. In the first group the suggestion is forgotten on awakening, in the second it is remembered. It will be explained in the theoretical section that the loss of memory in the first group is only apparent. I shall thoroughly discuss this group first, as it is the more important and inte-resting.

The moment for the fulfilment of the suggestion can be decided in several ways. To one subject I say, "An hour after you wake you will hear a polka played; you will believe you are at a ball, and will begin to dance." To another, whom I wake at eight o'clock, I say, "When the clock strikes nine you will take the water-bottle from the table, and walk up and down the room three times with it. The moment of fulfilment is decided differently in these two cases. In the second case the moment is decided by a concrete external sign; in the other an abstract term, an hour, is fixed.

The suggestion in this second example, where the moment of action is decided by some external sign, nearly always takes effect, especially after a little hypnotic training. The first more rarely succeeds. There are some subjects, however, with whom such suggestions take effect punctually. But the greater number are not only unpunctual, but often do not execute the suggestion at all, if some external impetus is not given; others carry out the suggestion, but inexactly—in forty-five minutes instead of one hour, &c.

I will point out a frequent source of error in these time experiments: this is the behaviour of the spectators. They look at the clock at the appointed time, or make some other unconscious signal that the right moment has arrived. This has sometimes happened in my own experiments.

There is a third way of appointing the moment for the execution of a post-hypnotic suggestion, which has been carefully experimented upon by Gurney and Pierre Janet. In many respects it is like the first method. I say to a subject (X.), "When I rub my foot along the floor for the tenth time after you awake, you will laugh." The subject wakes, and does not remember my order. I talk to him, and rub several times without his paying any attention; at the tenth shuffle he laughs. Consequently the suggestion has taken effect. I make the experiment again, but at the fourth shuffle I ask X. if he has not heard the noise. He says, "No." Nevertheless at the tenth shuffle he laughs, though he is quietly talking to me. In most experiments the result was less exact. The suggestion succeeded, but not at the right moment.

Many deferred suggestions resemble these suggestions in which the moment of fulfilment is fixed by counting. Post-hypnotic deferred suggestions can be made in two ways; for example, on the 3rd of May I say to a person who sees me every day, "On the 6th of June, when you come into the room, you will see me with a black face, and you will laugh at me." The suggestion succeeds. But here a fixed date is named which helps the subject to carry out the suggestion, in the same way as the striking of the clock in the case first quoted. Delbœuf, in particular, has pointed out the importance of this. In this case also we have a concrete sign. It would have been another matter if I had made the suggestion thus: "On the 35th day, reckoning from to-day, you will come into my room and see me with a black face," &c. According to Gurney's observations, suggestions of this kind succeed, and a few of my own experiments confirm him. An example may make this sort of suggestion clearer. I suggested once to X., "You will come to my house on the sixteenth Tuesday, reckoning from last Tuesday, and will abuse all the people present," &c. This suggestion succeeded completely, although no fixed time was named. I shall return to an explanation of this later on.

I have as yet only discussed the manner of deter-
mining the point of time for the carrying out of the
post-hypnotic suggestion. The question now is,
What is the condition of the subject while carrying
out the post-hypnotic suggestion ? So far as I
know, Dumontpallier, Beaunis, and Liégeois were the
first to remark that post-hypnotic suggestions were
certainly not carried out in a waking state, even if the
action took place after the awakening from hypnosis.
The question has led to lively discussion ; Forel and
Gurney have made the best and most numerous observations in regard to it ; in particular they have
shown that the post-hypnotic suggestion may be
carried out in very different states.

To give the reader an idea of these states, I will
show some examples. A man (X.), thirty years old,
is in the hypnotic state. I say to him, " When
you wake, directly I cross my knees you will take
the inkstand from the table and put it on the chair."
He wakes at my order, and I talk to him. After
a time I cross my knees ; he begins to stare at the
inkstand and hardly answers me. He goes to the
table, takes the inkstand and puts it on a chair ; upon
which I suggest to him that he sees his brother, that
he is eating his luncheon, &c., all of which suggestions he accepts. I am obliged to re-awaken him to
put an end to this new state of suggestibility. After
waking he remembers absolutely nothing. This
case is characterized by loss of memory of all that
happened during the state, and further by susceptibility to suggestion. I do not know how this state
is to be distinguished psychologically from a true
hypnosis, and to my mind Delbœuf is right when he
says that to make a post-hypnotic suggestion is really
to order a new hypnosis at a fixed moment, and the

11

carrying out of the suggestion in this new hypnosis. There are other very different cases. I say to a hypnotized subject, " When you awake, directly I rub my hands together, you will forget your name. When I separate my hands you will remember it again." The order is obeyed ; we talk to one another, but when I bring my hands together the subject forgets his own name. He is, however, completely awake, and incapable of accepting any further suggestion. When I separate my hands he knows his own name, and knows also that he had forgotten it a moment ago. Directly I bring my hands together he forgets it again. He goes away, and in a few days we meet again ; but now he remembers his name, however I hold my hands. But he remembers perfectly that the other day he was several times unable to say his own name. He maintains that he was awake all the time.

We are not justified in calling this case one of hypnosis. There was no mental symptom of hypnosis, no loss of memory, no suggestibility, no fatigue; the subject did not think he had been asleep ; nothing remains but to consider the state a perfectly normal one, except on one point. Whether such a state may be regarded as normal, generally speaking, is another matter. I shall discuss this when I come to the legal question, for which these cases are very important (Bentivegni).

It appears from these examples that post-hypnotic suggestions may be carried out in various different states. Between the two extremes—the one case in which there were all the mental symptoms of a new hypnosis, and the other in which there were none— there are many degrees which will now be discussed.

Here is another example. A woman is hypnotized.

A. and B. are present. I say to the subject, "When A. speaks to you after you wake you will laugh at him. When B. speaks to you, you will put out your tongue at him. Wake!" The suggestion is exactly carried out. A. speaks to the subject and she laughs. I ask, "Why did you laugh just now?" "I did not laugh." And she positively insists that she did not laugh. A. speaks to her again and again ; she laughs, and again at my question she denies having laughed. She puts out her tongue at B. when he speaks to her, and the moment after, when I question her, she says that she did not do it. I suggest that she hears a barrel-organ ; but she says she does not, and is insusceptible to other suggestions. She remembers everything else that has happened, and knows perfectly what I have said to her. All that is forgotten is the post-hypnotic act and what is connected with it ; *i.e.*, the words which A. and B. spoke to her. She can repeat what I said to her, and her replies ; everything, in fact, unconnected with the suggestion. She knows nothing about the time during which she carried out the suggestion ; at the same time she recognizes no gap in her memory.

In this case there is complete loss of memory of the post-hypnotic act, and no further suggestibility ; the loss of memory extends simply to the post-hypnotic act. This is, then, a third way in which post-hypnotic suggestion is carried out, and it is not rare.

In other cases the subject remains susceptible to suggestion while he performs the act, but wakes directly it is over and remembers nothing about it. It is difficult to distinguish these cases from those just described ; on that account I shall not make a separate group of them ; for it seems that subjects

like the person described in the third example are
really always susceptible to suggestion while they
are carrying out the act, but that in many cases
the act takes place too quickly to allow of a fresh
suggestion being made. The post-hypnotic act is
completely forgotten, while the state of the subject
before and after the action is quite normal. Liégeois
thought this a separate state, which he called "*condition prime.*" He gave up this later, and now calls
the state "*condition seconde provoquée ;*" Beaunis calls
it "*veille somnambulique,*" Gurney, "trance-waking." I
think, however, that these states must be considered
true hypnoses (Delbœuf). Evidently, the suggested
idea is so powerful in them that it produces a state
analogous to that in which it was first implanted.
When the idea vanishes the state also vanishes.

Here is a fourth case. I suggest to X. to take a
chair and put it on the table five minutes after he
wakes. The suggestion is carried out. While he is
putting the chair on the table I call out suddenly that
a dog is biting him. He believes it, kicks away the
imaginary dog, and wakes spontaneously. He remembers moving the chair and remembers the dog,
but says the whole thing was like a dream.

Consequently this state is characterized by suggestibility during the carrying out of the post-hypnotic
suggestion ; but there is also memory. It is true that
X. feels as if he dreamed it. He has a consciousness
of having slept through the performance, and of
having waked when it was ended. This consciousness of having slept is very important (Delbœuf). We
often have some life-like experience in a dream, and
yet know directly we wake that it was a dream. I
think that the last-described post-hypnotic state must
be considered a hypnosis. The suggestibility is very
characteristic.

In order not to complicate the question I will re-capitulate. Amongst the post-hypnotic states we have studied—(1) a state in which a new hypnosis charac-terized by suggestibility came on during the carrying out of the suggestion ; loss of memory afterwards, and no spontaneous waking ; (2) a state in which no symptom of a fresh hypnosis was discoverable, although the suggestion was carried out ; (3) a state in which the post-hypnotic suggestion was carried out, with complete forgetfulness of the act, with or without fresh susceptibility to suggestion, and from which the waking was spontaneous ; (4) a state of suscepti-bility to suggestion with loss of memory following. In judging of these states I think the chief symptoms are, firstly, the fresh suggestibility, and secondly, the subsequent loss of memory. Whether the subject wakes spontaneously or has to be again awakened, is of secondary importance, as spontaneous waking is observed in ordinary hypnoses.

Gurney has directed attention to a particularly important device for estimating the mental state during the carrying out of a post-hypnotic suggestion. We have seen that the renewed suggestibility is of great importance in deciding whether a fresh hypnosis has been induced or not ; and Gurney has made use of this post-hypnotic suggestibility for solving the question.

The subject (X.) is shuffling cards. We wish to find out in what state he is, and he is therefore told while he is shuffling, that when the clock strikes he will jump up three times. He has finished shuffling and is quite awake. There is nothing to show that he is still in hypnosis; he is not susceptible to suggestion. He does not remember shuffling the cards, and con-tends that he has not done it ; but directly the clock strikes he jumps up three times. From this post-hypnotic susceptibility to suggestion we conclude that he was not in a normal state when he was shuffling the cards. Whether this state was hypnotic, or was another peculiar mental state, as Beaunis and Gurney suppose, is another question. I incline to think it a true hypnosis.

Gurney thinks that in order to properly estimate and characterize this state we must take memory into consideration also. We have seen that subjects in later hypnoses remember what has occurred in earlier ones. If now the events of earlier hypnoses should be present in the post-hypnotic state we should consider it a fresh hypnosis. Now I have often found that there was a complete recollection of the events of earlier hypnoses while the post-hypnotic suggestion was being carried out. This fact also favours the supposition of a fresh hypnosis.

Finally, there are cases in which physical symptoms may be found. It would be interesting to observe these during post-hypnotic suggestion. The fixed look and blank expression often seen during the carrying out of the suggestion also favour the idea of fresh hypnosis.

It may be concluded from what has been said that post-hypnotic suggestions may be carried out in various different states. This is the case not only when we compare one subject with another, but when we observe the same subject under the influence of different suggestions. The questions upon which it all hinges are — 1. Does the subject remember later on what he has done, and does he remember the events of earlier hypnoses while carrying out the suggestion ? 2. Whilst doing what has been suggested is he susceptible either to suggestions to be carried out at once, or to new post-hypnotic suggestions? 3. Has he the look, the manner, the physical symptoms usual in hypnosis or not?

The question becomes even more complicated when we consider the following experiments of Forel. Forel said to a nurse, " Whenever you say ' Sir ' to the assistant physician you will scratch your right temple with your right hand without noticing it." The nurse did so, talking clearly and rationally all the time. She did not notice that she was scratching her face.

Here the subject behaves normally, and yet the post-hypnotic suggestion is executed during the conversation with complete loss of memory. When the subject acts once with loss of memory, is this state hypnosis or is it some other state? I think it should be regarded as a normal part of waking life, for it would be a mistake to conclude a hypnosis from the mere forgetting of one act, without susceptibility to suggestion. Gurney points out that loss of memory alone cannot be taken for proof of an abnormal state, because in normal life we perform actions and see objects without remembering them afterwards. If the action is a purely mechanical one, such as winding a watch, we often remember nothing about it.

I have purposely in the last section only discussed movements and acts executed post-hypnotically. But all sorts of delusions of the senses, positive and negative, can be induced post-hypnotically at pleasure. We can cause whole scenes to be gone through ; the subject will go to a ball, or dinner, &c. The state of the subjects during the realization of a post-hypnotic delusion may differ considerably. But in my experience it is almost a rule that the induction of a post-hypnotic delusion should induce a fresh hypnosis with susceptibility to suggestion and subsequent loss of memory.

It is possible besides to influence subjects in these states in any way (Forel). For example, we may make the suggestion thus : " You will see a dog five minutes after you wake ; but you will remain awake and not allow anything else to be suggested to you." The subject may be in this way protected from further suggestion ; he will then carry out the first suggestion, but for the rest will appear fully awake. Messrs. X. and Y. are at my house. I hypnotize Y. I say to him, " When you wake X. will be sitting on this chair ; you will remain awake." When he wakes he believes that he sees X. in the chair, and talks to him, &c. I draw his attention to the real X. and say, " Which is the real X. ? You see one in the chair and one standing before you." Y. feels the chair and the real X. to find out which is air and which is reality. He feels about and finally concludes, " He is in the chair." And yet Y. is not susceptible to suggestion on other points.

In what precedes I have discussed the state of the subject during the carrying out of the post-hypnotic suggestion. It will not take long to consider the state between waking and the execution of the suggestion. The subject is then nearly always fully awake, and insusceptible to suggestion ; the state is, in fact, the same as if he had been wakened without previous post-hypnotic suggestion. However, there are some cases in which the awakening is not complete so long as the effect of the suggestion lasts ; this occurs particularly when the suggestion is repugnant to the subject's character and will. Such subjects look tired and sleepy, and often say themselves that they are not

quite awake. I have had cases in which I was obliged
to cancel the suggestion before I could completely
awaken the subject. However, this has never occurred
when the post-hypnotic suggestion had a therapeutic
aim, but only in experiment. I think the resistance
of the subject is partly to blame. In other cases I
have observed a subjective discomfort instead of the
feeling of fatigue, till the suggestion was executed.
This subjective discomfort is sometimes felt without
the suggestion being carried out. One lady to whom
it had been suggested that she should put a book on
the floor woke in great discomfort, but it did not
occur to her to put the book on the floor. She recovered herself however when, at my request, she had
put the book on the floor in a waking state. Another
subject complained of a twitching in the arm after
waking ; I had suggested to him to give me his hand
when he woke. He did not do it till I asked him
again in the waking state ; he was aware of nothing
but the twitching.

As in all the above cases of post-hypnotic suggestion the command was not remembered, it is particularly interesting to observe how the subjects try to
account for their execution of the suggestions.
Naturally, I shall here only consider the cases in
which the action is not immediately forgotten ; in the
others the subjects do not try to find reasons for
actions which they have forgotten.

Let us take an example. I say to a hypnotized
woman, "After you wake you will take a book from
the table and put it on the bookshelf." She wakes
and does what I told her. When I ask her what she
has been doing, she answers that she has moved the
book from the table to the shelf. When asked for her

reason, she answers, " I do not like to see things so untidy ; the shelf is the place for the book, and that is why I put it there." In this case I suggested an action to the subject ; she does not remember my order but believes she has so acted of her own accord, from love of order. This phenomenon has often been observed (Richet), and is so common that some consider it the rule. This, however, can hardly be said (Forel). Let us go on with our experiment. I suggest to the re-hypnotized subject to take the book from the shelf and lay it under the table, which she does. I ask her why she did it ; she can give no reason. " It came into my head," she answers. I repeat the experiment several times. To a new request for her reason she finally replies, " Something made me feel as if I must put the book there." In this case the subject, who at first believed she was acting freely, came by degrees to recognize the constraint put upon her ; she, perhaps, suspected the suggestion, but was not sure of it.

Another case. I suggest to a hypnotized man to use an insulting expression to me when he wakes. He wakes, and after a pause of a few seconds, during which his face expresses an inward struggle, he calls out " Donkey ! " When he is asked why he so insults me, he makes many excuses, and explains, " I felt as if I must say ' Donkey ! ' "

Here we have to do with a paradoxical action ; the man knew at once that constraint was being put upon him ; the woman who performed the simpler act above described only perceived the constraint after several experiments.

However, in a great number of cases the result is different. I tell a hypnotized subject that when he wakes he is to take a flower-pot from the window, wrap it in a cloth, put it on the sofa, and bow to it three times. All which he does. When he is asked for his reasons he answers, "You know, when I woke and saw the flower-pot there I thought that as it was rather cold the flower-pot had better be warmed a little, or else the plant would die. So I wrapped it in the cloth, and then I thought that as the sofa was near the fire I would put the flower-pot on it ; and I bowed because I was pleased with myself for having such a bright idea." He added that he did not consider the proceeding foolish, he had told me his reasons for so acting. In this case the subject carried out an absurd post-hypnotic suggestion ; he was unconscious of the constraint put upon him and tried to find good reasons for his act. Most experimenters have observed that their subjects try to find reasons for the most foolish suggested acts.

It is also to be observed that when the subjects are questioned as to their motive they make different answers ; they either believe that they have so acted of their own accord, and invent reasons for their proceedings, or they say they felt impelled to act so, or they only say, "It came into my head to do it." We can use suggestion here also. When the original suggestion is being made, it may, at the same time, be suggested to the subject to believe he has acted of his own free-will, or to believe that constraint was put upon him.

When such a suggestion is not made, it depends upon the subject's power of self-observation which reason he gives—whether he perceives the constraint, or invents false reasons for his conduct. Something also depends upon the frequency with which the experiment is made, and particularly upon the greater or less absurdity of the suggested act.

This endeavour of the subjects to find a motive for their apparently free acts is very instructive ; since, though they believe themselves free, they are really acting under constraint. This mistaken feeling of freedom has been used by several psychologists lately to demonstrate the powerlessness of human will. A state has been produced by experiment, in which the subject is convinced that he is acting freely, while in reality his will has been directed in a particular manner, unconsciously to himself. Ribot, Forel, and others especially point this out. Spinoza's saying, " The illusion of free-will is nothing but ignorance of the motives for our choice," appears to find support in these hypnotic experiments (Forel) ; it is certainly proved that one of the chief supports of the doctrine of free-will, *i.e.*, our feeling that we might have acted otherwise, is not enough to prove free-will. The following experiment, which I have repeated in various ways with several subjects, shows this. I suggest a post-hypnotic act to a subject—for example, I tell him to lay an umbrella on the ground. The subject now wakes, and I tell him to do anything he pleases ; but at the same time I give him a folded paper, on which I have written what he is to do. He does what I have suggested, and is much astonished when he reads the paper afterwards. He declares that this time he was quite sure he would do something else than what I had suggested.

However, I believe that in spite of these hypnotic experiments, we should hesitate to draw general conclusions about free-will ; for though hypnosis is not a pathological state it is an exceptional one, from which we must not draw general conclusions. Few who have made such experiments often can fail to feel occasional subjective doubts of freedom of will, but from these doubts to scientific proof is an immense step. Further, it should not be forgotten that we do not by any means find these deep hypnoses and subjective delusions of the judgment in all subjects. On the contrary, such subjects are in the minority. Also, after repeated experiments they begin to observe themselves, and are aware of the constraint put upon them, particularly when the suggested action is opposed to their natural disposition. Before we can draw final conclusions we must find analogous cases in ordinary life; which, indeed, has often been done. We will go back to the art of conjuring. A well-known trick of the conjurer is to allow a card to be drawn from a pack and to guess it. The trick is thus explained: the spectator thinks he has freely chosen the card, but in reality the conjurer has directed him to one in particular, and compelled him to select it. The conjurer often attains this end by putting the card he wishes chosen where it will naturally be the first to be taken up. It need hardly be mentioned that I do not draw conclusions against freedom of will from this example.

We can then with certainty, by means of post-hypnotic suggestion, compel many actions which the subject in normal circumstances would refuse to perform. We may, in consequence, consider such acts purely compulsory. I ask a man to tell me something which he would never voluntarily do; he replies that he would never throw a sofa cushion at my head; all the same, when I suggest this to him in hypnosis he does it, after a short resistance. These compulsory acts have a great resemblance to the impulsive acts which we sometimes see performed in pathological states. When the signal for the carrying out of the post-hypnotic suggestion is given the subject feels an impulse exactly like that felt by many morbid persons, in whom the sight of a sheet of water arouses a desire to commit suicide or murder (Cullerre). The same effort to resist the impulse may be observed in these patients as in hypnotic subjects. Bentivegni has lately pointed out the analogy between these pathological impulses and the above-mentioned post-hypnotic suggestions. The patients dominated by this imaginary necessity are fully aware of their unfortunate state, but are none the less impelled to action (Maudsley) ; in the same way a subject dominated by a post-hypnotic suggestion often recognizes its folly, but finally succumbs.

Post-hypnotic suggestions are of especial value for the induction or prevention of future hypnoses. In this way an easily hypnotizable subject may be prevented from allowing himself to be hypnotized by another person. Post-hypnotic suggestion is an excellent means for protecting susceptible people and guarding them against unexpected hypnosis, as Ricard pointed out with regard to the somnambulic state. Mr. X., whom I had often hypnotized, had also often been hypnotized by Mr. A. I suggested to X. that he should in future only allow himself to be hypnotized by doctors, and on no account by Mr. A. After this Mr. A. could no longer hypnotize him. However, I do not believe that this is a perfect protection in all cases. But the chief danger, which does not arise from susceptibility to hypnotism, but from susceptibility to hypnotism against the subject's will, is thereby guarded against. On the other hand it is possible to throw a subject into an unexpected hypnosis by means of post-hypnotic suggestion. I say to a subject, " Directly I say the word 'to-day' you

will fall into a fresh hypnosis." I then wake him,
and he remains awake till I say "to-day"; upon
which he is instantly thrown into a fresh hypnosis.

It is difficult to say to what length of time the
carrying out of a post-hypnotic suggestion may be
deferred, since this depends upon the patient's
character and the method employed. The longest
post-hypnotic suggestion I have seen was executed at
the end of four months; no hint had been given to
the subject in the meantime. The longest which has
ever been described, as far as I know, was in a subject under Liégeois and Liébeault; in this case
exactly a year elapsed before the suggestion was
carried out. The case of the photograph, mentioned
on p. 140, in which the photograph remained visible
for two years, is rather different, as it appears that the
suggestion was often recalled to the subject's memory
in the meantime. The case mentioned by Dal Pozzo
is, perhaps, of the same kind: a person who was afraid
of thunderstorms was cured of the fear by suggestion;
the effect is said to have lasted twenty-six years
(Belfiore).

These deferred suggestions are not very common,
and depend upon the power of the subject's memory.
But by clever management of the association of ideas
they can often be obtained; I have observed them in
nearly all hypnotic subjects belonging to the second
group. I am surprised that Binswanger has only
observed one such case, in spite of his more numerous
experiments.

I have hitherto only discussed those post-hypnotic
suggestions in which there is loss of memory after
waking from the hypnosis. This loss of memory
greatly favours the carrying out of the suggestion.

But loss of memory is not absolutely necessary; post-hypnotic suggestion succeeds also in light hypnoses, where there is complete recollection after waking. These cases, though more rare, are highly interesting, because the compulsion can be better observed in them. The subject may be able to say to himself, "The suggestion was made to me in hypnosis; I remember it perfectly, but I cannot help obeying it." One of my colleagues, a doctor, was in the hypnotic state ; I suggested abnormal movements to him with success ; sense delusions did not succeed. I told him that after he woke he would be unable to say his name whenever I laid my hand on his forehead, and further that instead of his own name he would always say mine. The suggestion succeeded perfectly. When he woke from the hypnosis, whenever I put my hand on his forehead he said his name was Moll ; he knew his right name also, but was unable to say it. He remembered my order about it, and did not believe in any supernatural force ; he knew that the effect was mental, but could not help himself. It is the same thing with sense delusions ; they also can be induced post-hypnotically, in spite of the fact that the suggestion is remembered. It is true that the effect of the sense delusion is in such cases often not to be seen, because, as the order is remembered, reasoning is possible, and thus the suggestion is nega-tived. Nevertheless, sense delusions with remem-brance of the suggestion are rarer because sense delusions with loss of memory are rarer, even though memory can always be restored by suggestion, as we have seen. In any case the subjects who remember the suggestion are always more conscious of the com-pulsion which it exercises upon them than those who do not ; these often believe they have acted of their own accord. Sometimes suggestion only succeeds with difficulty and after a long struggle, in consequence of the subject's resistance and control of his consciousness.

We have now studied the memory and the post-hypnotic suggestions dependent upon it. We have seen that the faculty of memory is an important one in hypnosis ; it is also a chief condition for the continuance of mental activity. This is certainly much circumscribed by suggestion in the deep hypnoses.

But a certain adherence to rule in the chain of ideas, conditioned by the laws of association, exists in many deep hypnoses. When, without hypnosis, we form in our own minds a mental image—of a fir-tree, let us say—a number of other images are formed in connection with it : we think of Christmas Day, presents, &c. An analogous process takes place generally in hypnosis. A suggested idea does not remain isolated ; on the contrary, it at once awakens new ideas dependent upon it.

I suggest to A., " Here is a pack of cards." A. believes it. The mental picture of the cards arouses the idea that he is playing a game, and also another idea—that he is at a restaurant with his friends B. and C. The single suggestion of the cards has sufficed to call up a whole scene before A., by association of ideas. A new suggestion suffices to destroy this association at once. I tell A., while he still thinks he is holding the cards, that he is in the train, and the chain of ideas connecting the cards and the restaurant is at once put an end to. However, in many hypnotic subjects a certain rational coherence of ideas persists, so that a suggested idea calls up others in one way or another connected with it. A large

12

number of the phenomena of hypnosis depend upon this principle. Many mentally induced paralyses, of which I spoke on p. 63, also depend upon it; the idea of a motor paralysis produces anæsthesia, vaso-motor disturbances, &c. I would emphatically say that the fact of their independence of the will has nothing to do with their being an indirect result of suggestion.

This mechanical associative process shows no real mental activity. The mental activity only appears when we destroy the natural associations, and see how the subject exerts himself to create a new sequence of ideas. In the example quoted above I told the subject as I gave him the cards that he was in a train. In order to bring these ideas into some logical connection, the subject A. now explained that he had bought the cards for a birthday present for the friend he was travelling to meet.

The fact that the subject sometimes allows himself to be persuaded to do something, if a reason is given to him for it, shows even more plainly that the thinking process is not always arrested in hypnosis. It is often necessary to suggest a false premiss to the subject before he will do what is wanted. X. cannot be induced to spill a glass of water in my room, but when I tell him that the room is on fire he does it at once.

On the other hand it should be said that even delusions of the senses are sometimes corrected purely by a reasoning process. A subject declines to believe that he sees a wolf in my room; or, rather, he explains that he sees an image of a wolf plainly enough, and could point out the exact spot. But he knows quite well that it must be a delusion, as I should certainly not allow a wolf to come into my sitting-room. Macnish says that people can guard themselves against bad dreams and control them in sleep by a process of thought.

The following very interesting phenomenon which I have observed in the various hypnotic states, even the deepest, demonstrates the activity of the mind in hypnosis. The subjects say they know quite well that the influence exercised upon them is a purely mental one, even while they obey it. One, in whom all kinds of sense delusions can be induced, said to me, " I know quite well that you do not exercise any extraordinary magnetic faculty ; I am sure it is my own imagination which deprives me of my will ; my own imagination obliges me to obey you ; but I cannot help it."

In a great number of cases the subjects are thrown into hypnosis in this way. Some of them, perhaps, are influenced by their belief in the experimenter's possession of a peculiar magnetic force ; on the other hand many are convinced of the subjectivity of the phenomena, and yet are thrown into hypnosis. If it happens that A. is easily hypnotized by B., and with difficulty or not at all by C., this is by no means always because A. believes in B.'s peculiar power ; it is rather an indefinite, and at present inexplicable, mental influence which unites A. to B.—an influence which reason often considers imaginary, but which is none the less constraining.

We see this every day in ordinary life, and particularly in love affairs. It happens often that one person is attracted by another and repelled by a third, without being able to discover his reasons for it. Reason often points out the perversity of his inclination ; and yet he cannot overcome the strong mental influence which attracts him. *De gustibus non est disputandum.* I have brought forward many facts regarding personal influence in hypnosis, in suggestion, and in ordinary life, in my work, *Der Rapport in der Hypnosis* (Leipzig, 1892).

It is particularly interesting, however, to observe how the hypnotic subject makes a logical use of slight external impressions. Few people think of the existence of these impressions, which yet often suffice to put a subject on the right track. Much apparent "clairvoyance" is a consequence of this heightened faculty for drawing conclusions. Many subjects are helped also by the hyperæsthesia of their organs of sense, which enables them to perceive things ordinarily overlooked. Let us take a very common experiment, often made to prove the existence of animal magnetism. The magnetized subject knows whether he has been touched by his magnetizer or another person. It is astounding to observe the accuracy with which such subjects, when their eyes have been bandaged, can distinguish one person from another. Ochorowicz, who believes in animal magnetism on other grounds, gives a number of interesting examples of this. The hypnotic subject observes the smallest details—the differences in the strength of pressure, in temperature, in the posture of the person touching him, in the sounds he makes with his shirt-cuffs ; nothing is overlooked, and a logically exact conclusion is drawn. Many observations and much information as to the increased acuteness of the mental faculties in the magnetic sleep can be found among the old investigators of mesmerism. Léonard considered this acuteness characteristic of the magnetic state. It may very well happen in such cases that the subject himself is not clearly conscious of drawing his conclusions from these details. This phenomenon is very common in normal life. Suppose a man sees another person for the first time. How often it happens that at first sight he draws a conclusion as to the character of the stranger, and is at the same time unaware of the

details from which he draws it. We often divine the
meaning of a face without knowing how : we think
that it is a stupid or a clever face ; we recognize an
expression of happiness or sadness at once, without
realizing the details of our impression. Thought
transference, of which I shall speak later, may commonly be referred to this ; the subject reads the wish
and thought of the experimenter even in a gesture,
in the involuntary movement of the lips, in the
direction of his eyes (Carpenter), particularly when
he has had some hypnotic training in this line.

The prophecies and predictions of somnambules
and other such persons often depend upon the logical
utilization of such insignificant impressions. A
peculiar mental quickness is not always necessary,
as is shown in the case of a man who was told by
one of these persons that he had lately suffered a
severe loss in his family. This was true.. The man
was astonished at the soothsayer's cleverness, till a
friend drew his attention to the fact that he was
wearing crape (Fonvielle).

This mental activity, and particularly the mechanical associations described above, show themselves
most clearly when suggested ideas are changed. New
ideas arise and attach themselves to the dominant
one, as I showed above. But it is exactly the quickness with which the subject can be transferred from
one situation to another, and with which he accepts
the suggested idea, which demonstrates that he is only
the plaything of the experimenter. Just as the ideas
of dreams transport us in a second from one situation to another, so do suggested ideas. Pleasure is
changed into pain in a moment ; the moods change
as quickly as they usually do only in children. The
subject now thinks he is in my room ; the next

moment he believes he is in bed ; directly after he is
swimming ; now he believes he is ninety years old,
and in the next second he is back in his tenth year.
Now he is Napoleon I., then a carpenter, then a dog,
&c.   This change of ideas takes place in a moment ;
the corresponding ideas arise at once through association.   Few people are able to do this in waking
life, even when they have a talent for acting.   A
certain opposition is sometimes made to this rapid
change of ideas in hypnosis, but this is rare.   When
it happens, the suggestion must be often repeated
before the subject will allow himself to be dragged
out of his earlier sphere of ideas.   The quick change
of these dominating ideas is so common that I was
astonished to read (in Malten) that a legal specialist
in Vienna, Ferroni, has been led by it to conclude that
thing is simulation.

This dominant idea, which calls up others, may be
looked at in another light.   We may say that it is the
idea to which the subject's attention is especially
turned.   In such a case this phenomenon of hypnosis must be regarded as a rapid change in the
direction of the attention, caused by the suggestion
of the experimenter, and not by the will of the
subject.   In deep hypnoses the subject's attention is
first directed to one point only, *i.e.*, to the experimenter, so that other objects hardly exist for him.
When this phenomenon is clearly marked, we speak
of *rapport.*

This *rapport* is an important phenomenon of
hypnosis.   We saw in the fourth experiment (p. 33)
that the subject only answered me, and apparently
ignored the other persons present.   This is the
common hypnotic phenomenon called *rapport.*   In
hypnotic *rapport* the subject responds to the hypno-

tist only. The old magnetizers were acquainted with this fact, and some investigators on the objective side, particularly Noizet and Bertrand, have tried to explain *rapport*. They thought that the subject fell asleep thinking of the experimenter, and with his whole attention directed to him, and that on this account only the idea of him remained active in the consciousness during hypnosis. Consequently he alone could make suggestions. As suggestions are most easily made through the muscular sense and the hearing, when *rapport* exists it is made most clearly evident by means of these senses. I lift up the arm of a subject ; it remains raised in suggested catalepsy. Another person (A.) makes the same attempt without result; the arm always falls down loosely (*cf.* Experiment IV.). A. now tries to bend the cataleptic arm, but is prevented by its rigid contracture, while I easily succeed. In the same way we have seen (p. 92) that only the hypnotist can obtain apparent reflex contractures by stimulation of the skin. The school of Charcot also maintains that only the hypnotist can relax a continuous contracture in somnambulism by renewed stimulation of the skin. As has been said, this experiment seems to prove that these contractures do not take place without some mental action ; for if we had only to do with physical stimuli, any one could produce the same result. All this becomes even clearer in the transference of *rapport*. The command of the experimenter suffices to put A. and B. in *rapport* with the subject. But the stimulus applied by A. and B. before the command is, from a physical point of view, exactly the same as they apply after it ; and any explanation of these things is impossible, unless we take refuge in the supposition that some mental action takes place in the production of catalepsy and contractures. The circumstances are analogous in verbal suggestion. The experimenter says when he has lifted the arm, " Now it bends, now it falls, now it is stretched out," and the effect at once follows. The commands of others are thrown away if they have not been put in *rapport* with the subject by the experimenter. Phenomena like those of *rapport* in hypnosis have been observed in spontaneous somnambulism (Macario).

According to the opinion that was formerly commonly received, *rapport* showed itself solely in this, that only one person was heard or felt by the hypnotized subject. In my work on *rapport* I have shown that in reality there is often only an apparent inability to hear other persons, and that it can be shown in various ways that they are heard. The kernel of *rapport* lies in the fact that the suggestions of others are not obeyed. This is shown even in light hypnosis, although it is only in the deeper stages that apparent failure of perception appears. *Rapport*, indeed, offers as many stages as the phenomena of suggestion.

From all the phenomena hitherto discussed it must have been gathered that there can be no question of loss of consciousness in hypnosis. Of course I mean loss of consciousness as it is understood in psychology.[1] We have seen that the subject in hypnosis remembers the events of earlier hypnoses. Consequently impressions were received into the consciousness in these earlier hypnoses. We cannot, therefore, talk of loss

[1] Psychologically, loss of consciousness is a state in which no kind of psychical process takes place ; in the penal code abnormalities of consciousness are included under loss of consciousness (Schwartzer, Casper, Liman).

of consciousness because loss of memory exists after the awakening (Forel), apart from the fact that suggestion in hypnosis will prevent the loss of memory. This temporary loss of memory is an every-day occurrence, and we could not conclude a loss of consciousness from it in ordinary life.

I will not speak of the daily mechanical actions we perform without attention and forget directly. I will take quite another case, in which we act with full consciousness and attention. I will choose an example out of my own experience, a thing which we have all doubtless observed in ourselves. I take a book and put it in a particular place, so that I may find it when I want it. At last I want it, but I cannot remember where I put it. I think in vain. Only when I replace myself in imagination at the moment when I put it away (a method which every one knows) do I remember where it is. And yet, in spite of temporary loss of memory, I did not put the book away in a state of loss of consciousness; it was rather that I was at the time in another state of consciousness. This is in many respects analogous to hypnosis, the events of which are remembered only when the subject is again in the same state of consciousness, *i.e.*, in a new hypnosis. Thus, in all these cases, we have not to do with an unconscious state, since all impressions remain in the memory.

But it might be asked, "Are there not perhaps unconscious states in hypnosis?" In my opinion this question only concerns the forms of lethargy, and only the lethargy which Charcot describes as such, and the lethargy which Bernheim calls hysterical, of which I have spoken (p. 48). As concerns the latter, it must be absolutely distinguished from hypnosis; it has nothing to do with the phenomena

of hypnosis, and is in any case extremely rare. With
Charcot's lethargy the case stands thus : apart from
the numerous cases of lethargy here described, and
which even the pupils of Charcot admit are associated
with movements caused by command, there remain
very few cases worthy of consideration. I doubt,
however, whether there is the loss of consciousness in
these cases which Charcot describes. The cases
which I saw in Paris convinced me of the contrary. The quickness with which these lethargic
subjects fall into catalepsy when Charcot merely
touches their eyelids makes me imagine that these
apparently unconscious persons have been attentively
waiting for the moment in which they are expected
to become cataleptic. Consequently the loss of consciousness seems to me more than questionable.
This point is of great importance because Charcot's
pupils maintain that the phenomena of the muscles
and nerves in the lethargic state are not induced by
suggestion. The experimenters conclude that the
state is one of lethargy without having proved it,
and it appears from their statements that, when
demonstrating this loss of consciousness, they did
not absolutely avoid discussion of the experiments
in the presence of the subjects. As a matter of
course these lose some of their evidential force in
consequence.

Even the states mentioned on p. 81, in which no
response could be obtained to questions and commands, do not prove loss of consciousness ; for—(1)
post-hypnotic suggestions could be made, and were
effectual, which proves that there was consciousness ; (2) these subjects woke directly they were told
to do so (Bernheim), which also shows that they were
conscious.

But though we cannot speak of a loss of consciousness, we must, however, suppose an abnormal state
of consciousness ; for if some one believes he sees
things that are not present, or fails to see things that
are present, he is certainly in an abnormal state of
consciousness. If a man forty years old believes he
is ten years old, his consciousness is certainly abnormal. We find such phenomena continually among
the second group of hypnotic subjects ; we must consequently here suppose a material abnormality of
consciousness. It need hardly be mentioned that
the will in these cases is also not intact, since,
without normal consciousness, free-will is not
conceivable. In the first group of hypnoses the
case is rather different. We must conceive these
states as involving less power of the external
activity of the will,[1] *i.e.*, as a disturbance of the
voluntary movements ; here there is no other abnormality of the consciousness. The subject knows
exactly where he is ; he knows what is being done
with him ; he makes the movements commanded
because he cannot help it ; his limbs are paralyzed
at command. A complete catalepsy may be induced
by suggestion, and yet the subject will be fully aware
of all that goes on. Some of Hack Tuke's subjects—
for example, North, a physiologist in London—have
given very interesting information with regard to the
interference of the will experienced during the experiments, which makes them unable to resist, though
otherwise fully conscious.

---

[1] The activity of the will is of two kinds : (1) the subjective,
which can arbitrarily arouse certain ideas, pictures of memory,
&c. ; (2) the objective, which is shown in the external movements which depend upon the will (Wundt).

In spite of this it would be a great mistake to think of the subject as an automaton without a will, set moving only by the experimenter. On the contrary, the will of the subject expresses itself in manifold ways, and this expression of the will presupposes consciousness, since without consciousness there can be no will, at least in the sense in which I here regard it. We will now consider in what ways the will of the subject can express itself.

Often the decreased power of will shows itself merely in slow and lingering movements. In these cases any movement can be made, but the subject takes longer to perform them than he does in normal circumstances. An inexperienced person is easily inclined to overlook these things, and to fail to recognize the hypnosis ; he generally thinks the experimenter mistaken in calling this state a hypnosis. Further, it has been already said that in many persons only certain muscles can be controlled by suggestion (p. 73). But in many cases it is necessary to repeat the suggestion often before the result is attained. For example, a subject can lift his arm in spite of the command of the hypnotizer ; but repetition of the command ends by making the movement impossible. This is an example of the way resistance expresses itself.

Expressions of the will which spring from the individual character of the patient are of the deepest psychological interest. The more an action is repulsive, the stronger is his resistance (Forel, Delbœuf, De Jong). Habit and education play a large part here ; it is generally very difficult to successfully suggest anything that is opposed to the confirmed habits of the subject. For instance, suggestions are made with success to a devout Catholic, but directly the suggestion conflicts with his creed it will not be accepted. The surroundings play a part also. A subject will frequently decline a suggestion that will make him appear ridiculous. A woman whom I easily put into cataleptic postures, and who made suggested movements, could not be induced to put out her tongue at the spectators. In another such case I succeeded, but only after repeated suggestions. The manner of making the suggestion has an influence. In some cases it must be often repeated before it succeeds ; other subjects interpret the repetition of the suggestion as a sign of the experimenter's incapacity and of their own ability to resist. Thus it is necessary to take character into account. It is often easier to induce some action by suggesting each separate movement than by suggesting the whole action at once (Bleuler). For example, if the subject is to fetch a book from the table, the movements may be suggested in turn ; first the lifting, then the steps, &c. (Bleuler).

It is interesting to observe the way in which resistance is expressed, both in hypnotic and post-hypnotic suggestion. Beaunis has observed that an attack of hysteria is sometimes the answer to a repugnant suggestion. I myself have observed the interesting phenomenon that subjects have asked to be awakened when a suggestion displeased them.

Exactly the same resistance is sometimes offered to a post-hypnotic suggestion. It is possible in such a case that the subject, even in the hypnotic state, will decline to accept the suggestion. Many carry out only the suggestions to which they have assented (Pierre Janet). Scripture reports a case observed at Brown University. The post-hypnotic suggestion was given to a person to pronounce *a* always like *ee*— *e.g.*, " feether " instead of " father " ; on being awakened

she was asked about her parents, but always avoided
using the word "father," speaking instead of "the
husband of my mother." Pitres relates an interesting
case of a girl who would not allow him to wake her,
because he had suggested that on waking she would
not be able to speak. She positively declared that she
would not wake till he gave up his suggestion. But
even when the suggestion is accepted as such, a decided
resistance is often expressed during its post-hypnotic
execution. This shows itself as often in slow and
lingering movements as in a decided refusal to perform
the act at all. The more repugnant the action, the
more likely is it to be omitted. In order to induce
subjects to carry out post-hypnotic suggestions more
easily, it is well to choose an external stimulus which
will recall the idea of it more and more vividly to the
memory. It is suggested to Mr. X. to say "fool" to
one of the persons present directly the clock strikes.
X. does not do it; the idea occurs to him when the
clock strikes, but he declines to carry it out. But if,
instead of the striking of the clock, I choose some
other more lasting stimulus which keeps the idea
alive, I attain the desired result. For instance, the
suggestion succeeds if I say to the subject, "You will
say 'fool' to that man when you wake and see me
rub my hands." When X. wakes I rub my hands,
and the idea arises in his mind; he represses it for
some time successfully. However, I go on rubbing
my hands for more than a minute; X.'s resistance
becomes weaker and weaker, and finally the suggestion is executed.

In other cases it is well to suggest a false premiss
directly resistance is offered to some suggestion (as I
mentioned on p. 178, in discussing mental activity).
The order will then be more easily obeyed. I will

choose an example from Liégeois. A subject was to be induced to steal a watch. He refused. But when it was represented to him that the watch was his own, and that he would be only taking it back again, he obeyed the command. Or the subject may be told that the laws are altered, that stealing is no longer punishable, &c.

There are numerous cases of post-hypnotic suggestion where the suggested act is not performed ; but the idea, and the impulse to carry it out are so powerful that the subject feels them for long (Forel). The impulse often only subsides when the action is performed or the suggestion withdrawn.

These explanations concern delusions of the senses, as well as movements and actions, though subjects in deep hypnosis often resist delusions of the senses less than movements and actions. However, I have often seen unpleasant and improbable delusions resisted when contrary ones succeeded. This shows the great influence of the consciousness and will ; in a great number of cases they triumph over the power of the experimenter. The following is an example. The subject (X.) was forty-one years old. I told him, "You are now thirteen years old." He answered, "No, I am forty-one." But directly after he accepted the suggestion that he was twelve or fourteen years old. However, I failed to make him believe he was thirteen years old ; he refused the suggestion. He was superstitious, and disliked the number thirteen. His notion that thirteen was an unlucky number accounted for his resistance ; on that account he would not be thirteen years old.

The experimenter may unconsciously increase the resistance merely by the tone in which he speaks. Fontan and Ségard rightly maintain, for example,

that many hypnoses may be continued or put
an end to by the tone in which the operator speaks.
When we say to a subject, " Try to open your
eyes ; they are fast closed, you cannot possibly
open them," the kind of emphasis may alter the
effect. If the emphasis is laid upon " Try to open
your eyes," the last part of the suggestion is more
easily overcome, and *vice versâ.* Here is an example.
I say to a subject, " Try to lift your arm ; you cannot,"
he remains motionless ; he is to a certain degree
influenced, even though he believes afterwards that he
so acted to please me. But if I now add, in as impressive a manner as possible, " Try all you can, try
with all your might to move your arm," the subject is
all at once able to move. It is just these states which
most clearly show the gradual transitions from the
lightest stages to the deepest. I raise a man's arm ;
the arm remains raised so long as I say nothing.
Directly I tell him that if he tries to drop his arm he
will not succeed, he does it nevertheless, though at
first with some stiffness. This shows that the state
was not quite a normal one. In this case, as in many
others, the subject passively allows his arm to remain
as it was fixed, he makes no effort of will either for or
against. But the moment I induce him by verbal
suggestion to make an effort of will, he does so, and
shows that he can exert the will against my orders,
even though the hesitating movement plainly shows
that he was influenced. It is the same thing with
continued movements, which are sometimes made
passively without an act of the will, and sometimes
cannot be inhibited by the strongest effort of will, as
I have explaned above (p. 81).

Many persons temporarily show substantial variations in susceptibility to suggestion. One declares

at one moment that his name is Moll, and does what
I command him ; directly after he is himself again,
without any certain or apparent cause. He says
afterwards that he perceives two opposing wills in
himself, and that sometimes one and sometimes the
other conquers.

Hypnotic subjects give us another proof that they
are conscious to a certain degree, when they tell us
they know they are asleep, or in an altered state
(Richet, Pierre Janet). This is also clearly shown in
ordinary sleep. We are occasionally conscious in
dreams that we are asleep and dreaming. Almost all
hypnotic subjects of the second group have this consciousness of being asleep, and it is remarkable that
when they are asked if they are asleep or awake, they
almost always give the right answer. When, as
sometimes happens, the awakening is incomplete they
also rightly say that they are not quite awake. The
continuance of susceptibility to suggestion may then
generally be established. I have mentioned that
subjects occasionally ask to be awakened when they
are uncomfortable in hypnosis, or when an unpleasant
suggestion is made to them.

I again lay stress on the fact that many hypnotic
subjects are conscious of an ability to resist. I say
to X., "You cannot lift your arm ! " " Yes, I can," he
answers, and experiment shows that he is right. But
the contrary sometimes happens ; the subject often
knows exactly the minute when his power to resist is
at an end, when he must obey and cannot help himself. X. announces after a time that he is at this
point : " Now the hypnosis is deep enough," he says.
I say to a person thirty years old, whom I have often
hypnotized, " Now you are a little child." The subject replies, " It is not enough yet, you must wait a

13

little." After a time, when I ask, he says that now he is at the right point. Many people have this feeling of deficient will and increased suggestibility in deep hypnosis ; they often know the moment when a suggestion will succeed and when not.

The consciousness and will of hypnotics may express themselves in other ways, in the case of in-determinate suggestions (*suggestions indéterminées*, as Beaunis calls them). In such suggestions no definite action is commanded, but the subjects are left to choose among a number. Here is a man with a violent bronchial catarrh. I suggest to him in hypnosis to do something or other which will benefit his health. He at once fetches himself some catechu. I tell another to do some foolish action after he wakes. He wakes and blows the lamp out. From this it is to be concluded that the subject was to a certain degree able to reflect.

Although the above examples show that there is no complete loss of will in hypnoses, yet in all of them the will was set in action by some external impulse. Let us consider whether spontaneity, an independent activity of thought and will, may not exist in hypnosis, apart from external impulse. To this question we must answer "yes," so far as the first group of hypnoses is concerned. Only the second group need be considered. Baillif, Obersteiner, and others describe independent hallucinations, arising without external suggestion, in the first group. But the question is complicated by the fact that we are not always able to exclude external stimuli, which also induce many dreams in ordinary sleep. For example, without any suggestion from me, a hypno-tized subject jumps up and says he has seen and heard a mad dog. The cause of this is the unintentional creaking of the boots of one of the people present. I had not observed the creaking, but as often as it was repeated the same result followed. The subject misinterpreted an impression of the sense of hearing, which aroused a certain chain of thought in him. I have often observed such phenomena in impressionable and lively persons.

But I have found spontaneous hallucinations and actions in the deepest hypnosis, when no suggestion had been made, and which I was unable to refer to any stimulus of the senses. In particular, any events which had much occupied the subject during the waking state continued to affect him in hypnosis. One of them, for example, related anecdotes which he had heard somewhere else a day or two before. While his mind was full of them no experiments could be made with him ; he was as uncomfortable as a diner-out, who only feels at ease when he has got rid of his whole stock of stories. I believe that in this and other such cases we have to do with independent mental activity, because I could never discover any external stimulus. Of course I cannot mathematically prove that these spontaneous actions did not result from some external impulse; for the external impulse might have been an almost imperceptible sound, and even the slight pressure of clothes on the skin may act as a stimulus and induce apparently independent actions in the subject. I do not believe that hypnotic subjects in the deep stage often have independent currents of thought. I have been much impressed by observing the contrary. Durand de Gros has even made a classification of somnambulists into those who act with, and those who act without, spontaneity.

I have hitherto purposely avoided much mention of the transitional forms. But I shall now say something about them, as certain transitional forms are of importance in psychology, and also in discussing the question of simulation, particularly as they are extremely common. A hypnotized man makes all the movements I command him. I say, "Eat this beefsteak," and he performs all the necessary movements with hand and mouth. I say, "Push that dog away," and he makes the appropriate movements of the legs.

And yet we have only here to do with suggested movements, and the subject by no means believes in the reality of the dog or beefsteak, or thinks he sees them. Consequently this case belongs to the first group of hypnoses. There are two ways of judging correctly of these phenomena: firstly, from observation, and secondly, from the later recollections of the subject. As regards the last, the subject says to me directly I have awakened him, "I knew perfectly well there was no dog and no beefsteak; I did not see them; however, I could not help making the movements you commanded, though I knew I must look utterly ridiculous." This is, then, a case of lessened power of the will without loss of consciousness. This will become clearer if we watch the subject during the hypnosis. The movements are not so quick as they would be if produced by a hallucination; they have a clearly marked character of constraint. There is nothing in the expression of the face which points to a hallucination. The subject often laughs at the foolish movements he is making, and makes corresponding remarks; for example, he says, "This is not a beefsteak," and shakes his head. All this plainly proves that it is not a case of sense delusion.

Again in other cases the subject is quite passive, and does everything the experimenter commands without resistance. When a sense delusion is suggested to him he says, "yes"; which is a sign that he is too passive even to accept the suggestion. For instance, when he is told that a tiger is in the room his behaviour is not affected; he does not run away, and is not frightened, but simply answers that he sees the tiger. In this case only the assent was suggested, and not a sense delusion, as the subject's later recollection shows. He says he only said "yes" because it was easier, but that he did not see a tiger.

Although this case is clear, in others there are important difficulties. These may arise from the fact that the movements themselves generate sense delusions. This is a consequence of the known reciprocal relations of movements and ideas. We have already learned that ideas can call up certain movements in waking life as well as in hypnosis. Now we have to show that particular movements may, on the contrary, excite particular mental processes (Dugald Stewart, Gratiolet). I choose first an example from ordinary life : an attitude expressing anger is assumed; a real feeling of anger very often follows, especially if words are also used ; it is known that people can talk themselves into a passion. In this case a particular mental state is induced by movements of particular muscles, and especially by speaking. Something exactly like this occurs in hypnosis. The suggestions made through the muscular sense, observed by Braid and Charcot, are founded on this (*suggestions d'attitude*, or *suggestion par attitude*) ; if a subject's arms are put into the attitude of prayer, the face soon wears an expression of religious devotion.

The following is a favourite experiment of Charcot. If the subject's hand is raised to his mouth as if he were throwing a kiss, he smiles. If the fist is closed and raised in a threatening attitude, he looks angry. Charcot and Richer maintain that the experiment may be reversed. If the muscles used in laughter are stimulated by faradization, so that a laughing expression is induced, the movement of throwing a kiss with the hand follows. If the muscles which produce an angry expression are stimulated, the arm is raised as in anger. But I believe it may be safely said that suggestions of this kind are affairs of hypnotic training.

However, movements may be used with advantage to help the induction of sense delusions, because movements influence the ideas.

I give an imaginary glass of bitter liqueur to a subject. He says that there is no glass of liqueur, and that he has nothing in his hand. Without noticing this objection, I raise his hand to his mouth, that he may drink. He obeys slowly and hesitatingly; but when his hand reaches his mouth he makes swallowing movements, and the expression of his face shows that he has a disagreeable taste in his mouth. When I ask him what is the matter, he answers that he has an unpleasant taste, as if he had just drunk something bitter. Nevertheless he had been quite sure at first that no liqueur had been given him; the suggestion took effect during his compulsory movement; without this movement the result would not have been attained. In another case I make the subject move his fingers as if he were playing the piano, and suggest at the same time that he is playing. He does not believe it, but continues the movement. While he does this the idea of piano-playing really arises by degrees in his mind, and at last he makes the movements in the firm belief that he is playing the piano. I have often observed that it was easier to induce sense delusions by accompanying movements than by verbal suggestion alone, and I would recommend this as a means of deepening the hypnosis in suitable cases, as I have often employed it successfully myself. It is often impossible to define the exact moment when the sense delusion supervenes; it is impossible, therefore, to decide whether the delusion was really in existence before, or whether it was called up by the compulsory movements.

Besides this an existing delusion may sometimes be corrected by the subject's consciousness, or rather by his reasoning powers, as I have stated above (p. 178). Although the delusion sometimes disappears more quickly by this means, in other cases it may persist, in spite of the correction made by the reason. If the correction is complete, the delusion will have no results; it will not influence the actions following. And yet the delusion will continue in full force. I ask a man before I hypnotize him, to tell me of something which in his opinion would never be found in my room. He says he would never believe there was an owl in my room. In hypnosis I make him the post-hypnotic suggestion that there will be an owl in my room. He wakes and says he sees the owl plainly; it is chained by the foot, and he describes it exactly. Although he knows and says that the owl is only a hallucination, it is so real to him that he hesitates to put his finger on the spot where he imagines it to be.

It is not always easy to recognize the mental state of a hypnotic subject, particularly in suggested sense delusions; for it is by no means necessary that a sense delusion should dominate the whole consciousness. If in many cases all thought and action is dependent on the delusion, in other cases the effects are less complete. I even believe that most subjects while the delusion lasts retain a dim consciousness that they are in a fictitious situation. For example, I suggest to a subject that he is in a battle and must fight. An imaginary struggle begins at once and he hits at the air. When I suggest that a cloth on the table is an enemy he strikes at this. I suggest that one of the persons present is an enemy, but in continuing the fight the hypnotic takes care not to strike this person. Naturally this looks like simulation, and I was at first inclined to think so myself. However, a repetition of such experiments forced me to conclude that these were real typical hypnoses, in which, in spite of the sense delusions, there was a dim dream-consciousness existing which influenced the actions of the subject. This dim consciousness of his real surroundings prevented the subject from striking a human being, but left him free to hit a cloth. Many may, perhaps, regard this behaviour of the hypnotic as pure automatism. As we when walking in the street and reading a newspaper automatically avoid knocking against passers-by, so the hypnotic avoids hitting another person, although he is only dimly, or not at all, aware of his existence.

It is the same thing with negative hallucinations. As in the positive delusions a dim perception exists of their being only delusions, so the subject in negative hallucinations really recognizes the object which has been made invisible to him through suggestion ; even though he is unconscious of the recognition. Binet and Féré have said about this: " The object must be recognized, in order not to be perceived."

These authors made a series of experiments in support of their assertion, which I have been able to repeat with success, as an example of a negative hallucination. If ten sheets of white paper are taken and one of them marked, the subject can be made to believe that he sees only nine sheets, even when the sheet, whose invisibility was suggested, is among them. If he is asked to give up the nine sheets, he picks out the nine unmarked ones, and leaves the other, guided by the mark. Consequently, he is able to distinguish it from the others, although he is unconscious of making the distinction.

A series of experiments made by Cory are even better. I was able partly to repeat them, and obtained the same results. I took a sheet of paper, and drew a rather irregular line on it. I then suggested to the subject (X.) that the paper was blank. X. agreed that he saw nothing. I then drew fifteen straight lines on the paper and asked X. what he saw. He said, " Fifteen lines." I recommenced the experiment, but made the first line straight, and then suggested its invisibility ; upon which I added twenty more lines exactly like it and made X. count them. "There are twenty-one," he said. Therefore the line suggested as absent was only invisible to X. when he could distinguish it from the others. The following experiment resembles this : I took a match and marked its end with a spot of ink. I then suggested that the match was invisible. I took twenty-nine other matches and put the whole thirty on the table in such a manner that X. could see the ink spot. To my question X. replied that there were only twenty-nine matches on the table. I then, while X.'s eyes were turned away, moved the marked match so that X. could not see the spot. He looked at the matches

and said there were thirty of them. Thus the marked
match was only invisible so long as X. could distinguish it from the others.

From these and other such experiments it may be
concluded that the subject recognizes the object of a
negative hallucination, and that it produces a central
impression, even though there is no perception of it.
The automatic writing, of which I shall speak further
on, demonstrates this (Pierre Janet). Numerous experiments in this direction, which I have made in
company with Sellin and Max Dessoir, also confirm
it. I shall not give them in detail, as this would take
me too long. The results of the negative hallucination depend upon the strength of this central impression. If the central impression is very slight, then
the result will be the same as if the object causing it
did not exist. But if a certain dim consciousness of
the presence of the object exists (and this is usually
the case), then it may influence the actions of the
subject in spite of suggestion to the contrary. I
suggest to a subject that a table, which was between
him and the door, is no longer there ; the subject
goes to the door, but carefully avoids hitting against
the table. I suggest that the electrode, which is
armed with the very painful faradic brush, is invisible.
After closing the current I touch the subject with the
brush and he shows great pain. When I ask what
has hurt him, he says he does not know, for my hand
is empty ; but at the same time he takes care not to
touch the place where the brush is lying, or does it
hesitatingly, and with evident signs of fear. I tell
another that I am going out of the room ; he apparently neither sees nor hears me. Yet every suggestion that I now make to him is executed. I order
him to take the cushion from the sofa and throw it

on the floor. The order is obeyed though after some hesitation. To another, who also believes by suggestion that I am out of the room, I suggest sense delusions—the presence of a dog, &c. All the suggestions succeed, evidently because the subject hears what I say, though he believes me absent. I tell another, "Now you are deaf." Upon which he ceases to do what I tell him. But after I have several times repeated, "Now you can hear again," he obeys every command. We see in these cases, which I could multiply, that the organs of sense act normally, that a certain effect is produced, but that the impressions are not received into clear consciousness. I naturally do not maintain that this is the case in all positive or negative hallucinations ; on the contrary, in some the delusion is complete. This depends on character, and to a great extent on the manner in which the suggestion is made. I wished merely to describe the more incomplete and by far most common cases, because they are often ascribed to simulation, and till now have never been seriously considered.

All the phenomena of which I have spoken hitherto are very variable. I have purposely only mentioned the most common and most important, lest my work should grow too long. But hypnotic education or training needs a particular discussion. I would ask every one who watches hypnotic experiments to give it particular attention. All the phenomena of hypnosis may be interpreted falsely by a mere spectator if sufficient attention is not paid to this point. When hypnotic experiments are shown to outsiders, subjects are as a rule selected who have gone through a hypnotic training in some particular direction, and as the directions are various, the results also are various. The experimenter A. keeps in view a particular symptom, *a*, and reinforces it at each experiment; in the same way experimenter B. cultivates symptom *b*. In the first case *a* is fully developed and *b* receives little attention; and in the second case the reverse happens. The Breslau investigators, for example, developed the imitative movements, while others did the same with the effects of the movements on the feelings (*suggestions d'attitude*)

He who only regards the final results and pays no attention to their gradual evolution will be inclined to believe that the two parties of investigators are engaged with different things; though it is in reality only difference in training which gives a different appearance to identical states. Each experimenter now only demonstrates such symptoms as he has cultivated by training, especially as this training commonly produces most interesting phenomena; the heightening of certain faculties in particular. The outsider is unaware that this is a mere result of hypnotic training, and is easily misled. Children who repeat to strangers the piece of poetry they know best, do exactly the same thing. Experimenters produce certain objective symptoms by means of training, and any one seeing them for the first time is apt to make mistakes. But every experimenter produces different objective symptoms—one, for example, a lasting catalepsy, another a perfect *écholalie*. These things strike the stranger, who cannot estimate the effect of training. Thus it happens that different experimenters discover different objective symptoms. The question of training is of immense importance. Many have suspected simulation because of the apparent variety of hypnotic states. This variety is really only the result of different training, if we put aside differences of character. The experimenter influences the development of the hypnosis (Delbœuf, Jendrássik). Unimportant phenomena such as *écholalie* are developed as much as possible and are at last wrongly considered to be essential hypnotic phenomena.

Training is the great source of error for the experimenter in hypnotism, because the subject is inclined to divine and obey his intentions, and thus unconsciously misleads him. Unknown to himself, the tone of his voice may induce the subject to present the phenomena which he expects. The subject is also greatly influenced by his surroundings, and by watching other subjects (Bertrand). Imitation is also of great importance here. I hypnotize X., and suggest that he cannot speak, at the same time inadvertently touching his left shoulder with my right hand. Y., in hypnosis, sees this, and every time I touch his left shoulder with my right hand he, too, is unable to speak. Y. believes that this is the signal for loss of speech, and behaves accordingly. Training enables a hypnotic subject to divine all the experimenter's wishes. The latter need not speak ; the least movement betrays his wish. A long training is not necessary ; Delbœuf artificially induced the stages of Charcot in one of his own subjects in a few hours. My object in making these remarks is to warn against attributing great importance to demonstrations, particularly when these offer certain symptoms apparently objective and impossible to imitate. It should always be kept in mind that many such symptoms can be produced by training ; and can, perhaps, be imitated by practice even without hypnosis.

Hitherto I have used the word " training " only for the artificial cultivation of certain symptoms ; but it also means the production of such particular modifications of hypnosis, as are seen after frequent repetition of the state.

As has been said already, it is sometimes necessary to make several attempts before the hypnosis appears. Husson, in 1831, said this with regard to the magnetic sleep. It may be very long before hypnosis is produced. Sometimes deep hypnosis only ensues after a process of training by several sittings. In one case which I have seen hypnosis with sense delusions only resulted after eighty attempts, though lighter states had been earlier attained. Training not only makes the hypnosis deeper, but makes it appear more quickly. But, undoubtedly, a deep hypnosis may occasionally be induced at a first attempt; and Forel is right when he warns against exaggeration on this point. One of my relations fell into so deep a hypnosis in a minute on a first trial, that I could at once induce post-hypnotic negative hallucinations. And this person is a perfect specimen of a healthy young man.

But in most cases it is necessary, as I have said, to give the subject a hypnotic training, in order t make the state as deep as possible. For this I wish to recommend a particular method, as otherwise the deepening is not always attained. Let the first suggestions be simple, so as not to shock the subject's sense of probability. The first suggestions should be possible, and progress should be gradual. More will be attained in this way than by suggesting impossible situations at first which the subject will not believe in. And if a suggestion is often declined, there is apt to arise in the subject the auto-suggestion that he is refractory to this suggestion, or perhaps to any suggestion. This is often lastingly prejudicial, and may lessen susceptibility to suggestion in all later hypnoses. I therefore strongly recommend a slow and gradually increasing method for post-hypnotic suggestion. Perhaps Binswanger's experiments in post-hypnotic suggestion failed because he overlooked this point. A man is in the hypnotic state. I suggest that when he wakes he shall call me an insulting name; he does not do it, but is perfectly ready to carry out another post-hypnotic suggestion; for instance, to tell me that he is quite well. Here there is only a slight degree of suggestibility at first, but it is quite possible by frequent repetition and slow increase to get much more complicated suggestions carried out.

This concludes the symptoms of hypnosis. I believe I have given a sufficient sketch of its essential phenomena in the foregoing pages. In the following chapters I shall refer again to the importance of some of them. We have seen that the symptoms are of manifold kinds, and I may add that they are hardly ever identical in two different persons. In spite of conformity to law one human body is never exactly like another, the mental state of one man is never exactly like another's. It is the same in hypnosis: one man displays this symptom with greater clearness, another that. We shall never be able to find a subject in whom all the symptoms are united, just as we cannot find a patient who has all the symptoms of an illness as they are theoretically described.

CHAPTER IV.

COGNATE STATES.

WE always try to advance the study of a state which has hitherto been little known and examined, by comparing it with other states, with whose symptoms we are better acquainted. We will therefore try to find points of correspondence with hypnosis.

Even the name selected by Braid shows that there is a resemblance between sleep (*hypnos*) and hypnotism; and the Nancy investigators, Liébeault, Bernheim, Brullard, as well as Forel, of Zürich, consider hypnosis an ordinary sleep; they think that a person who falls asleep spontaneously is in *rapport* with himself, while a hypnotized subject is in *rapport* with the person who hypnotized him; in their view this is the chief difference between sleep and hypnosis.

I believe, however, that we cannot so easily agree to an identification of the states. We must begin by distinguishing the light and deep hypnoses. We see that in the light hypnosis there is merely an inhibition of the will, which affects the movements; the memory is not at all affected. Now we always presuppose a great decrease of self-consciousness in sleep. But it is just this self-consciousness which remains intact in light hypnosis; and in this state the subject is perfectly aware of all that goes on, and, as a rule, forgets nothing on waking. Consequently I do not think we can make a close comparison between sleep and hypnosis; nor do I think it possible to make a fruitful comparison between these light hypnoses and the states of drowsiness and fatigue which precede sleep. In any case we have seen that a feeling of fatigue is not uncommon in these hypnotic states. Besides which we have also seen that the loss of voluntary muscular movement is one of their chief phenomena. There is hardly a hint of this in the drowsy state ; there is only a general fatigue of the muscles and heaviness in the limbs. In spite of this the sleepy person can move as he pleases ; at the most he only feels dull, but the lessened power of the will shown in hypnosis is entirely wanting.

Further, these light hypnotic states are distinguished from the early stages of sleep by the decreased activity of consciousness in these latter. The current of the ideas, of images of memory, &c., is less under the control of the will, while in the light hypnotic states only the voluntary movements suffer change. In the early stages of sleep sense impressions do not develop into conscious ideas in the usual way ; much that generally excites our interest and attention is overlooked, while there is often reverie independent of the will. But almost all this is entirely absent in the light hypnotic states.

On this account I here protest against a terminology, which has been to a great extent adopted, and which many doctors have helped to propagate, but which is none the less erroneous. For example. it is often said that hypnotized persons are "asleep," and the two states have been partly identified. I think this a misuse of words, since, as has been explained, there are a whole series of hypnotic states in which not one symptom of sleep appears, and mis-

14

taken conclusions are often drawn from the mistaken terminology, with resulting confusion.

The case in deep hypnosis is essentially different. It is characterized by numerous sense delusions, which, however, are just the same thing as our nightly dreams. In order to carry out the comparison, it will perhaps be well to consider the mode of origin of dreams in ordinary sleep. Dreams are divided into two classes, according to the manner of their origin (Spitta) : (1) dreams induced by nerve stimulation, and (2) dreams induced by association of ideas. The first—by far the most numerous—are induced by a peripheral stimulus of the nerves, affecting the brain. Here the nerve stimulus is certainly felt; a memory picture arises, and a perception results. This picture does not, however, correspond to the actual stimulus, which could only be accurately estimated by full waking attention.

It is difficult to say what memory picture will be aroused and what dream will result, as it depends upon several factors which as yet escape our observation. Scherner's numerous attempts to explain this are not very convincing. The memory picture aroused by a stimulus in the manner sketched above attaches itself in a number of cases to a previously existing dream. "When an orator dreams he is making a speech, he takes every noise for the applause of his imaginary hearers" (Walter Scott).

Dreams can be artificially called up by nerve stimulation. If a sleeping man is sprinkled with water he will dream of a shower of rain (Leixner). Maury has made a number of experiments on himself during sleep. When Eau de Cologne was held to his nose he dreamed that he was in Farina's shop at Cairo. Preyer, Prevost, Harvey, Parish, and Tissié have published such experiments.

The second kind of dreams are dreams from association of ideas; they are supposed to follow on a primary central act. The memory picture is supposed to be caused by some primary central activity, and not by a peripheral stimulus. Between these two classes of dreams there is another which I may call suggested dreams. In these no stimulus is applied to the nerves of the subject which he may work out according to his fancy; but a dream is suggested to him verbally (Reil, Maury, Max Simon). An acquaintance of mine told his daughter that she saw rooks, upon which she dreamed of them and related her dream on waking. On other occasions the attempt failed.

It would seem that certain stages of sleep are fitter for this than others. Delbœuf believes that the transitional stage between sleeping and waking is the best. He even supposes that many nervous and mental disorders originate from natural suggestion made at this time, and that they develop themselves like post-hypnotic suggestions. As regards the mode of origin, these suggested dreams are identical with the suggested sense delusions of hypnosis.

But the mode of origin of other dreams in sleep does not differ essentially from their mode of origin in hypnosis. This is particularly clear when we compare the hallucinations induced by nerve stimulation mentioned on p. 195 with them; these hallucinations are identical with dreams induced by nerve stimulation. Here is an example. I hypnotize a person, and blow with the bellows close to him, without speaking. The blowing causes a central excitation, and the subject believes he hears a steam engine. He dreams he sees a train; he believes he is at the railway station at Schöneberg, &c. This

is exactly the same thing as a dream produced by
nerve stimulation, in which the falling of a chair
makes the dreamer think he hears a gun fired, and is
in a battle. Besides, in hypnosis as well as in sleep
such stimuli are enormously over-estimated by the
consciousness ; a slight noise is taken for the sound
of a gun, and a touch on the hand for the bite of a
dog. I have made many such suggestions in hypnosis. I drum upon the table, without speaking ;
the subject hears, and dreams of military music, and
that he is in the street, and sees soldiers, &c. Tissié
mentions that in sleep visual impressions seldom lead
to dreams, since we sleep in the dark and usually
with the eyes entirely closed. We can, however,
produce dreams in ordinary sleep with the help of a
source of light. It is interesting to find, nevertheless,
that recent investigations on sleep (Mary Whiton
Calkins) show that the nervous stimulation comes
preferably through the ear, as in hypnosis.

One thing is clear from the comparisons I have
made : it is a mistake to think, as many do, that no
intercourse with the outside world takes place in
sleep. The opinion that by far the greater number
of dreams are induced by sense stimuli gains more
and more adherents (Wundt, Weygandt). This re-
ceptivity to stimuli which reach the brain, unregulated
by the consciousness, and mistakenly interpreted, is a
phenomenon of both sleep and hypnosis.

It is evident from what has been said that the
method employed to make external suggestion in
hypnosis often suffices to induce dreams in sleep.
At the most there is only a quantitative difference,
since most sense delusions are directly suggested in
hypnosis, while in sleep dreams are caused by some
peripheral stimulus, which undergoes a special elabo-

ration in the brain of the sleeper. A qualitative distinction is not here possible, although Sully separates sleep and hypnosis on the ground that dreams arise in the former differently from hallucinations in the latter.

The purport of dreams, as well as the way they originate, is alike in sleep and hypnosis. It is naturally impossible to go into details. But as in sleep we believe ourselves in another situation, and encounter all sorts of sense delusions, so also in hypnosis. And as a subject in hypnosis can be replaced in earlier periods of his life, so in dreams also. Many habitually dream that they are again undergoing the final examination at college many years after. Complete changes of personality also take place in dreams. An officer who greatly admired Hannibal, told me that he had dreamed he was Hannibal, and had fought an imaginary battle in that character. Another man was even less modest; he dreamed that he was God, and was governing the world.

We cannot decide whether there is more dreaming in hypnosis than in sleep, because we can never know how many dreams happen in sleep. While some say that dreams only occur during a short period of sleep, others, like Kant, Forel, Exner, and Simonin go so far as to deny that there is any sleep without dreaming; they say that dreaming is continuous, but that most dreams are forgotten.

As we find that the origin and purport of dreams are the same in sleep and hypnosis, it follows that in all probability the dreams of hypnosis are no more injurious to health than the dreams of sleep.

In spite of all this, we can find a difference between the phenomena of deep hypnosis and of sleep in several points—(1) in the apparently logical connection between the suggested idea and the hypnotic subject's own thoughts ; (2) in the movements of the subject, and particularly in his speech, since there may be a conversation between experimenter and subject (Wernich).

With regard to the first point, we have seen (p. 178) that a series of ideas sometimes link themselves logically to another particular idea. Consequently the difference from sleep is only apparent. As long as the suggested idea prevails in hypnosis, other ideas will often link themselves logically to it. This linking is, however, on the whole, merely mechanical, the result of habitual association of ideas. This logical connection can be broken at any moment with the greatest ease by suggestion, as I have shown ; in the same way the whole current of ideas may change at any moment. It at once appears from this that the consciousness is unable to unite the ideas actively, as the smallest external influence suffices to tear them asunder at once. The logical connection mentioned above lasts only as long as the experimenter permits. In the dreams of the night, which Radestock refers to the pause in logical thought, there is not usually such a logical connection, because it only rarely happens that they centre in a definite idea as in hypnotic suggestion. In hypnosis the attention of the hypnotic subject is directed to the experimenter ; the ideas given by the latter are accepted, others are not. In sleep the most various sensations are conducted to the brain ; as the sleeper's attention is not usually directed to a special point, it is much less easy for a definite idea to gain supremacy. That, however, when once a definite idea is predominant, a certain logical sequence arises, may be shown by the cases in which effective mental work is accomplished in dream-consciousness. Those cases in which the dream-consciousness carries on some planned mental work show that there may be a logical connection with the dominant idea even in dreams.

I will not go into details of examples. It is known that Voltaire wrote poetry in sleep, that mathematicians sometimes solve problems when asleep, and that the well-known physiologist, Burdach, worked out many scientific ideas in sleep. Maury has also pointed out that apparently disconnected dream-ideas are yet related to each other by certain associations.

I mentioned the movements in hypnosis as a further apparent contrast between this state and sleep. But this assuredly forms no qualitative distinction, since it is known that people move in sleep (Hans Virchow). The activity of the muscles in sleep is often an automatic continuation of movements begun awake. This happens with people who fall asleep in making one particular movement ; they continue the movement in sleep. Coachmen will go on driving, and riders will hold the bridle without falling off : here the movement begun has made an unconscious impression strong enough to make the muscular movement go on. Birds also go to sleep standing.

In all these cases the muscular action is very like the contractures and automatic movements described on p. 81 Besides this, certain external stimuli may cause movements during sleep. It seems probable to me that they do not happen without consciousness. If part of a sleeper's body is uncovered, he will draw the cover over it ; if he is tickled, he will rub the place. Even if these are regarded as physical

reflexes without any accompanying mental action,
which is not proved, the case is essentially different
with the movements which children make in sleep,
at command. If a child is told to turn over,
he will do it without waking (Ewald). This is
an act which, as Ewald remarks, may fairly be
compared with the phenomena of hypnosis, in which
movements the same in kind, if greater in extent,
are made at command. It shows how movements
may be caused in sleep by external mental stimuli.
These movements become plainer when they are not
called up directly, but are purely the consequence of
a dream. Dreams often cause movements. Many
persons, particularly children, laugh in pleasant
dreams. The same sort of thing has often been
observed. A lady I know dreamed that she was
blowing out a lamp; she made the corresponding
movements with her mouth. She was awakened,
and related the dream which had no doubt caused
the movements of the mouth. Every one knows
that children in especial often scream when they
are dreaming.

The persons we call somnambulists (sleep-walkers,
night-walkers) show these movements, which are
characteristic. The resemblance between hypnotism
and somnambulism is so great that the name somnambulism is used for both (Richet). Hypnotism
is called artificial somnambulism, and the other
natural somnambulism, or, better, spontaneous somnambulism, since artificial somnambulism is really
as natural as the other, as Poincelot insists. All
sorts of movements are made in spontaneous somnambulism. Three stages are generally distinguished—(1) that in which the sleeper speaks; (2)
that in which he makes all sorts of movements but

does not leave his bed ; (3) that in which he gets up, walks about, and performs the most complicated actions. In my experience the first two stages are found in persons of sanguine temperament who are decidedly not in a pathological condition. It is not yet finally decided whether the third state appears under pathological conditions only. From my own experience I am inclined to think that it is occasionally observed when there is no constitutional weakness, especially in children. If we want to show these states, we can do it with the healthiest subjects. As regards these movements in sleep, my own experience is that the persons who are most restless in natural sleep, who talk, or throw themselves about, are the most inclined to lively movement in hypnosis. In any case the movements are also displayed in sleep. I think we ought to call the last states sleep, especially the two first stages of somnambulism. Consequently the movements of subjects in hypnosis do not offer a fundamental contrast to sleep, especially when they are caused by suggested delusions of sense.

The fact that a subject in hypnosis can carry on a conversation is not enough to mark off hypnosis from sleep, as Werner erroneously supposes ; for many persons answer questions and obey in sleep (Lotze, Bérillon). According to my experience, and that of others, certain persons easily answer in sleep when some one they know well speaks to them. A child will speak to its mother, and bedfellows to one another. A conversation is easily carried on when the waking person follows the sleeper's chain of thought and insinuates himself, so to speak, into his consciousness (Brandis). A lady I know dreamed aloud of a person (X.), and when her husband talked to her as if he were X. he was answered, but when he spoke in his own person he was ignored.

Finally, there are many persons who can hardly be induced to move in hypnosis, though they can be made to dream anything.

I hope that what has been said makes it clear that hypnosis by no means needs to be sharply distinguished from sleep, in spite of its apparent differences.

Even post-hypnotic suggestion finds an analogy in sleep (Liébeault, Tissié, Exner). Of course the effect of dreams upon the organism is not so easy to observe as the effect of suggestion, as most dreams are forgotten. However, I will mention some of these analogous cases. People who dream of a shot, and wake in consequence, continue to hear the reverberation clearly after they wake (Max Simon). Others after waking feel a pain of which they have been dreaming (Charpignon). I will merely mention certain phenomena which resemble these—the dreams which are continued into waking life, which may be compared to continuative post-hypnotic suggestions. There are well-known vivid dream-pictures which are not recognized as dreams, and which are taken for reality even after waking (Brierre de Boismont). It is certain that even the most enlightened persons are influenced by dreams. Many are out of humour the whole day after having been annoyed by unpleasant dreams. The experiments lately made by Friedrich Heerwagen, of Dorpat, have proved that persons who have dreamt much are in an unpleasant frame of mind the next day. I know patients who are much worse after dreaming of their complaints ; a stammerer will stammer more after dreaming about it. We find analogies with post-hypnotic suggestion everywhere. There are well-known cases in which persons have dreamed of taking an aperient, with effect.

Perhaps a case mentioned by Féré may be referred to here. A girl dreamed for several nights that men were running after her. She grew daily more exhausted, and the weakness in her legs increased till a hysterical paraplegia of both legs declared itself. In mental diseases doctors have often mentioned an analogous phenomenon ; they say that the earliest signs of mental disorder may show themselves first in dream. Griesinger says that delirium often begins in dream. Esquirol says that in acute mania it has been observed that the patient thinks he is ordered in a dream to do something, which afterwards he actually does. To this class belongs a case, recorded by Sauvet and Moreau (de Tours) in 1844, in which a man in ordinary sleep had visions which gradually influenced him in waking and induced him to abandon his home. Tonnini mentions a rather inconclusive case of a woman who was induced by a dream to do something. Of course such cases are difficult to observe ; but it is very probable that dreams have an after-effect on even thoroughly healthy people. Aristotle maintained long ago that many of our actions had their origin in dreams.

Although, as we have seen, deep hypnosis and ordinary sleep are closely related, and especially as regards dreams stand very close to one another, we must not therefore accept the identity of sleep and hypnosis. Dreams are only *one* symptom of sleep ; we cannot consequently regard a comparison of dreams and suggested hallucinations as sufficient to demonstrate identity. I believe that even in deep hypnotic states we have clear grounds for concluding that the condition is not identical with sleep ; for in order to

assert an unconditional identification we must take
into consideration not only the psychological picture,
but also the physiological symptoms.   Now we know
that during sleep, the pulse, the respiration, and other
physical functions are changed, and exhibit a greater
regularity and prolongation.   If we do not find this
in deep hypnosis, it is a proof that the physiological
condition in hypnosis is not identical with that in
sleep.   Francke finds, indeed, that pulse, respiration,
and sweat-secretion show greater regularity, but his
observations are not convincing since he tells us
nothing more definite concerning the other symptoms
of hypnosis as he observed it.   In any case, however,
Francke saw a remarkable resemblance between the
curves of sleep and hypnosis.   I have only seen in a
few cases of hypnosis the slowing of the respiration
and pulse observed in sleep.   I believe, therefore,
that the state in which this is not observed cannot,
on the grounds already mentioned, be identified with
sleep.   Certain pathological conditions argue an even
wider separation of sleep and hypnosis.   The spasm
in chorea and the tremulous movements in paralysis
agitans cease in ordinary sleep.   I have hypnotized
patients suffering from these diseases without causing
the movements and tremors to stop.   I believe that
this also favours a distinction between sleep and
hypnosis.   In such cases I have even been unable by
suggestion to produce any notable lessening of the
movements—a phenomenon which, for such cases at
all events, justifies in a high degree the separation of
hypnosis and sleep.

   From various sides (Bernheim, Delbœuf, Max
Hirsch) it has lately been asserted that the hypnotic
subject is not asleep, but that he believes he is asleep,
that the illusion of sleep produces the increase of

suggestibility. A somewhat different, and perhaps
more correct, view has been expressed by Schrenck-
Notzing. He divides hypnoses into those in which
there is no sleep, those in which there is an illusion of
sleep, and those in which actual sleep is present.

The similarity of the means used to induce sleep
and hypnosis is often insisted upon as a proof of
their identity. But a distinction must be made. It
is said that monotonous stimuli induce both sleep
and hypnosis. Purkinje, therefore, thought that
Braid's methods would also produce sleep. But we
should never conclude an identity of states from the
identity of their causes. We should observe whether
the symptoms are identical. To decide the question,
we should ask, Is the subject who is sent to sleep
by monotonous sense stimulation without a primary
mental act susceptible to suggestion or not? I have
seen cases in which the subjects fixed their gaze but
did not concentrate their attention. The subsequent
state was an ordinary sleep, out of which the subjects
awoke when I made verbal suggestions to them,
however softly I spoke. It is the same thing when
we wish to decide whether a tedious speaker hypnotizes his audience. Many people grow sleepy, or
even fall asleep, in such a case. Unluckily it would
be hardly practicable to make a suggestion to a man
who had fallen asleep under such conditions, and yet
this would be the only way to decide whether he was
hypnotized or not. But sleep comes on without concentration of the subject's thoughts. If he concentrates
his thoughts on the orator, he will not go to sleep ; in
this case his state of partially strained attention much
resembles hypnosis. If the state is strongly marked,
negative hallucinations may arise (for instance, with
regard to noises), as in hypnosis. In many works on

oratory, even in Cicero's, this effect of a fine speech is
referred to.   I am also in doubt whether those states of
loss or disturbance of consciousness, induced by vertigo,
e.g., by spinning round quickly, should be reckoned
as hypnoses.   Erdmann has identified the states induced by vertigo and by tedium in his well-known
ingenious manner.   But I must repeat that it does
not matter how the states are produced ; the point
is whether their symptoms are alike.

Hypnosis has been often compared to mental disorder as well as to sleep.   Rieger and Semal, as well as
Hack Tuke (so far back as 1865), called hypnosis an
artificially induced mental disorder.   In the first
place I would remark that it is of no consequence
what hypnosis is called.   Even in therapeutics this
is a matter of no moment.   Suppose the use of
morphia were denounced because morphia is a
poison, and because the sleep induced by morphia
is an effect of poisoning.   As Rieger justly says,
we need not trouble ourselves about names.   We
might call hypnosis a mental disorder if we also
regarded sleep and dreams as such.   And we find
that when doctors in psychological practice wish
to discover analogies to mental disorder, they always
have recourse to dreams.   This resemblance has
struck many observers, but no author has maintained
that in order to lose one's sanity it is only necessary
to go to sleep.

The most different mental disorders have been
compared to hypnosis, which shows what confusion
there is about it.   For example, Rieger and Konrád
say that hypnosis is nothing but an artificial madness.
Meynert maintains that it is an experimentally-
produced imbecility.   Luys compares it to general

paralysis of the insane, and others to *melancholia attonita*. These different comparisons show the want of unanimity among authors, for the forms of mental disorder we call imbecility and mania are as unlike as a pea and a rose, which are both plants, but of utterly different kinds. No two states of mental disorder could be more unlike than imbecility and mania.

When hypnosis is thus compared to mental disorder it is generally forgotten that susceptibility to suggestion is the chief phenomenon of hypnosis. But it is a mistake to think that susceptibility to suggestion is an essential phenomenon of mental disorder; if it were, mental disorders could be cured by suggestion, which is hardly ever possible. Suggestibility is a symptom of sleep, and we have seen that the dreams which follow on stimulation of the nerves may be induced by suggestion. By means of suggestion in hypnosis forms of hypnosis may be induced which resemble mental derangement, *i.e.*, spontaneous mania, or *melancholia attonita*, besides forms of imbecility, &c. But we can also induce paralysis and stammering by suggestion, and yet hypnosis is not a state of paralysis or of stammering. We can suggest pain in hypnosis, yet hypnosis is not a state of pain. And how the light stages of hypnosis, in which only certain motor effects are caused by suggestion, can be called states of mental disorder is not clear to me, unless a person is to be called mentally unsound simply because he cannot open his eyes. But even the susceptibility to suggestion which exists in such mental disorders as delirium tremens (Möli, Pierre Janet), or the Katatonic of Kahlbaum (Jensen), must not be without further ceremony identified with the susceptibility we find in hypnosis. I need only say

"Wake!" to the hypnotized subject, and the state ends; but there is no disease which can be guided and ended at a moment's notice like hypnosis.

Of course no author would call hypnosis a mental disorder merely because it may be occasionally a delusion in insanity. Freud is right when he says that meat does not lose its flavour when an enthusiastic vegetarian calls it carrion; why should a mental influence, such as we have found hypnosis to be, lose its value or interest because it is sometimes called mental disease?

A remark of Griesinger shows how capriciously all such terms are used; he thinks a somnambulism of short duration is a sleep, and a longer one a mental disorder.

It is no new thing to see hypnosis brought into connection with hysteria and regarded as an artificial hysteria or neurosis. Demarquay and Giraud-Teulon have pointed out analogies, and Charcot has lately called his three stages a "*grande névrose hypnotique.*" Dumontpallier also thinks that hypnosis is an experimental neurosis. I would make the same remark upon this as upon the mental disorders. Charcot has called up the complete type of a neurosis, and specially of hysteria, by suggestion. This was comparatively easy in his cases of "*grande hystérie,*" because phenomena which are common in the subject in waking life are more easily induced in hypnosis than others (Grasset). I repeat, it would be easy to suggest stammering in hypnosis, and then draw the conclusion that hypnosis is a state of stammering. Besides, Charcot has never maintained that the states, as they exist apart from his three stages, and as they have been observed by the school of Nancy, are neuroses; on the contrary, he expressly excludes them from neuroses.

Other states have also been occasionally compared to hypnosis. I may mention catalepsy, a disease, or symptom of disease, in which the limbs keep any given position; and lethargy, a strange state of sleep, in which artificial awakening is difficult or impossible, and to which a disease called *hypnosia* or sleeping sickness, observed in the negroes of West Africa, appears to be related. That the unconsciousness in lethargy, as in Charcot's lethargic stage, is only apparent, is shown by an observation of Encausse, who in a case of this kind was able to produce awakening by suggestion. Thomsen's disease, in which a contracture follows voluntary movement, is also compared to hypnosis, and so are epileptic disturbances of consciousness. Effertz has lately described hypnosis as an induced hystero-epileptic attack, but has brought forward no evidence for this view. I pass over the phenomena of intoxication by alcohol, chloroform, ether, opium, and particularly haschisch, which are often compared to hypnosis on account of the delusions of sense which occur in them. Haschisch intoxication has lately been described in detail by Régla. There are many phenomena in this state which recall hypnosis, and suggestibility can go so far as to produce a change of personality. Régla has made experiments on himself; and on one occasion, for instance, he believed that he was a pregnant woman on the eve of confinement. Narcolepsy must also be mentioned. In this disease there are periodical attacks of sleepiness. It has been described by Gélineau, Rousseau, Ballet, and others. Certain cases of what Drosdow calls *Morbus Hypnoticus*, whose resemblance to hypnosis is unmistakable, may be included in this tolerably undefined narcolepsy. These states might be regarded as auto-hypnoses. Vizioli has published an account of an auto-hypnosis,

15

in which he succeeded in making even post-hypnotic suggestions to the subject. Naturally, the terminology is very arbitrary in these cases; these states might be ascribed to spontaneous somnambulism arising directly out of waking life, and not in sleep, as usual. The famous case of Motet, which was so important from the legal point of view, would then belong to this class. A man committed a criminal act in a state of self-induced hypnosis, to which he was subject. On Motet's recommendation he was acquitted. A case of Dufay's is nearly identical. It would be extremely illogical, besides, to call hypnosis a morbid state merely because a morbid imitation of it is to be found in many forms of *Morbus Hypnoticus.* It would be as great a mistake as if we were to take yawning for a disease because there are people who suffer from attacks of yawning, and who yawn to an abnormal degree (Ochorowicz). *Lata* often resembles hypnosis (Bastian, G. Ellis, Forbes). The word *Lata* properly means the sufferers from this complaint, not the disease. The disease is found among the Malays; the patient imitates every movement made in his presence, as in " fascination." The same thing has been seen in Maine among the " Jumpers " (Beard), and in Siberia, where the sufferers are called " *Mirya-chit* " (Hammond). Obersteiner mentions the interesting observation of Kaschin that a troop of Siberian soldiers once repeated all their commander's orders, without obeying them, and even imitated the threats which he uttered against them.

I lately had an opportunity, at the large Arab hospital at Cairo, of seeing a case which doubtless should be mentioned in this connection. The subject was a negress, some thirty years of age, then in the hospital. Besides her own negro tongue she understood some French. The chief symptom of her disorder was that while she sat passively in the same place all day long she repeated whatever was said to her, whether in her own language, in French, or in other languages of which she knew nothing whatever. I made trials with German and other languages ; even difficult sentences she repeated mechanically, the first time usually with omissions, but when she had again gone over it every syllable was clearly uttered. She also imitated movements to a certain extent. If I put out my tongue she did the same, if I showed my teeth she also showed hers, if I clapped my hands she clapped hers, though after a longer interval. It was, however, generally first necessary to attract her eye before performing an action.

Once more, the chief feature of hypnosis is increased susceptibility to suggestion. By means of this we can induce counterfeits of all sorts of diseases, which appear identical with the real thing. But none the less, hypnosis should not be identified with these diseases. The two characteristics of hypnosis are suggestibility and the power of ending the state at pleasure. We do not find them united in mental disorders, nor in neuroses ; but we find them in sleep, in which suggestion induces dreams by means of stimulation of the senses, and from which the subject can be aroused at any moment by an external stimulus. Although no identification of hypnosis and sleep would be justifiable on the above grounds, I must again point out that, in spite of their apparent differences, they are closely related, at least so far as hypnoses of the second group are concerned.

The different phenomena of hypnosis have been also observed in normal waking life, and this makes a comparison of the hypnotic states with other abnormal states considerably more difficult. For example, a symptom which A. shows in hypnosis he does not show in his normal state ; but it may

be observed in B.'s normal waking life. This may
be referred to the phenomena of suggestion, which
exist normally, as I showed on p. 69, but which are
increased in certain cases during hypnosis. People
differ greatly in their susceptibility to suggestion in
waking life ; I have spoken (p. 69) of suggestions in
ordinary life, from which hypnosis cannot be concluded. Besides which a number of phenomena of
suggestion, which are generally regarded as a peculiarity of hypnosis, have been found in waking life.
Braid, the American electrobiologists, Heidenhain,
Berger, Richet, Lévy, Bernheim, Beaunis, Liégeois,
Herzog even in 1853, and Forel, are among those who
have made observations in this field.

These phenomena are shown by subjects who have
been hypnotized as well as by those who have not.
Contractures, paralyses, dumbness, and all kinds of
motor disturbances can be induced by suggestion in
the waking state. According to some authors it is
even possible to induce hallucinations without hypnosis. However, many of the experiments, and particularly the conclusions drawn from them, seem to
me to have two defects. Those who talk of suggestions in the waking state (*suggestions à veille*) forget,
first, that sleep is by no means always indispensable
for many hypnotic suggestions. Authors often confuse hypnosis with sleep in speaking of suggestions in
the waking state. We have seen that the light hypnotic stages do not much resemble sleep ; consequently we must not conclude that a state of
contracture, &c., is, or is not, a hypnosis because it
resembles sleep or not. The second point which these
authors generally overlook is this : they think that
hypnosis is excluded in these cases of waking suggestion, because none of the usual methods of inducing

hypnosis have been used. But the methods are not absolutely necessary for the induction of hypnosis. We cannot make the question, whether hypnosis is present or not, depend on the means employed. If we refused to believe in any particular state unless the usual means had been used to induce it, we should revolutionize science. In my opinion we ought to consider the state and its symptoms separately. For if we take a certain degree of suggestibility, loss of memory, &c., for a symptom of hypnosis, nothing remains but to regard as hypnoses many—I will not say all—of these states which are generally described as suggestions without hypnosis. The chief phenomenon of hypnosis is that a certain accepted idea leads to a movement or a delusion of the senses, &c. We have further seen that the experimenter can change the subject's dominant idea very quickly, *i.e.*, he can suggest one thing quickly after another. If, then, we can do the same without, apparently, previous appearance of hypnosis, we must call the state a hypnosis all the same, particularly if there is subsequent loss of memory.

In reality a hypnogenic method is employed, because in such suggestions the subject generally remembers an earlier hypnosis ; and the idea of hypnosis is enough to induce it. Therefore we often need only to repeat a suggestion made in an earlier hypnosis to cause a new one (Marin).

The fact that paralyses, contractures, &c., can be produced by suggestion in this new hypnosis, shows that it is as real as the first. In the deeper states, when delusions of sense can be induced, loss of memory usually follows. The changed expression of the subject's face also shows there is hypnosis. Finally, the presence of a real hypnosis is proved by the *rapport* between subject and experimenter.

For the reasons above mentioned I think we should
call many of these states true hypnoses, not suggestions without hypnosis. The school of Nancy, and
particularly Liégeois and Beaunis, have to a certain
extent acknowledged this. But they certainly have
not given to the point all the importance it deserves.
They thought many of these states were intermediate
forms between sleeping and waking, which they
identified with the *veille somnambulique* described
above (p. 164).

I know that from what I have said it might be
concluded that all these suggestions were made in
hypnosis. It is, in truth, very difficult to find clear
diagnostic symptoms in certain cases. My explanation aims only at pointing out that there may really
be hypnosis, though none of the usual methods have
been employed to bring it on. I have, besides, tried
to prevent suggestion in waking life, and especially to
make delusions of the senses impossible.

It is often very difficult to decide whether there is
hypnosis or not, because isolated hypnotic symptoms
are often seen in certain people who are not in hypnosis. I may refer here to a case of Carpenter's
mentioned by Finlay. A gentleman placed his hands
on the table and for half a minute directed his attention to them. When the suggestion was then made
to him, in decided tones, that he could not remove his
hands, he was in fact unable to do so. I have
frequently observed the same thing, especially after
hypnotic exhibitions. I have, for instance, seen inability to move a limb, to withdraw the outstretched
tongue, or to close the mouth. New suggestions, however, only succeed after the attention has been drawn
to them for some time. There are even delusions of
the senses without hypnosis, sleep, or mental disorder,

when circumstances influence the mind in a particular way. The common hallucination of smell is an example. People often imagine that they still smell things which have been removed. Delusions of sight are just as common. Many people have taken trees for men when walking in the twilight. Goethe's self-induced hallucinations of sight are well known. Delbœuf also describes a waking hallucination of sight; he thought he saw his dead mother, but corrected his impression by reason. If there are even delusions of the senses without hypnosis, it is evidently difficult to argue the presence of hypnosis from a single symptom.

I should call the following the chief points in settling the question whether a suggestion is made in hypnosis or not : 1. Of what kind are the suggestions ? Are they of such a kind that they rarely occur normally? 2. After one suggestion has succeeded, can other suggestions be made as quickly as in hypnosis, or is a long preparation necessary for each suggestion ? The quick success of the following suggestion would be in favour of hypnosis. 3. After the suggestion has succeeded, can the subject prevent further suggestion by an act of will, or not ? If he cannot, it favours the supposition of a hypnotic state. 4. Is there *rapport ?* That is, can the subject be influenced by anybody or by only one ? *Rapport* favours hypnosis. 5. Are there bodily symptoms of hypnosis ? 6. Are the events subsequently forgotten ? Loss of memory also favours the supposition of hypnosis.

The many transitional states between waking life and hypnosis will often make the question difficult to decide ; none of the points above mentioned will alone suffice to settle it.

It sometimes happens that we try to induce a
person to do something by looking at him fixedly ;
we then see how slight is the division between the
hypnotic states and waking life. A teacher who
thinks his pupil is lying, looks at him fixedly to ascer-
tain the truth, just as is done in fascination. This
fixed gaze affects the will of the person looked at, as
we have seen in hypnosis. We recognize an analogy
on one hand, on the other we see how difficult it
must always be to decide where hypnosis begins and
waking life ends.

States resembling, or perhaps identical with, hypnosis, are also found in animals, and can easily be
experimentally induced. The first experiments of
this kind are referred to by the Jesuit Kircher ;—the
so-called *experimentum mirabile Kircheri.* Kircher
described these experiments in 1646. But according to Preyer the experiment had been made by
Schwenter several years earlier. The most striking of
these experiments, which are being continued in the
present day, is as follows : A hen is held down on
the ground; the head in particular is pressed down.
A chalk line is then drawn on the ground, starting
from the bird's beak. The hen will remain motionless. Kircher ascribes this to the animal's imagination ; he said that it imagined it was fastened, and
consequently did not try to move. Czermak repeated the experiment on different animals, and
announced in 1872 that a hypnotic state could be
induced in other animals besides the hen. Preyer
shortly after began to interest himself in the question,
and made a series of experiments like Czermak's.
Preyer, however, distinguishes two states in animals—
cataplexy, which is the effect of fear, and the hypnotic

state. I believe that Preyer is here decidedly in the right. Various recent reports on hypnosis in animals more correctly belong to paralysis from fright or similar conditions. Lysing records some facts bearing on this point. Regnard observed that when dynamite explosions took place in the water, fish that were not in the immediate neighbourhood of the charge would lie as if dead, though a slight touch would restore movement. Laborde found the same true of trout, which could thus be caught. Heubel, Richet, Danilewsky, and Rieger, besides the authors mentioned above, have occupied themselves with the question.

Most of the experiments have been made with frogs, crayfish, guinea-pigs, and birds. I myself have made many with frogs. This much is certain : many animals will remain motionless in any position in which they have been held by force for a time. There are various opinions as to the meaning of this. Preyer thinks many of these states are paralyses from fright, or cataplexy, produced by a sudden peripheral stimulus. In any case they vividly recall the catalepsy of the Salpêtrière, also caused by a strong external stimulus. It is said a sudden Drummond lime-light produces the same effect on a cock as it does on hysterical patients (Richer). But in general the external stimulus used with animals is tactile, as in seizing them. Heubel thinks that these states in animals are a true sleep following on the cessation of the external stimuli, and Wundt seems to agree with him.

Rieger has especially shown that the frog will remain rigid when upright, if it is kept from falling, as well as when lying on its back. The hind leg of a frog lying on its back may be pulled out, and the animal will not draw it in again as it usually does.   Richet, however, says that it is drawn in again at once, if the spinal cord is divided below the *medulla oblongata.* It is interesting that when a " hypnotic" frog is placed in a certain position it will at first move after a short time, but the more often the experiment is repeated the longer the frog lies without moving.   I have seen frogs lie on their backs in this way for hours, and have even often seen them die without turning over.   The deeper the state is, the less the animal responds to external stimuli; it ends by not moving at tolerably loud noises or even stimulation of the skin.   Danilewsky made a series of experiments, from which he concluded that there were regular changes of reflex excitability; but Rieger was unable to confirm this.   Danilewsky has lately made some more deeply interesting experiments, which it is to be hoped he will carry on.   He says that when the brain hemispheres are taken away the frog assumes cataleptoid postures, and further that these turn into hypnoses in animals who have rotatory movements after injury of the semi-circular canals of the ear.

Harting's experiments also deserve mention ; after repeated hypnotic experiments with fowls he observed hemiplegic phenomena in them, according to a communication by Milne-Edwards to the Paris Academy of Sciences.

I will not try to decide the question as to the nature of the state revealed by these experiments on animals.

Another series of observations, which were chiefly made for practical purposes, may be mentioned here. They also may be regarded as hypnotic phenomena.

I speak or the so-called "*Balassiren*" of horses, introduced by the cavalry officer Balassa. This process
has been introduced by law into Austria for the
shoeing of horses (Obersteiner). It consists chiefly
in looking fixedly at the horse, just as in "fascination."
It has also been stated that restive horses may be
checked by hypnotism (Glanson). Czinski is said to
have hypnotised dogs, cats, and monkeys; Bruno,
cats and doves. Stoll believes that in other ways we
work by suggestion on our domestic animals. He
regards the influence of the rider on the horse or the
mule, especially when particular tricks have to be
combated, as suggestive, since scarcely anything can
be accomplished here by brute force. A kind of
counter-suggestion, appropriately brought to the
animal's intelligence, would thus oppose his idiosyn-
crasies and auto-suggestions. The numerous experiments of Wilson should also be mentioned; he is
said to have hypnotized elephants, wolves, horses,
&c., in London, in 1839. Fascination is used by
beast tamers, who stare fixedly into the eyes of the
animal they wish to tame. Many think that the
charming of birds by snakes is fascination. Hart
and Lysing, however, believe that the animals are
not hypnotized, but that, as the snake gazes at them,
they hypnotize themselves. Liébeault and Forel
think that the winter sleep (hibernation) of animals
is an auto-hypnosis; and so, perhaps, is the strange
sleep of the Indian fakirs, which sometimes lasts for
weeks and months (Fischer).

A number of trustworthy witnesses and authors
(Jacolliot, Hildebrandt, Hellwald) tell us even
stranger things about these fakirs, which set any
attempt at explanation on the basis of our present

scientific knowledge at defiance ; that is, if we decline
to regard them as mere juggler's tricks. Hildebrandt
among other things relates that he saw a fakir sitting
in a Hindoo temple ; he was crouching down with his
left arm stretched upwards ; the arm was dead and so
perfectly dry that the skin might easily have been
torn from it. Another fakir had held his thumb
pressed against the palm of his hand till the nail had
grown deep into the flesh. It is said, besides, that
some of these people can make plants grow very
quickly. Görres mentioned this. These fakirs are
also said to have been apparently buried for weeks
and months, and yet have returned to normal life.
Kuhn holds this to be an undoubted fact, the condition of the fakirs being that of hypnotic catalepsy.
Of course these things must be listened to with sceptical reserve. Yet even a scientific investigator like
Hellwald thinks that though no doubt there is a
great deal of jugglery, yet some of the phenomena
remain at present inexplicable.

Many other observations recorded by ethnologists
and travellers show striking resemblance with auto-
hypnotic conditions. Stoll records many such facts,
as, for instance, the auto-hypnotic state of the
shamans or priests of various Siberian peoples, as
recorded in the travels of Pallas and Gmelin. An
Armenian doctor, Vahan Artzronny, mentions a
disorder which attacked a whole race, the Ezidi, in
Armenia. When any of the people were brought to
a spot and a circle drawn round them with a stick,
they would die rather than step out of it. There
would seem to be some suspicion of a superstition in
this case ; but it may have been a matter of fascination.

I have made but brief mention of these matters and of the experiments with animals ; details would take me too far. Any one who is interested will find material enough in Preyer's book, " Die Cataplexie und der thierische Hypnotismus."

CHAPTER V.

THE THEORY OF HYPNOTISM.

IT will appear from what has been said that the symptoms of hypnosis are extremely complex, and the question now is, "Can the phenomena of hypnosis be explained?" Before we reply to this, we must agree what we mean by "explanation." To explain a hitherto unknown thing, we must trace it back to what we do know. And as we know nothing of the real nature of our mental processes, it is useless to expect any satisfactory information regarding the mental state during hypnosis. It seems then that at present we must content ourselves with such an explanation as may be got by comparing the phenomena of normal life with those of hypnosis. We must settle what are the true, and what the apparent, differences between hypnotic and non-hypnotic life, and then we must find the causal connection between the peculiar phenomena of hypnosis and the means used to induce it. This last is the main point. An example will make this clearer. I will suppose that we want to find an explanation of a hypnotic negative hallucination of sight. We must first of all find some parallel phenomenon in a non-hypnotic state. If we find a case in which, without hypnosis, an object has not been perceived, though the eye must have seen it, we must then ask what difference there is between this phenomenon and the same phenomenon in hypnosis. We shall then find that in hypnosis objects are not perceived only when the experimenter forbids the perception ; but that to forbid the perception of an object in waking life would be to ensure its being perceived. This point of difference must be kept in view for a proper explanation. It will be explained by the existence in the one case of a peculiar state of consciousness—the so-called dream-consciousness ; and we must then ask how the origin of hypnosis explains the formation of this dream-consciousness. If we cannot find phenomena parallel to the methods of origination of hypnosis anywhere, we shall be obliged to give up the attempt at explanation for the present.

I believe that we can already explain many of the hypnotic phenomena, if "explanation" is taken in the above sense. In any case, such numerous analogies to the phenomena of hypnosis have already been found that we need no longer think them mystical. We need no longer think the methods of hypnosis incomprehensible, as was the case a short time ago. This progress has been made by following the method Obersteiner recommended ; *i.e.*, by carefully observing the transitional states between hypnosis and normal life. We have been able to connect many every-day occurrences with hypnosis, and have found many more connecting links with normal life than is generally supposed. I even believe, as I have said, that we can already explain certain hypnotic pheno- mena by means of analogy, and I think that many of the post-hypnotic phenomena are capable of ex- planation in the above meaning of the word.

But much remains to be done ; one method of in- vestigation in especial should be more used ; *i.e.*,

self-observation.   It is a great disadvantage that
strict self-observation often prevents the induction of
hypnosis ; but on the other hand I think that our
neglect of self-observation is the reason of our failure
to explain many hypnotic phenomena clearly.   It is
true that some trustworthy investigators, Wilkinson,
Bleuler, Forel, Obersteiner, North, Heidenhain, Wundt,
etc., have helped a little by their accounts of their
personal experiences in the hypnotic state ; but such
observations should be made oftener by intelligent
people ; they would be valuable to investigators.   An
explanation of hypnosis drawn from the material
already accumulated cannot be given in a few words,
since the symptoms alone are so complex.   Besides, I
think it probable (and Braid was of the same opinion)
that a great number of different states are included in
the concept "hypnosis," and that an exact classification
of them is not possible at present, though it surely
will be later.   Under these circumstances I think it
best to discuss the most commonly observed and best
established phenomena of hypnosis singly, and to
explain them when possible.   I must give up any
attempt at completeness and detail in order not to
make the theoretical explanation too long ; I reserve
this for another work.   The chief points which I
shall try to explain in what follows are—(1) the
phenomena of suggestion as regards voluntary movement ; (2) positive and negative delusions of the
senses ; (3) *rapport* ; (4) the phenomena of memory ;
(5) post-hypnotic suggestion.   I will discuss these
points one by one and try to explain them in the
manner described above.   It may be thought, on a
superficial view, that it would be more important to
examine the way the methods employed induce
hypnosis than to explain the separate symptoms ;

but to discuss this would be to dispute about words, because hypnosis hardly ever appears suddenly, but rather develops itself by degrees out of a series of symptoms. For example, the eyes close first; then suggestion induces a heaviness in the arm, and then the arm is paralyzed; a suggested sense delusion follows. Hypnosis develops itself nearly if not quite always in this way; one symptom is added to another. Consequently to explain the separate symptoms is to explain the mode of production of hypnosis; the reader will find that the one explanation involves the other. This fact will become clear when the abnormal functions of the muscles are explained.

We shall understand the different symptoms of hypnosis much more easily if we first examine two phenomena. These phenomena might be laid down as laws of the psychical states of human beings, though they would be laws with many exceptions. They are not generally enough considered, but they are of immense importance to psychology, physiology, and medicine, as well as to hypnotism. These rules are— (1) men have a certain proneness to allow themselves to be influenced by others through their ideas, and in particular to believe much without making conscious logical deductions; (2) a psychological or physiological effect tends to appear in a man if he is expecting it.

Let us begin by considering the first point. There are people who believe that they can escape external psychical influences; but they are wrong, since observation shows that every one is more or less influenced by ideas (Bentivegni, Bernheim). Life is full of such influences, and they will work so long as there is mental activity among men. The desire for society,

the necessity of exchanging opinions, show the need
we feel of influencing and being influenced by ideas.
If we want to convert a political opponent we try to
influence him by arousing certain ideas in him.   It is
not mentally deficient people who are thus accessible
to ideas.   There is in every man a gap where these
ideas can enter.   It is well known that the greatest
people and most distinguished scholars are often
dominated by some inferior individual who has discovered the gap where his ideas will enter.

   In the same way men have a tendency to believe
things without complete logical proof ; we will call this
quality credulity.   Those who contend that men are
not credulous, show that they are themselves incapable
of reflection (Forel).   There is no man who believes
only what has been logically proved to him.   Our
sense perceptions show us this in the clearest way ;
we hardly ever consciously reason upon them, and yet
the thing which we take for an external object is
only in reality an act of our minds, which in no way
corresponds with the unknown object, the "thing
in itself," as Kant calls it.   Most people confuse
the subjective idea of an object with the object itself
(Spencer).   This mistake, which we make incessantly
with regard to our sense perceptions, proves that we
do not use conscious logical thought.   But when we
consider our behaviour with regard to dogmatic assertions, and to assertions often repeated, this credulity
is made particularly clear.   It leads us to dogmatic
belief.   Children are most influenced by it, but adults
are also under its jurisdiction.

   As children are particularly credulous of dogmatic assertions,
and as such credulity is strongly marked in hypnosis, this state
has often been compared to childhood (Copin, Miescher,
Cullerre, Wernicke).   But I must point out that in this com-

parison childhood and infancy are confused. To make the comparison possible we must choose a period of childhood in which ideas can be incorporated into the existing consciousness, not the period of infancy, in which consciousness is hardly formed.

I will give a simple example of the credulity of childhood with regard to dogmatic belief. I was told at school that the North Cape was the north point of Europe. This was not logically proved to me; yet I believed it because it was in the book, and more especially because the teacher said so. Dogmatic assertion influences not only children but adults; and the constant repetition of an assertion has also a great power. This is shown in the clearest way by an incident which is particularly interesting to us. A few years ago it was believed that there was really no such thing as hypnotism, and that those who believed in it were deceived. But since that time opinion has entirely changed. The representations made by different people in authority as to the reality of the hypnotic phenomena, and particularly the repeated assertions of numerous investigators, have caused a complete change of view. Doctors and others have changed their minds about hypnotism, not because it has been proved to them, but exclusively because they have been influenced by constantly hearing and reading the same assertions about it, and by their faith in authority.

I hope that the above explanations, which every one can add to from his own experience, sufficiently prove what I said above—that all men are credulous to a certain degree. Now for the second of my propositions—*i.e.*, that an effect on himself which a man expects tends to appear. We can find a great number of these phenomena in ordinary life; they

are mysterious and astonishing only when we neglect
to consider this tendency. Carpenter, Hack Tuke,
and many English investigators have besides admitted
that these phenomena are of great importance. I
will now describe some of them.

People who suffer from sleeplessness have often
been sent to sleep by taking something which they
were told was a sleeping draught, but which was
really some inert substance. They slept because
they expected to do so. When they learn that the
medicine is not a sleeping draught they no longer
expect sleep, and do not sleep. It appears from this
that to expect a state, and to wish for it, are essentially different things; which fact is often strangely
enough overlooked. A great many people wish for
sleep, but as they do not expect it, it does not come.
Some other examples will show that this principle is
generally valid; for example, the fatigue that is felt
at the usual bedtime may be mentioned. We see
how much habit has to do with it; when people have
been long used to go to bed at a certain time, they
generally feel tired just at that time (Forel). The
rule holds good for the functions of the motor organs
as well as the others. We will take a case of hysterical paralysis; it is well known that such a paralysis
is sometimes cured at the exact moment the patient
expects. Many mysterious effects may be thus explained. Hysterical patients can often foretell an
improvement in their paralyses. This gift of prophecy need not astonish us if we think of this rule;
the connection is not what believers in the gift of
prophecy think; for the hysterical patient is cured
at a particular time because he expects to be—the
prophecy causes its own fulfilment. It also occurs
that people vomit when they expect to, or if they

think they have taken an emetic; impotence also may come on if it is anticipated; and stammering may be induced in the same way.

Of course there are exceptions to the rule. However much a sufferer from severe myelitis may expect his paralyzed legs to move they will not do so, because the impediments are too great to be overcome by this natural tendency of expectation to produce an effect. There are other impediments which, though they do not interfere with the tendency as such, prevent its taking effect.

Many observations show that the above rule holds good for the organs of sense under particular circumstances; the following case of Carpenter's is related by Bentivegni. A judicial disinterment was to be made; the grave was opened, and the coffin raised; the official who was present said that he already smelt putrefaction, but when the coffin was opened it was found to be empty. Here expectation caused a distinct sense perception. There are many examples of this. Yung has made a series of experiments, and has shown that the sense of touch and the sense of temperature are particularly subject to delusion, and that certain perceptions occur when they are expected without external stimuli. I myself have often repeated the following experiments of Braid, Weinhold, and others. I blindfolded certain persons, doctors among the number, or I simply made them close their eyes. I then told the subject that he was going to be mesmerized; and even when this was not true, he generally imagined he felt the current of air caused by the passes; he believed he knew the exact moment when the passes were begun. Here again we see expectation produce a perception. Many people begin to feel the pain of an operation almost before the knife has touched them, simply because their whole attention is fixed upon the pain and the beginning of the operation.

The principle has other effects. Forel and many others mention that there are certain popular methods of slightly retarding menstruation. In one town many of the young women tie something round their little finger if they wish to delay menstruation for a few days in order to go to a ball, &c. The method is generally effectual, but when faith ceases the effect also ceases.

I hope that what has been said sufficiently explains the second rule mentioned above.

I go on to discuss single phenomena of hypnosis ; the functional disturbances of voluntary movement first. These are seen in every hypnosis, as I said before in speaking of the symptoms ; they are almost always the first symptom, even when there are other changes. The principle just developed, that an expected functional abnormality comes on when expected if it is not hindered by mechanical or other insuperable obstacles, best explains the abnormalities of the voluntary movements. But to understand this thoroughly, the hypnosis should be induced by slow degrees, as in this case the motor disturbances are plainer.

Now, the previous discussion makes it evident that to produce any motor disorder in a subject (X.) who is at present in a perfectly normal state, we must first of all draw his attention to the desired effect, and make him firmly expect it; that is, we must be able to place the conviction in the foreground of the subject's thoughts, or, as Fechner and Wundt express it, in the range of his inner perspective. If we succeed in capturing the subject's attention to such a point that he firmly believes something—*e.g.*, that his arm will be paralyzed—the paralysis will generally happen.

It would evidently be unfavourable if the subject should reflect and criticize while the attempt to direct his attention was being made. If he does so an effectual concentration of his attention is impossible. Numerous other conditions must be fulfilled before we can make an idea dominate the subject's attention ; these conditions are for the most part the same which I mentioned as favouring the coming on of hypnosis, when I was speaking of its production. It is clear, therefore, that the surroundings, the subject's mental state as well as the manner of the experimenter's entrance, play a great part. The favourable influence of imitation is also easily explicable ; for these things may greatly influence the subject's expectation of the effect. For example, a person who has seen paralysis induced by certain passes in another subject's arm, will be much more likely to let the same phenomenon be induced in himself, than would another who had not seen it.

Supposing such a paralysis induced, the subject's mental balance is already disturbed. If a man cannot voluntarily move his arm he feels at once that his will is weakened ; a mental state ensues which Pierre Janet often calls "*misère psychique*" ; a peculiar feeling of weakened will-power. This feeling is very important ; by means of it the subject's power of resistance is lessened more and more. When one limb has been paralyzed it is easier to paralyze a second, because the subject already doubts his own will-power. Thus, when the subject can no longer voluntarily move a limb, or part of it, very much has been gained for further susceptibility to suggestion, because the consciousness of weakness favours the acceptance of later suggestions. The development of suggestibility need no longer astonish us, since we have found the clue to its production.

I have endeavoured to explain the disturbances of the muscular functions in their gradual development, as it were; this development is in many cases nearly identical with that of hypnosis, which, as we have seen, is often merely an inhibition of the voluntary muscular functions. Many of the methods used to induce hypnosis are alike in one particular—they direct the subject's attention to some change in the functions of the muscles. The method of the school of Nancy consists chiefly in making the subject expect the closing of his eyes as strongly as possible, though this method also aims at producing the dream-consciousness, of which I shall speak later. But other methods induce abnormalities in the functions of single limbs in just the same way. For example, an arm or leg loses its power to move when I concentrate the attention of the subject upon the loss of power to move. In fact, it is quite unnecessary to begin with the eyes, as the school of Nancy does; we can begin with any member, as Max Dessoir rightly insists.

As a fact, it does not matter whether the first motor disturbance is a muscular action performed against the subject's will—*i.e.*, a certain movement which the subject makes at command—or whether it is an inability to move, caused also by a command. The great thing is to gain enough influence over the subject. In any case we should begin with the disturbance which is the easiest to induce, because one success increases the experimenter's influence. Now as a rule it is easier to inhibit an action than to cause it, as daily observation 'shows. An example may make this clear. We assure a person whose arm is stretched out that he is tired and cannot hold it out any longer. In almost all cases there is a momentary pull down-

.

wards ; *i.e.*, there is an inclination to lower the arm. This shows that there is often susceptibility to suggestion without hypnosis. I will briefly recapitulate ; the disturbances of voluntary movement induced by suggestion in hypnosis are caused by the experimenter's directing the attention of the subject as strongly as possible to the desired effect. When the attempt has once succeeded, further disturbances may be more easily induced, since the subject is already persuaded of his inability to resist.

This principle of the effects of expectant attention illustrated above is nowhere shown more plainly than in the voluntary movements. It is even not always necessary that a movement should be very attentively expected ; the idea of the movement will induce it. Let a man bend his arm at the elbow at right angles, and think that the arm will bend quickly, without expecting it to do so ; if he fixes his whole attention on this idea the movement will very soon follow. This shows again how great is the tendency to make a certain movement when the subject concentrates his whole attention on that one point. If expectation is added to attention the effect will be so much the greater.

I now come to the discussion and explanation of sense delusions ; first of all, of the positive kind. Are we not exposed to such delusions otherwise than in hypnosis ? Take first a very simple example of Max Dessoir's. I say to some one who is quite awake, " A rat is running behind you." The man can assure himself at once by turning round that there is no rat, but according to experience he will have a mental image of a rat for a moment, because I spoke of it ; *i.e.*, there is already a trace of hallucination.

Modern psychology, following such men as Dugald Stewart and Taine, generally supposes that every idea includes an image, *e.g.*, the idea of a knife includes an image of a knife. As further every central image tends to externalize itself, as Stuart Mill in particular has explained, when an idea is aroused, there is always a tendency to externalize the corresponding image, *i.e.*, there is a tendency to hallucination. We have thus a tendency to take the remembered image for real objects (Binet, Féré, and especially Souriau in *La Suggestion dans l'Art*).

So in the case of the rat there is a transitory hallucination. Its persistence is prevented in two ways. Firstly, the man could convince himself by means of his senses that no rat was there. Secondly, reflection and the logical grouping of former pictures of memory would convince him that no rat was present. The two factors would suffice to prevent the persistence of the suggested delusion. A simple consideration shows that sense perceptions are not always needed to prevent hallucination. Tell a person whose eyes are shut that a rat is running in front of him. Without opening his eyes he is convinced of the contrary, and says it is not true. Although the image of the rat arises in his mind for a moment, it does not grow into a definite sense delusion, because reflection and memory prevent it. It is not the sense perceptions which prevent it; calm, critical reflection is enough. This is often of more value in preventing a threatening hallucination than the perceptions.

We have thus learned to distinguish the different effects of a suggested hallucination in the waking and in the hypnotic states; we have seen that in the latter the hallucinations arise absolutely without any new factor. They increase in strength and persistence because they are not hindered by sense perceptions or critical reflection. It must now be asked, Are there states analogous to these also?

We must make it perfectly clear that we have a dream-consciousness completely distinct from the waking consciousness (Ed. v. Hartmann), in which feelings and perceptions do not occur at all in the same way as in the waking consciousness. When we wake from sleep we are able to distinguish dream-consciousness from waking life simply by recollection. We know whether what we dreamed was only a dream, or whether it was real (Bentivegni). It is true that in dreams ideas are reproduced and perceptions felt, but in two respects (according to Wundt) this consciousness differs from that of waking life. In the first place the remembered ideas have a hallucinatory character, *i.e.*, we try in dreams to objectify the images of memory ; we do not recognize that they are images of memory as we do in waking life, but believe that we see, feel, &c., the real object to which they correspond. In the same way external impressions do not produce normal perceptions, but illusions. In the second place, in dreams what Wundt calls apperception is changed ; *i.e.*, the power of judging the experiences of which we are conscious is essentially altered. It is just this peculiarity of the dream-consciousness (mentioned by Wundt) which is found in the consciousness of such hypnotic subjects as are accessible to suggested sense delusions. There is no need to enter into details on this point, as it has been thoroughly discussed in the chapters on " Symptoms " and " Cognate States." The chief point is the hallucinatory character of the images of memory ; faintly indicated in normal states, in dream-consciousness it is extremely plain, and appears in hypnosis in connection with illusions, to which dream-consciousness is also favourable. But we may be sure that such a dream-consciousness is by no means a strange and

new thing, since it is often found in ordinary sleep ;
or, rather, it seems to be habitual in sleep, as has just
been shown. The production of this peculiar dream-
consciousness is one of the chief points in hypnotizing.
The question is, how is it brought about ; is there
a causal connection between dream-consciousness and
the induction of hypnosis? I need not discuss this at
length, since we already know that children may be
talked to in sleep. In adults dream-consciousness only
appears in hypnosis when they have been sent to
sleep by some methods like those used to induce
ordinary sleep. As we have seen, hypnosis is generally induced mentally. Now, Forel, Liébeault, and
many other investigators say that natural sleep is the
immediate result of a mental process—an auto-suggestion of sleep, in fact. I do not contend that the
products of tissue waste in the body may not produce
sleep without arousing the idea of it, but it is a fact
that in many cases—whether in all must be left undecided at present—we fall asleep merely because we
have the idea of sleep, and are convinced we shall
sleep. As sleep is only a particular state of consciousness, it is not clear why we cannot induce certain people to sleep by telling them to do so, when
we are hypnotizing them. We can talk people into
all sorts of states of consciousness ; the priest, the
popular orator do so every day. Why can we not
induce dream-consciousness in a like way, as is often
done as a matter of fact when children are put to
sleep?

It is true that in many cases dream-consciousness can
be induced in hypnosis by means which have nothing
to do with the induction of sleep ; for example, when,
a hypnotic subject fixes his gaze and his eyes finally
close, this does not appear to be the induction of a

state of sleep. Nevertheless,I think that sleep comes
on, even when it is not purposely suggested. Sleep may
be brought on by the feeling of heaviness in the eyes,
through association of ideas (Forel); for some people
are in the habit of staring fixedly at a point in order
to tire their eyes and bring on their ordinary sleep.
For these reasons, about which I cannot enter into
more details here, I believe that when a hallucination
happens in hypnosis, some means of inducing dream-
consciousness have always been used. Even those
hypnoses in which hallucinations happen without
previous closing of the eyes do not contradict this,
since the dream-consciousness is not necessarily connected with the closing of the eyes. It sometimes
comes on when the eyes are open, as is seen in cases
of spontaneous somnambulism. After what has been
said we can find an explanation of sense delusions in
the analogy between these hypnotic states and sleep.
Certainly we do not know why sense delusions
happen in ordinary sleep. I have not space to enter
into the different attempts at explanation which have
been made, and, besides, it would be useless. But I
think it will provisionally help us in examining hypnosis if we take the hypnotic states in which there
are pronounced sense delusions, as completely corresponding with ordinary sleep and its dream-
consciousness. In both states certain impressions
of external origin (memory pictures, or mere stimulations of the senses) induce sense delusions. It is
only necessary that the impression which causes the
delusion should affect the sleeper deeply enough.

These conclusions lead to a discussion of *rapport.*
This *rapport* causes the subject to be more influenced
by certain impressions than by others, and to respond

to them by corresponding sense delusions.   I shall
speak of *rapport* briefly, as I have elsewhere dealt
with it at length.   According to Noizet and Bertrand,
who have been joined lately by Liébeault, Bernheim,
Forel, and others, *rapport* is a state of sleep in which
the attention of the subject is fixed exclusively
upon the hypnotizer, so that the idea of him
is constantly present in the subject's memory.   On
this account Bertrand compared these processes to
the falling asleep of a mother by her child's cradle.
She continues to watch over it in sleep ; she hears the
least sound it makes, but no other sounds.   This
analogy may explain the peculiar influence which a
hypnotizer has over his subject.   The subject has
fallen asleep with the thought of the hypnotizer in
his mind, and hears only what he says, as in the case
of the mother and child.

It is also not strange that this influence should
increase in the course of hypnotic training, as we see
that the influence which one person has over another
in normal circumstances grows with exercise. No
new psychical law is to be found in hypnosis.

(When we go on to discuss the negative hallucinations and the way they originate in hypnosis, we
remark two things: firstly, that the subject does
not see certain objects or hear certain noises, &c. ;
secondly, and more particularly, that the objects he
does not see are just those he is forbidden by the
hypnotist to see. I have mentioned that many things
are not seen and heard in normal circumstances when
the attention is not directed to them.) These facts
are not astonishing, but the way they originate in
hypnosis is striking. If I tell a waking man who
has a chair in front of him, " There is nothing there,

neither chair nor table," he will see the chair in spite of what I say ; but the hypnotic subject will not see it, at least if he is susceptible to negative hallucination. Now we can regard this process in the hypnotic as a diversion of the attention, like that in the waking man who fails to perceive things which stimulate his organs of sense.

This is shown in particular by those hallucinations which vanish the moment the attention is drawn to the hallucinatory object. We can see clearly in such cases that the negative hallucination was caused by the diversion of the attention from the object, and that the direction of the attention to it was a counter-suggestion. I say to a subject, " When you wake, X. will have gone away." When he wakes and is asked how many people are present, he says, " Two ; you and I." I then point out X., and tell the subject to look at him. Then he sees X., and the suggestion has lost its effect.

But in any case the mode of origin is remarkable. For just because I told the hypnotic subject the chair was not there, he did not see it ; but if I told a man in the normal state that the chair was not there, he would be all the more certain to see it. My remark would draw his attention to it. How can we explain the completely opposite result with the hypnotic subject ?

According to Binet and Féré, another factor must be added to the diversion of the attention ; before it can be attained a conviction that the chair is not there must be first established in the subject. Without this there would hardly be a negative hallucination.

It is a certain fact, observable without hypnosis, that such an established conviction favours negative hallucinations.

Let us suppose a man occupied with work in some place which is generally quiet, and where he does not expect noise ; let us suppose some noise is made ; the man will not perceive it. Yet he would have heard the same noise if he had known before-hand that it would be made. In just the same way he would fail to see a spark of light if he had the conviction beforehand that no light was there, but would perceive it if he expected it. The expectation of an effect is very favourable to its appear-ance. Consequently we have here another analogy between hypnotic and non-hypnotic processes.

We see, then, that under normal circumstances the conviction that a thing is not there makes it probable it will not be perceived. If we make use of this principle to explain negative hallucinations in hyp-nosis we must ask, How is the conviction that a thing is not there established in the subject ? We must come back to his subjective feelings of weakened will and dependence. A whole series of experiments which have convinced the subject of his weakness has generally been made before the negative hal-lucination succeeds. When he is once that everything really happens which the hypnotist says, he will believe him more and more. The hypnotist has generally made many suggestions of movement to him, and has induced in him the positive hallucina-tions of which I have given an explanation above. Consequently we cannot feel surprised that the sub-ject inclines to believe him when he is told by him that some object is not there.

Nevertheless these two factors, the diversion of the subject's attention and the conviction established in him, do not suffice to explain negative hallucinations. However firmly he believes the hypnotist, without such motives as would induce belief under normal circumstances (as Bentivegni rightly points out), this does not alone explain such mistakes of the sense

perceptions as are found in negative hallucinations.
A completely changed state of consciousness must be
added if we wish to understand negative hallucinations ; the dream-consciousness again, which helped
us to understand positive delusions of the senses.
For dream-consciousness is not only distinguished by
the reappearance of former memory pictures as hallucinations ; it is also characterized by the fact that
sense impressions which under normal circumstances
become feelings and perceptions induce in it no feeling or perception.   To recapitulate : there are three
factors for the production of negative hallucinations :
firstly, dream-consciousness ; secondly, the conviction established in the subject of the absence of an
object; and thirdly, the diversion of the attention
which results from this.

We can explain the analgesia of some hypnotic
subjects in a like manner.   It is known that an
expected pain is more acutely felt than an unexpected one.   When any one believes that the effect
of some stimulus will be painful he will feel the pain
much sooner than he would if he did not expect it
and believe in it.   We see this in operations ; the
subject feels much more pain when he expects the
stroke of the knife and sees it than when it takes him
unawares ; in the latter case he often feels hardly any
pain.   It is the same thing with analgesia in hypnosis.   I still doubt whether there is ever an entirely
spontaneous analgesia without suggestion, though
I have mentioned it above.   In any case analgesia is
more usually induced by suggestion.   Here again we
may take it that the hypnotic subject has been pre-
convinced by the repeated assertions and suggestions
of the hypnotist, and that he has in consequence an
unreasoning credulity.   If now the hypnotist firmly

17

insists upon the analgesia, the subject will soon
believe in and expect it, and this will greatly help
him to it.

The phenomena of the memory must now be considered. Such a derangement of the memory as
sometimes happens in hypnosis is certainly very
striking, though it is clear at once that we can find
many analogies in ordinary life. I need not, of
course, discuss those hypnotic states in which there is
no derangement of the memory.

But there are persons who, after waking from hypnosis, remember nothing of what has happened. It
is also a well-known fact that we forget certain events,
apart from hypnosis. We entirely forget certain mechanical actions, such as the winding of a watch. But
some things done with reflection and in perfect consciousness are occasionally forgotten. We have here,
then, an analogy to the forgetfulness of the hypnotic
subject. But these analogies by no means explain
the sudden and often nearly systematic forgetfulness
in hypnotic states. We studied this phenomenon
when discussing the memory before, and we also saw
that the subject in hypnosis remembered all the
events of preceding hypnoses, and of his waking life ;
we called this " double consciousness." This requires
special consideration. It is, indeed, a striking phenomenon that two complete and thoroughly separate
states of consciousness can be induced and distinguished in a human being; so that in one, the waking
life, the events of waking life only are remembered ;
and in the other, the hypnotic state, the events of
preceding hypnoses and of waking life. If we think
of the life of such a being as divided into several
periods, $a, b, c, d, e, f, g,$ in the periods $a, c, e, g,$ only

the events of those periods will be remembered, so
that in period *c* he will remember only what happened
in *a*, and in period *e* what happened in *a* and *c*. On
the other hand, in the periods *b, d, f,* both what has
happened in them and in *a, c, e,* will be remembered.
This is very remarkable, particularly when it happens
spontaneously, *i.e.,* without suggestion.

In order to explain this double consciousness I
must return to Max Dessoir's theory of the "Doppel
Ich," or double Ego ; I must, however, describe it
exactly before it can be applied to our subject.

Max Dessoir supposes, with Pierre Janet, that
human personality is a unity merely to our consciousness, but that it consists really of at least two clearly
distinguishable personalities, each held together by
its own chain of memories. He chooses several ways
of establishing this principle. According to him
many actions are done unconsciously, though of
mental origin. I do not notice many automatic
movements, *e.g.,* rubbing the hands when they are
cold, &c. The experiment made by Barkworth is
more complicated than this. He can add up long
rows of figures while carrying on a lively discussion,
without allowing his attention to be at all diverted
from the discussion. Recently some American investigators (Speir, Armstrong, Child) have brought forward
interesting statistics of unconscious cerebration. It is
shown that during this activity, though it goes on in
the lower consciousness, most people have a distinct
feeling of effort. If, for instance, one cannot recall
a name, and purposely refrains from trying to do so
in the hope that it will recur later, these statistics
show that there is still very frequently a certain sense
of effort.

This shows that, in the first place, there is an un-

conscious intelligence in men, as is seen in the rubbing
of the cold hands, and in the second place, that there
is an unconscious memory; for Barkworth, for example, must have at least two groups of figures in his
memory, to make a third out of them; he must retain
the third to add a fourth. But this chain of memory
is independent of the other chain, by means of which
he carries on the conversation (Max Dessoir). As.
according to Max Dessoir, consciousness and memory
are the two elements of personality, he supposes that
in the above-mentioned case of Barkworth there are
the elements of a second personality. The mental
processes which take place consciously to the man
are called the primary consciousness, and those which
go on without his knowledge the secondary consciousness; the action of both together is a state of double
consciousness, or "doubled consciousness" (Max
Dessoir). Thus in Barkworth's case the primary
consciousness carried on the conversation, while the
secondary one mechanically performed the addition.
It must of course be understood that we cannot
assume, as is done by some psychologists, that the
individuism is made up of several entirely separate
personalities, that, for instance, a gentleman whom we
usually know as Mr. M——, carries within him also
the personality of a Mr. S——. The double Ego must
not so be conceived, and if, as a few incline to do, it
is so conceived, we fall into danger of accepting an
absurd conception of human consciousness. For our
object the double Ego is only a diagram to indicate
the fact that psychic processes may go on within us,
unobserved, and often yielding no evidence of themselves except their results. This is, indeed, the
kernel of Max Dessoir's theory.

To prevent confusion it should be impressed on the reader that what has hitherto been habitually called consciousness will for the future be called primary consciousness. Generally speaking "consciousness" means the sum of subjectively perceived mental processes. We must now give it a wider meaning. Consciousness falls into two halves, primary and secondary, and the primary consciousness is consciousness in the older sense of the word.

In the case above mentioned both consciousnesses exist together, but they may, under certain circumstances, follow one another. Max Dessoir tells of a case in which a person took up his dream on a second night where he had left off on the first. Here, then, the dream-consciousness tended to form a new chain of memories. The same author puts the following case of Macario's with the last : A girl who was outraged during an attack of spontaneous somnambulism knew nothing about it when she woke, and only told her mother of what had happened in her next attack. Such cases occur under morbid pathological conditions (*cf.* p. 144).

These cases in dream and in morbid conditions show the two consciousnesses following one another as the Barkworth case showed them co-existing. Max Dessoir mentions other examples in support of his view, but I am unable to go into them here.

To return to hypnosis. We have now to explain the state of double consciousness. Max Dessoir thinks that hypnosis simply exhibits the hidden half of our mental life ; the part which is called secondary consciousness and which can occasionally be observed in ordinary life, or more plainly in pathological states, that hypnosis represents experimentally this part of life. According to Max Dessoir's theory, the condition of double consciousness is no absolutely new

phenomenon, but only the experimental representation
of a definite psychic relationship, such as may occasionally be observed even in normal persons. Whatever
we may think of this theory, Max Dessoir's explanations are none the less valuable for the consideration of the double consciousness in hypnosis.
It is not necessary for our purpose to generalize
this theory, as, though double consciousness is sometimes observed in hypnosis, it is by no means so
common as some authors suppose. Even if we
suppose that hypnosis is simply the demonstration
by experiment of the pre-existing double consciousness, the question of the causal connection between
the origin of hypnosis and this demonstration still
remains unanswered. Perhaps we may call in dream-
consciousness again ; it may be that it is induced by
the originating of hypnoses, and may complete the
secondary consciousness. Delbœuf, who by no means
accepts the sharp division of the primary and secondary consciousness, identifies the hypnotic phenomena
entirely with nightly dreams, as far as the subsequent
recollection is concerned. In this case we could explain the causal connection between the production
of hypnosis and the appearance of double consciousness in the same way as we explain sense delusions
by the experimental induction of dream-consciousness. I will not go into further details with regard
to the phenomena of memory during hypnosis, as I
have already mentioned many analogies in speaking
of the symptoms.

The post-hypnotic suggestions will occupy us a
little longer, because, in a certain sense, they can be
explained by analogy. For this purpose I will choose
some action induced by post-hypnotic suggestion, and
will suppose it to be a case of hypnosis without subsequent loss of memory.

Here is an analogous case in waking life. I give a letter to X., who has called on me, and ask him to post it on his way home, if he passes a letter-box. This he does.

I now give exactly the same commission to Y., who is in a hypnotic state, without subsequent loss of memory.

In both cases my commission is executed. Now the question is, What is the difference between the two cases? In the case of Y., one circumstance may strike us, *i.e.*, that he did the act without, or perhaps against, his will.

The fact that Y. posted the letter *without* willing to do so does not distinguish his case from X.'s. X. walked home with Z. and talked all the way. He passed a pillar-box, and though he continued to talk, and apparently did not notice the box, he mechanically threw the letter into it. Later it occurred to him that he had the letter to post; he had a faint recollection of having done it. He could, however, convince himself of the fact by feeling in his pocket for the letter. We see, then, that he executed the commission without conscious will.

It would be more striking if X. should do some such action *against* his will. In the action described this was not the case. He would not have executed the commission if his will had not consented. Also, he would have remembered the action if his will had opposed it. There must always be consciousness when the will is exerted to prevent something. There must be an idea of the action to be performed. What is striking in post-hypnotic suggestion is exactly the fact that it is carried out against the will, in which case the subject of course knows what is to be done, and has an idea of it. It is this idea which causes a post-hypnotic action to be carried out in spite of the will.

The question now is whether we can find an analogy to this in waking life, whether an idea can in this case cause a motor or other effect in spite of the will. The answer must be, "Very commonly."

We saw, when talking of suggestion in the waking state, that an idea is sometimes enough to cause an action or a particular state in spite of the will. This is a common occurrence. We will suppose that A. has lost a dear relation. A. is in consequence sad and depressed, and cannot refrain from tears. Months pass, and he grows calm; but when the anniversary of the death arrives he falls again into the same state of mental excitement and tears, which he cannot conquer. The vivid idea has been enough to throw him, against his will, into a certain state.

A person who stammers is in the same case. Alone at home he can speak quite well, but a stranger comes in and he begins to stammer. He stammers because he thought he should stammer, and his will is powerless both over the thought and the stammering. We see the same sort of thing constantly, and certain states of illness are induced merely by a vivid expectation of them; they then come on in spite of the will. Accordingly it is not astonishing that a post-hypnotic suggestion should succeed against the subject's will.

The post-hypnotic movements and actions carried out in spite of the will—or, to speak more exactly, in spite of the wish—have a great likeness to the instinctive movements well known in Psychology, which are often made to satisfy a pleasure which follows from the act. Such instinctive movements are entirely independent of the will; they take place in spite of the wish. For example, the raising of the hand to ward off danger is an instinctive movement (Wundt). Here there may very well be an idea of the movement, though deeper mental processes compel its execution, as in many cases of post-hypnotic suggestion carried out in spite of the will. It is the same thing in cases of so-called impulsive mania. The patients act without clear ideas of their motives. Their actions appear to be impelled by instinct though they are consciously carried out (Schüle).

I have now considered why post-hypnotic suggestions are carried out without, or in spite of, the will. I supposed a case in which the subject remembered the order given him in hypnosis after he woke; *i.e.*, I considered only those cases in which there was no loss of memory in waking. It is a more enigmatic question, why post-hypnotic suggestions are carried out when there is loss of memory after waking, and the subject in consequence is apparently unconscious of having received the command.

For explanation let us return to the case of waking life, where X. was to post a letter. I point out that X. did not keep the request continually in his consciousness, and that he even apparently posted the letter unconsciously; yet he would not have performed the action at all if he had not really remembered my request.

It is the same in post-hypnotic suggestion. It really remains in the memory, and the unconsciousness is only apparent. All post-hypnotic suggestions are merely apparently forgotten between waking and fulfilment. To prove this I must digress a little and go back to the primary consciousness, which is the name given to our subjective mentally perceived processes, while the unperceived ones are called the secondary consciousness.

The state of the primary consciousness is not uniform, but, on the contrary, subject to constant changes. In one period we are conscious of ideas which are wanting in others. One period comprises more than another. Now, if we call the sum of mental processes perceived in one state a sphere of consciousness, we may suppose a number of such spheres. But not to complicate the subject too much, we will suppose two spheres, which will answer our purpose.

We saw, when discussing the memory, that the hypnotic subject who forgot the events of hypnosis in waking life remembered them in later hypnosis. But he remembered the events of waking life also in hypnosis, though in waking life he was only conscious of the events of that life. We have, then, two different spheres of consciousness here: one comprises the events of hypnosis and of waking life, the other only those of waking life. They follow one another.

During waking life there are only memory pictures of this life in the primary consciousness; in the secondary consciousness there are memory pictures of the hypnotic state, *i.e.*, the impressions of hypnosis are received, but do not rise into the primary consciousness. But it must not be thought that the two consciousnesses are completely separated. Impressions made on the secondary consciousness occasionally rise to the primary. Upon this fact depends the restoration of memory through association of ideas, spoken of on p. 141 It can also be proved that the impressions of hypnosis by no means disappear in waking life, but are really firmly established in the brain.

To prove this I must digress again, and mention automatic writing. I owe my knowledge of this to Dr. Max Dessoir, whom I again thank for his unselfish and genuinely scientific help in the writing of this book. This automatic writing is of great interest and importance. It has been also observed among uncivilized peoples (Doolittle, Bastian).

I have had frequent occasion to speak of automatic movements and actions. To prevent confusion of ideas it should be expressly mentioned that I do not mean here by automatic movements, those so called by Liébeault and Bernheim, which Max Dessoir more justly calls continued movements (*cf.* p. 82). By automatic movements I here mean those of which we are unconscious at the moment they are made, though they show all the symptoms of a mental causation. When I walk my movements are nearly always automatic; I walk without being conscious of making the individual movements.

With regard to automatic writing, it should be mentioned that there are men who habitually move their fingers on the table while they are talking or thinking. When such people take a pencil in their hands they make all sorts of scribbled marks without observing it, while they are thinking of other things. This scribbling may be regarded as the beginning of automatic writing. It may take a certain rational form. Schiller says that when reflecting he has often covered whole sheets of paper with little horses (Max Dessoir). Other people automatically write letters and words, and this process is called automatic writing ; it is evidently guided by a species of intelligence, as without it no rational words could be written. But this intelligence resides in the writer, though it may not be conscious in the ordinary sense of the word ; it is the secondary consciousness, which carries on movements and actions as does the primary consciousness, although the person concerned does not remark them. In any case the intelligence is innate in the person, and is part of him, and not an external force or spirit, as the spiritualists, who are also acquainted with it, and call it mediumistic writing, say it is.

I ask the reader to follow me through some experiments with automatic writing. I give a person who is not in hypnosis a pen or pencil and ask him to answer some question in writing—for example, what he had for dinner yesterday ; he is, however, to leave his hand passive and not write on purpose ; at the same time I put the point of the pencil on paper. It would not be strange that the person should write down something he is thinking of. It would remind us of the experiments in thought-reading described (p. 68). The person thinks of roast veal and the hand makes corresponding movements. But the process becomes rather different when I talk quietly to the writer meanwhile. I speak of the theatre, the weather, &c.; in the meantime the hand writes "roast veal." It appears that this was yesterday's dinner. In this case the hand wrote without concentration of thought on the writer's part; and this is already different from the usual thought-reading. A rational and true answer has been given to a direct question while a conversation was being carried on. As the writing was not noticed it follows that it was automatic. This automatic writing is certainly striking.

Now, though the writer did not know he was writing, he knew the fact which he unconsciously wrote down; *i.e.*, he knew that he had had roast veal for dinner yesterday. But there are also persons who will answer questions through automatic writing about things they do not know at all, *e.g.*, when somebody is asked what he had for dinner every day last week, he will write down the whole list of dishes, though he does not know them himself, *i.e.*, though they are not in his primary consciousness.

Such experiments are very good when made in hypnosis, and sense delusions, especially the negative ones, are made more intelligible by them, as was pointed out on p. 200. I suggest to X., in hypnosis, that A. and B., who are really present, have gone away. X. ceases entirely to respond to A. and B.; he neither hears nor sees them. When I ask him who is present he says, "Only you and I"; upon which I give him a pencil and paper and command him to answer the question in writing. He writes, "Dr. Moll, Mr. A., Mr. B., and myself." Consequently he has answered the question intelligently, without knowing that he is writing. This shows that A. and B. were really perceived, but that X. was unconscious of the perception.

We will now return to the starting-point of our discussion.

By means of automatic writing it can be proved that the impressions of hypnosis are really firmly lodged in the brain; Gurney, F. Myers, and Pierre Janet have made a series of very good experiments on this point. X., for example, is waked from hypnosis and remembers nothing that has happened ; but when he is ordered to write automatically what was said to him he does it. Now, as he could not tell these things, and they are not to be found in the primary consciousness, these experiments in automatic writing prove that the impressions exist all the same. They disclose themselves in the automatic writing.

We have now to show why the post-hypnotic suggestion is carried out in spite of loss of memory. We have seen that this loss of memory only exists so far that the hypnotic events and the post-hypnotic suggestion are to be found in the secondary consciousness only. In any case, as I have shown, the loss of memory is only apparent, and the post-hypnotic suggestion is lodged in the secondary consciousness. And this, as I have also shown by automatic writing, acts with a certain intelligence, and without confusion in its proper chain of thought.

The foregoing explanations show, firstly, why a post-hypnotic suggestion is carried out without the will or in spite of it ; and, secondly, why it is carried out in spite of the apparent forgetting of the command. A further question is this—Why is a post-hypnotic suggestion carried out at the right moment? The answer will differ according to the manner in which the moment for the execution of the suggestion is decided. We already know (p. 159) that the moment may be appointed in numerous ways ; either by a concrete external sign—*e.g.*, the striking of the clock—or by fixing an abstract period, or by counting signals or days.

In the case of the striking clock we shall find no new mental law ; we find the same process quite com-

monly in normal life, it is a result of the association
of ideas. The striking of the clock often reminds us
of something we wanted to do at that particular time.

The same thing happens when we tie a knot in our
handkerchiefs to remind ourselves of something. It
occurs to me that I must write a letter to-morrow ; I
make a knot in my handkerchief to remind myself of
it. The knot and the letter are then associated in my
consciousness, and when I see the knot the idea of the
letter rises from my secondary into my primary consciousness. Memory is caused by association of ideas.
Now we see the same thing in the example of post-
hypnotic suggestion on p. 159. The striking of the
clock made the subject remember to take the water-
bottle and walk up and down with it. This process
of association is so powerful that it often takes effect
even when the suggestion is not punctually carried out.

I hypnotize a man on Saturday and tell him, "When
you come in on Tuesday I shall cough three times ;
you will then give me your hand and remark, ' That is
too stupid.' " The man does not come till Thursday,
but the suggestion is carried out, merely because I
cough.

We will take the second case where an abstract
period of time was given instead of a definite sign.
Here the idea lay in the secondary consciousness till
it resulted in the corresponding action. An approximate but inexact calculation took place in the
secondary consciousness.

For this also many analogies may be found in
ordinary life. I say to A., "Remind me in an hour
to write a letter." A. is busy, and thinks no more of
the letter, but nevertheless reminds me of it after
some time. But as he has not looked at the clock, he
is not punctual : the case is quite analogous to post-

hypnotic suggestion, where there is generally no perfect punctuality.

Some people suppose that in the few cases of striking punctuality, some unconscious calculation of time takes place, like the unconscious regularity of our pulse and breathing. However that may be, there are certain persons who can calculate time with some exactitude when they are awake, and others can do the same in sleep ; they can wake themselves at a definite time without hearing the clock strike. In any case it is unnecessary to suppose that hypnotic subjects possess a peculiar faculty for fixing time which others do not. Delbœuf, also, is not led to this conclusion by his experiments. He made post-hypnotic suggestions to various persons, by telling them to perform a certain act after so many minutes, say a thousand minutes. In many cases, even with persons who were otherwise not able to estimate time rightly, striking punctuality was shown.

According to Child, there are many people who can voluntarily awake from their usual sleep at any hour they please. Brandis also remarked long ago that no one who observes himself can fail to recognize this power of noting time during sleep.

The older mesmerists, Nasse and Eschenmayer for example, made investigations about this faculty of somnambulic subjects for exactly reckoning time. The ancient Hindoos studied it industriously. This subjective faculty for calculating time is sometimes called the mental clock (*Kopfuhr*) (Du Prel).

The third way of fixing time is by counting signals or days (*cf.* p. 159). Gurney's explanation of this is grounded on the division of the consciousness into primary and secondary, which I have explained above. While the primary consciousness is busy talking to the experimenter the secondary consciousness works on independently. It remembers the command and

counts the signals given ; *e.g.*, the shuffling of feet, &c.
When the tenth signal is given the suggestion is
carried out, just as other suggestions are carried out at
an appointed signal (*cf.* the example on p. 159).

Gurney endeavours to explain many long-deferred
suggestions in just the same way. As we have seen,
in these also the execution of the suggestion may
be ordered at the end of a series of days and weeks
instead of on a definite date (p. 159). This may be
explained in two ways. Perhaps the subject cal-
culates the date after he has been told the number
of days or weeks. Against this there is the fact that
the subjects, when hypnotized in the intervening time,
cannot tell the date. On this account Gurney supposes an action of the secondary consciousness in
such cases. He thinks that the subject counts the
days in his secondary consciousness just as we consciously count days in waking life, and thus is able
to carry out the suggestion. He thinks this all the
more likely because when the subjects are hypnotized
in the intervening time, they can count the days
which have elapsed, and are to elapse, before the
suggestion is carried out, though they do not know
the exact date.

These different spheres of consciousness enable us
to better understand those post-hypnotic suggestions
which are carried out in a state of complete loss
of memory ; for the suggested command is always
accepted, even when the subject remembers nothing
about it subsequently. The punctual execution of
such a command is only comprehensible if, besides
the primary consciousness, a secondary consciousness
works intelligently in us.

The preceding explanations are chiefly intended
to approximate as much as possible post-hypnotic

suggestion to certain habitual occurrences. There is no question of a complete identification of them; for many post-hypnotic suggestions can apparently be distinguished from all known processes of waking life in two ways. The subject does not remember the command when the hypnosis is over; he is apparently unconscious of the idea of executing it; if he is spoken to about it after waking the idea cannot be recalled to his mind; and yet, in spite of this, it arises at the time fixed. We forget much in ordinary life also; but the recollection of a thing at a certain moment, which no hints or efforts can recall in the intermediate time, appears to me to be the first prerogative of many post-hypnotic suggestions; a second is that it is not the command itself but the idea of its execution which is remembered.

And yet even these striking phenomena are by no means an absolute prerogative of hypnosis. We are reminded, in the first place, of those dominant ideas which are often pathological, and whose origin is for the most part unknown (Bentivegni). These ideas sometimes impel to actions (Krafft-Ebing) which the person concerned becomes under some circumstances powerless to control. Sometimes the origin of the idea is not to be discovered by questions or by any other means. If we hold fast to the principle of Locke, " *Nil est in intellectu, quod non prius fuerit in sensu,*" we shall be obliged to suppose that some external event has formerly influenced the mind of the person concerned, but that the event itself is forgotten. None the less, it has an effect, which sometimes takes the form of a dominant idea and sometimes of an action caused by it (murder, suicide, incendiarism, &c.) (Krafft-Ebing). Here, exactly as in post-hypnotic suggestion, the external prompt-

ing impression is forgotten in the intervening time,
as well as at the moment when the idea arises or the
action is carried out.

But I think that it is not only under pathological
conditions that some externally induced idea influences our actions, feelings, &c., without our being
able by any means to remember how the idea was,
so to speak, implanted in us. Let us suppose that
a child two or three years old is often in the society
of A. and B ; A. is kind and gentle, B hard and
unkind, so that the child gradually learns to like
A. and dislike B. Let us suppose that the child sees
neither for a long time ; nevertheless when it does
it will still like A. and dislike B. The child, who
is now several years older, will not know its own
reasons ; it will not remember the former conduct
of A. and B. ; no questions will bring this back to
its memory ; yet the effect of the old impressions
remains, and shows itself in the child's behaviour
to A. and B. It is certain that the same thing
happens after childhood. Sharp-sighted observers
think it likely that a man may owe his preference
for a particular profession—painting, for example—
to some childish impression, such as dabbling with
colours ; in this case also the early impression is forgotten by the adult.

Besides, this occurrence is by no means confined
to childhood. We are often influenced by unimportant expressions we have heard, though later
we cannot trace back the effect to its cause. Our
conduct with regard to persons, circumstances, and
things is very often the effect of early unconscious
impressions.

We now know that those hypnotic states in which
there is subsequent loss of memory are by no means

unconscious states, but that the impressions received are at the most only sub-conscious. Therefore the fact that the impressions received in hypnosis influence the waking conduct of the subject, though he has forgotten them, need no longer be an enigma to us. Like the waking people in the examples given, he will rather fully assimilate the external influence, will forget it, and act as if spontaneously; or he will yield to an impulse, as in the cases of a dominant idea, without being conscious of its external cause.

I have hitherto spoken only of post-hypnotic movements and actions, and have endeavoured to explain the most important phenomena by means of analogy. I have still a few words to say about post-hypnotic sense delusions, which are less easy to explain. It is true that those which occur in a fresh hypnosis hardly present any substantial difficulty. We have seen that the subsequent loss of memory is only apparent, and that consequently the idea remains in the consciousness, though only in the secondary consciousness. Consequently it is not surprising that the suggested idea should at an appointed time transform itself into a sense delusion in a fresh hypnosis, which fresh hypnosis comes on through association when the idea reappears; we must then explain the sense delusion by means of the dream-consciousness, as I have shown above.

It is quite another thing when the sense delusion appears without a new hypnosis. For example, I say to some one in hypnosis, "When I cough after you wake, you will see a pigeon sitting on the table; you will remain thoroughly awake." The suggestion takes effect; the subject sees a pigeon where no pigeon is; but it is impossible to make him accept a further suggestion. That one point excepted, he seems perfectly normal. Whether, in spite of this, the total mental state of such people is really normal, will be discussed when we come to the legal side of the question. Bentivegni speaks very clearly on this point. Now, how can we explain this particular sense delusion? We can hardly consider the dream-consciousness its cause, as this apparently is not present while the suggestion is taking effect. Eduard von Hartmann, however, believes that dream-consciousness always co-exists with waking consciousness. But we find like occurrences under different circumstances. I do not mention the hallucinations of insane persons, because it is exactly the addition of other disorders to their sense delusions which distinguishes them from the above case. But we find the same kind of sense delusions under other circumstances in persons who for some reason or other "are disinclined to correct the creations of their own imagination," as Krafft-Ebing puts it. This author mentions the hallucinations of several famous men— the case of Socrates and his Dæmon, and Luther, who threw an inkstand at the devil. Statistical investigations on hallucinations among normal persons have lately been carried on by the English Society for Psychical Research. These results were presented by Sidgwick at the Congress of Experimental Psychology in London, and are published in full in the Proceedings of the Society for 1894; they are discussed by Parish in his work on *Hallucinations and Illusions*. Parish holds that hallucinations in themselves are no indication of disease, but that usually when they are present an abnormal psychic state may be demonstrated. Such delusions are

often caused by strong expectant attention, of
which I have already spoken. This is very clearly
seen in spiritualistic manifestations, which may be
ascribed in great part to hallucinations of the spectators, who think they see spirits or other things
in consequence of abnormal processes in their own
brain. Eduard v. Hartmann has carefully discussed
the theory of hallucination in spiritualism, though
he explains the origin of the hallucinations in a
peculiar manner. In any case there are persons who
have hallucinations of sight, hearing, &c., without
being hypnotized ; they result from a particular
mental state which in some cases may be called a
state of expectation. It thus appears that the induction of sense delusions by means of post-hypnotic
suggestion brings about a mental state when the idea
reappears, which has a great resemblance to this state
of expectation, and is even perhaps identical with
it. In this way, perhaps, these cases of sense delusion
may be classed with facts with which we have long
been acquainted.

Several attempts have been made to explain hypnosis from the point of view of psychology ; but their
common defect is, that they try to explain too many
different phenomena by attention, the change in
which is most striking during hypnosis. I have
formerly tried to explain hypnotic phenomena in a
like manner. As the different theories referring to
this are often met with, I shall develop them further
in what follows. The ensuing explanations are not
in contradiction with what has been already said, but
are, on the contrary, supplemented by it, particularly
by a careful consideration of the dream-consciousness.

Susceptibility to suggestion is the chief phenomenon
of hypnosis. We have seen how easily a hypnotic
suggestion is carried out. The externally suggested
idea of a movement induces the movement, the idea
of an object causes a corresponding sense hallucination. However strange and paradoxical the phenomena of hypnosis may appear to us at first sight,
we may be sure that there is no absolute difference
between hypnotic and non-hypnotic states. Psychology has lately shown that a certain degree of susceptibility to suggestion is normal. If A. tells B.
to lift his arm B. is inclined to do it, though he probably controls the impulse by his own will. The
following example may make this clearer. When
two people look at each other they both often begin
to laugh, if one assures the other he is going to
laugh. But the idea of laughter is a necessary condition for its appearance, and the stronger the idea
the quicker will laughter ensue. We seek to prevent
the laughter by arousing in ourselves the contrary
idea. Probably many of my readers have made the
following observation in their own cases, as I have
in myself: when I feel inclined to laugh I can prevent it by causing myself some physical pain, *e.g.*,
by pricking myself with a needle. The pain drives
away the idea of laughter, and so prevents it. This
is an example of the way in which laughter may
be prevented by arousing an opposing idea.

Now it appears that this occurs often in ordinary
life; the idea of a movement results in a movement
(Johannes Müller), if it is not opposed by a contrary
idea. The idea of a movement called up in a subject
in or out of hypnosis has a tendency to induce the
movement. But in waking life this idea is made
ineffectual by the voluntary idea of the subject that
he will prevent the suggested movement; the hypno-

tized subject cannot do this. Thus in hypnosis certain ideas are inhibited, and even the inhibitory ideas can be inhibited. We have to thank Heidenhain for having first pointed out the importance of inhibitory processes in hypnosis. The case is of course the same with suggested paralyses. Here the idea of inability to move is suggested. In ordinary life we can oppose this and make it ineffectual by means of voluntarily produced opposing ideas ; but in hypnosis the suggested idea cannot be supplanted by the voluntary one, and in consequence the idea of inability to move transforms itself into a real inability.

Let us see if the process in sense delusions can be looked at in the same light. To my mind it is possible. When we hear some one say, "There is a dog," we are inclined to believe it, as I have said above. Our sense perceptions, feelings, and memory pictures prevent the suggested idea becoming a perception, so that we decline to believe in the dog. But in hypnosis the sense impressions do not change into feelings, except such external impressions as the experimenter allows to change into conscious sense ideas ; consequently the memory pictures in hypnosis do not follow their normal course and are not justly estimated. The normal course is interfered with. This limitation of the normal course of the ideas allows the idea of the dog to become a perception because the idea cannot be corrected. It is the same with negative hallucinations, which we may consider as caused by the inability of the normal course of ideas to correct the suggestion.

We may, then, consider every hypnosis as a state in which the normal course of the ideas is inhibited. It matters not whether the ideas have to do with movements, or with sense impressions. We have seen that their normal course is always inhibited. In particular, the subject is unable to control the external ideas or to put forward his own ; the external ones dominate his consciousness. Psychologically speaking, what we mean by attention is the power of fixing certain ideas in the mind and of working with them. Consequently we may say that there is an alteration of attention in hypnosis.

But attention may be either spontaneous or reflex (Ed. v. Hartmann). When by an act of will we choose one of several ideas and fix our attention upon it, this is spontaneous attention ; but when one idea among several gets the upper hand through its intensity or for some other reason, and thus represses other ideas, and draws exclusive attention upon itself, this is reflex attention.

Now it is only spontaneous attention which is altered in hypnosis, *i.e.*, the subject's ability voluntarily to prefer one idea to another is interfered with, while reflex attention is undisturbed, and it is through this last that a suggested idea, the choice of which has not, however, been left to the subject, comes into prominence. Many investigators conceive hypnotism in this way. The works of Durand de Gros, Liébeault, and more lately of Beard, Richet, Schneider, Wundt, and Bentivegni, are in the main directed to this point, as latterly were Braid's also.

We may hope besides that further investigations in numerical[1] psychology will throw light upon the state of the attention in hypnosis. Measurements of the time of reaction should be the chief point considered ; they have hitherto been undertaken in insufficient

---

[1] In Max Dessoir's classification of psychology he calls that part which occupies itself with calculating the time of reaction, &c., " numerical psychology."

number. By reaction-time we mean the time that elapses between the moment of making a sense impression, and the moment when the impression manifests itself by some external sign (Wundt). It is known that a number of different processes take place in the consciousness during the time of reaction. I shall the less enter into them, that the researches which have hitherto been made into the time of reaction during hypnosis have given contradictory results. Marie and Azoulay have measured the time of reaction of suggested sense delusions in hypnosis ; they found it longer than when the object was a real one. Perhaps this is because the points of recognition (*points de repère*) have to arouse the suggested picture [1] before it can be received. The time of reaction, according to my experience, may last so long—to return to the experiment with the photographs on p. 116—that we might even speak of a search for the picture. The subject looks till he finds the points of recognition, which at once recall the picture to his memory. This search may be united with a dim consciousness on the part of the hypnotic that the whole thing is a delusion. It is quite a mistake to think this search a sign of fraud.

Other experimenters have examined the time of reaction for real objects. Stanley Hall found that for real objects it was considerably shortened in hypnosis. He found before hypnosis, 0·328 seconds ; during hypnosis, 0·193 seconds ; half an hour after, 0·348 seconds. The time of reaction during hypnosis is thus sensibly diminished here ; but William James's experiments have not confirmed Stanley Hall's. He

[1] I am doubtful if in this case we ought to talk of time of reaction, as this expression is generally used only with regard to perceptions of real objects.

nearly always found an increase of the time of reaction during hypnosis, sometimes to an important extent. He gives this as the average on one occasion : before hypnosis, o˙282 seconds ; during hypnosis as much as o˙546 seconds ; after hypnosis, o˙166 seconds. But as there are many contradictions in James's different experiments, no conclusion can be drawn. He himself believes that the contradictions are to be ascribed to the fact that so many different states are included in hypnosis, and that we should be careful not to generalize from single observations. Beaunis, who has also made these experiments, is just as cautious. The only conclusion he draws from his partly contradictory results is, that the time of reaction in hypnosis may be shortened by suggestion. Similar results are given by the investigations of Henika, Worotynski, and Bechterew. These observers also found a lengthening of reaction-time in hypnosis as compared with the waking condition.

It should be already clear from all the foregoing explanations that the phenomena of hypnosis have many more points of contact with ordinary life than would be concluded from the discussions and articles written to satisfy a mere longing for sensation. Some of the phenomena, *e.g.*, motion without will, only appear mysterious on the most superficial observation, for we have seen that an idea of a movement is enough to cause a movement without an act of will. The explanations could only be given in outline, not to lengthen the chapter too much, but they have to a great extent approximated hypnosis to waking life, as well as to the nightly state of dream. The thoughtful reader will have recognized that phenomena which were often considered the prerogative of hypnosis, *e.g.*, the movements without will, appear spontaneously in ordinary life. I will, therefore, here express my conviction that all good observers may find "hypnotic phenomena" in daily life. They result spontaneously from a chance concurrence of the necessary conditions. There are further analogies to hypnosis which can easily be developed out of the preceding discussions, and which show us that *many symptoms of hypnosis often appear spontaneously in ordinary life*, or, what is the same thing, that ordinary life often displays phenomena, which we find again in hypnosis. Hypnosis, or at least many hypnotic states, is merely a means of easily and safely producing symptoms which, under other circumstances, are not easy to produce because all the necessary favourable conditions do not concur at the same time.

An explanation of one side of hypnosis, *i.e.*, the psychological, has already been given in vart, and can in part be deferred for a time. But I do not believe that every one will be content with an explanation in this sense of the word. Thus Wundt has referred to the defects in the attempts at psychological explanation hitherto offered. He points out that the various analogies between hypnosis and waking life which I have emphasised, certainly exist, and show that hypnosis is a less strange phenomenon than was imagined, but that they do not suffice to explain it. He remarks, not without justice, that my exposition brings out the actual psychological condition of hypnosis, especially the one-sided concentration of passive attention, or, as Wundt now prefers to call it, the contraction of consciousness; but that the main point lies in the question why this contraction

comes about, and that this explanation psychology
has not yet been able to offer. Wundt believes that
psychology is not to-day able to offer any explanation
without the aid of physiology. The physiologists
also make very definite demands. They want an
answer to the following questions: 1. What is the
state of the central nervous system and the other
organs during hypnosis? 2. What is the causal
connection between this state and the phenomena of
hypnosis? 3. What is the causal connection between
this state and the methods which induce hypnosis and
put an end to it?

Unluckily the physiology of the nervous system
has been built up on such a weak foundation that
we can expect no explanation from it at present, or
perhaps, as Leixner thinks, for ever. In spite of
the great progress which physiology has made, we
must admit to ourselves that we know much less
about the psychical functions of the different elements of the brain than would appear from our
physiological text-books. The hypnotic experiments
of which I have spoken will not help us to reach our
goal. However carefully such experiments may be
made, it would be very daring to draw conclusions
from them about mental action in men. Heidenhain
believes that hypnosis may be explained by means of
experiments on animals, since animals can be hypnotized. But we cannot hope much when we remember
that hypnotism is essentially a psychical process.
The investigation of mental processes may, as we
have seen, be undertaken in two ways—(1) by
observing indviduals, and (2) by calling the subject's
memory to our aid. This last could not be done in
the case of animals. But any observation of animals
must be very elementary ; we can very seldom under-

stand the processes of their consciousness. For these reasons I at present believe that experiments with animals will give us very little help. We may, further, be perfectly sure that the successful electrical stimulation of any portion of the brain does not prove that an act of will originates in that spot. Heidenhain and Bubhoff have made a number of experiments in electrical stimulation of the cortex of the brain on dogs poisoned by morphia. But when these authors draw conclusions about the action of will in men from such experiments, I must pronounce them mistaken till it can be proved that the impulse of the will is an electrical stimulation. For the above reasons I consider Heidenhain's comparison of these experiments on dogs with hypnotic experiments on human beings too hazardous; no conclusion can be drawn from them.

The attempt to give a physiological explanation of hypnotism on the foundation of our present knowledge of physiology has often been made.

Heidenhain must here be mentioned first, though I believe that Heidenhain's theory is built up on a mistaken premiss. Heidenhain supposes that the cause of the hypnotic state is an inhibition of the action of the ganglion cells of the cerebral cortex, induced by continuous weak stimulation of certain nerves. Heidenhain thinks this inhibition is analogous to reflex paralyses, as in these also the functions of the ganglion cells are impaired by peripheral stimuli.

But even if we take the inhibition of the action of the ganglion cells for granted, Heidenhain's theory does not explain the connection between this and the means used to induce hypnosis. For (1), according to the views of most authors, mere fixed attention, apart from an idea or representation, will not induce hypnosis; (2) in any case there would be no causal connection here between the purely psychical methods and hypnosis.

Besides this, Heidenhain starts from a mistaken premiss when he supposes an inhibition of the action of the cerebral ganglion cells. He concludes this inhibition from the lowered state of consciousness during hypnosis. But consciousness expresses itself in many ways during hypnosis. The processes of consciousness seem merely to be concentrated on one point, which is removable at the experimenter's pleasure. Heidenhain maintains, like Despine, that the subject is not conscious of the external stimuli. This erroneous view has lately been taken by several physiologists; *e.g.*, by Landois. Heidenhain was led to take it by his almost exclusive observation of the movements of imitation. He supposed that the subject received a sense impression of a movement and copied it, though it did not result in a conscious idea (as in fascination). From what does Heidenhain conclude that the sense impression was unconscious? From the subsequent loss of memory? But he says himself that the subjects often remember what has happened when some hint is given them. Even when this is not the case, loss of memory does not prove that we have to do with an unconscious movement (Forel). Besides, the subjects generally remember in the hypnosis the imitative movements they have made; they remember them also in later hypnoses, and finally, a suggestion made during the hypnosis will cause subsequent memory.

In 1880, when Heidenhain declared his views about the imitative movements, O. Rosenbach explained that the processes were certainly mental, and not, as Heidenhain thought, unconscious physical reflexes. Unfortunately Rosenbach did not at that time explain his own views in detail. Berger and others agreed much later that these processes were mental. I also was enabled to study the imitative movements. They only take place when the hypnotic subject is conscious of them, and knows that he is intended to make them. If they were unconscious reflexes, the subjects would imitate any person's movements. But they only imitate the one person who exists for them, *i.e.*, the experimenter, and only him when they know they are intended to do so. A clear idea of the movements to be made is the first condition. I do not contest that when such experiments are often made, the imitation may not become mechanical in later hypnoses, as happens in waking life. However, at first a clear idea is necessary ; but we regard the cerebral cortex as the seat of ideas, and there is no reason for placing them in another part of the brain in hypnosis ; so that there can be no doubt of the inaction of the cerebral cortex. Forel, who is one of the greatest authorities on the brain, also holds this view. But perhaps there are mental processes in the subcortical brain-centres during waking life, about whose extent we know nothing. We know just as little whether, or in what degree, the cortex takes part in unconscious activity. In his very careful work, *Die Mehrheit geistiger Personlichkeiten in einem Individuum*, Landmann attempts to localize the processes of hypnosis in various regions of the brain. His work loses in value, however, because he makes undemonstrated assumptions in favour of his views. In any case there is no need to suppose that mental processes in hypnosis take place in another part of the brain than in waking life.

For these reasons I recur to the comparison between hypnosis and the state of Flourens'[1] pigeon when its brain was removed. It sat quite still unless it was touched, when it flew, ran, &c. But some external impulse, some mechanical stimulus probably unaccompanied by an idea, was necessary. For this reason all pigeons behave alike under the circumstances. It is otherwise with the hypnotic subject. He sees the movement he is to imitate; but the stimulus is only effectual when he knows he is to make the movement; if he has seen that another subject did not imitate the movement he also does not do it, because he does not understand the stimulus as a command. It is true that a subject often continues to walk forward automatically when he has once been set going. But this does not prove the inactivity of the cerebral cortex, for he goes on when he believes he is intended to go on; if he continues to take steps automatically, he does it as we do it in waking life; once moving, we go on, paying no attention to our separate steps. This phenomenon, consequently, is no reason for supposing that the cerebrum is less active in hypnosis than out of it. I will take this opportunity to remark that partially paralyzed persons whom I hypnotized, and in whom the *capsula interna* had been injured by a fit of apoplexy, made no imitative movements in hypnosis with the paralyzed side, any more than out of hypnosis. But in this case exactly that part was excluded in which we place the conscious ideas of movement, *i.e.*, the cerebral cortex; the centres which cause the unconscious reflexes were not excluded. As, however,

---

[1] Flourens experimented on pigeons, whose cerebrum he had removed. Untouched they remained quiet, but when excited they made all sorts of movements, as if to walk, fly, &c.

there were no imitative movements, this shows that without that part of the brain in which ideas are produced, no imitative movement takes place. None the less, I should as yet hesitate to say that Heidenhain's theory of the inhibition of the cortex was false. I wished only to prove that his reasons do not justify it. I thought these explanations all the more necessary as Heidenhain's supposition that the hypnotic subject is influenced by unconscious sense impression is often accepted. Even such a prominent authority on mental diseases as Mendel has been led astray by this. It is the cause of the mistaken views taken of suggestion, the chief phenomenon of hypnosis. *There is no suggestion without consciousness.* It makes no difference whether the suggestion is made through imitation (imitative automatism) or by a command (the commanded automatism of Heidenhain) (Max Dessoir). I likewise think Bernheim altogether mistaken when he compares certain functions, such as breathing and the action of the heart, which we assume to occur without mental action, to the phenomena of suggestion.

My reasons for not completely rejecting this opinion of Heidenhain on the inhibition of the cerebral cortex are as follows. Although single ideas, single processes of consciousness, are not absent in hypnosis, yet the influence of the will upon their course is limited. According to the present views of physiology the cause of this absence of the power of the will must be sought in a functional disorder of the cerebral cortex.

Cullerre, supported by Ferrier's experiments, thinks there is a functional disturbance in the front half of the cerebral cortex during hypnosis. He thinks that though this is not the seat of the motor centres, the centres here have a regulating influence on the motor

19

centres, but that this influence is removed in hypnosis.

Others do not try to localize the hypnotic subject's
loss of will. Dr. J. Hughes Bennett, who, as Preyer
tells us, put forward a very interesting physiological
theory as early as 1851, is one of these. He recognized more clearly than many present investigators
that it is not the genesis of separate ideas which is
prevented in hypnosis, but the voluntary synthesis of
them. And as the ideas originated in the ganglion
cells, Bennett supposed a functional disturbance during
hypnosis in the nerve fibres which connect them. We
know that these nerve fibres are called the fibres of
association.

Jendrássik takes somewhat the same view at the
present day. At least he tries to account for hypnosis by a disturbance of the nerve fibres of association.

Other investigators went further ; they did not ask
merely what parts of the brain are inactive ; they
tried to find the cause of the inactivity. Naturally,
one of the most probable causes was a change of the
circulation of blood in the brain. Braid thought of
this, and sought the cause in the altered circulation
in the brain and spinal cord. Carpenter supposed
cerebral anæmia, as Hack Tuke has more recently
imagined a partial spasm of the vessels. Rumpf
expresses a like opinion.

Heidenhain also at first supposed that anæmia of
the brain was the cause of hypnosis. He soon gave
up this opinion, for two reasons. 1. The investigations of Förster with the ophthalmoscope discovered
no sort of change in the vessels at the back of the eye
during hypnosis. I can confirm this by my own
experiments. Luys and Bacchi, in opposition to

these observations, describe hyperæmia of the retina
during hypnosis. 2. Heidenhain saw hypnosis appear in spite of inhalation of nitrite of amyl,
which causes hyperæmia of the brain. Salvioli and
Bouchut have, on the contrary, found cerebral
hyperæmia during hypnosis. Krarup finds a narrow-
ing of the internal carotid, an enlargement of the
external carotids and of the vertebral artery during
hypnosis. Tamburini, Seppilli, and Kaan also investigated the circulation of the blood during hypnosis,
but only in connection with the three stages of
Charcot. In the same connection Meynert investigated circulation during hypnosis; he speaks, however,
of a strong muscular cramp in the lethargic stage, so
that his theory does not seem to me very clear. The
three other last-named investigators used several
methods: 1. Mosso's method, which determines the
volume of an extremity, and concludes from a
decrease in the mass of blood contained in it,
an increase in the mass contained in the brain.
2. The action of cold and hot compresses on the
head (Kaan), which cause anæmia or hyperæmia.
From the resulting changes, *i.e.*, from the cessation or
modification of the hypnosis, a conclusion is drawn as
to the causal connection between this and the mass
of blood contained in the brain. 3. Ophthalmoscopic
investigations of the vessels of the retina. I do not
enter into the details of the different experiments, (1)
because they are valid for the stages of Charcot alone;
(2) because the influence of hypnotic training was
not enough regarded, *i.e.*, in the application of warm
and cold compresses; (3) because cause and effect
are not distinguished clearly enough.

The last point is often overlooked. Even when
there is really a change of circulation in the brain It

is a mistake in logic to think the changed circulation causes the changed functions. As a muscle needs more blood when it is at work, but does not work more because more blood flows to it ; as the stomach when digesting needs more blood than when it is inactive, it is also not improbable that the brain, or portions of it, when they are active, need much blood, and when they are inactive but little. Then if we take the vasomotor disturbances as proved, it is by no means proved whether they are the cause or the effect of hypnosis.

In fact, Cappie takes the opposite view. He thinks that the increased activity of the motor centres in hypnosis draws too much blood to them, thereby causing anæmia of the other portions of the brain which are necessary to consciousness. Of course this is no explanation, apart from the facts that the author arbitrarily opposes the motor centres to the parts of the brain necessary for consciousness, and that there is consciousness in hypnosis. The principle from which Cappie starts is the one put forward by Brown-Sequard. He thinks that hypnotism is a sum of dynamo-genetic and inhibitory acts ; *i.e.*, that the increased action of certain parts of the brain (dynamo-genetic act) causes decreased action of others (inhibitory act).

Just as Cappie assumed that there is during hypnosis an altered activity of certain centres and associated changes in the circulation, so Wundt has suggested as the physiological basis of the phenomena of hypnosis a double interaction, neurodynamic and vasomotor. The irritability of any central element depends not only on its own condition at the moment of stimulation, but also on the condition of the other elements with which it is in association ;

in such a way that excitation of the neighbouring element lowers its own excitability, while a condition of inhibition in the neighbouring element favours discharge of energy.   This is the neurodynamic reaction.   At the same time, according to Wundt, there is a vasomotor reaction, since for the most part the blood contents and functions of the organs stand in such a relation to one another that increase of function produces increased flow of blood, decrease of function, depression of the blood-flow.   Wundt further argues that neurodynamic compensation favours vasomotor compensation, and *vice versâ*, and in this way seeks to explain the phenomena of hypnosis, by viewing the chief symptoms from this standpoint.   He then refers to the centre for apperception, which, hypothetically, he regards as the substratum of the process of apperception.   He believes that in hypnosis, when active attention is alone inhibited, there is partial inhibition in the apperception centre.

As I have already mentioned, Wundt has raised against my attempts at a psychological explanation, the objection that I have not answered the question why in hypnosis consciousness is contracted.   I have, however, put the questions which must be met by physiological answers (p. 283).   The third question I put is this : What is the causal connection between this state and the methods which induce hypnosis and put an end to it ?   I do not find that this question is in any way answered by Wundt's physiological theory, and against Wundt's physiological explanation, must raise the same objection as he has raised against my psychological speculations.   If Wundt enables us in certain respects to conceive the condition of the central system during hypnosis, the question as to why this condition arises on the application of certain definite methods remains absolutely unanswered.

Finally, I mention the theory of Preyer, which is indeed cleverly thought out, but is, as Bottey insists, in no way confirmed; and Bernheim objects that it cannot explain the hypnotic states. Preyer puts the matter thus: An activity of one hemisphere of the brain results in hypnosis; fixed attention causes a rapid accumulation of waste tissues in the parts of the brain which are active, and by this a quick local consumption of the oxygen of the blood is caused. In consequence of this, favoured by the failure of the ordinary change of stimulus of the nerves of sense, there is a partial loss of the activity of the cerebral cortex. The partial loss of activity of one region would then explain the increase of activity of the other, because the inhibition would disappear. Bernheim justly objects to this that it does not explain a rapidly induced hypnosis, for it is hardly conceivable that waste matter should accumulate so rapidly. But, in particular, the sudden termination of hypnosis is not consistent with this. As we have seen, the one word "wake" is enough to end the hypnosis at once. We should be obliged to suppose that the simple idea of waking was able to dissipate the waste matter or make it of no effect.

I do not think that these physiological theories can be regarded as sufficient. As long as the physiologists fail to consider what an enormous influence an idea, roused for example by the word "wake," exercises, their theories will be unable to explain the phenomena. It is here necessary to show how the word acts, and why it is enough to put an end to the state. I even

think we ought to set our faces decidedly against the
way in which certain physiologists play with words, as
if the enigma of consciousness were child's play for
them. Lotze is said to have ironically stated that,
according to his own statistical reckoning, the great
discoveries of physiology had an average existence of
four years (Max Dessoir). This may not be exact.
I think better of physiology, though I do not wish to
fall into the extravagance of Meynert, who has asserted
that cerebral physiology is no longer a problem. But
when Mendel, speaking of hypnotism and the phenomena of suggestion, explains that we have to do with
a strong stimulation of the cerebral cortex, and
Ziemssen declares the exact contrary, *i.e.*, that the
cerebral cortex is too little stimulated and the subcortical centres too much, we are startled at such
contradictions, and are compelled to hope that in
future less will be asserted and more will be proved.
Such contradictions as those between Mendel and
Ziemssen would be inconceivable if it were not for
the presence in their works of just such speculations
as those with which medicine is in the habit of
reproaching philosophy.

CHAPTER VI.

SIMULATION.

I NOW come to the question of fraud, or simulation. As is well known, hypnosis has only lately been generally recognized. The scepticism which once reigned, and which is an advantage so long as it does not pass into *a priori* prejudice, has been overpowered by facts. But it took some time to attain this result. At present, when it is generally acknowledged that " there is something in it," it is not necessary, when discussing simulation, to consider whether there is such a thing as hypnotism at all. We have only to consider the question of " simulation or hypnosis " for each separate case.

Those who believed in hypnosis were for a long time regarded as deceivers or deceived. It was occasionally less harshly supposed that any man who busied himself with hypnotism must be suffering from some loss of mental health or balance ; which was said of some of our best-known investigators. Latterly, Mendel, in a popular lecture, has expressed himself in this sense. He brings forward no names, but his charge would apply to such men as Forel, Bleuler, Obersteiner, Wundt, and even to Mendel himself. Such methods of controversy are outside the bounds of legitimate scientific discussion.

In the first place, fraud is much rarer than is generally believed. It has been too much the habit to look for one physical symptom or another, and settle

the question of fraud from its presence or absence.
And yet this is exactly the opposite of what is
generally done in judging of mental states; *e.g.*,
when we want to diagnose a case and decide whether
it is insanity or not, no authority on mental disorders
would suppose fraud simply because some bodily
symptom was absent. He will consider and weigh
the case as a whole. Even when each symptom
taken separately might be fraudulent they would be
weighed against one another and a diagnosis formed
from them. If the doctor finds also some symptom
which cannot be simulated, he will weigh this too,
but he will not conclude fraud from its absence. It
is true that in this way the conviction may be only
subjective, or rather it will be clear only to those who
have studied mental disease. The outsider may often
be able to raise the objection that this or that symptom
may be feigned. But no doctor of mental diseases
would allow himself to be influenced by this.

If we apply this to hypnosis, which is also a mental
state, it follows that only he who has studied hypnosis
practically is in a position to diagnose it. The idea
has gradually grown up that every one is able to
judge of hypnotism, and may express his opinion and
demand consideration for it, however ignorant he may
be about hypnotic experiment. Kron and Sperling
have very rightly contested this supposition. It is not
correct to diagnose fraud in hypnotism from a certain
bodily symptom. Even when each separate symptom
may be feigned, the experienced experimenter will
diagnose by summing up the different symptoms and
comparing their relation to each other. It is satisfactory if he finds an unfeignable symptom besides; this
is an objective proof, convincing even to those who
have no practical knowledge of hypnosis. But it is

to be said that objective physical symptoms are more seldom found in hypnosis than in mental diseases. The first is a transitory mental state, in which objective physical change is less likely to happen than in mental disorders, which last for months and years.

However, we must of course try to find bodily symptoms in hypnosis. Many authors have done so, among them Charcot in particular, who threw the weight of his name into the scale for hypnotism. The school of Nancy also sought for objective symptoms and found them, though different from Charcot's; I mean the blisters, &c., produced by suggestion. As a mistaken notion is beginning to take root, that the question of fraud forms the point of difference between the two schools, because that of Nancy had found no objective symptoms, I will here point out the real difference between them.

To exclude fraud we look for symptoms which cannot be voluntarily simulated; it is indifferent whether these are produced by suggestion or not. Now, there are phenomena which are produced by suggestion and which are independent of the subject's will. And in these the chief difference between the two schools lies.

The Nancy school believes that *all* the symptoms are caused by suggestion, even those independent of the will, while the school of Charcot finds bodily symptoms which are independent of the will and of suggestion. Consequently, *suggestion* is the main point on which they differ.

I shall show that the questions of suggestion and fraud are very different. The case of Siemerling teaches us this. His subject was hemianæsthetic, both with regard to sight and feeling, *i.e.*, the power

of sight was limited on the side on which the skin was
without feeling. The field of vision was concentrically
narrowed, so that anything beyond a certain distance
from the point on which the eyes were fixed could not
be seen. Now in hypnosis the sense of feeling on
the hemianæsthetic side was restored by suggestion,
and directly feeling was restored the eye on the
corresponding side became normal, without direct
suggestion. Westphal and Siemerling thought this
an objective proof of hypnosis, and I also believe that
such a proof might satisfy even somewhat strained
demands, since the power of sight is independent of
the will And yet this effect was produced only by
suggestion, though by indirect suggestion. Krafft-
Ebing had a case like this ; mental paralyses with
objective symptoms were produced by suggestion,
and the symptoms were those mentioned by the
school of Charcot as happening in mental paralyses.

Objective symptoms can be produced by suggestion. It is doubtful whether they happen without
suggestion. We see that the suggestion need not be
direct ; the symptom may be produced by an indirect
and partly unknown mental influence. Siemerling
said to his patient, " Now you can feel again " ; when
the patient recovered sight as well as feeling, this was
the effect of an indirect suggestion, induced by a
certain mental interdependence between the anasthesia
of the eye and that of the skin. Both organs were
functionally disordered, and this common disorder
disappeared, when the function of one organ was
restored by suggestion Krafft-Ebing's case is like
those mental paralyses studied by the school of
Charcot. In these, when the subject is told, " Your
arm is paralyzed," vasomotor disturbances follow on
some mental process, with which we are at present

unacquainted.   As the vasomotor disturbance is the
direct consequence of the paralysis we are obliged to
think that some mental communication causes both
phenomena.

To return to the objective symptoms of Charcot.
We see that there are certain bodily phenomena in
the three stages.   Thus the point of difference
between the two schools is this : Are these bodily
symptoms a result of suggestion or not ?   I believe
(as I said, pp. 94, 95) that suggestion plays an important part in most of the symptoms, but I by no
means maintain that they have no objective value,
though I am not quite sure.   For phenomena might
be produced by practice, even without hypnosis,
which at first sight would seem impossible to simulate
(p. 103).   This is the point of difference between the
two schools.   I have discussed it here in order to
show that objective symptoms may be caused by
suggestion, and that, consequently, the objective
symptoms in themselves do not separate the two
schools, although the symptoms mentioned by each
are rather different.

Let us now ask what symptoms should help us to
decide the question of fraud.   In the first place we
must notice how the eyes close, and how the subject
tries to open them.   This closing of the eyes is difficult to describe.   The gradual falling of the lids is
important, and the action of the muscles of the forehead when opening the eyes, in a way like that after
sleep, as well as the convulsive rolling upwards of the
eyeballs, which is often seen.   The fibrillary twitching
of the eyelids is, on the contrary, of no importance, as
it often happens without hypnosis.

In cases where the eyes are open their expression

is most important. The look is often blank and meaningless, the mask-like expression and the attitude of the subject are often characteristic also. He moves his limbs slowly and heavily when commanded. But I should mention that in certain cases, particularly of light hypnosis, these symptoms are wanting, and the movements in especial are quick and lively. The expression during sense delusions is also very important. Every one knows how difficult it is to place oneself in an imaginary situation so that the expression, the attitude, and the actions should correspond to the idea. This is the great art of actors, and everybody knows how seldom an actor is able to represent a scene by the mere exertion of his own will ; but it is still more difficult to change the mood in a moment, and pass from one situation to another in a few seconds. It is extremely difficult for a person awake, but the hypnotic subject does it easily. It is astonishing that outsiders should regard this very ability as a sign of fraud, as a competent judge once did at Vienna (*cf.* p. 182). It is surely one of the most difficult things to do, and it would be wonderful that all the suspected persons should devote themselves to the thankless part of fraud, when with such talents for acting a very different career would be open to them. The expression of pain, the smiles, the chattering of teeth and shivering at different suggestions of pain, pleasure, cold, &c., would be no easy task to the supposed impostor.

The waking in many cases is just as characteristic ; the astonished face with which the subject looks round, as if to find out where he is. His behaviour in post-hypnotic suggestion is likewise important.

The impostor generally exaggerates, like a person pretending madness. In spite of the variability of

the symptoms of hypnotism there is a certain conformity to rule in its development. The impostor
usually accepts all suggestions very quickly, while the
experienced experimenter knows that susceptibility to
suggestion increases with a certain uniformity. It is
very easy to simulate analgesia to slight feelings of
pain, as this analgesia is mistakenly thought to be
a common symptom. An unexpected pain causes
the usual reflexes in the face and eyes, and yet the
impostor will declare that he felt no pain. It is the
same with sense delusions, where the suggestion
generally requires to be emphasized before it takes
effect. The impostor usually exaggerates here also.

Let us consider certain objective symptoms which
have been said to be particularly characteristic.
Charcot and his pupils lay great stress on the
curves of the muscular contraction and respiration
in the cataleptic stage. Charcot says there is no
essential difference in the duration ; a cataleptic
person cannot hold up his arm longer than an impostor. But when the curve-tracings from the raised
arm and the respiration are noted, there is an important difference ; the impostor soon shows that he
is tired by irregularity in the arm and respiration curves ; the hypnotic subject, on the contrary
breathes calmly and evenly from beginning to end
and there is no perceptible trembling in his arm.

Other people say that a cataleptic posture is sometimes maintained a very long time, and therefore
offers an objective proof.

Charcot mentions increased neuro-muscular irritability as a particular characteristic of lethargy. It
is not to be denied that this is impressive when seen
for the first time. It cannot for a moment be supposed that a person can thus bring single muscles,

and also groups of muscles supplied by single nerves, into contraction. But these contractions would only be important if they appeared instantaneously from the first.

Charcot does not think that the contractures induced by stimulation of the skin in the somnambulic state are of much value, and in fact they might easily be simulated. Apart from these symptoms of Charcot's stages we must, in judging of fraud, consider some abnormal muscular actions—*e.g.*, the cessation of the uncertain, staggering gait in cases of locomotor ataxy, which Berger described and I also have observed—and other like phenomena.

Binet, Féré, and Parinaud have made particular investigations on the sense delusions of sight. They say that a prism doubles the hallucinatory object as it would a real one; and in hallucinations of colour, the complementary colour is said to be seen afterwards. But Charpentier and Bernheim have refuted these experiments, particularly those with the prism, which from the first seemed very improbable. They showed that the apparent doubling of the hallucination was due to some *point de repère*, which the subject found for himself. He first saw some real object doubled by the prism, and concluded from this that the suggested hallucination should be doubled also. In any case, the great point is that the prism only produces the doubling when a real object can be seen through it. If there is no such *point de repère ;* *i.e.*, if the experimenter is in a dark room, or if he shows the subject a perfectly blank, white screen, the doubling does not happen.

According to Charpentier and Bernheim the experiments with complementary colours were not more exact ; and the same is the case with other experiments of Binet and Féré on colours, from which they drew the conclusion that in suggested perceptions of mixed colours the effect was the same as with real optical images.

The phenomenon presented by the pupil of the eye, which they mention, seems to me more valuable. In suggesting a hallucination, *e.g.*, that of a bird, the suggested approach of the object causes a contraction of the pupil, and *vice versâ.* At the same time there is often convergence of the axes of the eyes, as at the approach of a real object. But it must be remembered that some people are able to produce this phenomenon in themselves by an effort of will (Hack Tuke, Budge).

Bernheim lays great weight on the analgesia of hypnotic subjects. I agree with him. If a completely analgesic subject is touched with a faradic brush he shows no trace of pain. There are no impostors who could repress the expression of pain under these circumstances, particularly if the contact were unexpected. But we must consider that such a high degree of analgesia is very rare in hypnosis. Naturally, this true analgesia must be distinguished from the simulated analgesia, which I mentioned on p. 302. The anæsthesia of the mucous membrane, *e.g.*, of the membrane of the nose, with regard to ammonia, is to be tested. There is no need to say that certain rare phenomena, *e.g.*, secretion of tears and sweat, flushings, changes in the heart's action and organic changes produced by suggestion, are of the highest value. Finally, I shall direct attention to a phenomenon whose absence may be of some importance ; I mean the absence of movements which I should prefer to call movements caused by tedium (Langweiligkeit). As is known, a waking man is unable to retain any posture for a long time, even when all his muscles are relaxed. In the latter case the movements cannot be caused by fatigue of particular muscles; it is rather that when one position is long maintained, a lively feeling of discomfort ensues, that is subjectively felt as tedium. This, it seems to me, induces certain movements difficult to describe, the movements from tedium. Their absence is strong evidence of the presence of hypnosis, and I think this an important and almost unmistakable symptom. They are best observed when the subject has been left for some time to himself.

From two points of view, however, all these symptoms have only a relative value. In the first place their presence is important, and is in favour of hypnosis, but their absence is unimportant. *We are never justified in concluding fraud from the absence of any particular symptom.* In the second place we must consider whether any symptom might not be produced by practice without hypnosis, and whether the subject could use this practice, or whether there may not be a special capacity for the voluntary production of this symptom.

On the first point I should say that in some cataleptic postures there are perceptible tremors, that complete analgesia is rare, and that neuro-muscular hyper-excitability is but rarely found.

The second point is often overlooked; for it is not yet decided whether by practice some persons might not produce even all the above-mentioned symptoms without hypnosis. Perhaps there is no hypnotic symptom which has not been observed in some person or another without hypnosis. For

20

example, neuro-muscular hyper-excitability is found in hysterical patients, so that it is not enough to prove hypnosis. And the most strained cataleptic attitudes can be produced by gymnasts, by means of practice. Some persons have been known to influence the action of their hearts without a change of breathing; though, according to Beaunis. a distinction can be found here : the hypnotic obeys suggestion at once, while out of hypnosis a short time must always elapse before the will can exercise its influence.

The local flushings of Mantegazza are a more extreme case. Mantegazza says that at one time in his life he was able to induce local reddening of the skin simply by thinking intently of the spot ; he even adds that wheals sometimes appeared. It has often been asserted that people can perspire at any place they please. Delbœuf says that he can influence the secretion of saliva by his will or ideas. It is well known that this last is much under the influence of the ideas.

I have purposely made these remarks, because mistakes about the objective symptoms are made on all sides. For this reason I think that the first question to be decided is the one mentioned above : whether the subject could not produce the symptoms by practice, without hypnosis. I know well that I thus lessen the value of my earlier explanations ; but I think it is more honest to say that we do not know enough about the objective symptoms of hypnosis.

I have as yet only spoken of such symptoms as take the form of bodily functions; but according to Pierre Janet these symptoms, contractures for example, are of much less importance to the question of fraud than the mental ones ; the memory in particular.

Gurney also thought the memory of great importance here. The postulate from which these authors start is that there is loss of memory after waking from hypnosis, and that consequently the subject remembers nothing that has happened during the state. Now this loss of memory is to be used to decide the question of fraud. An example will make this clear.

I tell X., whom I have hypnotized, that when he is going to bed he is to dip a handkerchief in warm water and tie it twice round his throat. When he wakes he seems to remember nothing about it ; upon which I repeat the command, but omit the doubling of the handkerchief. When I ask him what he is to do, he answers, " I am to dip a handkerchief in warm water and wrap it twice round my throat." It will be seen that I gave the order differently before and after hypnosis ; yet X. repeats the command as it was given in hypnosis.

According to the views of Pierre Janet and Gurney, this would very likely be a case of fraud ; for X., who had apparently completely forgotten everything after waking, yet mentions the one point omitted in the second command. But must we really consider this a case of fraud ? I believe not, and I appeal to a long series of experiments with perfectly trustworthy subjects, in whom I often observed objective bodily symptoms also. The subject may very well make such a statement as the above about the twice-folded handkerchief quite automatically, neither remembering nor remarking it ; but he may also make it consciously, as a previously forgotten idea may be suddenly called into consciousness by the law of association mentioned on p. 141.

On account of their practical importance I shall speak of other symptoms which, according to experience, are often wrongly considered by outsiders as proofs of fraud. I begin by insisting that there are very few hypnoses which really correspond to the outsider's ideal picture of a hypnosis. At least the inexperienced often think that the apparent impostor is forgetting his part when some symptom appears which, according to them, ought not to appear.`

First, the laughter of hypnotic subjects. Of course many subjects laugh, just as a waking man does. In the light stages the subject is quite aware that he is playing a somewhat absurd part, *e.g.*, he makes all the movements of eating an apple, and feels compelled to make them, but knows quite well that he looks rather ridiculous ; therefore it is not odd that he should laugh. But there is often a trace of consciousness even in deep hypnoses ; the subject separates himself, so to speak, into two parts, one of which acts the suggested part and the other observes it and laughs.

I have already spoken of the trembling of cataleptics. I add that the subject sometimes makes movements unforeseen by the experimenter, and which sometimes interrupt the suggestion. I stretch out a subject's arm and suggest that he cannot move it. It remains as I placed it. But now a fly settles on the subject's forehead and he moves his arm at once to rub the place. This is a common occurrence. Rubbing when one is tickled has become a habitual, rapid, unconscious act. So that if the first suggestion has lost its vividness, the new impulse causes a change of posture. I have seen people put their hands to their faces when they sneezed, as we habitually do, though the hands had previously been made motionless by suggestion. Besides, many movements which

have been prevented by suggestion become possible
when the subject does not think of the suggestion ; if
he is forbidden to say " *a*," he can use it unconsciously ;
he only cannot say it when he thinks about it (Laver-
dant, Hack Tuke, Max Dessoir).

There are many phenomena of this kind. I say to
the subject, A., "You are a rope-dancer, and are on
the rope." He believes it, and I pretend to cut the
rope, on which he falls down ; but he falls so as not
to hurt himself. This is caused by a normal, mechanical, nearly unconscious process which is always
going on in us. We always use our hands to shield
ourselves when we fall. This habitual mechanism
works on in hypnosis regardless of the suggestion.
Hysterical paralytics for this reason seldom hurt
themselves when they fall. Hack Tuke told a subject
that he was dead ; he fell without hurting himself.

I will further point out that the eyes sometimes
open very quickly. I have seldom seen this, but can
safely assert that it happens in genuine hypnoses.
An impostor will also often open his eyes when he
thinks he is not observed ; the hypnotic subject does
it whether he thinks he is observed or not. I must
also direct attention to those sense delusions in which
a dim dream-consciousness persists, which prevents
the full effect of the delusion. In such cases fraud is
often suspected ; *e.g.*, the case mentioned on p. 199
where the subject fought with an enemy, taking pains
not to hit him.

Further, a complicated suggestion may be misunderstood or half-forgotten, in which case it will be
carried out imperfectly. A post-hypnotic suggestion
can naturally only be fulfilled when it is remembered.
As memory is the first condition for the success of a
suggestion, a person with a good memory (*ceteris*

paribus) will execute a suggestion better than another.
If the post-hypnotic suggestion is badly remembered
it will be badly carried out, as the memory only acts
in a natural way. I mention this though it seems a
matter of course, because I have heard the existence
of hypnosis doubted, purely in consequence of such
mistakes. To a man whom I have hypnotized in the
presence of A., B., C., and D., I make the post-
hypnotic suggestion that when A. speaks he is to say
" Ha ! " when B. speaks, " He ! " when C. speaks, " Hi ! "
and when D. speaks, " Ho ! " It is not surprising that
he is confused in carrying out the suggestion, and
makes the wrong exclamation to each person. For
all depends upon the strength of the memory, and its
power to retain and reproduce the suggestion. To
the class of imperfectly realized suggestions belongs
also a case of Joire's. He suggested to a person that
the name Marie was written on a piece of paper.
When the paper was turned upside down he seemed
to see the letters backwards—eiraM. But, in reality,
if the word had actually been written on the paper,
not only would the word have appeared backward,
but each separate letter would be upside down. We
must bear in mind that these things only depend on
strength of the memory, and on the way in which a
person preserves and reproduces it.

Finally, a subject will sometimes confess to imposition, or to having acted to please others. Such a
confession must be judged with caution. Many who
have made hypnotic experiments have observed that
subjects will often say after the hypnosis that they
have been pretending, though their actions were
really compulsory. I need not say that there are
people who think they show weakness of will by
allowing themselves to be hypnotized ; then they

consciously tell untruths.   Another group is more
interesting psychologically.   Their self-deception is
the same as we have found in some cases of post-
hypnotic suggestion.   They think they could have
acted otherwise if they had pleased (F. Myers).
Heidenhain mentions such a case; a doctor said,
after the hypnosis, that he could have opened his
eyes if he had pleased ; but when the hypnosis was
renewed he could no more help himself than the first
time.   I could add a number of personal observations.
One case was that of a doctor, who often asserted
after the first hypnosis that he could have behaved
otherwise ; but in each fresh hypnosis his will was
inhibited.   Finally he himself became aware of his
loss of will-power.   In another case I hypnotized X
at least ten times before he would agree that the
suggested paralysis of his arm had really made him
unable to move it; he previously believed that he had
so behaved to oblige me.

All this makes it evident how difficult it is to
decide the question with regard to fraud.   It seems
to me to occur more often with children, but the
transition from simulation to true hypnosis is so
gradual that even an experienced experimenter is
sometimes uncertain.   For example, when a subject
shuts his eyes to be obliging, it is not the same
thing as if he shut them to deceive ; or he shuts them
because he is tired of fixing them on something, but
could open them by a strong effort, though he keeps
them shut because it is more comfortable.   It would
be a great mistake to identify this with simulation.
Others do what the experimenter wishes, to please
him, but not to deceive him.   This is not pure fraud
either, for the wish to deceive is absent.   And there

is another complication; for people in hypnosis sometimes pretend, just as it is known insane persons do.
Thus a hypnotic will say he sees something when he
does not. It is naturally very difficult to say where
deceit begins and ends in such a case ; but, generally
speaking, practice will enable us to judge the mental
state of the subject with some certainty. There is no
doubt that even the most experienced deceive themselves or are deceived ; the most experienced doctor
of mental diseases is in the same case. Obersteiner
justly observes : " A group of morbid symptoms, such
as an epileptic fit, may be so exactly reproduced by a
skilful simulation, that even the most skilful expert
(Esquirol, for example) may be deceived. And yet,
unfortunately, we must still unconditionally recognize
the existence of epileptic fits." But just as, in spite
of such occasional deception, the alienist learns
to diagnose by experience, so will the experimenter
in hypnotism. The fear of being deceived has
prevented many from interesting themselves in the
subject. But no advance can be made unless the
fear is put on one side and the question examined. It
is possible to maintain a complete scientific reserve.
The question of fraud must be treated in a scientific
manner, as mental diseases are treated. We must
not make impossible demands in order to exclude
imposition ; to do so would prove neither scepticism
nor a scientific spirit ; it would, on the contrary, be
unscientific. And yet I have heard a " cultivated "
man, who thought himself scientifically sceptical, say,
when watching a hypnotic subject, that he would
believe in the reality of the hypnosis only if the subject could see through a non-transparent substance ;
e.g., if he could see through a man as if he were
glass !

CHAPTER VII.

THE MEDICAL ASPECTS OF HYPNOTISM.

IT is certain that the present interest in hypnotism depends chiefly upon its therapeutic utility, although its value for experimental psychology must not be underrated. The attention of doctors has never been directed to it so much as at present; in spite of all differences, it becomes more and more clear in medical circles that a thorough examination of it is necessary.

We have already seen that Bernheim and Liébeault think that hypnotism means suggestion, and suggestion is truly the chief agent in it. Bernheim's definition of hypnotism makes its therapeutic value more comprehensible. He believes that hypnosis is a particular mental state, in which susceptibility to suggestion is heightened. It follows from this that suggestibility exists apart from hypnosis, and that consequently there is no contradiction between the therapeutics of suggestion in, and out of, hypnosis; one is the natural complement of the other. It is the school of Nancy which has pointed out that there are many suggestions without hypnosis, and it was the first of all to recognize the therapeutic value of purely empirical suggestion.

The therapeutics of suggestion are founded on the

premiss that a number of diseases can be cured or relieved merely by making the patient believe he will soon be better, and by firmly implanting this conviction in his mind. Every able practitioner knows this suggestive treatment, which is as old as disease. Preyer mentions the healing of King Jeroboam, whose hand, the Bible tells us, was motionless, but recovered the power of movement through the prophet's words. Most of the miraculous cures one hears of we may now consider the results of empirical and often unconscious suggestion. We can at all events refer many of the results procured by the mesmerists to psychic operation. When Bailly wrote his report, in 1784, he thought of the power of imagination, to which he ascribed Deslon's phenomena. About the same time John Hunter expressed a similar opinion as the result of his own experiments. From ancient times this mental influence has been used. Ancient medicine, which was partly in the hands of the priests, and in which many religious ceremonies were used, is full of this mental influence. The temple sleep of the old Greeks and Egyptians was a means to facilitate the effect of suggestion. The sick lay down to sleep in the temple, and were told by the god in dreams of something that would cure them. We find the same kind of thing again and again. The belief in some particular medicine is an important agent in healing. There is no need to recount the miraculous deeds of each century. But in later times I may mention the well-known Greatrakes, whose cures astonished all England in the seventeenth century. He healed by laying on of hands, but seems also to have used verbal suggestion. I may mention, also, Gassner, the exorcist, at the end of the last century. The reports make it clear that Gassner used suggestion; for though he spoke Latin, it is evident that he made his patients understand him; nobody misunderstood his famous "Cesset"; they knew that the pain, &c., was ordered to stop. I was interested to find in Sierke that Gassner once sent a patient to sleep by command. He told her to sleep, and when to wake, and in fact induced what we should at present call a hypnosis.

Lichtenberg reports that during the last twenty years of the eighteenth century, a certain Frau Starke in Osterode created some excitement by performing many cures through stroking and touching the patient's body, and by so-called charming.

Among other wonder-workers I may mention Prince Hohenlohe, at the beginning of this century; a Catholic priest, who aroused much attention by his cures in Bavaria, after 1821. The mesmerists supposed he was one of those persons who possessed a peculiar force, while on other sides religious faith was called in as an explanation. One school of mesmerists, that of Barbarin, of Ostend, took up an odd middle position. Barbarin maintained that the influence was a purely spiritual one, and that the right way to induce sleep was to pray at the patient's bedside (Perty). Even to-day many adherents of vital magnetism hold like views; for instance, Timmler thinks religious faith valuable and necessary for obtaining the result.

I will not multiply examples of suggestive therapeutics. I will but mention the authenticated cures which have occurred at Lourdes and other holy places quite recently. Everywhere and in all times suggestion has been effectively and unconsciously used. When we see that it is exactly those people who use suggestion who are the most successful, we are justi-

fied in giving it a high place in modern therapeutics.
For no one who reads the stories with unprejudiced
mind can doubt that Gassner and many others were
more successful than many a scientific physician;
though they are unjustly called swindlers. It may be
that some of the diseases were hysterical, but there
were many others. It is at least certain that nearly
all of them were diseases which the usual medicinal
treatment had failed to heal. Weil mentions the
case of a doctor who lived in a large town in Saxony.
This doctor cured many patients by strictly ordering
them to go to bed at a certain hour, at the same time
telling them that they would perspire profusely and
that this would cure them; by this suggestion he is
said to have obtained remarkably successful results.
If suggestion is to succeed, the patient must firmly
believe he will be cured. This belief must be
impressed upon him, and the question is how this
can most surely be done. It is not always possible
for a doctor to implant this idea, however great his
patient's faith in him may be. Hypnotism is a means
of attaining this end, in spite of opposition. No
patient, be he ever so intelligent, can resist the influence of hypnotic suggestion if only the hypnosis is
deep enough. An idea implanted in hypnosis takes
root like a belief in Lourdes in a faithful Catholic.
The idea of a cure should, however, be instilled into
the patient during hypnosis. If it is allowed that the
idea of a cure effects a cure in many cases there can
be no doubt that suggestion is an integral part of
therapeutics.

We have to thank Liébeault, of Nancy, for having
been the first to use suggestion methodically in
therapeutics. It is true that verbal suggestion was
occasionally used by the old mesmerists, Kluge,

Lausanne, Jobard, and others, as Du Prel and Pick justly point out. But method was entirely wanting. It is often maintained that Braid recognized the value of suggestion in medicine, but this is an error. It is clear that Braid saw and used suggestion, but he did not recognize its great significance.

I must not forget to notice that in 1880 Friedberg, and more especially Berger, concluded that hypnosis was a therapeutic agent. Berger saw a hemiplegic patient make movements in hypnosis which he could not make awake. He saw sufferers from locomotor ataxy cease to stagger during hypnosis and for a short time after. It is true that he did not use hypnosis systematically. The simplified method of Liébeault was unknown to him; he knew nothing of the Nancy methods, nor of verbal suggestion, nor of the great importance of suggestion. Many people, unknown to Liébeault, had seen that, from a medical point of view, a state in which contractures and paralyses, analgesia and pain, &c., could be induced and removed, must be of immense importance; but Liébeault was the first to find the right path, while Bernheim and Forel developed the methods and made them known to physicians.

It is not astonishing that objections have been made to the therapeutic use of suggestion. No essential progress has often been made in the science of medicine without a struggle. Every one knows how the use of quinine, and vaccination, and particularly of emetics, especially in France, was contested; and how the cold-water cure was rejected, and how Remak was attacked in Germany before the galvanic battery was accepted in the medicine-chest. Every one knows how *massage* was laughed at.

And all these methods have finally succeeded, in spite of opposition and childish laughter.

The difficulty of judging of the therapeutic value of hypnosis is much increased by the hazy definition of "hypnotic suggestion." Thus, some oppose suggestive treatment, and some hypnotic suggestive treatment, while others object sometimes to suggestion in general and sometimes to hypnotism, *e.g.*, Ewald, Mendel, S. Guttmann. I think that the latter are right, in spite of their false point of view, because it is impossible to draw a sharp line between suggestion and hypnotism.

It has often been asked why so many authorities have pronounced against suggestive therapeutics. There are three answers—(1) Even an authority may be wrong, and generally it is the authority which believes in its own infallibility; (2) all so-called authorities are not necessarily authoritative; (3) many who are authorities in one field are just for that reason not so in another. The last two points are important in medicine, and we may consider them further.

In all sciences, besides the real authorities, there are men who are mistakenly supposed to be so. It is interesting to observe in the history of culture how fashion makes "authorities" out of those who have no real scientific greatness. A man is called an authority; but when it is asked what he has done there is shrugging of shoulders, for often he has done nothing. Such pseudo-authorities are much inclined to pass judgment on questions they have not examined. There have always been such persons; they are the drag on the wheel of science. Their position and credit is due to a faculty, which a clever writer, Karl von Thaler, a short time ago called the art of putting oneself on the stage. Their judgments are of no value.

But I do not mean to say that all who have opposed the therapeutic use of hypnotism are pseudo-authorities; on the contrary, true authorities, such as Meynert and others, have expressed themselves decidedly against it. But as regards the third point above-mentioned, I will say that because a man is an authority on one matter it does not follow that he has a right to claim authority on another. A great historian or astronomer is not in a position to pass judgment on medicine. Now, many of those who have objected to the therapeutic use of hypnotism are authorities on matters that have nothing to do with therapeutics. Physicians as well as laymen often lose sight of this. A man may be eminent in the histology of the brain, and yet be incompetent in therapeutics. And there is nowadays no more connection between the art of healing and the histology of the brain than there is between it and astro-nomy. If I may call the art of healing a science, the histology of the brain is something quite apart from it—at least, in the present day. Perhaps a connection between them may be discovered later ; perhaps the histology of the brain may be of use to the science of healing ; but at present there is no such inner connection. Therefore I consider the judgment of a man who may be an authority in his own branch as of little weight here as the judgment of an astronomer would be. I would on no account have it thought that I depreciate the investigations of such men. On the contrary, investigations on the histology of the brain, for example, are necessary and immensely valu-able ; but as yet they have not affected the art of healing. Whether they ever will the future will show. Feuchtersleben, whom no one will accuse of dislike to medicine or anatomy, since he was their most ardent admirer, has expressed the opinion that the art of healing should not be confused with the knowledge of anatomy.

Besides, scientific opposition has always advanced science. A serious, unprejudiced opposition prepares the way for a scientific investigation of new questions; only the investigation must be permitted, not rejected absolutely, as was done in some quarters in the case of hypnotism.

Every investigator should test as a matter of course, if he wishes to judge clearly. But unluckily this is not done. When the author demanded such an examination, that the value of hypnotism might be tested, many "scientific investigators" protested against the demand in the most energetic way. While

Virchow, &c., considered a long and thorough examination necessary, others were already prepared
with an *a priori* judgment, for which they could
not offer a shadow of reason. But, indifferent to
condemnation, new observers came forward to test
the healing power of hypnotism and of the suggestion and mental treatment so closely connected
with it. When it became evident that the question could not be easily put aside, and it was
recognized that the absolute refusal to examine
was unscientific, an endeavour was made to support
the original *a priori* decision by false assertions.
Those who had first defended the therapeutic value
of hypnotism were accused of having asserted the
discovery of a universal panacea. It is a pity that
those who, as the representatives of science, ought
to seek for truth, should take such a way of
justifying their original refusal. These tactics are
pitiable, and deserve to be branded. Neither the
serious investigators at Nancy nor those in Germany,
Switzerland, and Austria, have ever wished to make a
universal panacea out of hypnotism.

We will consider singly the objections made to
hypnotism as a therapeutic agent.

A chief objection was made by Ewald, of Berlin,
who "decidedly protested against calling suggestion
medical treatment." He did this in the interest of
physicians. Forel's reply to him will make it clear
what he meant. It refutes his objections better than
I could do.

"Ewald protested against the expression 'medical
treatment by hypnotism.' He said that medical
treatment meant the medical art and medical knowledge, and that every shepherd - boy, tailor, and
cobbler could hypnotize ; only self-confidence would

be necessary. I, for my part, think it right to protest against this way of treating a scientific question.
Has not medicine drawn a countless number of its
remedies from the crudest empiricism, from the tradi-
tions of the 'shepherd-boys'? Cannot every cobbler
inject morphia, apply blisters, and give aperients if
he has the material? Yet we do not despise these
remedies, nor baths, nor massage, &c. But Prof.
Ewald deceives himself greatly if he believes that
a delicate agent like hypnosis, which affects and
modifies the highest and most refined activities of
our minds, could be manipulated by a shepherd, or
ought to be handed over to him. Medical science
and psychological knowledge, the ability to diagnose
and practise, are all necessary to its use. It is true
that laymen have succeeded with it, just as charla-
tans have succeeded, and continue to succeed, in all
provinces of medicine. Should we on that account
leave the practice of medicine to them? Long
enough, much too long, science has left the important phenomena of hypnosis to 'shepherd-boys and
their like'; it is high time to make up for the
delay, and to devote ourselves to a thorough examination of the series of phenomena which can complete our views of psychology and of the physiology
of the brain. Medical therapeutics must not remain
behind when great result are to be obtained. But
these results can only be obtained by a thorough
study of the proper hypnotic methods."

A second objection is the danger of hypnosis. I
long ago pointed this out, and earnestly warned
people not to consider hypnosis absolutely safe.
Mendel and others have said the same thing later,
but have somewhat exaggerated the danger. This
point must be seriously weighed. But it is

21

never asked whether a remedy might not be dangerous ; we only ask if we cannot avoid the
danger by careful and scientific use of it.   Rust
asserts, in speaking of artificial somnambulism, "the
best assertion that can be made about a remedy or
method of cure, is, that it might also do damage ;
for what can never do positive harm can never do
positive good." This assertion is to a great degree
justifiable, though perhaps exaggerated ; for I think
I may say that there are few remedies in medicine
which would not injure if carelessly and ignorantly
used.   There are even medicines which may injure,
however carefully used, because we do not know
exactly under what conditions they become hurtful
I need not speak of morphia, strychnine, and belladonna, which have sometimes done injury even when
the maximum dose was not surpassed, nor of the
deaths from chloroform, the reason of which has not
been explained.   Thiem and P. Fischer, with praise-
worthy scientific frankness, have quite recently
published a case of the fatal after-effects of chloroform ; death followed on the fourth day.   These
authors say that there is at least one death for every
thousand administrations of chloroform. Neither will
I speak of the dangers of surgical operations ; I need
only point out that an apparently harmless medicine
may have very likely already done more mischief
than hypnotism.   Many deaths have resulted from
the use of potassium chloride, and unfortunately this
drug can still be bought in retail without a medical
prescription. Severe collapse has been observed after
the use of antipyrine.   I will add to these one of the
most recent medicines—sulfonal—which is supposed to
be a perfectly harmless hypnotic drug.   A friend and
colleague has told me that he has seen sad consequences

follow from its use, and that there were some patients to whom he never gave it, for fear this "harmless" drug should work great mischief. And again, as to Mendel's treatment by suspension, which a few years ago became almost a fashion, and from which certain enthusiasts really expected the cure of locomotor ataxy. It is now certain that it may cause great injury, or even death. Many published reports show that even the presence of a doctor does not prevent evil consequences. And Billroth has also pointed out great dangers from carbolic acid, which is constantly used. If we gave up the use of these remedies we might give up medicine altogether, as everything employed may do harm.

Whether or not there are dangers in the use of drugs is not the question. We must ask : 1. Do we know under what conditions the danger appears? 2. Can we remove these conditions and the consequent danger? 3. And if we cannot, does the advantage to be gained by the patient outweigh the danger he runs? The answer to these questions is in favour of hypnotism ; we know perfectly well under what conditions it is dangerous, which we do not know about some drugs ; we are able in certain cases to exclude these conditions by using the proper and harmless methods, and thereby preventing danger ; and supposing that these perfectly harmless methods fail, we can ask ourselves if we shall or shall not use the methods which are not harmless. I think the small discomforts to which the patient is exposed—a short headache, watering of the eyes, and depression, are infinitesimal compared to the advantages which may result from the hypnosis. The future will decide here also, but I will remark that nearly all the men (Gilles de la Tourette, Ewald, Mendel, Rieger, Bin-

swanger), who have said the most about the dangers
of hypnotism, and are in general against it, by no
means themselves refrain from hypnotizing. By this
they allow that it is not hypnotism itself, but its
misuse, which is mischievous.

The danger of hypnotism has been enormously
exaggerated. The inhabitants of a little town once
left off eating potato soup because a woman fell
downstairs and broke her neck half an hour after
eating some. Conclusions have been drawn in the
same way here, and this sort of reasoning is not uncommon. If a person was hypnotized, and later on
had some ailment or other, straightway the ailment
was ascribed to hypnotism. If we reasoned thus we
should have to say that Carlsbad causes apoplexy, for
Mr. X. had an attack of apoplexy a fortnight after he
returned from Carlsbad, &c. Many things could be
proved in this way.

I should hardly have thought it possible that such
logic should be used in scientific circles. It is
true I have often heard that when patients come
back from a watering-place without having been
cured — which must happen sometimes — they are
dismissed with the comforting assurance that they
will feel the effects later. Till now I thought this
was a bad joke, or at best an effort to console the
patient ; I never believed that such a principle was
really credited in the medical world. If a patient
got better or worse six months after his return from a
watering-place, I should not be inclined to ascribe the
effect to the baths, because in the interval other
things might have affected the patient. Like Pauly,
I must on these grounds reject the connection found
by Binswanger, Ziemssen, and others, between hypnosis and ailments long subsequent to it. Besides,

if I were to accept their sophisms, it would be easy for me to prove in the same way that modern medicine makes mankind ill; for what medicine might not produce important results half a year after its administration? What doctor has ever argued in this way? Recently Friedrich, formerly an assistant of Ziemssen's, has written at length on the dangers of hypnotism; he has, however, been refuted by Forel, Schrenck-Notzing, and Bernheim, who show that he made the crudest mistakes. And when the cases in which hypnosis is supposed to have had dangerous results are published in careful detail, it becomes clear—as in the cases of Séglas, Briand, Lwoff, &c.—either that important precautions were neglected, or else that a connection between hypnosis and the disease was assumed according to the principle, *post hoc ergo propter hoc.*

However, I by no means deny that there are certain dangers in the improper use of hypnotism.

Mendel maintains that it induces nervousness; that nervous people grow worse, and sound people nervous through its use; but Forel and Schrenck-Notzing think this is a mistake of Mendel's, caused by his using the method of Braid instead of suggesting hypnosis verbally. I agree that fixed attention too long continued may have unpleasant effects. It may be followed by nervous debility or nervous excitement. But I have never seen any one become "nervous" whom I hypnotized verbally, and to whom I made no exciting suggestions. This also is important (Bertrand). Whoever has seen the difference between a subject who has received an exciting suggestion and one who has received a soothing one, will agree that as much good can be done

in one way as harm in the other. A man who
makes absurd suggestions to amuse himself and
satisfy his curiosity, without a scientific aim, need
hardly be astonished if he produces ailments.
Sawolshskaja is right in warning against such sports.
I have observed that patients are often worse on days
following bad dreams. Can we be astonished that a
person who has awaked from hypnosis during an
imaginary fire should feel ill after it? Such suggestions should not be made at all, or with the
greatest caution, taking care to do away with the
suggestion and soothing the subject before the
waking. This is the most important point. I think
that even if these mistakes are made it is of little
consequence, provided the subject is thoroughly and
properly wakened in the manner used at Nancy and
by all who follow the prescriptions of that school.
I should like to ask those who talk of the dangers
of hypnotism if they have taken care that the
awakening should be complete? I know that most
people are not at all aware that they should do away
with the suggestion entirely. They think it enough
to blow on the subject's face, and are astonished that
he does not feel well after it. I am surprised that
more mischief is not done in consequence of insufficient technical knowledge. It is this that is
dangerous—not hypnotism. No wonder that there
are sometimes unpleasant consequences. It is as
necessary to know the right way in this case as
in using a catheter.

To show how a suggestion should be done away
with I will suppose that an exciting suggestion has
been made to a subject, who is disturbed in consequence. One should say something like this : " What
excited you is gone ; it was only a dream, and you

were mistaken to believe it. Now be quiet. You feel quiet and comfortable. It is easy to see you are perfectly comfortable." Only when this has succeeded should the subject be awakened ; and this should not be done suddenly ; there are reasons for thinking it better to prepare the patient for waking (Sallis). I generally do it by saying, " I shall count up to three. Wake when I say three." Or, " Count to three, and then wake." I add (and this is also important), " You will be very comfortable, happy, and contented when you wake."

Further on I will give some other precautionary rules which should be used before the awakening to prevent disagreeable consequences.

I have spoken of the nervousness which hypnotism is supposed to produce, and have tried to show that it is not hypnotism which causes it, but its improper use. These rules should especially be followed : I. To avoid continuous stimulation of the senses as much as possible. 2. To avoid all mentally exciting suggestions as much as possible. 3. To do away with the suggestion carefully before the awakening. The proper method will not cause nervousness. Hypnotism offers less dangers on this point when properly used than electricity, for example, which has made many people " nervous." A lady I knew became so nervous when electricity was applied to her larynx by a very competent doctor, that she was obliged to give it up.

It is asserted that hypnotism causes hysteria (Guinon), or hysterical convulsions (Anton), even in people who have never had them. It is not to be denied that hystero-epileptics are sometimes thrown into hysterical convulsions in hypnosis, but I contend decidedly that the convulsions are not caused by the hypnosis. The slightest mental affection causes convulsions in such persons : electricity causes them ; they fall into them even when they hear a noise, such as a falling book, a bell, &c. But it is preposterous to say the electricity causes the convulsions ; the mental excitement of the patient about the electrization is the real cause ; timid patients sometimes faint when they are electrified (E. Remak). Besides, the main point is whether the convulsions of the hystero-epileptic are permanently aggravated or not, and experience shows that this is not the case. On the contrary, when once a complete hypnosis has been obtained we have in our hands a trustworthy means of permanently lessening the convulsions; and, in truth, an attack of hysteria is not so important that it need be regarded as one of the chief dangers of hypnotism. Hysterical attacks are sometimes artificially induced merely for the sake of experiment or demonstration.

Certain cases of Sperling and Krakauer show that hysterical attacks are of no importance, and do not indicate the necessity of stopping the hypnotic treatment ; in these cases there were attacks at first, yet cures were obtained ; and they also show that the attacks are by no means permanently aggravated, even when they take place at the first or second attempt to hypnotize. If Krakauer, in his case or hysterical deafness, had allowed himself to be thus hindered from making further experiment his patient might be as deaf to-day as she was two years ago. And I will further mention that Mesmer and Deslon even thought the hysterical convulsions (*crises*) necessary if the magnetizing were to do any good ; which was certainly a mistake. So far as I know, in no single case has a person hypnotized according to the above rules ever had convulsions in hypnosis, unless he had had them before. Solow in New York has certainly reported a case in which this apparently happened. Tremors and convulsions appeared, followed some days later by disturbance of memory. It plainly appears, however, from the report that the most elementary precautions were overlooked ; and, in addition, the hypnosis was only produced to amuse those who were present.

Among other dangers which have often been mentioned I may name insanity in various of its forms. It is even said that delusions may result from hypnosis. Now we know that many people suffer from morbid delusions. When, therefore, any one who has been frequently hypnotized becomes the victim of delusions, we must be on our guard not to assume too hastily any causal connection, especially if a long interval has elapsed since hypnosis was practised. It is well known that delusions are influenced by the ideas of the time ; it is, therefore, not surprising that in recent years we have frequently met with the delusion of being magnetized or hypnotized. Such delusions occur in persons who have never been hypnotized. I have seen many cases in which persons believed that they were influenced by the operations of people at a distance. We must not, therefore, conclude that such delusions show any connection between hypnosis and insanity. I have even observed delusions of thought-transference effected from a distance among persons who had scarcely even heard of hypnotism.

It has been mentioned as a special danger of hypnosis by some, Sioli, for instance, that after repeated hypnotism an inordinate desire for its repetition may be set up ; on the other hand, Smidt has objected that an undue dependence of the subject

on the experimenter is established.   But as Forel
points out, it is easy to deprive such objections of
their power by the use of proper precautions.

But I should like to mention some slight accompanying ailments which are sometimes found after
hypnosis, though they cannot be tnought a real
danger, and are often the result of auto-suggestion
(Forel), or of a bad method.   There may be
fatigue and languor, heaviness of the limbs, &c.,
after waking.   It is easy to prevent these by suggestion in deep hypnoses.   It is different in the
light ones, though I believe a clever operator can do
it by post-hypnotic suggestion even here.   In other
cases I think it better to prevent fatigue by suggestion before the awakening ; in any case it is a good
plan to get rid of it at the first sitting, as otherwise it
increases by auto-suggestion at each sitting, and can
finally be hardly overcome.   This feeling of fatigue in
the light hypnoses is the same we sometimes have
after an unsound sleep.   All these inconveniences are
slight, and can for the most part be avoided.   Drosdow made of these phenomena a particular stage of
the hypnotic state, characterized by headache, pains
in the limbs, faintness, &c., but he was no doubt misled in 1881 by the then want of knowledge of the
methods of Nancy.

The main dangers of hypnotism are not those just
mentioned, which appear relatively seldom even when
improper methods are used.   The real ones show themselves more easily in such a case.   They are : the
increased tendency to hypnosis, and heightened susceptibility to suggestion in the waking state.   This too
great susceptibility to hypnosis shows us how careful
we should be with the method of Braid, which is the
most frequent cause of this; for accidentally fixing

the eyes on some object may cause a sudden hypnosis, simply because the idea of an earlier hypnosis
is thereby vividly recalled.

The last-mentioned danger can be guarded against
by repeatedly making some such suggestion as
follows to the subject before awaking him: "Nobody
will ever be able to hypnotize you without your consent; you will never fall into hypnosis against your
wish; nobody will be able to suggest anything to you
when awake; you need never fear that you will have
sense delusions, &c., as you do in hypnosis, you are
perfectly able to prevent them." This is the surest
way to avoid the danger. Such are the dangers of
hypnotism, and such the methods of meeting them
Their antidote is suggestion, and they are no hindrance to hypnotic treatment. They can be avoided
by a proper use of hypnotism.

But it may be objected that though a short use of
hypnotism may not be hurtful, a long one, involving
a repeated induction of the state, might be so. The
objection is justifiable. But it might also be made
against the use of various drugs, since we do not yet
know whether a long use of them might not cause
severe chronic poisoning. Experience is the only way
to decide such questions. Now Liébeault, who has
used hypnotism therapeutically in France for about
thirty years, has watched cases for a long time, without finding bad consequences. Forel has done the
same thing, though for a rather shorter time; I myself have hypnotized persons for several years without
evil results.

I will not enter into a purely theoretic discussion of
the dangers of hypnosis. Mendel fears over-action of
the cerebral cortex from it, while Ziemssen and
Meynert fear just the contrary, that is, a loss of

power of the same part. The contradictions in
which they are involved are evident ; to suppose that
they meant the same thing would show a great want
of reflection.

In the foregoing I have discussed and refuted two
objections made to the therapeutic use of suggestion
and hypnotism : first, the assertion that hypnotism
should not be called medical treatment; and secondly,
that it has too many dangers to allow of its practical
use.

It is further added that its mysterious side should
prevent its being used. Benedikt maintains this, and
thus contradicts Mendel, who finds its healing value
especially in the mysterious impression it causes. I, on
the contrary, believe, as I have explained before, that
the mysterious impression plays a subordinate part,
and that there is less mystery about the matter than
is generally believed. Apart from this, it would be
perfectly indifferent to a practitioner whether a drug
took effect from the mysterious impression it made, or
through suggestion, or through chemico-physical influence. The point is that it shall act, not in what
manner it acts.

When Benedikt maintains that, in order to lessen
the impression of mystery, hypnosis should be
induced by the use of a magnet instead of the
ordinary methods, he would do better if he showed
how this is possible. He should prove his assertion
that the magnet produces hypnosis by publishing
his experiments. I have applied the magnet to
hundreds of persons and never induced hypnosis.   -

If I believed that in some cases a mysterious
agent would be useful to the patient I should not
for a moment hesitate to use it; for were I to do
otherwise I should be neglecting my duty as a doctor,

which is of more importance than any scientific sign-
board. For example, I should think it right in certain
cases to send patients to some miracle-working spot,
e.g., Lourdes, if they expected they would be cured
there ; and, in fact, fifty or sixty patients are yearly
sent to Lourdes from the Salpêtrière (Constantin
James). That Charcot was convinced of the healing
power of faith is well known. It cannot be denied
that faith and emotional excitement produce many
results at Lourdes. We may well believe Rom-
melare's statement that the water from Marseilles
cured a patient who believed in it. But even if
hypnosis was effectual only from its mysteriousness
—which is not the case—it would none the less be
well to use it.

Among the remaining objections to suggestive
therapeutics the assertion that they do not produce
any lasting improvement or cure may be mentioned.
This may be answered as follows. The results are
by no means transitory ; on the contrary, a large
number of lasting cures have been observed and
published. The author has seen many cases where
there was no relapse for years. One cannot ask for
more. The objection that the improvement may
be only temporary is thus not justified. But even
were this so we must still rejoice to have found a
way of procuring even temporary relief (Purgotti,
Schuster). For instance, in difficulties of menstruation, it is a great thing if we can succeed in
subduing pain for a time. If the pain returns a new
hypnosis may be induced ; it is always to be had,
and as it generally becomes deeper the more it is
used, it is less likely to lose its effect (even in relapses)
than drugs, which often do so quickly (Sperling). In
any case therapeutics are not yet so far advanced as

to give us the right to reject a remedy merely because
it only affects symptoms or has often merely a temporary value.   If we were to reject remedies which
suppress the phenomena of disease for a time only, we
might abandon a large part of therapeutics, perhaps
the whole.   Besides, from some methods of treatment
nothing but a temporary improvement is expected,
and yet this temporary improvement is considered to
prove the value of the method.   How often it happens
that a patient who has benefited by a stay in Carlsbad
or Aix, &c., is recommended by his doctor to go back
there when his ailment returns, because his health was
improved the first time.   Remedies should not be
weighed and measured by different standards.

Another objection to the therapeutic use of hypnotism is that it cannot be generally applied because
everybody is not hypnotizable.   I should like to add
that in many cases, even when a hypnosis is induced,
it is not deep enough to be used therapeutically.   I
pointed out these two defects several years ago,
without, however, exaggerating their importance.
After all, it is the same with other remedies.   For
instance, under some circumstances a journey to the
North Sea, or among mountains, or, perhaps, in some
states of collapse, a few bottles of Madeira, are supposed to be excellent remedies.   I think that many
more people can be hypnotized than can be sent to
bathe in the North Sea.

A further objection to treatment by hypnotic
suggestion is that there may be suggestions without
hypnosis.   But this is exactly the standpoint which
the school of Nancy and I myself have always taken
up, although, as I have pointed out, it is often difficult
to distinguish between hypnosis and suggestion.   This
is the heart of the present movement, which shows us

how extensive is the empirical use of suggestion in therapeutics. It is also the real reason of the strong opposition to hypnotism. We hereby see how often suggestion occurs spontaneously in ordinary life and medical practice. Hypnotism, by means of which we can make suggestions artificially, shows us what a great mistake has been made in estimating previous therapeutics, since we have neglected to consider the mental element in the action of the various drugs. The physiological effect only was regarded; it was quite forgotten that many remedies have only a suggestive value.

Now, when it is asserted that there is suggestion without hypnosis, and that suggestion in medicine is no novelty, let it be remembered what Ewald said a short time ago—*that suggestion oversteps the bounds of medical treatment and trenches on the field of psychology.* We also see that some of the opponents of suggestion generally fail to recognize mental treatment as a factor in medicine. According to them suggestion is no affair of the physician as such. I maintain, on the contrary, that *a physician can only do good, only attain his aims, when he is a psychologist,* and that this is at least of as much importance as what we call medical art and science.

There are, then, as the school of Nancy has shown, many suggestions without hypnosis; but, in spite of this, artificially induced hypnosis makes suggestion possible in many cases where it would otherwise fail. Therefore when any one, in objecting to hypnotic suggestive therapeutics, says that there is also suggestion without hypnosis, he is merely confirming what the school of Nancy has always maintained. This "refutation" of hypnotic therapeutics is as if one were to say that a doctor is no longer needed in

confinements, because many births take place spontaneously and very well without one.

Hardly anybody thinks the temporary loss of will
is an objection to hypnotic therapeutics. The main
point is to choose only an experienced and trustworthy experimenter, as we should do in taking
chloroform.

About the indications for suggestive treatment
there is not much to be said with certainty. This
is why Ewald will not concede the same rank to
suggestive treatment as to other methods, *e.g.*, electro-therapeutics, treatment by drugs, &c. Mendel
decidedly opposes Ewald and thinks the indications
clear ; unluckily he does not say what they are. I
think that the indications are not yet clear, but that
it cannot be expected they should be, when the
method of treatment has been under examination
for a time relatively so short. But Ewald is certainly
mistaken in thinking that fixed indications are
to be found in internal disease at all. Medicine
consists to a great extent in trials of various treat-
ments. Strictly speaking, there are indications in but
few cases as may be clearly seen by comparing various
text-books, and from the numerous contradictions
among different doctors. I think that indications
for suggestive treatment are at least as exact as those
for treatment by electricity, by massage, by drugs, by
baths, which are all supposed to cure a great number
of definite diseases, if the too favourable explanations of the text-books and essays in journals are to
be believed. In any case I think that this belief is
to be found hardly anywhere but in medical students,
who generally greatly over-estimate the power of
therapeutics (Unverricht). Any one who keeps his
eyes open in practice may soon convince himself that

there unluckily are not many so-called accurate indications for the treatment of internal diseases, and particularly for nervous disorders. It is by no means a contradiction to this that there are doctors who in certain cases can find the proper remedy at a glance. It rather confirms what I have said, and is a consequence of the fact that therapeutics are less a science than an art, although many representatives of "exact medicine" suppose the contrary. Though this has often been said before, it is, unfortunately, not sufficiently considered nowadays. On the whole, to exclude any misunderstanding, I should expressly declare that I recognize definite indications in certain cases of internal disease, but they are very rare when compared to the total number of diseases.

So far as we have hitherto been able to judge, functional neurosis is the chief field of suggestive therapeutics, *i.e.*, nervous disorders not founded on anatomical derangements. These must not be too readily confused with hysteria or with neurasthenia. It is true that these ideas are so blended, and hysteria in particular is conceived in so many different ways, that we might almost say, "What we cannot define, that we call hysteria." "Hysteria" is used in many senses; the term is used in one sense or another at pleasure, and thus sophisms are constructed which even many doctors fail to penetrate. I will here give two meanings of the word "hysterical."

In the first place, hysteria is a name for an illness which has no anatomical foundation, which has numerous and variable symptoms—now headache, now ovarian pain, now pain in the side, and now weakness in the legs. The patient is called "hysterical" as well as the symptoms. As such patients are sometimes obstinate and capricious, and like to

22

make themselves interesting, this word "hysterical" has a somewhat unpleasant after-taste ; some authors go so far as to say that a tendency to falsehood and hypocrisy is a chief symptom of such hysteria. This is evidently an unfair generalization. At all events, the multiplicity and variability of the symptoms are the main characteristics of "hysteria" taken in this sense. Hysteria in the other sense is quite different. In many quarters any symptom is called hysterical when there is no anatomical cause for it and it is merely "nervous," *e.g.*, headache, pains in the muscles, certain tremors, frequent vomiting, &c. ; even when the symptom is solitary and constant. Now, if in such a case the patient, as well as the symptoms, is to be called "hysterical," we have two entirely different meanings for the term "hysterical patient," from the interchange of which, at pleasure, all sorts of subtle sophisms result. The meanings of the term are changed to suit the discussion. For example, an author says in one place that any hysterical symptoms can be removed by hypnosis, *i.e.*, such as are marked by quick spontaneous changes. That is hysteria No. 1. But as soon as some one asserts he has seen a person, without any other symptom of hysteria, freed by suggestion from a severe pain in a muscle—the biceps, for example—then, to suit the discussion, the second meaning of the word hysterical is adopted, and it is said that the symptom was hysterical. But a prudent silence is maintained with regard to the fact that the patient suffered from one merely local pain, had no other hysterical symptom, and consequently was not hysterical in the first meaning of the term. Anything can be proved or refuted if the word "hysteria" is thus treated.

To give another proof of this I return to a letter which Charcot once addressed to Gutmann, and in which he asserted that only hysteria can be treated by hypnosis. If this means that hysteria in sense No. 2 can also be thus treated, there is nothing to say against it, and the most different authors would agree upon the point. But, in fact, Charcot, as Nonne remarks, understands much more by "hysteria" than is understood in Germany. Thus Charcot says, in contradiction to two German authors, Oppenheim and Thomsen, who think the variability of the symptoms the chief mark of hysteria, that in his view this is not a characteristic of hysteria.

To avoid error it should be mentioned that Charcot admits suggestive therapeutics conditionally in his letter. He even says that a good effect may be hoped from them in hysterical phenomena. It is true that these parts of Charcot's letter about suggestive treatment are sometimes omitted when the letter is repeated, while every impartial observer must see in this passage rather a defence of suggestive therapeutics than an attack upon them, if "hysteria" is understood in the second sense given above. Moreover, while Charcot expresses himself decidedly in favour of the hypnotic treatment of hysteria [Ziemssen, who is supposed to have the same standpoint, maintains that such treatment makes it worse.]

Even though Charcot's authority is appealed to, if erroneously, against suggestion, it should not be forgotten that a short time ago Charcot was attacked and laughed at ; that his hypnotic experiments were mocked at ; that Rieger, among others, energetically opposed hypnotization in the Salpêtrière ; that Mendel said his subjects were "prepared"; that according to Ewald the said subjects obtained all sorts of advantages from submitting to the experiments (though he did not talk of fraud); and that Ewald expressed himself in a manner not altogether appreciative about Charcot's experiments with the magnet ; that he described the antecedents of his subjects unflatteringly, &c. From all which it appears that the side which now claims him as an ally against hypnosis was attacking him vehemently hardly a year earlier.

From this digression, which was intended to make clear what is meant by "hysteria," I return to the question of the indications for suggestive thera-

---

peutics. I will give them here, so far as my own experience permits, with the help of trustworthy authors, especially of Forel. Particularly suitab'e ones are all kinds of pains which have no anatomical cause (headaches, stomach-aches, ovarian pain, neuralgic and rheumatic pains, even with effusion in joint, according to Block, but we must not confuse with hysterical effusion); sleeplessness; hysterical disturbances, particularly paralyses of the extremities and aphonia; hysterical vomiting (Freud); polyuria (Mathieu, Babinski, Debove); disturbances of menstruation (Brunnberg); spontaneous somnambulism; uneasy dreams; loss of appetite; vomiting of pregnancy (Choteau); alcoholism (Forel, Lloyd Tuckey, Wetterstrand, Neilson); morphinism (Wetterstrand, Marot, &c.); nicotinism and allied conditions.

Many authors, and especially Kraepelin, have of late years advocated the use of hypnosis in alcoholism and morphinism. The results have been more favourable with the former than with the latter. Corval points out that in alcoholism any injurious effect of abstinence can thus be avoided. It has been disputed whether in morphinism a gradual or sudden disuse of the drug should be produced. Bérillon and Tanzi are in favour of the gradual method. Forel, Wetterstrand, and others, have reported good effects in various drug manias. Bérillon and Jennings hold that auto-suggestion is a great factor in producing the difficulty of treating morphinism, the auto-suggestion that he cannot do without morphia leading the patient to desist from treatment. A controversy regarding the treatment of morphinism has arisen between R. Binswanger and Wetterstrand. Binswanger disputes the great efficacy which Wetterstrand attributes to suggestion. Landgren, a Swedish physician, has hereupon published his own history; in consequence of acute pains due to inflammation of the joints, he had become accustomed to the use of morphia. Wetterstrand succeeded in curing him with remarkable rapidity, and Landgren states that the severe pains which assuredly followed every attempt to discontinue morphia were remarkably shortened.

Whether suggestion can be of any essential use in neurasthenia is a question that has often been raised of late. Bérillon reports brilliant results which have, however, been criticized by Schrenck-Notzing. R. Binswanger justly points out that the suggestive treatment of neurasthenia is often a waste of time. Bernheim has seen no good results; but this is not the experience of Van Eeden. Many believe that neurastheniacs are not very suggestible, an opinion which is not shared by Bérillon, Mezeray, and Mavroukakis.

Among other indications for hypnotic treatment, I may mention nervous asthma (Brügelmann); stammering (von Corval, Ringier, Wetterstrand, Pauly); chronic constipation (Forel, Bénard, Schmidt); nervous ocular disturbances (Forel, Möllerup, Chiltoff); and nocturnal incontinence of urine. In this last connection Ringier relates that a little girl of five became subject to incontinence of urine after other children had told her that she would wet the bed because she had plucked a certain flower, the meadow crow-foot. The flower in question, *Ranunculus acris*, is in Switzerland commonly called *pisse-en-lit*. It is easy to see that a disorder which can thus be caused by suggestion may most easily be cured by suggestion.

Other indications are: pruritus of the skin of nervous origin; sexual perversion if not congenital (Krafft-Ebing, Schrenck-Notzing, Ladame); ringing in the ear: writer's cramp, vaginismus (Barbaud); chorea, especially if the cause is psychic (Dumont-pallier, Leroux); paramyoclonus (Scholz); the neuroses of traumatism and emotion (Hirt); agoraphobia (De Jong), and other obsessions (Hirt). To the obsessions belong also cases of nosophobia, in which the patient is dominated by the fear of disease. It is well known that the symptoms of serious illness may be produced by auto-suggestion; Mavroukakis has lately shown that attacks closely resembling epilepsy may thus arise, as well as phenomena which recall disease of the spinal cord. There can be no doubt that in all such cases suggestion is the proper method of treatment.

In reference to an experiment by Heim, in which suggestion was successfully used to ward off sea-sickness, Forel mentions a similar successful case. I believe, with Rosenbach, to whom we owe an admirable discussion of sea-sickness, that we have here to distinguish two causes, of which one is fear and excitement. In this respect a favourable influence can certainly be exerted by psychic treatment and suggestion. But the second cause is made up of physical causes, the movement of the ship, etc. That suggestion may sometimes render these physical influences inoperative appears from some published cases; whether it can always succeed seems to me doubtful.

Affections which can scarcely be called diseases may also yield to hypnotic suggestion. I may mention a case brought forward by David. A lady for many years had been liable to burst into tears at every occurrence, however slight; this condition improved under suggestion, and five years later there had been no relapse.

' Hysteria (in the sense of definition No. 1) is not easily curable. Consequently we try as much as possible to obtain an improvement in the symptoms. As far as our experience goes, this is at least as easily done by hypnotism and suggestion as by any other method. Much depends upon the depth of the hypnosis, and upon the degree of susceptibility to suggestion, &c. But I am decidedly of opinion that hysterical patients are less susceptible to suggestion than others. Forel thinks that a sound brain is above all things necessary for hypnosis; the sounder it is, the sooner we may hope for results. In hysterical patients the brain is often by no means sound.

For the same reason it is difficult to treat insane persons by hypnotism. However, improvements have been obtained in the lighter forms of mental disease, *e.g.*, of melancholia and mania (Forel, Burckhardt, A. Voisin, Séglas, Burot, Dufour). But generally the effect is less than in the neuroses. This is partly because insane persons are not good subjects for hypnosis (A. Voisin, Percy Smith, A. T. Myers). Tokarski rightly protests against the powerful hypnotization which has by some—such as A. Voisin, Herrero, Caryophilis—been applied to the insane, children, and criminals. Even when the hypnosis is deep, insane ideas and delusions of the senses are much more difficult to remove than nervous troubles, such as sleeplessness and headache, which often precede psychoses (Forel, Robertson). Although there may sometimes be organic changes which cause the mental disturbance, and which explain the resistance to suggestion, yet the chief reason is to be found in the tenacity of the patient's diseased ideas. These might often be rightly called auto-suggestions. A.

Voisin, Locojano, and Repoud say that they have
seen good effects produced in cases of severe mental
disorder; but Forel is unable to confirm this.

The therapeutic successes which hypnotism has
had in neuroses have been confirmed in so many
quarters that a doubt of the trustworthiness of
their source is hardly possible (Forel, Krafft-Ebing,
Obersteiner, Hirt, Eulenburg, Möbius, Bernheim).
Those who dispute the successes do so generally
a priori, without having scientifically and patiently
tested the matter. It is a mistaken assertion that
only such cases of illness can be benefited which
could easily be benefited in other ways. At least
I must contend that this was not so in a number of
cases in my own experience, where the cold-water
cure, massage, electricity, surgical operations, or
drugs had been tried in vain, while suggestion, and
hypnotic suggestion in particular, was successful.

Besides, even when one of the above methods is
successful, we should be careful how we draw the
conclusion that suggestion had nothing to do with
it; for numerous remedies appear to be effectual
only through suggestion; they succeed because the
patient believes in them, as even Mendel, one of the
most decided opponents of suggestion, has admitted.
It is in the nature of things that drugs, even when
they only act by suggestion, should sometimes succeed better than verbal suggestion, because many
people are more easily influenced by something
tangible than by words only. Some very practical
investigators (Krafft-Ebing and others) even attribute
a merely suggestive value to drugs in certain diseases,
e.g., in neurasthenia and hysteria.

With regard to organic diseases, in which we find
anatomical changes in the organs, as opposed to

functional derangements, we have before us a number of accredited observations, from which it follows that important functional improvements were made possible, *i.e.*, the consequences of the disease could be partly removed by hypnosis. Thus in a case of *tabes dorsalis,* though the disease continued, the severe pains were subdued (Lloyd Tuckey). It may, no doubt, be objected that the diagnosis was mistaken, and that a functional derangement was mistaken for an anatomical lesion. But the examination of sections of the spinal cord contradicted this in one such case. Bernheim saw an apoplectic paralysis rapidly improved by suggestion. The patient died later of disease of the lungs, and the seat of the original disease was discovered on dissection. Besides this confirmation by anatomy there is another method by which we can sometimes decide a doubtful diagnosis. For example, in chronic rheumatism of the joints, with clearly visible and tangible swellings, there can be no doubt about the diagnosis. If suggestion removes the pain, we have obtained an important improvement in an organic complaint. But many such cases have been published. I can confirm it from my own experience in a case of articular rheumatism.

Among other diseases accompanied by organic injury I have seen a very painful eczema of the ear, in a child of eight, made painless by post-hypnotic suggestion. I observed this case in the company of my friend and colleague Friedemann, of Cöpenick, whom I have to thank for a number of interesting experiences in hypnotism. The child in question could not bear the slightest touch. An order given in his first hypnosis had such an effect that he could afterwards endure even strong pressure on the spot.

What are the counter-indications against hypnotic

treatment, *i.e.*, what conditions forbid the use of hypnotism? In particular cases it may be that when certain phenomena produced by auto-suggestion cannot be avoided, the use of hypnotism is counter-indicated. Fear of hypnosis may also justify delay in attempting hypnotic treatment, at all events until the anxiety has disappeared. However, the therapeutic effect we wish to obtain is of so much more importance than a chance attack of hysteria, &c., that in general we should not allow ourselves to be restrained by it. In any case there are no more counter-indications against this treatment than against any other.

How can the effects of hypnotism be explained? Some think that it is in itself healing and beneficial; this is the opinion of Beaunis, Obersteiner, and especially Wetterstrand. The general view is that suggestion is the healing agent.

To make the operation of suggestion clear I will take an example. We wish to cure a headache by arousing in the subject the idea that the headache is gone. Spontaneous reflection would prevent this in most waking people, but in hypnosis ideas are more easily established. If the subject accepts the suggestion we may be sure that in the hypnotic state he does not feel the pain. But now we have to prevent the return of the pain after waking. Either external post-hypnotic suggestion or auto-suggestion will do this. We can make the patient continue to think the pain is gone after he wakes. He need not be conscious of this idea in the sense of remembering it. On the contrary, the less conscious the idea is, the more effect it will have, because reflexion will not struggle against it (Forel). Auto-suggestion is the

second plan. The patient, finding himself without
pain in hypnosis, may convince himself that pain is
not a necessary consequence of his state, and this
idea may under some circumstances be strong enough
to prevent the return of the pain.

The more easily an idea can be established in the
subject, the quicker a therapeutic result can be induced.
And the deeper the hypnosis, the more easily ideas
can be established. It does not follow, of course, that
the light stages are of no value. Apart from the fact
that they often become deeper, they are often useful
in therapeutics, especially when we have to do with
motor disturbances. Much depends upon the subject's
character. For example, A. may be as susceptible to
suggestion in the light stage as B. is in the deep one.
However, it is not to be contested that suggestibility
increases in some persons with the depth of the hypnosis. Beginners frequently regard the light stage as
useless for therapeutic purposes. This is a mistake,
as Hirt and others have shown. I cannot, however,
agree with those who regard the light stage as equally
useful therapeutically with deep hypnosis. Liébeault
has rightly insisted of late that the best results are
obtained in deep hypnosis.

In methodical suggestion lies the key to suggestive
therapeutics. When the hypnotized subject refuses
the suggestion, which sometimes happens, no therapeutic result will be obtained.

Neither is the effect to be attributed to the patient's
confidence in itself, though it plays a large part.
Misrepresentation has aroused so much distrust of
hypnotic treatment that in some cases there is no
confidence at all. But the immense power of hypnotic
suggestion is shown by the fact that it succeeds in a
large number of cases in spite of mistrust ; for mis-

trust is a powerful auto-suggestion, and auto-suggestion is the greatest foe of external suggestion. The success of hypnotic suggestion will be greater the more distrust disappears, and when it has been recognized that hypnotism properly used is as harmless as electricity properly used. Then only will the power of hypnotic therapeutics be practically estimated. I have little doubt what that estimation will be. Hypnotism and suggestion will outlive many remedies whose praises fill the columns of medical journals at present.

To avoid misunderstanding, I will briefly state in what way the improvement of organic diseases by hypnotic suggestion is to be explained (according to Bernheim). I only mention this because Binswanger and Seeligmüller mistakenly represent Bernheim as having maintained that the original organic injury is done away with by suggestion (Corval). Apoplexy is an example. If a part of the brain, *a*, is injured, then the functions of the nerves served by *a* are interfered with. Now it is a well-known experience that when *a* is injured the functions of another part of the brain, *b*, are often influenced. Then the functions of the nerves served by *b* are also interfered with ; *b* itself is not organically injured, only its functions are inhibited. Now suggestion can restore these functions. It can sometimes also produce a functional amelioration in an organic disease. In any case it need not be supposed that suggestion has an immediate influence on the organic lesion. Under the name of suggestion-gymnastics, L. Lehmann has described a method of gymnastics for the paralyzed with the object of rendering undestroyed nervous paths permeable by the will. The chief point is for the patient to concentrate his will on the movements to be performed, and to learn to believe in the results of his own activity.

Delbœuf has expressed the opinion—supporting it by some cases, especially of eye disease—that even organic changes may be effected by suggestive therapeutics. Braid, Hack Tuke, and others, have already come to the same conclusion. Bernheim s explanation may, *mutatis mutandis*, be called in for other cases. Sperling believes that electricity only does good in apoplexy by restoring the inhibited functions of parts which are anatomically sound. He is known to have experience and ability in the field of hypnotism and electro-therapeutics, such as are possessed by few, but does not believe that the part of the brain injured in apoplexy has ever been restored by electricity.

In cases of organic lesion it is possible in hypnosis to carry out movements which cannot be executed in the waking condition. In this connection Stembo has lately suggested a very ingenious theory. He believes that the recollections of movement are lost in the waking condition, when they have long since ceased to be executed. Consequently they cannot be carried out even when the lesion is repaired. In hypnosis, however, there is a heightening of memory by which the mechanism of movement is again recollected and so set in action.

It would take too long to give all the rules for hypnotic treatment, and Baierlacher, Bernheim, Hirsch, and Forel have already done so. I will merely mention a few of the chief points. A certain mental preparation is usually necessary. This preparation, as Bourdon remarks, must not begin by telling the patient who complains of pains, as is sometimes done by the inexperienced, that he has no pains. A sensible patient would simply laugh at his doctor and go to some one else.

There is, further, a difference between preparatory and therapeutic experiments. Practice will enable us to decide whether the hypnosis in particular cases is deep enough to be used therapeutically, or whether further trials are needed to increase susceptibility to suggestion. In most cases preparatory experiments are necessary.

When the suggestion has been given, care must be taken not to remove it by irrelevant and stupid questions. This sometimes happens unconsciously. Remarks like "The suggestion will only help you for the time," &c., may injure the patient like chemical poisons. Forel is right when he expresses the wish that only a doctor should give a patient methodical suggestions.

Sometimes the object of treatment can best be attained by pursuing a slightly roundabout way. Laurent mentions cases in which persons have been weaned from tobacco, not by direct command, but by suggesting that the smell of tobacco is unpleasant. In other cases I have found it an excellent plan to place the hypnotic subject back into earlier periods of life. I have sometimes been unable to remove acute pain even during deep hypnosis. But if I placed the patient back in a period when he suffered no pain, it has been possible in many cases not only to remove the pain during hypnosis, but to find that it does not return on awaking.

Russel Sturgis recommends, at all events in such cases of "fixed ideas" as he treated, that the suggestions should be noted down before hypnosis and communicated to the patient in order to exclude any misunderstanding of the suggestion; he further recommends frequent repetition of the suggestion during hypnosis, and its communication in a present, not a future form.

Since intense pain often renders hypnosis impossible, it is desirable, at the first attempt, to select a lull in the pain. Later, hypnosis can be induced even during acute pain. It is often necessary, after cure or improvement has been obtained, to repeat the suggestion occasionally, to prevent relapse.

Various authors have recently recommended the practice of collectively hypnotizing several patients. Liébeault has done this for many years. He finds that the psychic contagion becomes stronger, and that hypnosis is rendered easier. Other hypnotists, for example Wetterstrand and Grossmann, have made the experiment. I have myself adopted it in particular cases, and find it advantageous. It must, however, be carefully planned, or the advantages will be outweighed by the disadvantages. We must first, as Hirsch has done, bear in mind the question of professional secrecy. I know, for instance, of a doctor who by such collective hypnosis allowed some patients to know what others were suffering from, that this one was a morphinist, that a dipsomaniac, &c. Schrenck-Notzing also remarks that people of the better social classes very often object to such collective hypnosis. There is also a danger, as I know, that the personal operation of the hypnotist on individual cases may be lost. This is specially to be feared if the doctor leaves hypnotized persons alone for a time. A single person in the group feigning hypnosis may also act as a disturbing element. I know of some "hypnotized" persons who, when the doctor left the room, began to talk to each other, and this may naturally destroy the suggestions given to the others even in deep hypnosis. Mavroukakis

refers to what he calls indirect suggestion, a different
kind of indirect suggestion from that mentioned in
Chapter III. Thus A. may be influenced by a
suggestion given to B. But if A. is suffering from
narcolepsy, or a pathological tendency to sleep, and
B. from insomnia, the suggestion to B. to sleep more
will not work very favourably on A. But such action
cannot always be excluded. On all these grounds I
conclude that while hypnosis in common is a sparing
of time for the physician, it is not always advantageous for the patient. With careful selection, however, the method may be used successfully.

Hypnotism does not necessarily succeed at once.
If the hypnosis is deep a result may be very quickly
obtained ; in other cases patience and method are
wanted, and the time the illness has lasted must be
taken into consideration. The more the idea of pain
has taken root, the more difficult is it to overcome.
Liébeault and Liégeois were only able to cure a patient
with a confirmed tendency to suicide after about sixty
sittings, of which each lasted over half-an-hour.
Why hypnotism should be measured by a different
standard than other methods of treatment is inexplicable to me. A doctor is often satisfied to obtain
a result after weeks or months of electro-therapeutic
treatment, and how often, after months of persveve-
rance, it fails to appear. Why, then, should we
expect suggestive therapeutics to succeed in one
day ? Patience on the side of both doctor and patient
is often required.

I likewise deny that hypnotism should be regarded
as a sort of last hope in the treatment of diseases.
The longer they have lasted .the more difficult they
are to cure, because the idea of the disease has
established itself firmly. It is the duty of every one

who believes that hypnotism is harmless when
properly applied to use it where he thinks it will be
of service, and before it is too late. For some
diseases become incurable simply because they were
not rightly treated at first. The illness develops
into an auto-suggestion, more and more difficult to
overcome. The more a patient thinks of his pain,
the less his attention is turned from it, the less
possible it is to remove it later. We might hesitate
to make long preparatory experiments with people
difficult to hypnotize (Grasset). But it is to be wished
that hypnosis should be used when hypnosis can
easily be induced, and when the method is indicated,
rather than that a hundred other methods, all disagreeable to the patient, should first be tried in vain.

It has been asked whether hypnotism and suggestion are of real value to the art of healing. To
answer this we must consider whether a larger
number of patients are cured or improved by this
means than by exclusively physical and chemical
treatment. It is difficult to decide. If we suppose
that 50 per cent. are cured or improved by the usual
treatment—which is by no means the case—and that
2 per cent. are cured or improved by suggestion, these
figures would not mean much, as the percentage would
only be raised from 50 to 52. But if we suppose that by
the ordinary methods only 1 per cent. of functional
neuroses are cured or improved—which is nearer the
truth—and that 2 per cent. are cured or improved by
suggestion, this would be a great progress, since the
percentage would be raised from 1 to 3 per cent.,
i.e., the number of successfully-treated patients would
be tripled. I have chosen two extreme cases, to show
how difficult it is to settle the question. I think that
very few neuroses—I will consider only these in the

23

first place—are cured or improved by any treatment
not mental; perhaps one per cent. is too high a
figure.

Such questions are hard to decide, since we are not dealing
with fixed quantities. I have spoken on purpose of improvement as well as cure, because cure is understood in different
ways. Mendel calls a disappearance of the symptoms a cure,
without regard to the time during which they have disappeared.
He said that a person who was periodically deaf-mute had been
cured by hypnotic treatment, because he spoke and heard for
several days, though a few days later there was a relapse. I
should make the idea of cure depend upon the disappearance
of the tendency to return of the disease. But this is a scientific
theoretical notion, while the other springs from practical need.

But I certainly believe, with Krafft-Ebing, F.
Müller, and others, that no important effect can be
obtained in most functional neuroses without suggestion. Therefore I consider suggestion an immense
step in advance in this direction; suggestion without,
as well as with, artificially induced hypnosis, which,
however often materially helps its effect. I think
that hardly any of the newest discoveries are so important to the art of healing, apart from surgery, as
the study of suggestion. This will be specially pointed
out in a later work. In any case, the conclusion that
neither hypnotism nor suggestion will again disappear
from the foreground in medicine is justified. This
hope is grounded on the fact that there are in
Germany a number of practical doctors, not carried
away by enthusiasm, who study suggestion, and do
not look for hasty successes and "miraculous" cures.
They are all the more careful inasmuch as many
opponents of suggestion watch their cases in the hope
of forming an opinion of their failure. This is the

only proper and scientific way, which the most decided opponents have not always followed.

Naturally, care must be taken to examine character as in all therapeutics. Men are no more alike mentally than physically, and I believe that their mental differences are greater than their bodily ones. Therefore it is not astonishing that doctors who have psychological knowledge should succeed, while others, who treat by hard and fast rule, fail. The investigations of many authors show what results may be obtained by a clever use of suggestion ; they have succeeded in most unpromising cases. Forel is one of these. It is true that few have it in their power to experiment as he has done. It is very unscientific to impugn the successes of others because one has failed oneself. Perhaps it may be mentioned that an eminent Swedish alienist—Oedmann—says that he recognizes the good effects of suggestion in alcoholism, but that as he is unable to produce them he sends such patients to Wetterstrand (Corval).

No doubt experience is the best teacher. It is incomprehensible why some people deny the therapeutic value of hypnotism simply because their own few experiments have failed. It is the same with all instruments ; a practised operator succeeds where an unpractised one fails. So an experienced and conscientious hypnotist will remove ailments by suggestion, while an unpractised one may induce them from want of experience. It is certain that people who are suggestible and easy to hypnotize may be influenced by any one. But in more difficult cases a doctor, who has experience and psychological knowledge, will succeed where others fail.

There is, of course, no need to cease using other means, while hypnotism is being used (Sperling) ; on

the contrary, in each case the indications must be
followed. No method of healing will be driven out
by hypnotism ; that is, if it is accepted in practice.
Suggestion will not supplant other methods of healing, but complete them (Bourdon).

Naturally, whatever might injure the prognosis, or
make suggestion ineffectual, must be avoided in suggestive therapeutics ; and, before all, the fear of hypnosis. There is no doubt that this may do more
injury and produce more unfavourable effects than
hypnosis itself. Therefore it is advisable not to use
it when the patient is excited and frightened about
it ; Tokarski and Faber are of the same opinion. But
other mental excitements should be avoided as much
as possible. Krafft-Ebing's case plainly proves that
excitement may make suggestion ineffectual.

Bernheim has attempted to use hypnosis for purposes of diagnosis. There are cases in which the
diagnosis between functional and organic trouble are
not clear. If the trouble—aphonia, for instance—
disappears under suggestion, then the affection is not
organic. This opinion of Bernheim's contradicts his
own observation that even organic disease may be
temporarily improved by suggestion. Gorodichze
also speaks against any over-valuation of the application of hypnosis. Delbœuf, Brunon, and Ernould
have, however, published cases in which the surgical
diagnosis of the cause of disease has been rendered
easier by hypnosis. And on the other hand, suggestion is certainly a valuable aid to diagnose functional
disorder when it suffices to remove the trouble, as in
a case, mentioned by Schibbye, of hysteria localized
in the urinary sphere.

I believe that the study of hypnotism will much

enlarge our point of view in other ways. We shall now be able to solve many a riddle that has puzzled us. Now that it has been proved that even organic changes can be caused by suggestion we are obliged to ascribe a much greater importance to mental influences than we have hitherto done. I think that the diseases which are generally called imaginary are much more common than is supposed. I think that improper surroundings cause or increase many maladies. There are few people who are not impressed when they are assured on all sides that they look very ill, and I think many have been as much injured by this cumulative mental process as if they had been poisoned. Just as suggestion can take away pain, so it can create and strengthen it. It is small comfort to call such pains imaginary. And even if the pain is "only" imaginary it troubles the patient as much as if it were real.

Besides, I believe this expression "imaginary pain," which is used by physicians as well as laymen, is scientifically false. One author has excellently compared "imaginary pains" with hallucinations. Now we can say that the hallucinatory object is imaginary, but it is false to say the perception is imaginary; it has a central cause. It remains the same whether the object is imaginary or not; so does the pain when it is felt, *i.e.*, when there is a central process. It is a matter of indifference whether this central process is caused by a peripheral stimulus or by suggestion by a spontaneous mental act. The pain exists in both cases, and is not imaginary. If in the latter case the patient were to refer it to an external stimulus he would be wrong, but the pain as a subjective feeling is not imaginary. We may call such a pain, without objective symptoms, what we please, but we may be sure that it is a necessary consequence of some central processes. Certain subjective ideas cause pain as much as a wound causes pain. The removal of these is as much the doctor's affair as healing a wound.

Forel mentions a case in which a patient suffered from headache during a whole year, because it was, as he believed, said to him, when suffering from inflammation of the lungs accompanied by headache, that this would never pass away. Whether or not the patient misunderstood the doctor, the working of suggestion appears here. Forel succeeded by hypnosis and counter-suggestion in rapidly removing the headache. From other sides we also hear it asserted, perhaps with some exaggeration, that auto-suggestion may produce disease. I may recall here the traumatic neurosis which Charcot and others explained by auto-suggestion, a view which Meynert has opposed. Krafft-Ebing attributes great importance to auto-suggestion in hysteria, neurasthenia, and traumatic neuroses. Brügelmann shows that many asthmatic attacks only occur because the patient believes he cannot breathe ; he awaits with anxiety the moment for the attack to appear, and this anxiety brings on the attack. A powerful diversion of the attention may suffice to prevent the attack.

A case of Krafft-Ebing's shows what mental influence without hypnosis can effect. The patient, fully awake, thought she had been poisoned by belladonna. A dangerous collapse followed, which was finally cured by hypnotic suggestion.

Suggestion is not only a key to the origin and aggravation of maladies, it also explains the working of drugs. If medicines have different effects when prescribed by different doctors, we shall not find the cause of this in chemical differences. We should rather ask if the manner of the prescription, the impression made by the doctor, and other mental factors have not some effect ; it has been proved in many cases. We shall have to consider this influence of unconscious suggestion as of much more weight than we have done. The powerful mental influence of surgical operations has been pointed out, especially by L. Landau. The psychic influence of electricity has been emphasized by Möbius, who has found both opponents and followers. To the latter belongs especially Delprat, who on the ground of statistics came to the conclusion that electricity made no difference, the cure being no more rapid. On the other hand, Eulenburg, Sperling, Löwenfeld, Müller, Lagner, Remak, and Wichmann have opposed Möbius. Eulenburg shows by a series of cases that electricity may certainly work psychically, but that there is often an action independent of suggestion. Forel has demonstrated the degree to which suggestion must be taken into consideration in the use of chemical methods. Many new studies show that hypnotism exerts considerable influence in this respect. I may refer to the criticisms brought against Brown-Séquard's testicular injections, Massalongo and many others regarding their operation as purely suggestive. Some ascribe the efficacy of homœopathy to suggestion, against which Roth emphatically protests ; and I believe that many of the successes and failures of allopathy may also be laid to the account of suggestion. When the practical importance of mental influences become more generally recognized, physicians will be obliged to acknowledge that psychology is as important as physiology. Psychology and psychical therapeutics will be the basis of a rational treatment of neuroses.

The other methods must group themselves around this; it will be the centre, and no longer a sort of Cinderella of science, which now admits only the influence of the body on the mind, and not that of the mind on the body.

Auto-suggestion also, to which many people are exposed, even men of science, will receive new light by the study of suggestion. Soury has published a study on a case of scientific auto-suggestion affecting several Italian physicians. Rainaldi and Giacomo Lumbroso had believed that it was possible to excite certain brain centres, and contract the related muscles, by mechanically irritating the scalp above those centres. Soury shows convincingly how doubtful the doctrine of localization is, and that every author always succeeds in causing contractions in accordance with his own views as to motor centres.

The use of hypnotism in surgery has already been mentioned. Its use in inducing analgesia is not new; one inventive genius even imagines that God took the rib from Adam while he was in a hypnotic sleep, since he would certainly have waked had it been a natural one. The first methodical surgical operations in the magnetic sleep were begun in 1821, by Réca- mier. Such operations were often performed in the Paris hospitals under the direction of Baron du Potet. Mesmerism has since occasionally been used for the same purpose. Cloquet used it in 1829. He related his experiences to the French Academy of Medicine, but Lisfranc, the celebrated surgeon, put him down for an impostor or a dupe. Oudet was no better received in 1837, when he told the Academy of the extraction of teeth in the magnetic sleep.

In 1840 Esdaile performed a number of operations

during mesmerically induced analgesia in the hospital at Calcutta. The wounds are said to have healed very quickly. (Hellwald has drawn attention to the quick healing of the wounds of the Arab pilgrims which are made in the hypnotic state.) Elliotson at the same time was using mesmerism in London. Braid, who was much struck by Esdaile's results, also used hypnotism in surgery. The opinion that mesmeric passes perhaps induce analgesia better than the other hypnotic methods has some adherents now. Azam brought Braid's method of inducing analgesia to Paris (p. 16) ; from thence it passed to Germany, but found little support. Preyer says that military doctors and others appear often to have used empirical hypnotizing methods for small operations, such as tooth-drawing. Bonwill observed that after a succession of deep respirations a brief anasthesia appeared ; this was confirmed by Hewson. Possibly this is an auto-hypnotic condition, or an auto-suggestive anæsthesia. Recently Forel, Voigt, Tillaux, Le Fort, Grossmann (for fractures and dislocations), Bourdon, Howard, Wood and Toll, Schmeltz have used hypnotic analgesia in surgical treatment. It has very frequently been made use of in the extraction of teeth (Bramwell, Andrieu, Hivert, Klemich, Sandberg). Lauphear has even used hypnosis for amputations.

The value of hypnotism for inducing analgesia, however, is not great. Analgesia cannot sometimes be induced at all, and sometimes only after repeated trials. The excitement before the operation increases the difficulty. At all events, the cases in which hypnotism can be used to make an operation painless are very rare ; the care with which every such case is registered by the daily press shows this. Besides which we have at present so many certain means of inducing analgesia—ether and chloroform, which, however, occasionally kill the subject—that hypnotism is little likely to be much used. When by chance a person who is to undergo operation is found to be susceptible, there is no reason why hypnotism should not be used. Hack Tuke and Forel think that hypnotism should be used in all cases where chloroform would be dangerous. Forel believes, besides, that analgesia is more easily induced than I suppose; it is possible that a clever hypnotist may obtain better results in this direction than I have been able to do.

I once hypnotized a patient in order to open a boil painlessly. I did not succeed in inducing analgesia, but the patient was almost unable to move, so that I could perform the little operation without difficulty.

Cases in which analgesia is induced by post-hypnotic suggestion, and the operation performed in the waking state, have a greater theoretical interest (Boursier).

The value of hypnotism in obstetrics is about the same as in surgery. Lafontaine and Fillassier among the mesmerists have put women to sleep during labour. Liébeault has done the same with hypnotism. A series of such cases has lately been published (Pritzl, Mesnet, Sechcyron, Auvard, Thomas, Varnier, Voigt, De Jong, Schrenck-Notzing, Tatzel, Grandchamps, Luys, Cajal, Menant de Chesnais. The effects were not unfavourable. The pains were regular and strong, and could often be made almost insensible by suggestion.

There is an interesting statement of Freyer's that Jörg, an eminent obstetrician, at the beginning of the century thought birth impossible in the magnetic sleep without a quick awakening; a view which is now disproved.

So much significance is now attached to suggestion that it is invoked even at the wrong time. A characteristic example is the reception which was given to Schleich's method of anæsthesia. Schleich showed that by the injection of water it was possible to produce such swelling of the tissues that a surgical operation might be painlessly performed. The reproach was brought against this method that it was only a phenomenon of suggestion. The criticism appears to be groundless, but it serves to show how nowadays every one has suddenly begun to think of suggestion, which a few years ago was entirely ignored.

Much has been said of the use of hypnotism in education. Reference may be made to cases of masturbation in children; and Bérillon refers to the habit of biting the nails (onychophagy), which is considered to be a phenomenon of degeneration, and, according to J. Voisin, is often associated with masturbation. This, however, belongs rather to pathology, though such distinctions are rather arbitrary. For example, a child gets chorea through imitating other children who have it. In such a case it is not easy to say where the bad habit leaves off and disease begins. The cases of Bérillon, who has cured various little tricks and bad habits in children by hypnotic suggestion, may be reckoned among diseases. It is indifferent whether we say that hypnotism is used in such cases to cure disease or in the interests of education; the point is, to know what is meant. But serious observers have by no means wished that hypnotism should be

introduced into schools, but that suggestive treatment
should be used by doctors to suppress the bad
instincts of children.   Only one author—Decroix—in
spite of all sorts of contradiction, says that such suggestion should also be made by laymen ; the unani-
mous opposition of Forel, Dekhtereff, and others
shows plainly that my view is just.   When an
anonymous German author thought he made the
thing ridiculous, or refuted French authors by banish-
ing hypnotism from the schools, he simply refuted an
assertion that was never made.   Other authors have
taken superfluous pains to do the same.   The French
authors (Bérillon, Hément, Netter, Leclerc, A. Voisin,
Collineau) merely mean that certain faults in children,
which in my view and that of others are pathological,
should be cured by medical hypnotic suggestion, particularly when other methods have failed.

   The frequent objection (Blum, Seeligmüller) that
children would thus become machines instead of independent creatures is erroneous.   Hypnotic suggestion
and suggestion out of hypnosis have the same aim :
to determine the subject's will in a certain direction.
He is to do right, not unconsciously and mechanically,
but with conscious will, which has got its direction
either from hypnotic suggestion or ordinary education.
Suggestion sets the conscious will in the right direction as education does.

   Education is only good when what is taught grows
into an auto-suggestion ; *i.e.,* when in particular cases
the well-taught person must consciously do the right
he has been taught to will.   But hypnotic suggestion
is also only good when it turns into auto-suggestion
(Forel) ; that is, when the same thing happens as
without hypnosis.   We see again that the false views
result from the fact that hypnotic suggestion is taken

for an unconscious process—a supposition which I
have already refuted (p. 286).

Cases of chronic alcoholism, which have been successfully treated by hypnotic suggestion by several
experimenters (Forel, A. Voisin, Ladame, Widmer,
Wetterstrand, Corval), belong here.

A decision can no doubt be arrived at only by
serious examination, such as the men just mentioned
have made.

I shall only briefly mention other scientific uses of
hypnotism. It will no doubt be of great use to
psychology, although psychologists in Germany seem
disinclined to approach the subject. In other
countries much psychological work, founded on
hypnotism, has been done. Beaunis goes so far as
to say that hypnotism is to psychologists what vivi-
section is to physiologists. Forel and Krafft-Ebing
think the same. Max Dessoir, in particular, has often
represented the great value of hypnotism to psychology.

I believe, indeed, that some of the facts are of the
deepest interest ; *e.g.*, the apparent freedom of will of
hypnotic subjects in post-hypnotic actions. The
French (Binet, for example), and to some extent
the English, have attempted to investigate the problems of human personality, not only by studies in
the field of pathology, but also by experimental
hypnotism. · Clemens Sokal and S. Landmann
consider that attempts to investigate plurality of
psychic personality in one individual by hypnotic
investigation form an essential part of recent French
psychology. Other authors, like Ribot and Wizel,
study psychic phenomena both in the hypnotic and
the waking condition. The subject cannot be pursued

here, but it may be mentioned that, according to these
authors, much more exact answers may be obtained
from the hysterical during hypnosis than during the
waking condition. In any case hypnotism offers a new
method for psychological investigation. Münsterberg,
one of the best known and least prejudiced of our
younger psychologists, has in his work, *Aufgaben und
Methoden der Psychologie*, admirably justified hypnosis
in this respect. Wundt, also, in spite of all opposition,
finally admits hypnosis into the region of psychological
investigation, together with dreaming and insanity.

Stoll believes that in ethnological psychology the
doctrine of suggestion is of great value, in two respects.
In the first place, we may thus explain many hallucinations in the waking condition ; in the second place,
we are enabled to understand the actions of large
crowds. Hypnotism is indeed a mine for the psychological investigator, for hypnosis is nothing but a
mental state. When we think that psychologists
have always used dreams so much in their investigations of mental life, and that experiments can be
better made in hypnosis than in ordinary sleep,
because it can be regulated at pleasure, we cannot
deny the value of hypnotism to psychology.

I will not enter further into the advantages which
other sciences may hope to gain from it. I confidently
hope that the study of it will help to clear up the
hitherto dim field of mental life, and that it will help
to free us from the mountain of superstition instead of
increasing it.

CHAPTER VIII.

THE LEGAL ASPECTS OF HYPNOTISM.

WE will now discuss the points which have a particular interest in law. Some of the old adherents of animal magnetism recognized the legal importance of the subject, though their point of view differed slightly from ours. Thus, the commission which investigated the matter in Deslon's time, besides their official verdict, sent in a private report to the king, which, it appears, came to light through the Revolution ; they thought that morality especially was threatened. The mesmerists in Germany—Kieser, for example—also touched upon the legal side of magnetism. Charpignon has occupied himself with the point lately. Liébeault also thoroughly discussed the question in his book in 1866, and his explanations are very valuable even now. Gilles de la Tourette, Liégeois, and particularly Forel, Reden, Lilienthal, Bentivegni, Bonjean, Reese, and Mesnet have studied the legal side of the question very recently.

The first point to be considered is the relation of hypnotism to crime. The crimes committed on, and by, hypnotic subjects must both be discussed. We will begin with the first.

The offences against morality to which hypnotic subjects are exposed, are important ; few such cases have hitherto come to the notice of the law. F. C.

Müller supposes that this may be because, from loss of memory, the subject is usually unaware of them. But Forel's supposition seems to me more probable; he thinks such offences are rare because experimenters know that the loss of memory is only temporary, and that the subject may unexpectedly remember the occurrences of earlier hypnoses. A number of such cases were brought to justice in Germany at the time when animal magnetism was flourishing. Wolfram published one in 1821. A doctor is said to have assaulted his patient during the magnetic sleep. He endeavoured to avoid the consequences by procuring abortion, and this brought him to justice; however, he was acquitted.

Lately several cases have been made known in France. A more exact collection of them may be found in Liégeois' book (" De la Suggestion," &c.). One case is that of a professional magnetizer of Marseilles, who, in 1853, assaulted a girl in the magnetic sleep. The experts, Coste and Broquier, with whom the well-known authorities on medical jurisprudence, Devergie and Tardieu, agreed, gave their opinion that a magnetized subject might be assaulted against her will and without her consciousness.

The case of Castellan in 1865, reported by Prosper Despine, is better known. An assault was committed on a subject in an obviously hypnotic state, though she retained her consciousness. Liégeois refers the case to suggestion; Castellan, the criminal, must have suggested to his victim, Joséphine H., to love him, trust him, &c. Castellan was condemned to twelve years' imprisonment, upon the opinion of Roux and Auban, with whom the doctors Hériart, Paulet, and Théus were associated.

The Lévy case, in 1879, is also interesting. A

dentist of Rouen, named Lévy, assaulted a girl in the magnetic sleep. The case is remarkable because the girl's mother was present and noticed nothing. Lévy had placed his dentist's chair so as not to be seen. Brouardel gave his opinion on the case and Lévy was imprisoned for ten years.

Bellanger mentions the case of a woman who was assaulted by a doctor, and a case in Geneva in 1882, in which Ladame gave evidence, may be mentioned ; the supposed offender was acquitted, as the accusation was possibly false.

There are some other cases in Liégeois, in Golt-dammer's Archives for 1863, and in F. C. Müller's book, " Die Psychopathologie des Bewusstseins." The number would be slightly increased if some cases of auto-somnambulism were counted among them.

The judgment of such cases would offer no diffi-culty if the state of affairs was always clear ; the same legal clauses would be used as in cases of narcosis by chloroform.

Among further offences against hypnotic subjects may be mentioned intentional injury to health, which in some cases might be caused by post-hypnotic suggestion. All sorts of paralyses, loss of memory, &c., may be thus caused ; even some paralyses with objective symptoms, such as the so-called paralyses dependent on idea, on p. 75. It is not probable that these will ever be important from a legal point of view, and Lafforgue's supposition that a man might try to evade military service by causing a disease to be suggested to him seems to me even more im-probable. At all events, the law provides for such cases.

I need hardly add that bodily injury may be caused

24

by inattention to the proper precautions, nor need I discuss the question of deprivation of will in cases when the subject is hypnotized without his consent

It has also been asked (Roux-Freissineng) whether suicide might not be caused by suggestion ; to which I say, " Yes, if the suggestion were adroitly made."

A case (that of Frau'ein von Salamon) has been published in recent years, showing that hypnosis may apparently lead to death. The case is not quite clear, but it seems probable that death occurred during hypnosis. It does not follow that death was a result of hypnosis. This person was employed by Neukomm in the hypnotic condition for clairaudient experiments. He was to diagnose symptoms of disease, and, as is well known, a person who thus diagnoses symptoms may himself feel them. In this case it was a question of diagnosing the disease of a man who, as it seemed to Fraulein von Salamon, was dying, and this made so strong an emotional effect on her that, by the influence of the vasomotors and the heart, the brain was emptied of blood and death resulted.

The hypnotic state might be used to get possession of property illegally. People can be induced hypnotically and post-hypnotically to sign promissory notes, deeds of gift, &c. I reported to the Society of Prussian Medical Officers a case of a man who in the post-hypnotic state promised a donation to the Society, and carefully explained in writing that he did it of his own accord, after I had suggested to him that he should think so. Testamentary dispositions might be influenced in the same way.

I shall speak later of the significance of such acts in civil law, when quoting Bentivegni. I cannot venture to decide whether the criminal law would interpose in such cases.

There are important differences of opinion about the offences which hypnotic subjects may be caused to commit. Liégeois, who has discussed the legal side of the question of hypnotism in a scientific manner, thinks this danger very great, while Gilles de la Tourette, Pierre Janet, Benedikt, Ballet, and others, deny it altogether. Liégeois believes that about 4 per cent. of the population can be influenced by criminal suggestion. According to him, 100,000 people in Paris, 60,000 people in Berlin, may be so influenced. Others, as already observed, consider the risk entirely imaginary. In any case we must not be too ready to believe the stories of robbery we find in the newspapers; they are often written rather to produce a sensation than to advance science.

There is no doubt that subjects may be induced to commit all sorts of imaginary crimes in one's study. I have made hardly any such suggestions, and have small experience on the point. In any case a repetition of them is superfluous. If the conditions of the experiment are not changed, it is useless to repeat it merely to confirm what we already know. And these criminal suggestions are not altogether pleasant. I certainly do not believe that they injure the moral state of the subject, for the suggestion may be negatived and forgotten. But these laboratory experiments prove nothing, because some trace of consciousness always remains to tell the subject he is playing a comedy (Franck, Delbœuf), consequently he will offer a slighter resistance. He will more readily try to commit a murder with a piece of paper than with a real dagger, because, as we have seen, he almost always dimly realizes his real situation. These experiments, carried out by Liégeois, Foureaux, and others in their studies do not, therefore, prove the danger.

On the other hand, Liégeois has made some such experiments in all apparent earnestness, and in the presence of officers of the law, by hypnotic and post-hypnotic suggestion, and even by suggestion in the waking state. He made a girl fire a revolver, which she thought was loaded, at her mother; and another put arsenic into the drink of a relation. Delbœuf shows good reason for not considering these experiments convincing. Yet we must admit the possibility that a crime may be committed in this way, as Eulenburg, Dalley, and Forel insist. On theoretical grounds I believe it is possible with some subjects. There may be much exaggeration. For example, few people are so susceptible as to accept the suggestion of a criminal act without repeated hypnotization. It is also true that many would refuse even after long hypnotic training (Delbœuf). Gilles de la Tourette insists, besides, that a criminal who suggested an offence would be no more protected from discovery than if he did the thing himself. A hypnotic subject is not a suitable instrument for the commission of a crime. For a person who would commit a crime by post-hypnotic suggestion would, generally speaking, not be a person of the most honourable character, since morally defective people are decidedly easier to affect in this way than those with strong principles (Forel). However, criminal suggestion is not impossible. Forel thinks the greatest danger is that at the time the suggestion is made the subject may be induced to believe that he is acting without constraint. But this should only be possible in the case of morally defective persons.

A succession of cases, in which suggestion is alleged to have played a part in the commission of crime, has of recent years attracted the attention of the press. To these belongs the case of Gabrielle Bompard, who was accused of murder, committed, according to some, under the influence of a suggestion received from her lover Eyraud. The Weiss and Chambige cases also attracted some attention. In the former, a Madame Weiss, in Algiers, endeavoured to poison her husband, and was condemned to twenty years' imprisonment, whereupon she committed suicide. Liégeois believes that this was a case of post-hypnotic suggestion received by the woman from her lover; but the possibility of this was not seriously investigated by the Court. In the other case, a married woman who had previously been a model wife and mother was killed by a man, Chambige, whom she had fallen in love with, and who afterwards attempted to kill himself. Liégeois's explanation is that the woman was hypnotised by Chambige, and then by suggestion induced to forget her husband and children, and fall in love with him, Chambige. Liégeois supports this argument by the defence made by the advocate Durier.

If such a case were brought to justice, the experts would need to consider the following explanations. As has been said, all suggestions, criminal and otherwise, can be made hypnotically or post-hypnotically, and the legal decision would differ accordingly.

Till now I have called those states "waking states" in which a post-hypnotic suggestion is carried out when the state was apparently normal, except on the one point. But I only did this to avoid complication; the question has been passed over, but Bentivegni has lately called attention to it. I will, therefore, now consider whether there is a mental state which may be called normal in spite of irregularity on one point, as is the case when post-hypnotic suggestions are carried out in an apparently normal waking state.

We will take a simple case. I say to X. in hypnosis, "When you wake you will give A. a blow in the ribs." X. wakes, and instinctively does what I told him. He perfectly remembers doing it, and will accept no other suggestion either before or during the act. Thus it appears that X. is quite normal, except on the one point. But the modern psychology, and medical jurisprudence in particular, say that a man cannot be mentally abnormal on one point only ; they rather suppose a mental disturbance showing itself on one point, which is a symptom of general mental disturbance (Krafft-Ebing, Bentivegni, Morel, Maudsley). Therefore the state in carrying out a post-hyp-notic suggestion would be abnormal, though it appeared normal, as Bentivegni insists. But this author rightly thinks that this cannot be supposed in all cases of post-hypnotic sug-gestion, otherwise we should be obliged to think every man who accepted a therapeutic post-hypnotic suggestion was in an abnormal state while he carried it out. Here is a case : Y. is hypnotized in my warm room, and I tell him to say in half an hour, " Your room is frightfully hot." Now, supposing that it is really hot in my room, the carrying out of this post-hypnotic suggestion would by no means suffice to prove the abnormal state of the subject.

Thus we see that in these cases—we are only considering cases in which there is no symptom of a new abnormal state— the suggestion is sometimes carried out in a changed mental state, and sometimes in a completely normal one. How can we decide which is which ? A diagnostic point is difficult to find, but it seems to me that Bentivegni's is the only practicable one at present, though it is rather vague. He says, " The state while carrying out a post-hypnotic suggestion can only be thought normal when the motive force of the suggestion is such as can also be explained by the normal disposition of the subject, and when it is not so opposed to reality that the normal individual would discover and correct it." According to the last clause, post-hypnotic sense delusions without a renewed state of suggestibility would at once prove an abnormal mental state ; according to the first, an abnormal state of consciousness must also be supposed for the carrying out of numerous post-hypnotic acts, even when there is no renewed state of suggesti-bility. Truly, in many cases it is difficult to decide whether a subject finds the motive force for his post-hypnotic act in his normal disposition or not. However, Bentivegni has found a point of view from which these post-hypnotic sug-gestions may be judged. I now apply this to the two above examples. One post-hypnotic suggestion was that X. should

give A. a blow in the ribs. Let us suppose that X. is a peaceful
man, who likes A. ; then the motive of X.'s act would be inexplicable from his normal disposition ; consequently, according
to Bentivegni, his post-hypnotic state would be abnormal.
Y.'s remark about the heat was different. It was a natural
remark, supposing that the room was really warm. Consequently we have no reason to conclude a generally abnormal
mental state. The question is no doubt difficult to decide,
because "normal disposition" is hard to define. However,
Bentivegni has brought us a good deal nearer to solution.

Desjardins in France expresses the strange opinion
that a person who commits a crime by hypnotic or post-
hypnotic suggestion is punishable, because he might
have foreseen the possibility of such a suggestion.

According to Lilienthal this position is quite
untenable. It would be a strange sort of justice
which punished a crime committed in unconsciousness
and without intention. The case would be different
if the subject had caused the criminal act to be
suggested to him in hypnosis, perhaps with the view
of carrying it out more courageously. Lilienthal
thinks that in this case he would be punishable. The
power of self-determination would be normal at the
moment of decision. The induction of the hypnosis
would be the cause of the act, and consequently the
subject would be guilty (Lilienthal).

Campili, who has thoroughly discussed the different
legal questions connected with hypnosis, distinguishes
between the standpoints of two schools, the classical
and the anthropological.[1] According to the first

[1] It may briefly be remarked, that in Italy these two schools
are decidedly opposed ; the classical school recognizes freedom
of will, and the anthropological does not. However, the last-
named also agrees to punishment in such a case ; but only
because the person concerned is dangerous to society, not
because his will is free when he commits the offence.

there is no guilt in the last-mentioned case, as there can be no reflexion when the crime is committed; according to the last the criminal must be punished because he is dangerous to society.

If hypnosis is considered to be a state of mental disease, then all actions in the hypnotic state must go unpunished. Punishment of an act committed in a state of mental disease would be at least a novelty. It is not the custom at present, even if the legal code did not prevent it.

The importance of hypnosis in civil law was not seriously considered at first. Most investigators passed it over, supposing that hypnotism could only be important in criminal law. However, Bentivegni has put forward the contrary in a detailed work. I am, unfortunately, no expert, and cannot decide the question. The main points of what follows are therefore borrowed from Bentivegni's work, which besides puts forward many new views in connection with hypnotism.

Bentivegni, in discussing hypnotism in its relation to civil law, distinguishes between responsibility in business and liability for damages. The first means such a degree of freedom of will as is necessary for the transaction of business in connection with legal affairs. Liability for damages means that degree of freedom of will which causes responsibility for unlawful acts.

As regards responsibility in business, Bentivegni thinks that a mere state of hypnotic suggestibility is enough to exclude it, since in such a case the power to act with reflection and reason is wanting. It is true he also takes the stage of hypnosis into account, for a very light stage would hardly exclude responsibility in business. It should be said that in opposition to earlier views, he thinks that not only such acts as are carried out through hypnotic suggestion are invalid, but that the mere existence of hypnotic suggestibility is enough under some circumstances to exclude business responsibility, even when the acts are not suggested. He thinks the same about most post-hypnotic suggestions, where he makes several distinctions. All transactions are invalid which are effected in a post-hypnotic state in which there is renewed suggestibility. Also, the state during the carrying out of a post-hypnotic suggestion, if it is united with post-hypnotic forgetfulness of the act, excludes responsibility, even if the suggestibility has ceased. But we saw (p. 162) that a person may be apparently quite awake and yet carry out a post-hypnotic suggestion without remarking it, without falling into a new hypnosis, and calmly talking meanwhile. Now we must ask whether such post-hypnotic suggestions affect responsibility in business. Bentivegni decides this according to the kind of suggestion. When the post-hypnotic suggestion is merely a movement or action which the subject often does automatically at other times, there is no reason to question the responsibility. Some persons, for example, have a habit of scribbling on paper. Now, according to Bentivegni, if he does this post-hypnotically, he is not in an unfit state for business. But he is unfit when he does post-hypnotically what he would refuse to do under normal circumstances. Bentivegni thinks that when the post-hypnotic act is done in an apparently waking state, *i.e.*, when there is no loss of memory and no susceptibility to suggestion, the question becomes very difficult. He thinks (p. 375) that in such a case all depends on the nature of the suggestion. The question is, Are the suggested acts, and their possible motives, of such a nature as to be willingly received into the conscious-ness of the subject, and to be compatible with the general content of his consciousness, or not? Ben-tivegni gives the two following examples: 1. A. owes B. £20, but has forgotten it; in hypnosis he is told to pay B. the money at the first opportunity, which he does, post hypnotically. 2. C., who is not in good circumstances, is told in hypnosis to make a present of his personal property to D., whom he does not like. He wakes, and the idea occurs to him when he sees D.; he resists at first, but finally formally obeys the order.

According to Bentivegni, in Example I. neither responsibility for the particular act nor the capacity for business in general need be doubted, because the sug-gestion was acceptable to the motives pre-existing in the subject's consciousness. But in Example II. there must be a revolution in the subject's consciousness before he will obey a suggestion so contrary to his interests. Therefore Bentivegni thinks the responsi-bility is doubtful, at least as far as the single act is concerned.

In other cases the incapacity is much more exten-sive, because delusive ideas may be post-hypnotically suggested, which, without doubt, cause incapacity for business so long as they last, in the same way as do the delusions of the insane. Bentivegni thinks it should be provisionally supposed that a subject who is under the influence of a post-hypnotically sug-gested idea must be considered unfit for business, when this idea is of such a kind that its spontaneous recurrence would partially or wholly do away with his responsibility.

Finally, besides the post-hypnotic suggestions

which do not interfere with consciousness, and those which alter consciousness, as insane ideas do, Bentivegni discusses a third category of suggestions. For example, a subject might be told in hypnosis that a particular engraving was an oil-painting. In such a case the error must be considered, *i.e.*, the inability to perceive the real facts. It is an important question whether such a suggested error is excusable; Bentivegni thinks it generally is. If the error is excusable, there could be no claim for damages.

Bentivegni next discusses liability for damages. This implies an illegal act committed in a responsible state, and the civil law punishes it with fine. According to the Prussian common law all illegal acts are irresponsible when the agent is not in possession of his reason and is unable to control his actions. Consequently the conclusions that Bentivegni draws with regard to irresponsibility in business hold good also for liability for damages.

They hold good for all acts done in a state of hypnotic suggestibility, such as in deep hypnosis and in some post-hypnotic states of suggestibility, and further for the post-hypnotic states in which there is loss of memory. If such a division of the consciousness occurs through post-hypnotic suggestion that a suggested act is done, independently of the normal activity, *e.g.*, if a subject after hypnosis, but under the influence of post-hypnotic suggestion, injures some other person, he will not be liable to damages if he is in an unfit state for business, as this state is described above. But any man who causes himself to be hypnotized, only that he may not be responsible for his misdeeds, must make reparation for every damage, as appears from a decision of the common law (Bentivegni).

Of course, I have been unable to enter into detail on all points. I have taken the chief facts concerning the legal importance of hypnosis from the learned work of Bentivegni, "Die Hypnose und ihre civil-rechtliche Bedeutung," as may be seen from the numerous quotations. I recommend the book to any one who wishes to study the question.

Retroactive hallucinations are of great import-ance in law. They can be used to falsify testi-mony. People can be made to believe that they have witnessed certain scenes, or even crimes, &c I have before pointed out the analogy between these retroactive suggestions and many phenomena of ordinary life. Lilienthal believes that the training of witnesses is the same sort of thing, and Forel explains the management of the different parties in a lawsuit by the counsel in the same way. Max Dessoir agrees with him. Bernheim and Motet believe that the Tisza-Eszlar lawsuit was the result of a retroactive suggestion made by Moritz Scharff without inducing hypnosis. As a matter of fact two parties often assert the exact opposite both in law cases and in ordinary life without conscious falsehood. An old proverb says, "The wish is father to the thought;" and each party imagines what it wishes. An honest delusion of memory is the consequence.

It has recently been pointed out by several authors —among others, Motet and Bezy—that children fre-quently tell untruths in law courts. The same has long been observed of the hysterical. This is partly due to auto-suggestion, and partly to external sug-gestion, leading to falsification of memory. Del-brück's work, *Die Pathologische Lüge*, deals very thoroughly with this question, and is certainly the best study of the matter which has appeared in recent years.

Bernheim insists upon certain rules of precaution for preventing witnesses giving false testimony purely in consequence of the method of examination. He thinks that the suggestibility of the witnesses should be tested, and that this could be done by suggesting a reply which could at once be proved incorrect. This advice, with which Forel agrees, may seem self-evident, but it is practically valuable. Every one knows how easily mistakes are made in legal cases from mental excitement. Any excited state lessens the power of cool reflection which is required for every act of memory.

Bernheim's wish certainly does not appear superfluous, when we recollect that he has succeeded in inducing complete delusions of memory by suggestion without hypnosis; he has made people believe they had witnessed thefts, &c., which were purely imaginary.

In a recent trial for murder at the Aisne Assizes, an alleged murderer was found innocent, in spite of the depositions, because the judge held that the chief witness might have been the victim of a suggestive falsification of memory.

The next question is, Can hypnotism be in any way made useful to justice? It cannot be denied that the point may become of practical importance at any moment. Is hypnotization in a court of justice allowable at present? Lilienthal says it certainly is under some conditions, and for some purposes.

It is interesting to note that as early as 1869 Erckmann-Chatrian, in their play *Le Juif Polonais*, represented hypnosis in a law court, in order to bring the murderer of the Jew to confession; the authors allowed this experiment to be crowned with success.

To the question occasionally asked, whether hypnotism may be used to obtain testimony from the accused or from witnesses which they decline to give in a waking state, we must certainly answer in the negative, in the present state of the law.

The practical value of such a proceeding has been much exaggerated. In the first place, very few people can be hypnotized against their will, and it is not to be supposed that an accused person would submit to the necessary conditions.

Besides this, I think it a mistake to suppose that a hypnotic subject would divulge all his secrets so easily. This supposition is copied from one book into another, but is none the truer for that. It is supported by a few well-known cases; for instance, that of Giraud-Teulon and Demarquay, who were obliged to wake one of their subjects who began to tell secrets; and a similar case is related by Brierre de Boismont. Though I do not contest the truth of these cases, I must insist that the phenomenon is rare. I have never observed it. According to my experience the subject keeps his individuality, and what he does not choose to tell he hides. A further question, whether the subject can be induced to tell by suggestion, must be answered in the affirmative, in a few cases. I have hardly any personal experience in this direction. I once observed a case of lock-jaw, when the subject feared some word would escape him. The spasm was so strong that it was impossible to end it artificially.

Lichtenstädt declared in 1816 that he knew of no case in which indiscreet questions were answered. Delbœuf goes so far as to say that the subject retains his own character even in hypnosis, and when he betrays what he should conceal, Delbœuf holds the apparent confession to be false. A woman who confesses infidelity under hypnosis, but denies it in the waking state, Delbœuf would regard as certainly faithful.

It is much easier to attain the end in a circuitous way than by suggestion ; by suggesting a false premise, for example, as I have mentioned on p. 178. Let the subject be told that some person is present in whom he would confide, or that the people he does not wish to tell are absent. This answers in many cases.

But all such statements must be received with caution, for I can safely assert that hypnotic subjects can tell falsehoods as well as if they were awake, and that subtle webs of falsehood are invented in hypnosis. Lombroso tried in one case to obtain a confession of a crime which had been proved, though the subject had always denied it. The attempt was useless ; the subject told the same tissue of lies as when awake. Delbœuf, Laurent, and Algeri give the same information. In any case, a statement made in hypnosis must be received with caution ; it might be an indication, but not a proof.

I have, however, made some experiments in another direction. Interested by Max Dessoir's experiments in automatic writing, I tried to obtain results in the same way, with a subject whose consent I previously got. I put a pencil into his hand, and ordered him to answer certain questions, but not to write purposely. The subject wrote everything I told him, and answered every question, betraying many family secrets without knowing it or wishing it. He did not know that he was writing. I have not space to enter into details of this case.

Thus, in law, hypnotism might be used to decide whether a person were hypnotizable or not, or to obtain a statement which the accused or the witnesses cannot give in the waking state. Such a case may occur, and, as a matter of fact, the question has already been of practical importance.

Such statements in hypnosis would be valuable because subjects remember in later hypnoses all that has occurred in earlier ones. Now, if it is suspected that the subject has been the victim or the instrument of a crime which he forgets in the waking state, it is evident that hypnotism should be judicially used, for re hypnotization might clear up the case.

But according to Lilienthal there is a legal limitation here. He thinks an accused person or subject may be hypnotized if he consents. But hypnotization is only permissible to confirm the fact of hypnotizability, and he thinks a judicial examination in hypnosis is illegal. However, the arrangement of criminal proceedings does not appear to me so carefully defined that a statement made in hypnosis might not be received in particular cases ; it is certain that in some circumstances such a statement might be very important. For, as so many persons are susceptible, a mere proof of susceptibility to hypnotism would not be worth much. Lilienthal thinks that such a statement is inadmissible, because the testimony of unsworn witnesses is only allowed in certain cases, and an oath could not be administered to a hypnotized subject, and it would not be possible either to make him swear to his statement after waking. The statements of an accused person in hypnosis are not admissible, because he should not be compelled to make statements against his will. However, I think that Lilienthal here overlooks the fact that when an accused person, who has forgotten the criminal suggestion in his waking state, demands

to be hypnotized that he may remember, he is not
making a statement against his will. At the most it
would only be a statement without his will. I cannot
venture to decide what scruples a lawyer might have,
neither do I feel competent to decide whether the
statement of a hypnotized witness is admissible in
law.

Goltdammer relates that this question of the use
of hypnotism in law called up a discussion in a court
of justice between the defending counsel and the
counsel for the crown, in a suit at Verona twenty-six
years ago. It was a case of assault in magnetic sleep.
There was loss of memory in the waking state. The
defending counsel opposed the counsel for the crown,
who proposed to re-magnetize the assaulted person, but
the court agreed to his doing so, as it considered the
induction of the magnetic sleep merely as a method
of proof. The victim made important statements in
the sleep, and in consequence of these the accused
was condemned.

We will now discuss what should be done when the
accused person pleads that he has committed the
offence through hypnotic or post-hypnotic suggestion,
or when he says he has been the victim of a crime in
hypnosis. If such a plea had never been made, hypnotism need never be judicially considered. The
point requiring consideration, as Forel points out,
is that when the crime is suggested it may also be
impressed upon the subject that he shall think he has
acted freely. However possible this may be, a consideration of it at present would lead to the most
monstrous consequences. If any regard were paid to
it, we should be obliged to take into consideration
that every case of crime might be a result of hypnotic

25

suggestion. This is always theoretically possible, especially when the crime does not in any way advantage the accused (Delbœuf). But at present—whether rightly or wrongly must be left out of the question—it is impossible for justice to weigh this point. We must confine ourselves to the consideration that this objection might be raised, greatly to the advantage of the accused (Riant).

Let us suppose that the accused says the crime was suggested to him, that he felt a subjective constraint, and that he has often been hypnotized, but that he does not remember the suggestion.

It would then have to be judicially decided—(1) whether the accused was really hypnotized; (2) whether a suggestion was made to him in this state; (3) who made the suggestion; (4) to what degree he was suggestible (Max Dessoir).

Now, if the statements of witnesses were insufficient, he could be hypnotized; but, as is easily to be seen, hypnotization would naturally prove nothing. I will therefore suppose that examination and statements made in hypnosis were legally admissible. Making use of the memory in hypnosis we should, first of all, ask who made the criminal suggestion. If no answer was obtained (since the originator might have also suggested loss of memory) an indirect method must be used, such as Liégeois mentions; the originator might be discovered by means of association, if any one is decidedly suspected. The subject might be told to laugh, cough, &c., when he saw the originator, or his photograph, or heard his name. I believe he could probably be got at in this way; but there must be a starting-point, such as suspicion of somebody.

If nobody were suspected the name of the originator might probably be got at in some other way; *e.g.,* by automatic writing.

I think it certain the aim could be attained by repeated suggestions, in spite of loss of memory ; for a suggested loss of memory can be made to disappear by repeated contrary suggestions in a new hypnosis. Finally, as I have said, the degree of suggestibility must be ascertained. This could also be done by fresh suggestions, which would have full play in a new hypnosis. But further, the author of the crime might suggest that the subject should not be hypnotizable by anybody but himself, as has been explained on p. 174; this would complicate matters. Although no experiments have yet been made on this point, my own experience makes it seem probable that even such a suggestion might be made ineffectual by repeated opposed suggestions in new hypnoses—supposing, of course, that a repetition of the original suggestion could be prevented.

The case would be the same if a subject asserted that he had been the victim of a crime; new hypnoses must be induced, and if there was loss of memory the question must be cleared up by examination during hypnosis, supposing the law allowed it.

All this shows what difficulties would arise if hypnosis should become an important question in law. New hypnotization would only result in a certain degree of probability, since (1) there is intentional falsehood in hypnosis ; (2) the assertions may be influenced by previous suggestions ; (3) the answers are readily influenced by the method of examination ; (4) previous suggestion may make new hypnoses very hard to induce.

All which shows that statements in hypnosis might be indications, but could never be proofs. Danillo even thinks such assertions so completely untrustworthy that he proposes to refuse to accept them.

As a matter of course all the other points should be
weighed, as in ordinary cases ; such as who benefits
by the crime; whether the subject has often been
hypnotized, &c. This would be the only way when
the person supposed to have been influenced by suggestion is already dead, as is conceivable in a will
case. Such a case does not seem to be unlikely, and
would be very difficult to clear up.

And in cases of legal hypnotization the possibility
of simulation must, of course, be considered, as well
as the possibility of a purposely false accusation
(Ladame). In judging of simulation the bodily
symptoms of the school of Charcot must on no
account be alone considered, as they are relatively
uncommon. Gilles de la Tourette ascribes a legal
importance to the stages of Charcot and their symptoms, which they by no means deserve.

Finally, Forel's opinion may be mentioned. He
thinks indirect extortion of money by an unprincipled
experimenter a much greater danger in hypnotism
than direct criminal actions, and that it would not be
difficult for such a man to avoid direct conflict with
the law.

Many proposals have been made for avoiding the
possible dangers of hypnotism to health as well as to
morality. Delacroix, in France, demands that hypnotization should be legal only for doctors, and then
only when at least two are present. Friedberg wished
in 1880 that hypnotic experiments should only be
allowed in the presence of a doctor ; [1] Grasset and
others agree with him.

[1] According to a short notice in the *Deutsche Med. Zeit.* in a
part of Russia any doctor who wishes to hypnotize is ordered
to have two other doctors present. This proposal--about which

All competent persons, including especially the lawyers (Drucker, Lilienthal, etc), believe that the use of hypnosis by doctors for therapeutic purposes should not be rendered difficult. This is recognised in the law which was proposed in Belgium by the Minister of Justice (Le Jeune); the hypnotizing of minors and the insane was only to be entrusted to physicians. Finally, on the motion of Soupart, it was agreed that by special authorization an exception might be made in favour of those who were not physicians. Hypnotic exhibitions are, however, forbidden by law in Belgium.

In free America, also, the objections to public representations are beginning to find favour, as we may see by the prohibition of exhibitions in Cincinnati.

It would certainly be well to avoid all dangers by means of a law. But to begin with, the term "hypnotism" is vague and hard to define, and this alone would raise all sorts of difficulties. And other difficulties would be raised by the fact that many people can hypnotize themselves (Preyer).

But hypnotization is by no means so dangerous as would be concluded from many novels, whose authors have naturally chosen the rarest and most sensational

I can find no further details—plainly shows a want of experience. On the ground of my own experiments I could make many objections, but content myself with the following : (1) Who is to pay the two doctors who are merely spectators? (2) Should a doctor, who is perhaps treating a poor man without any fee, pay the two other doctors into the bargain? (3) If there is only one doctor in a place is he to fetch doctors from one or two other places to witness an experiment which perhaps must be repeated daily? More recently, the application of hypnotism in Russia has been still further restrained, any public exhibition being now forbidden.

phenomena. There are in reality things more important than hypnotism from a hygienic standpoint. For example, it would be of great service if exact legal directions for disinfection were given to both doctors and laymen attending cases of diphtheria, and if disobedience to such directions were severely punished. This point seems to me much more weighty than the hygienic importance of hypnotism. How many people have communicated diseases by insufficient disinfection! The happiness of many families has been destroyed, and the guilty person has remained unpunished.

I think it indispensable that science should take possession of hypnotism. This is the easiest way to prevent its misuse. When I speak of science I naturally mean psychology as well as medicine, for hypnotism will never become a factor in medicine without a scientific psychological basis. Psychology is needed for the investigation of mental states just as chemistry and physics are needed for the testing of drugs and the investigation of electricity. But just as medicine is obliged in part to leave the study of chemical and physical agents to the representatives of other sciences, so it will be obliged not only to leave the investigation of hypnotism to psychologists, but to beg them to undertake it. But as it is necessary to have some physical and chemical knowledge in order to prescribe drugs, so it is necessary for a doctor to have some psychological knowledge before he can use hypnotism. In a time when the pillars of therapeutics, though apparently raised on a foundation of exact medicine, are crumbling more and more; when the supposed fixed indications— which many think are a prerogative of non-mental therapeutics—are more and more attacked; when

men like Unverricht, Arndt, and Hugo Schulz discover the errors and false conclusions of a system of
therapeutics supposed to be guided by fixed indications ; when the "exact" therapeutics of fever have
been more and more abandoned during the last ten
years, and knowledge of fever seems to be returning
to the standpoint of Hippocrates, we have no right
to be hostile to psychology. Nowadays, when ill-
grounded therapeutics are increasingly attacked by
doctors as well as laymen, an assertion such as was
lately made is untenable: "Mental treatment is outside the domain of medicine, because there are no
fixed indications for mental treatment." But mental
therapeutics are an integral part of medical treatment,
and as the study of hypnotism is a department of
psychology, it should not be superciliously rejected ;
hypnotism should be regarded as a department of
science in medical circles as well as in any others.

From this point of view medicine and psychology
should unite to study the question. In any case the
path is made plain already. Public exhibitions have
called the attention of science to these states, though
on the other hand the flavour of charlatanism in the
matter has repelled many. For this reason it is a
good thing that such public exhibitions have been
forbidden in Prussia. Nothing now prevents our
approaching the subject in a scientific manner.

I do not wish to depreciate the services of those
who have drawn attention to hypnotism by public
exhibitions. Just as I refuse to join in the general
condemnation of Mesmer, I try to judge men such as
Hansen, Böllert, and others, fairly. Though their
motives may not have been purely unselfish, they
have been of great service to science, since without
them we should probably still be ignorant of the sub-

ject. To the honour of those mentioned, to whom
Donato may be added, it should be expressly stated
that all three of them have been ready to help the
representatives of science in the most straightforward
way. Heidenhain, Michael, Wernicke, Morselli, and
many others have emphatically recognized this. None
the less, I oppose such exhibitions for the reasons
mentioned, and I do not think they are justified by
Delbœuf's supposition that they are the best means
of spreading a knowledge of hypnotism, and thus
lessening its dangers. It must be added that, from
the moral point of view, there is no justification for
putting people into a condition which deprives them
of will, for no higher object than for the amusement
of uncultured persons.

CHAPTER IX.

ANIMAL MAGNETISM, ETC.

THE following chapter aims at giving the reader an idea of some phenomena which are often mentioned in connection with hypnotism, although the connection is rather historical than essential. In my view they are the consequence of erroneously interpreted observations. But as they are often quoted, and it is necessary to know at least something about them, I will explain them in the following sections. I do not think that the conclusions drawn from them are just, but everything should be examined without prejudice. A scientific refutation helps truth more than *a priori* negation; and some of these things are related by eminent observers. An investigation is as much in place here as it was when Virchow consented to examine the case of Louise Lateau when the necessary conditions were fulfilled. As Virchow remarks, what we call the laws of nature must vary according to our frequent new experiences.

The phenomena are—(1) animal magnetism; (2) super-normal thought-transference, telepathy (*suggestion mentale*); (3) certain super-normal acts in somnambulism; (4) the effect of the magnet on hypnotic subjects; (5) the effect of drugs on approach or contact.

In animal magnetism the chief part is played by a personal influence, not resulting from suggestion, which A. exercises over B. The following examples will make this clear :—

A. tells B., " You cannot speak." B. hears, and cannot speak ; this is merely suggestion. If A. makes mesmeric passes down B.'s arm, and analgesia follows, this may be also suggestion. B. knows what A. is doing, and the result may be produced by B.'s imagination in a purely mental way. Let us suppose that C. comes on the scene, and makes passes over B.'s arm, and that analgesia does not follow ; suggestion explains this too. B. 'believes that A. can induce analgesia, and that C. cannot, and the results are in accord with his belief. But the case is different when B. does not know whether A. or C. is making the passes. According to the views of the adherents of animal magnetism—the so-called mesmerists—A. can produce analgesia by magnetizing and C. cannot. They therefore think that A. has some personal influence which suggestion does not explain. This influence is an inherent power in some people, and only such people can magnetize. This example shows what is at present understood by mesmerism or animal magnetism (vital magnetism, bio-magnetism, zoo-magnetism).

The mesmerists think that a man who has this power can cause local or general analgesia or contractures, or even cure diseases. He can even magnetize children under a year old, and influence them therapeutically. Liébeault, the founder of the Nancy school and of the method of suggestion, who disputed the magnetic influence in 1866, became a firm adherent of it later. In 1883 he published a book in which he describes cures of children under three years ; these cures caused the change in his views. He thought that though nearly all might be explained by suggestion, something remained which needed another explanation, and this he called animal magnetism or zoo-magnetism—a name used by Athanasius Kircher, and afterwards Bartels. Lately Liébeault has again abandoned his belief in animal magnetism.

Besides the effects named—induction of analgesia and contractures, the healing of diseases, and its influence on young children—other effects of this supposed animal magnetism are mentioned as proving the existence of the force. Du Prel, one of its decided adherents, gives the following : Firstly, animals can be magnetized, in which case he thinks suggestion out of the question. On this point I refer the reader to the hypnotic experiments on animals which I have described. Such a force cannot be concluded from them. In the first place, it is by no means proved that animals are not susceptible to suggestion ; *e.g.*, if an animal is held for some time, why should it not be able to conclude that it is unable to move, even after it has been released ? Many eminent experimenters hold this view. And further, certain stimuli applied to the nerves of the skin make movements impossible, though the stimuli are not caused by some unknown force ; and the fascination which the rattlesnake exercises on birds cannot be considered a proof, in Du Prel's sense of the word, any more than the fascinating gaze of a man can be considered to prove the possession of some force peculiar to himself. Secondly, Du Prel speaks of magnetic experiments on sleeping persons, *i.e.*, on persons who did not know they were being magnetized. But it must be remarked that sleep does not involve an absolute loss of consciousness ; consequently, that suggestion, in the psychological sense, is not impossible in sleep.   Thirdly, the same author can magnetize people at a distance, as well as asleep, in which case suggestion is also supposed to be excluded.   Fourthly, he says that plants can be magnetized and their growth thus influenced, as is said of some of the fakirs.   Fifthly, the magnetic force can be passed on to inanimate objects, which then have the same effect as the magnetizer.   Sixthly, Du Prel brings forward the super-normal thought-transference, which I shall shortly discuss, in proof of animal magnetism.

The magnetic influence is used by means of mesmeric passes, by touch, by fixed gaze of operator and subject, by breathing on the subject (Baréty), and some think by concentration of thought and will on the desired result (Puységur, Nasse).

The mesmeric passes described on p. 22 are most generally used.   Much information about the direction of the passes can be found in the books of the mesmerists.   The effect is supposed to be different according as the passes are upwards or downwards, or made with the back or palm of the hand, apart from suggestion.   The right and left sides have different effects.   The mesmerists all speak much about the polarity of the magnet, and Fludd, Hell, Mesmer, and Scoresby supposed a similar polarity in men. The same thing has been asserted more recently by Chazarain, Dècle, Durville, De Rochas, and Baréty. Baraduc has even devised an instrument to measure and formulate magnetic relations between men.   But the views are so opposed that for the present I ascribe the supposed polarity to unconscious habit.

The mesmerists have put forth many theories to

explain this personal influence. I pass over most of them for brevity's sake. But I will mention those of Mesmer, because many false views are widespread about them. He says the whole universe is filled with a fluid which is more subtle than ether, just as ether is more subtle than air, and air than water. This fluid conducts vibrations just like ether, air, and water. As the vibrations of the light-ether cause light, and those of air cause sounds, so the vibrations of this universal fluid cause other phenomena. The mutual influence which the heavenly bodies undisputedly exercise on each other and the earth are caused by the vibrations of this fluid. One animal body influences another by means of the vibrations of this fluid. Mesmer called this animal magnetism.

This theory of Mesmer's is often confused with another theory of a fluid. Mesmer was thinking of a universally extended fluid. Another theory supposes a fluid in the nerves, which is called outwards by movement. This is the assertion of Albrecht von Haller, the famous physiologist of the last century, who established his priority to Mesmer, although their theories are by no means identical. These are not mere notions invented and defended by swindlers and fools. Many clever men—A. von Humboldt, for example—thought that a force in the nervous system could produce effects at a distance, if not at a great distance. The well-known physician and anatomist, Reil, held a like view. In any case the mesmerists had the support of eminent scientists, who supposed a nervous fluid surrounding men. Mesmerism has even quite lately found some adherents among eminent men of science. Ed. von Hartmann is a convinced adherent of it, and founds his belief on personal experience.

I shall pass over the other theories of animal magnetism, merely mentioning that many persons did
not believe in the universal fluid.

The mesmerists maintain that sleep need not
always be induced before a person can be magnetically influenced ; that the subjects may be thoroughly
awake ; and that this is the distinction between mesmerism and hypnotism. But it should be said that
there is by no means always a true sleep in hypnotism. It is evident that the old mesmerists knew the
light hypnotic stages well ; they called them magnetic states. The mesmerists also did not use the
personal methods exclusively ; they used inanimate
objects for magnetizing, such as the *baquet* of Mesmer
and Puységur's favourite magnetized tree. They
thought that the magnetic force passed into the
object from the magnetizer. But when this was not
the case they were not at a loss. When no magnetizer
has touched the object, as is the case in the method
of Braid, then (as Moricourt thinks) the fluid of the
subject is reflected from the object gazed at, and he
is affected by his own fluid.

So-called animal magnetism has been made of practical
importance by its use by healing magnetizers, who are supposed to be able to cure diseases. The utter lack of criticism
among them, which makes scientific discussion impossible,
obliges me to renounce the attempt to give details, though I
am convinced that not one professional magnetizer has yet
proved that he possesses any particular power unexplained
by suggestion. On the other hand, many authors —*e.g.*, Göler
von Ravensburg—have pointed out great sources of error, so
that childlike faith would be required to take their assertions
seriously.

The phenomena of thought-transference, mental
suggestion, telepathy, or, as Mayerhofer calls it,
telæsthesia, are related to animal magnetism, and

are often spoken of in connection with it. Telepathy means the transference of thoughts, feelings, sensations, &c., from a person A. to a person B. by some means other than the recognized sense perceptions of B. Consequently such thought-reading is altogether excluded, in which one person guesses the thought of another by means of the tremors in his muscles, *i.e.*, by a recognized kind of perception. Telepathy has a certain relation to mesmerism (Ochorowicz).

In making the experiments, the person B., who is to guess the thoughts of A., is often mesmerized by A., as this is supposed to make the transference easier. Some English experimenters, Guthrie in particular, have made experiments when both persons were quite awake. The transference is supposed to be caused merely by a strong concentration of thought on the part of the agent. In the same way the subject feels the agent's sense perceptions. If A. is pricked, B. feels it ; if A. tastes salt, B. tastes it, &c. It is also said that A. can make B. act, merely by concentrating his thoughts on what B. is to do. Others think that it is the concentration of A's. will on B. which causes the action. Perronnet even maintains that it is possible to influence the pulse and cause vasomotor changes telepathically, by an effort of will. The nearer A. is to B. the better, but the phenomena are said to have been observed when subject and agent were separated by several *kilometres*. It is said to be even possible to hypnotize certain people at long distances by concentration of thought ; such experiments are said to have succeeded at Havre. Among authors who vouch for the reality of telepathy, and whose experiments deserve consideration, I mention Charles Richet, Ochorowicz, Pierre Janet, Gibert, F.

Myers, A. Myers, Gurney, Birchall, Guthrie, Van
Eeden, Glardon, and Podmore. However, these
experiments raise some doubts. I had an opportunity some years ago of being present at Mrs.
Sidgwick's interesting experiments at Brighton.
These experiments were remarkable for their extraordinary success. Two persons were in the hypnotic
condition, and one had to indicate a number thought
of by the other. The proportion of correct answers
was extremely large. As, however, the two persons
experimented on, though separated by a partition,
were somewhat near together, I do not consider the
experiments conclusive. I may mention that Mrs.
Sidgwick, who carried out the investigation in the
most earnest manner, recognized the justice of this
criticism. These experiments published by Du Prel,
Schrenck-Notzing, Mensi, and Welsch; contain so
little information about the conditions that it is
difficult to weigh the question. Du Prel's views on
scientific proof sometimes recall the logic that rules
in the nursery.

Clairvoyance is the perception of things distant
either in time or in space. Belief in it is as old as
history; I need only refer to the Bible and the
Oracles. The prophecies of the Pythia at Delphi
show that it was even then believed in. From what
has come down to us in history it seems that the state
of the Pythia was like deep hypnosis, although they
probably used toxic methods also; Kluge and Ed.
von Hartmann think that the state was somnambulism. It was the same thing with the Sibyl of
Cumæ. Other phenomena of antiquity must also be
included here, for example, the reports of Apuleius
about the prophesying of boys; as well as many

phenomena reported in recent times from various countries, and recorded in the works of various travellers. Stecker tells us that in the camp of King John of Abyssinia, in 1882, a boy in an apparently somnambulistic condition was employed to discover a thief.

The mesmerists think clairvoyance and the transposition of the senses of which I shall shortly speak are phenomena to be found in magnetized subjects. It is not certain whether Mesmer himself knew of the phenomena; but it appears from one of his letters (published by Du Potet) that he was acquainted with them, but did not enter into them, because they appeared to him inexplicable. Most of the commissions which have investigated clairvoyance have failed; but some great minds—Schopenhauer, for example— have believed in it. Even Braid, about whose views there are so many mistaken opinions, believed in clairvoyance, at all events at first. There is a passage in his *Neurypnology* (p. 22) which I can interpret in no other way. Braid thought clairvoyance proved, though he had never seen it and could not induce it himself; but he thought that a number of those who vouched for its reality were scientific and truth-loving enough to be believed; he expressly says so, and there can be no doubt about it. The magnetic state in which such phenomena as clairvoyance, thought-transference, &c., are found, is sometimes called somnambulism [1] by the mesmerists.

[1] Consequently the word somnambulism is used in several senses : 1. One of Charcot's stages is often called somnambulism. 2. The school of Nancy calls that hypnotic state somnambulism in which there is loss of memory after waking. 3. Some identify hypnotism with somnambulism. 4. Somnambulism is a natural sleep in which there are actions and movements. 5. The mesmeric state described above is called somnambulism.

In previsional clairvoyance forthcoming events are
foretold ; in spatial clairvoyance things are seen which
are so placed in space that normally they would be
invisible ; they are either separated from the seer by
some non-transparent substance, or they are too far off
to be seen.   To spatial clairvoyance belongs the
employment of somnambulists to diagnose disease.
A frequent experiment is the diagnosis by somnambulists of their own disease, the prediction of its
course, and the indication of the remedies. We may
see here the operation of realized post-hypnotic suggestions. Somnambulists also prescribe medicines for
other people. A Bavarian medical official, Wetzler,
in 1883 treated himself with medicines ordered for
his rheumatism by a somnambulist, and with good
results. We may perhaps trace here also the action
of auto-suggestion. More recently, we have the case
of Jost, who was tried and condemned for fraud.
Jost, who had formerly been a tailor, while in a state
of assumed hypnosis prescribed cures for hundreds
of sick people. On the testimony of medical experts,
the court found him guilty of simulated hypnosis and
fraud. To realize the absurd results to which such
practices lead, we need only consult mesmeristic
literature, new and old. In one book it is stated that
when things do not fit in, we must not take the
prophesyings literally but metaphorically.

In transposition of the senses, stimuli, which normally would only affect a particular organ of sense,
affect some other part of the body. For example,
letters are said to be read by means of the skin,
instead of the eyes, without a heightening of the
sense of touch, such as is found in the blind. On the
contrary, the part of the skin concerned is supposed

to be stimulated by the light rays, even without direct contact and when there is no hyperæsthesia of feeling. The supposed transposition of the senses is thus distinguished from hyperæsthesia of the sense of touch. One of the most commonly mentioned phenomena is reading or hearing with the pit of the stomach. I have seen a person who was supposed to read with his nose, even at a distance of several feet. When his nose was covered with wadding he failed. It is tolerably certain that he saw with his eyes; for though they appeared to be covered with wadding and bandaged, Braid has pointed out that such bandaging is of very doubtful use.

I will here mention some experiments of Heidenhain's which are generally misunderstood, and which at any rate may be easily misunderstood. He maintained that his subjects repeated whatever he said to them when a stimulus was applied to their stomachs ; it was necessary to speak close to the stomach to stimulate it. He even said that the part could be exactly defined, and that it was the region of the stomach. According to him the *vagus* nerve was set vibrating and the sound centres were stimulated, and thus a sound was made which exactly corresponded to the one heard ; but he thought the sound was heard by the ear and not by the stomach, the nerves of which merely stimulated the sound centres and thus induced imitation of what was heard by the ear. It might be concluded from many accounts of Heidenhain's experiments that he thought his subjects heard with their stomachs, but nothing was further from his thoughts. I have said on p. 93 that Heidenhain was probably wrong in his conclusions.

The law of the individual capacity of the sense

organs[1] would be violated by transposition of the
senses.   But I do not think the thing is proved.

I now come to the action of magnets, especially
during hypnosis.   The belief in the action of the
magnet on human beings is very old.   The Magi of
the East used it for curing diseases, and the Chinese
and Hindoos used it long ago.   Albertus Magnus
in the thirteenth century, and later Paracelsus, Van
Helmont, and Kircher also used it, as well as the
astronomer and ex-Jesuit Hell of Vienna at the end
of the eighteenth century.   We have seen that
Mesmer also used it at first.   Even then many
doctors—*e.g.*, Deimann, of Amsterdam—denied the
therapeutic action of the magnet, and asserted, as
others do at present, that brass plates did as well.
Reil, the well-known physician, used the magnet
therapeutically; in 1845 Reichenbach asserted that
some sensitive persons had peculiar sensations when
they were touched by a magnet.   He also said that
they saw light—the so-called *Od* light—at the poles
of the magnet: an assertion that was supposed to be
disproved, but which has lately been again made by
Barrett in London, and by Luys in Paris, on the
ground of experiment.   Jastrow and Pickering, basing
their conclusions on new negative experiments, have
opposed the revival of the *Od* doctrine.   Shrenck-
Notzing, also, has attempted to show that the curative
results obtained by Reichenbach with the alleged *Od*
were due to suggestion.   Maggiorani, in Italy, has
lately contended for the therapeutic use of the magnet
(Belfiore), and the school of Charcot has asserted

---

[1] According to this law each organ of sense has its own
appropriate stimulus, which has no effect on any other organ,
e.g., the eye is stimulated by light, but not the sense of touch or
the stomach.

the influence of the magnet on certain individuals. Benedikt, also, in opposition to American investigators, who had attributed the therapeutic action of the magnet to suggestion, advocated its specifically physical operation; his experiments are not conclusive, however, for he neglected the necessary precautions.

I have already spoken of the application of the magnet for inducing hypnosis, as well as of the action of the hypnoscope.

With regard to the action of the magnet during hypnosis, the phenomena of transference must first be mentioned. According to the school of Charcot, transference means that certain phenomena, influenced by some æsthesio-genetic expedient, particularly the magnet, change the place of their appearance. Charcot says that such phenomena are seen in hysterical patients. Thus, contractures on the right side can be transferred to the left by the magnet. Charcot, as well as a number of other experimenters, among them Preyer, thinks these phenomena quite proved, while in Germany a mental factor has been called in to account for them. It was supposed that the subject's expectation produced the effect and not the magnet ; and that (according to Westphal) sealing-wax, bones, &c., produced the same result, provided only that the subject expected it. The school of Charcot say that this transference takes place in hypnosis as well as in the waking state. The laws which Binet and Féré have laid down about it are as follows : When lethargy on one side of the body and catalepsy on the other have been induced by closing the subject's eyes, the approach of a magnet causes lethargy on the cataleptic side, and on the lethargic side catalepsy. In the same way, when the state is somnambulistic on one

side and cataleptic or lethargic on the other, the magnet
causes transference.   But also, in each particular
hypnotic state, symptoms can be transferred by the
magnet from one side to the other, *e.g.*, the individual
contractures in lethargy, and particular postures of
the limbs in catalepsy.   In somnambulism, contractures as well as hallucinations of one side, and hemi-
anæsthesiæ, can be transferred in the same way.
Binet and Féré say that when hypnotic subjects
write with the right hand, they reverse the direction
of the writing under the influence of the magnet
and write at the same time with the left hand.

Another method of influencing with the magnet is
called polarization.   It is a reversal of a functional
state (Belfiore).   For example, the magnet is supposed
to resolve a contracture induced by suggestion (motor
polarization).   It can banish a suggested hallucination
and can change the mental pictures of colours into
their complementaries.   If a subject believes he sees
blue, he thinks he sees yellow when the magnet is
brought close to him (sensory polarization).   The
magnet is said to change happiness into sadness
(mental polarization).   When a reversal of the state
takes place, *e.g.*, when "blue" is turned into "yellow,"
i.e., into its complementary colour, then this is called
polarization in a narrower sense, and an arbitrary
change of state, *i.e.*, the changing of "yellow"
into "red" is called "dispolarization" (Lombroso,
Ottolenghi).   Binet and Féré are the authors of
these experiments, which are confirmed by Bianchi
and Sommer, whose experiments, however, offer no
guarantee that sufficient precautions were taken ; at
least I have found nothing concerning this point in
their publications.

The phenomena of mental polarization were care-

fully examined by a special committee of the Medical
Congress at Padua. They were not confirmed; at least,
they could not be referred to the action of the magnet.
Tanzi especially opposes them, and thinks they are to
be referred to unconscious and unintentional suggestion.

Venturini and Ventra made a therapeutical experiment in connection with these phenomena. They say
they conquered a fixed idea, an auto-suggestion in the
waking state, by means of the magnet. Some experiments of Raggi belong to this class ; he says that the
approach of a magnet in hypnosis often causes subjective discomfort. In other cases the magnet is said
to have put an end to the hypnosis.

A third possible way of influencing the hypnotic
subject by the magnet is given by Tamburini and
Seppilli. They think that when the magnet is brought
close to the pit of the stomach it influences the
respiratory movements. Later on, Tamburini and
Righi found that other metallic bodies produced the
same effect ; the strength of the effect depended, however, on the size of the metal. The electro-magnet
is said to have the same effect whether the stream is
open or closed ; Tamburini supposes later that it is
only the temperature of the magnet which has the
effect, and that the magnetic force may have no
influence.

Lastly, there are Babinski's and Luys's experiments,
founded on a union of true magnetism and animal
magnetism. If a hypnotized subject and a sick person
are set back to back, a magnet put between them will
cause the sick person's symptoms to pass over to the
hypnotized subject. Hysterical dumbness and contractures have been thus transferred. But symptoms
of organic disease, *e.g.*, of disseminated sclerosis have
also been transferred in this way. As a matter of

course the phenomena must not be caused by suggestion. The hypnotic subject must not know what the
sick person's symptoms are. Luys goes still further.
He places a magnet on the patient's head; after a
time he places the same magnet on a hypnotized
person's head; now the morbid symptoms of the first
person should appear in the hypnotized person. The
whole arrangement of the experiments is so uncritical
that there can be no doubt about Luys's self-deception.

All these actions of the magnet appear to rest on
erroneous observations. But it is certainly singular
that the action of the magnet should have been
asserted by so many authors at so many different
times.

Little has been said in explanation of this supposed
effect. Obersteiner supposes that there may be a
magnetic sense, which may come into activity during
hypnosis, and which is, perhaps, localized in certain
terminal organs of perception whose functions are
still unknown.

The action of drugs at a distance is at the present
moment supposed to be disproved, though some
authors still assert it. This also is no new thing. The
belief has often arisen that certain persons could find
water or veins of metal with a divining-rod, through
some influence of the water or minerals at a distance.
Burq's *metalloscopie* and *metallothérapie*, in which,
however, there was contact with the metals, was the
same sort of thing.

Certain persons were supposed to be influenced by
particular metals—copper, for example—which even
caused symptoms of disease to disappear. The later
investigations on the action of drugs at a distance

apparently proved that certain drugs in hermetically closed tubes would, when brought close to human beings, act in the same way as if they were swallowed. Thus, strychnine was supposed to cause convulsions, ipecacuanha vomiting, opium sleep, alcohol drunkenness, &c. Experiments of this kind were made even in the last century Pivati of Venice believed that if odorous substances were shut up in glass tubes, the fragrance would penetrate the glass and exert a specific influence on human subjects as soon as the tubes were rendered electric by friction. Verati and Bianchi found this correct, and so did Winckler, professor of philosophy at Leipzig. As a result, such tubes were much used at Leipzig for therapeutical treatment in the middle of the last century. There were anti-apoplectic tubes, anti-hysterical tubes, &c. Abbé Nollet then went to Italy to investigate the phenomenon, but was unable to confirm it. He found that the idea was the outcome of inaccurate observation, exaggeration, and fraud. Bianchini, professor of medicine at Padua, came to the same conclusion (Lichtenberg).

Similar experiments were more recently made by Grocco in Italy, and Bourru and Burot in Rochefort. They experimented with both waking and hypnotized people; Luys and Dufour repeated the experiments with hypnotized subjects and confirmed them; so did Duplouy, Peter, and Alliot. The last-named even asserted, on the strength of experiments he had carried out on one subject with Caron and Martinet, that contact with gold would produce a burn of the second degree. So far as can be seen, the experiment was not very carefully carried out. Luys went further; he even found distinctions, according as the ipecacuanha was applied to the right or left sides. These experiments have been repeated in other quarters, *e.g.*, by Jules Voisin, Forel, Seguin, and Laufenauer, without result; Luys brought the subject before the French Academy of Medicine, which appointed a commission (Brouardel, Dujardin-Beaumetz, and several others) to test the question in the presence of Luys ; they came to a conclusion opposed to his. Seeligmüller has confuted the experiments in a much better and more scientific way, which appears to me the only proper one for coming to a decision. It consists of examining the conditions of the experiments ; the reports of commissions have no particular value. When we consider the history of animal magnetism we see that commissions always find what they wish to find ; the result is always what they expect. Commissions, in fact, are much influenced by auto-suggestion.

Although I have spoken of a number of enigmatical phenomena in this chapter, I have not done so because I wish to maintain their reality; I should expressly state that this is not the case. I thought it necessary to mention them briefly, on account of their connection with the history of hypnotism. It was further necessary to point out the many sources of error in such experiments.

One important condition in such experiments is that every word uttered should be taken down by some person present for the purpose. One apparently unimportant word may be enough to justify the chief objection made to such experiments—*i.e.*, suggestion.

And there is an absence of criticism in most of them. When a subject reads in a closed book, and it is not proved that he was unacquainted with it previously, I think it is at least *naïve* to speak of clairvoyance.

When the magnet causes transference in subjects who
know that the magnet is supposed to cause transference, it should be proved that the subjects could
not know of the presence of the magnet through their
organs of sense. When the approach of the magnet
changes a subject's perception of "blue" into "yellow,"
let it be proved that he did not know the magnet was
near, for a properly "trained" subject knows that
the magnet is supposed to change his perceptions of
colour. When it is asserted that drugs in closed tubes
have an effect, Bernheim's conditions should be
observed, the chief of which is that no one in the
room should know the contents of the tube. When it
is asserted that some persons can magnetize others by
means of a particular force, let suggestion be excluded.
The impression that A. makes upon B. is often impossible to calculate, and when A. can influence B.,
but C. cannot, it should be shown that A. does not
know whether B. or C. is magnetizing him. This is
of course very important ; for there is no doubt that
some people, by the manner in which they play their
part and by a thorough knowledge of the *technique* of
suggestion, can influence subjects who are refractory
to others. It by no means follows that they possess
a peculiar magnetic force ; suggestion will explain it.

The chief sources of error in the experiments
described in this chapter are as follows :—

1. Intentional simulation on the part of the subject
in or out of hypnosis. A simulation of hypnosis is less
to be feared, because if a person saw without using his
eyes, it would not matter whether he was in hypnosis
or not ; the main point is the seeing. But even when
there is hypnosis, the experimenter is not protected
from simulation on the subject's part, because lying
and fraud are possible even in deep hypnosis. This

may have been the case with Czermak's somnambulist, who prophesied that she was about to spit
blood. Czermak, Voigt, and Langer subsequently
showed, microscopically, that this was bird's blood,
which, of course, the somnambulist had previously
placed in her mouth. More probably, however, there
was here deception without hypnosis.

2. Unintentional simulation, if I may use an expression which is really contradictory. For example,
the subject hears something, and is not conscious that
the impression has been made on the usual organ of
this sense ; as is the case when subjects themselves
believe they hear with their stomachs. Or transference happens, when the subject has been induced
by training to produce this phenomenon whenever a
magnet is brought near him. The subject pays no
attention to the approach of the magnet, and is not
really conscious of it, and yet the effect appears. In
the same way the subject in thought-transference
learns to guess others' thoughts from many little
signs, but is not conscious that he does so. The
involuntary tremor of the muscles which every one
has when he concentrates his thoughts strongly, and
which betrays his thoughts to the subject, seems to
me a great point in these cases; Wernicke in particular has pointed out this source of error.

It should be especially guarded against in clairvoyance, because persons present, who can see the
thing which the clairvoyant is to see without using his
eyes, may give indications by involuntary muscular
movements, &c. Even Göler v. Ravensburg, who is
generally so practical, does not enough consider the
importance of this point.

3. The probability of chance success. As many
experiments fail, it should be considered whether

the number of successful ones exceeds probability.
Preyer, however, believes that for our objects statistics
of probability have little significance.

4. Coincidence. *E.g.*, a command given in thought
may be obeyed, because by chance, or for some
reason, experimenter and subject think of the same
thing. In telepathy the first order thought of is
nearly always that the right arm should be raised.
This source of error is both great and interesting. It
has lately been carefully examined by a member of
the American branch of the Society for Pyschical
Research, C. S. Minot. Thus it has been discovered
that every one prefers certain figures, &c., which recur
strikingly often, even when the choice is left open.
Now, when in a telepathic experiment one person is
to divine a number thought of by another, it would
be necessary to discover if they prefer the same
figures, if they have the same " number habit." This
must also be weighed in experiments with cards, in
which it appears to me the ace of hearts is very often
chosen. It is evident that great care must be exercised in drawing conclusions, and that the study of
" mysterious " phenomena leads to the recognition of
important laws.

5. Hyperæsthesia of the subject's organs of sense
often allows him to perceive things imperceptible to
others.

6. The increased power of drawing conclusions,
which I have spoken of before, must be taken into
consideration.

7. A special source of error is constituted by
illusions of memory; Christian has emphasized this
with regard to telepathic experiments. In clair-
audience, also, it may happen that when the phenomenon occurs one may believe that one had seen

or known it before. Imagination then easily dismisses the circumstances which stand in the way. Grützner well points out that certain accessory circumstances, as in conjuring, may easily escape the observer, and the more easily the more he is on his guard.

Wernicke emits the dubious supposition that different thoughts induce different effluvia from the skin, from which a properly trained subject can discover what the agent is thinking about.

When the published experiments are criticized by the rules given above, very few are left which are worthy of serious consideration. These are chiefly the experiments in thought-transference of Guthrie and Birchall, published by the Society for Psychical Research. I could discover no sources of error in them. As conscious deception is excluded, the supposition that the experiments did not really take place as published is out of the question. However, even here there was no regular registrar of the proceedings ; and besides, I am subjectively convinced that some sources of error were overlooked, and that suggestion was somehow or other called into play. Perhaps somebody else may be able to discover these. In any case the members of the society are too scientific and too honourable not to recognize sources of error which are pointed out.

There is nothing to be said against the present examination of inexplicable things. Almost all great steps in natural science have been made by some one who had the courage to contest existing views, in spite of the danger of looking ridiculous. Harvey was obliged to struggle with the prejudices of his colleagues for years before the circulation of the blood was accepted. The fall of meteors was long denied. Modern anatomy was founded by Andreas Vesalius, who fought the prejudices of his time often by improper methods. The fact that a thing is contrary to known laws ought not to prevent its being examined. The contradiction is often merely apparent, and even the laws of nature change from day to day, as Virchow has said. Theories never precede facts; observation first, and then theory. The electric current does not contract muscles because the book says so; the book says so because the current causes the contraction. As Herbert Spencer explains, experience comes first, and then theory.

Everybody may not care to approach this subject; but they should not blame others for their unprejudiced investigations. So long as science does not examine everything, practically and without prejudice, the great delusions of which animal magnetism, &c., makes use, will continue to exist. When careful examination has shown the sources of error, charlatanism will have lost its chief support. The indifference of science has always been the mainstay of charlatanism. The dread that many people have of investigating things of evil reputation is the chief support of imposture and error, and yet how much can be done to suppress them by a careful investigation of even what is improbable. The real enlightenment of the people can only be attained in this way.

It is incomprehensible to me that even scientific men should call those who interest themselves in hypnotism marvel-mongers. Any one who examines the question seriously will find, on the contrary, that the latest hypnotic experiments explain in a natural way much that has been called strange and supernatural. Stigmatization, for example, and automatic

writing, which seems to be almost unknown in most
scientific circles, and for this reason, and for want
of scientific examination, is a powerful support to
spiritualism and superstition.   The spiritualists think
that automatic writing proves some external force,
because a work showing design, and independent of
the consciousness of the writer, can only be produced
by an external force or a spirit.   But thanks to the
investigations of Taine, F. Myers, Gurney, Pierre
Janet, and Max Dessoir, automatic writing has now
received another explanation, as table-turning did
through Faraday.   It is the same with many other
phenomena which have been pressed into the service
of superstition.

Whoever reads the writings of the magnetic healers
and spiritualists will see how bitter they are against
the investigators of hypnotism, and how angry the
professional magnetizers become about suggestion,
which takes the ground from under their feet (Forel).
Truly great men try to avoid dogma and *a priori*
conclusions, in spite of scientific doubts.   If they cannot examine themselves, they yet consider a scientific
examination, even of the improbable necessary.   An
example which Delbœuf brings forward may be
mentioned.   Darwin once wished, it is said, to examine the influence of music on the growth of plants,
because such an influence had been talked of before
him, and he therefore made some one play the
bassoon for several days, close to some planted beans.
If this anecdote is not true, it is well invented.   Examination will conquer superstition sooner than an
a priori philosophy.   The non-recognition of dogma
distinguishes science from blind faith, but to say a
fact is impossible because it is opposed to the laws
of nature is to dogmatize.

We should be careful, besides, not to make the mistake of claiming supernatural powers for ourselves and denying them to others. When—as happened to me—an otherwise scientific man, X., of Berlin, said that the subjects of Forel and Bernheim were impostors, without having seen them, and without offering proof, he made the mistake of claiming clairvoyance for himself, though he denied its existence. I have often seen such self-contradictions.

Knowledge of nature is still in its infancy. Have the elementary mental processes yet been explained? Has any one ever explained how an ovum, fertilized but soulless, develops into a being with a soul? Has it been explained how the brain moves the muscles by means of the nerves? Do we know why an apple falls to the ground? The, most elementary processes are inexplicable wherever we look, and most people only do not think them inexplicable because they see them every day. Some one has justly said that dreams, as well as hypnotism, might be called an extravagant fancy, if they did not happen every day.

In spite of the progress which the exact sciences have made, we must not for a moment forget that the inner connection between the body and the mental processes is utterly unknown to us. Under these circumstances we should not refuse to examine the apparently inexplicable. Let us, however, impose severe conditions, and not accept any facts on authority without proof.

X

BIBLIOGRAPHY.

BIBLIOGRAPHY.

As I have read nearly all the authors I have quoted in the original, it would take too much space to mention them in detail. There are catalogues for certain periods—for the movement of 1880, those of Möbius in Schmidt's *Jahrbüchern* and Max Dessoir's Bibliography of 1888 ; these are for the later periods. The bibliography is continued in the periodical *Revue de l'Hypnotisme.* The following is a list of works particularly to be recommended :—

BELFIORE, *L'Ipnotismo.* Naples, 1887. (Contains much historical information which is wanting in most French books.)

BENTIVEGNI, V., *Die Hypnose und ihre civilrechtliche Bedeutung.* Leipzig, 1890.

BERNHEIM, *Hypnotisme Suggestion, Psychothérapie.* Paris, 1891. (Shows the universal importance of suggestion with and without hypnosis. Written for doctors.)

BINET and FÉRÉ, *Le Magnétisme animal.* Paris, 1887. (Treats hypnotism from the point of view of the school of Charcot.)

DESSOIR, MAX, *Das Doppel-Ich.* Leipzig, 1890 ; second edition, 1896. (Short psychological studies, partly connected with hypnotic experiments.)

ENNEMOSER, *Der Magnetismus.* Leipzig, 1819. (Contains much historical information about animal magnetism.)

FOREL, *Der Hypnotismus.* Stuttgart, 1889 ; third edition, 1895. (Short, very clear work, explaining the general importance of suggestion.)

GURNEY, Peculiarities of Certain Post-Hypnotic States (essay in the " Proceedings of the Society for Psychical Research," vol. iv., April 23, 1887). (Contains classical records of experiments, like almost all the works of Gurney and his friend Frederic Myers)

JANET, PIERRE, *L'Automatisme psychologique.* Paris, 1889. (Detailed psychological experiments on human consciousness, its analysis by means of hypnosis, &c.)

KRAFFT-EBING, V., *Eine experimentelle Studie auf dem Gebiete des Hypnotismus*, 3rd edition. Stuttgart, 1893. (Contains a detailed account of many physical and mental symptoms of hypnosis in connection with an interesting case.)

LEHMANN, *Hypnosen og de daemel beslaeglede normale Tilstände.* Kopenhagen, 1890. (Many noteworthy psychological details are contained in this book.)

LIÉBEAULT, *Du Sommeil.* Paris, 1866 ; new edition, 1889. (Psychological analysis of ordinary and hypnotic sleep. Much information.)

LIÉGEOIS, *De la suggestion et du somnambulisme dans leurs rapports avec la jurisprudence et la médecine légale.* Paris, 1888. (A rather diffuse book, containing much of deep interest.)

LILIENTHAL, V., *Der Hypnotismus und das Strafrecht.* Reprinted from the *Zeitschrift für die ges. Strafrechtswissenschaft*, 1887. (Based on the school of Charcot.)

MINDE, *Ueber Hypnotismus.* Munich, 1891. (An objective historical study, dealing especially with the older mesmeric literature.)

MOLL, *Der Rapport in der Hypnose.* Leipzig, 1892. (This work confutes, with the aid of numerous experiments, many opinions of the mesmerists, especially that which regards *rapport* as a proof of animal magnetism)

MORSELLI, *Il Magnetismo animale.* Turin, 1886. (An interesting book, written from a determinist point of view.)

MYERS, F , *The Subliminal Consciousness.* (A valuable study, contained in the "Proceedings of the Society for Psychical Research for 1892," on unconscious processes.)

OCHOROWICZ, *De la suggestion mentale.* Paris, 1887. (Though the book does not prove telepathy convincingly, it is written with scientific earnestness, and is clever and interesting.)

PODMORE, F., *Apparitions and Thought-Transference,* Contemporary Science Series. London, 1894. (A comprehensive summary of the evidence, on these and allied subjects, brought forward by the Society for Psychical Research.)

PREYER, *Der Hypnotismus.* Vienna and Leipzig, 1890. (Lectures, delivered at the University of Berlin, containing many historical facts.)

SCHAFFER, KARL, *Suggestion und Reflex.* Jena, 1895. (An experimental study of the cutaneous and muscular reflex phenomena of hypnosis, which the author regards as of great importance. While not denying the influence of mental suggestion, he thus seeks to harmonise the school of the Salpêtrien with the school of Nancy.)

INDICES.

—

INDICES.

I.

INDEX OF SUBJECTS.

The large figures point to the most important paragraphs.

INDEX OF NAMES.

A single date in the index means the year in which the author's work on hypnotism, or his most important work, appeared; two dates mean the times of his birth and death. When no date is added, the author's work has almost invariably been published during the last fifteen years.

Gascard, doctor, Paris, 131
Gasquet, J. R., alienist, Brighton, 21
Gassner, Joh. Jos., 1727-1779, Catholic priest, well-known exorcist in Regensburg, Ellwang, &c., 315
Gélineau, French doctor, 1880, 225
Gessmann, G., Vienna, 49
Gibert, doctor, Havre, 399
Gilles de la Tourette, neurologist, Paris, 18, 91, 323, 371, 388
Giraud-Teulon, 1816-1887, oculist, Paris, 17, 127, 382
Gley, Eugène, physiologist, Paris, 67
Gmelin, Eberhard, 1753-1809, physicist, Heilbronn, 10, 236
Goclenius, Rudolph, 1572-1621, doctor, professor of physics, Marburg, 6
Göler v. Ravensburg, art historian, Coburg, 398, 412
Görres, Jak. Jos., v., 1776-1848, prof., Munich, writer on mystical subjects, 236
Goethe, Joh. Wolfgang v., 1749-1832, 231
Goltdammer, *Ober-Tribunalsrath*, 369
Goltz, prof., Strassburg, physiologist, 80
Gowers, neurologist, London, 25
Grasset, prof., Montpellier, neurologist and pharmacologist, 49, 224, 353, 388
Gratiolet, Louis Pierre, 1815-1865, doctor and zoologist, comparative anatomist, Paris, 197
Greatrakes, Valentine, about 1670, "healer," Ireland, 314
Griesinger, Wilhelm, 1817-1868, alienist and physician, Berlin, 219

Grimes, 1848, New England, U.S.A., 16
Grossmann, Jonas, doctor, Berlin, 28, 351, 361
Grocco, 1882, Italian doctor, 409
Grützner, P., prof., Tübingen, physiologist, lecturer at Breslau in 1880, 100, 414
Gscheidlen, R., 1842-1889, prof. extraordinary at Breslau, hygienist, chemist, 56
Guérineau, 1860, doctor, Poitiers, 17
Guermonprez, prof., doctor, Lille, 48
Gürtler, 1880, doctor, Sagan, 128
Guinon, neurologist, Paris, 327
Gurney, Edmund, 1847-1888, psychologist, secretary of the Society for Psychical Research, London, 21, 60, 83, 156, 165, 167, 269, 307
Guthrie, Malcolm, merchant, Liverpool, 399, 400, 414
Guttmann, S., doctor, Berlin, 318

Hack Tuke, *see* Tuke
Hähnle, Karl, doctor, Reutlingen, Würtemberg, 52
Hall, Stanley, prof. of Clark University at Worcester, United States, eminent physiologist and psychologist, 281
Haller, Albrecht v., 1708-1777, prof. of anatomy at Bern and Göttingen, 397
Hammond, prof., neurologist and alienist, New York, 226
Hansen, Danish magnetizer, 18, 142, 391
Hart, E., doctor, London, 22
Harting, 1882, prof. at Utrecht, 234

Mendel, prof. extraordinary at Berlin, alienist, 289, 295, 296, 318, 332, 344, 354

Mendelsohn, 103

Mensi, Alfred v., author, Munich, 400

Méric, Elie, prof. at the Sorbonne, theologist, 133

Mesmer, Friedr. Anton, 1734-1815, doctor, Vienna, 6, 7, 8, 9, 11, 40, 79, 328, 391, 397

Mesnet, Ernest, alienist and physician, Paris, 362, 367

Meunier, Victor, French author, 135

Meyersohn, Bernhard, 1880, doctor, Schwerin, 18

Meynert, prof., Vienna, alienist, 222, 291

Michael, J., doctor, Hamburg, 24, 63, 392

Miescher, F., prof., Basle, physiologist, 242

Mill, John Stuart, 1806-1873, English philosopher and political economist, 250

Milne-Edwards, H., physiologist, Paris, 234

Minde, doctor, Munich, 25

Minot, Charles Sedgwick, Boston, U.S.A., 413

Möbius, Paul Julius, lecturer, Leipzig, neurologist, 23, 25

Möli, Karl Franz, lecturer, alienist, Herzberge, near Berlin, 223

Moleschott, 1822-1893, distinguished German physiologist, Rome, 84

Möllerup, Danish doctor, 341

Morand, J. S., French doctor, 49

Morel, celebrated French alienist, 374

Moricourt, J., doctor, Paris, 398

Morselli, prof., Genoa, alienist, 21, 58, 109, 392

Mosso, Ang., prof., Turin, physiologist, 291

Most, G. F., 1842, doctor, Stadthagen, 13

Motet, doctor, Paris, 380

Mouillesaux, 1787, French magnetizer, 157

Müller, F., lecturer, neurologist, Graz, 24, 354

Müller, F. C., doctor, Alexandersbad, 368, 369

Müller, Johannes, 1801-1859, eminent anatomist and physiologist, prof., Bonn and Berlin, 278

Münsterberg, Hugo, prof., psychologist at Harvard, United States, formerly at Freiburg, 29, 366

Myers, A., doctor, London, 343, 400

Myers, Frederic W. H., psychologist, Cambridge, 21, 28, 29, 45, 98, 124, 132, 269, 400

Nasse, Christian Friedrich, 1778-1851, prof., Halle and Bonn, physician, 271, 396

Netter, A., librarian of the University, Nancy, 364

Nietzsche, distinguished philosopher, &c., 3

Noizet, French general, 1820, Stenay, Paris, 12, 157, 254

Nonne, doctor, neurologist, Hamburg, 24, 57

North, W., lecturer on physiology, London, 187, 240

Nuel, prof., Liège, oculist, 154

Obersteiner, H., prof. extraordinary at Vienna, alienist and histologist, 23, 49, 194, 235, 239, 408

Ochorowicz, Julian, psychologist, 122, 399

Oedmann, alienist, Lund, Sweden, 355

Ibsen's Prose Dramas

EDITED BY WILLIAM ARCHER

*Complete in Five Vols. Crown 8vo, Cloth, Price 3s. 6d. each.
Set of Five Vols., in Case, 17s. 6d. ; in Half Morocco,
in Case, 32s. 6d.*

'*We seem at last to be shown men and women as they are ; and at first
it is more than we can endure. . . . All Ibsen's characters speak and act
as if they were hypnotised, and under their creator's imperious demand
to reveal themselves. There never was such a mirror held up to nature
before ; it is too terrible. . . . Yet we must return to Ibsen, with his
remorseless surgery, his remorseless electric-light, until we, too, have
grown strong and learned to face the naked—if necessary, the flayed and
bleeding—reality.*'—SPEAKER (London).

VOL. I. 'A DOLL'S HOUSE,' 'THE LEAGUE
OF YOUTH,' and 'THE PILLARS OF SOCIETY.'
With Portrait of the Author, and Biographical Introduc-
tion by WILLIAM ARCHER.

VOL. II. 'GHOSTS,' 'AN ENEMY OF THE
PEOPLE,' and 'THE WILD DUCK.' With an Introductory Note.

VOL. III. 'LADY INGER OF ÖSTRÅT,' 'THE
VIKINGS AT HELGELAND,' 'THE PRETEND-
ERS.' With an Introductory Note and Portrait of Ibsen.

VOL. IV. 'EMPEROR AND GALILEAN.' With
an Introductory Note by WILLIAM ARCHER.

VOL. V. 'ROSMERSHOLM,' 'THE LADY
FROM THE SEA,' 'HEDDA GABLER.' Translated
by WILLIAM ARCHER. With an Introductory Note.

The sequence of the plays *in each volume* is chronological ; the complete
set of volumes comprising the dramas presents them in chronological order.

LONDON : WALTER SCOTT, LTD., Paternoster Square.

Library of Humour

Cloth Elegant, Large Crown 8vo, Price 3s. 6d. per Vol.

' The books are delightful in every way, and are notable for the high standard of taste and the excellent judgment that characterise their editing, as well as for the brilliancy of the literature that they contain.' —BOSTON (U.S.A) GAZETTE.

VOLUMES ALREADY ISSUED.

THE HUMOUR OF FRANCE. Translated, with an Introduction and Notes, by ELIZABETH LEE. With numerous Illustrations by PAUL FRÉNZENY.

THE HUMOUR OF GERMANY. Translated, with an Introduction and Notes, by HANS MÜLLER-CASENOV. With numerous Illustrations by C. E. BROCK.

THE HUMOUR OF ITALY. Translated, with an Introduction and Notes, by A. WERNER. With 50 Illustrations and a Frontispiece by ARTURO FALDI.

THE HUMOUR OF AMERICA. Selected with a copious Biographical Index of American Humorists, by JAMES BARR.

THE HUMOUR OF HOLLAND. Translated, with an Introduction and Notes, by A. WERNER. With numerous Illustrations by DUDLEY HARDY.

THE HUMOUR OF IRELAND. Selected by D. J. O'DONOGHUE. With numerous Illustrations by OLIVER PAQUE.

THE HUMOUR OF SPAIN. Translated, with an Introduction and Notes, by SUSETTE M. TAYLOR. With numerous Illustrations by H. R. MILLAR.

THE HUMOUR OF RUSSIA. Translated, with Notes, by E. L. BOOLE, and an Introduction by STEPNIAK. With 50 Illustrations by PAUL FRÉNZENY.

THE HUMOUR OF JAPAN. Translated, with an Introduction by A. M. With Illustrations by GEORGE BIGOT (from drawings made in Japan). [*In preparation.*

LONDON: WALTER SCOTT, LTD., Paternoster Square.

Ibsen's Prose Dramas

Edited by WILLIAM ARCHER

*Complete in Five Vols. Crown 8vo, Cloth, Price 3s. 6d. each.
Set of Five Vols., in Case, 17s. 6d. ; in Half Morocco,
in Case, 32s. 6d.*

'*We seem at last to be shown men and women as they are ; and at first
it is more than we can endure. . . . All Ibsen's characters speak and act
as if they were hypnotised, and under their creator's imperious demand
to reveal themselves. There never was such a mirror held up to nature
before ; it is too terrible. . . . Yet we must return to Ibsen, with his
remorseless surgery, his remorseless electric-light, until we, too, have
grown strong and learned to face the naked—if necessary, the flayed and
bleeding—reality.*'—SPEAKER (London).

VOL. I. 'A DOLL'S HOUSE,' 'THE LEAGUE OF YOUTH,' and 'THE PILLARS OF SOCIETY.' With Portrait of the Author, and Biographical Introduction by WILLIAM ARCHER.

VOL. II. 'GHOSTS,' 'AN ENEMY OF THE PEOPLE,' and 'THE WILD DUCK.' With an Introductory Note.

VOL. III. 'LADY INGER OF ÖSTRÅT,' 'THE VIKINGS AT HELGELAND,' 'THE PRETENDERS.' With an Introductory Note and Portrait of Ibsen.

VOL. IV. 'EMPEROR AND GALILEAN.' With an Introductory Note by WILLIAM ARCHER.

VOL. V. 'ROSMERSHOLM,' 'THE LADY FROM THE SEA,' 'HEDDA GABLER.' Translated by WILLIAM ARCHER. With an Introductory Note.

The sequence of the plays *in each volume* is chronological ; the complete
set of volumes comprising the dramas presents them in chronological order.

LONDON : WALTER SCOTT, LTD., Paternoster Square.

Library of Humour

Cloth Elegant, Large Crown 8vo, Price 3s. 6d. per Vol.

' The books are delightful in every way, and are notable for the high standard of taste and the excellent judgment that characterise their editing, as well as for the brilliancy of the literature that they contain.'
—BOSTON (U.S.A) GAZETTE.

VOLUMES ALREADY ISSUED.

THE HUMOUR OF FRANCE. Translated, with an Introduction and Notes, by ELIZABETH LEE. With numerous Illustrations by PAUL FRÉNZENY.

THE HUMOUR OF GERMANY. Translated, with an Introduction and Notes, by HANS MÜLLER-CASENOV. With numerous Illustrations by C. E. BROCK.

THE HUMOUR OF ITALY. Translated, with an Introduction and Notes, by A. WERNER. With 50 Illustrations and a Frontispiece by ARTURO FALDI.

THE HUMOUR OF AMERICA. Selected with a copious Biographical Index of American Humorists, by JAMES BARR.

THE HUMOUR OF HOLLAND. Translated, with an Introduction and Notes, by A. WERNER. With numerous Illustrations by DUDLEY HARDY.

THE HUMOUR OF IRELAND. Selected by D. J. O'DONOGHUE. With numerous Illustrations by OLIVER PAQUE.

THE HUMOUR OF SPAIN. Translated, with an Introduction and Notes, by SUSETTE M. TAYLOR. With numerous Illustrations by H. R. MILLAR.

THE HUMOUR OF RUSSIA. Translated, with Notes, by E. L. BOOLE, and an Introduction by STEPNIAK. With 50 Illustrations by PAUL FRÉNZENY.

THE HUMOUR OF JAPAN. Translated, with an Introduction by A. M. With Illustrations by GEORGE BIGOT (from drawings made in Japan). [*In preparation.*

LONDON: WALTER SCOTT, LTD., Paternoster Square.

Great Writers

A NEW SERIES OF CRITICAL BIOGRAPHIES.

EDITED BY ERIC ROBERTSON AND FRANK T. MARZIALS.

A Complete Bibliography to each Volume, by J. P. ANDERSON, British Museum, London.

Cloth, Uncut Edges, Gilt Top. Price 1s. 6d.

VOLUMES ALREADY ISSUED.

LIFE OF LONGFELLOW. By Professor ERIC S. ROBERTSON.
LIFE OF COLERIDGE. By HALL CAINE.
LIFE OF DICKENS. By FRANK T. MARZIALS.
LIFE OF DANTE GABRIEL ROSSETTI. By J. KNIGHT.
LIFE OF SAMUEL JOHNSON. By Colonel F. GRANT.
LIFE OF DARWIN. By G. T. BETTANY.
LIFE OF CHARLOTTE BRONTE. By A. BIRRELL.
LIFE OF THOMAS CARLYLE. By R. GARNETT, LL.D.
LIFE OF ADAM SMITH. By R. B. HALDANE, M.P.
LIFE OF KEATS. By W. M. ROSSETTI.
LIFE OF SHELLEY. By WILLIAM SHARP.
LIFE OF SMOLLETT. By DAVID HANNAY.
LIFE OF GOLDSMITH. By AUSTIN DOBSON.
LIFE OF SCOTT. By Professor YONGE.
LIFE OF BURNS. By Professor BLACKIE.
LIFE OF VICTOR HUGO. By FRANK T. MARZIALS.
LIFE OF EMERSON. By RICHARD GARNETT, LL.D.
LIFE OF GOETHE. By JAMES SIME.
LIFE OF CONGREVE. By EDMUND GOSSE.
LIFE OF BUNYAN. By Canon VENABLES.
LIFE OF CRABBE. By T. E. KEBBEL.
LIFE OF HEINE. By WILLIAM SHARP.
LIFE OF MILL. By W. L. COURTNEY.
LIFE OF SCHILLER. By HENRY W. NEVINSON.
LIFE OF CAPTAIN MARRYAT. By DAVID HANNAY.
LIFE OF LESSING. By T. W. ROLLESTON.
LIFE OF MILTON. By R. GARNETT, LL.D.
LIFE OF BALZAC. By FREDERICK WEDMORE.
LIFE OF GEORGE ELIOT. By OSCAR BROWNING.
LIFE OF JANE AUSTEN. By GOLDWIN SMITH.
LIFE OF BROWNING. By WILLIAM SHARP.
LIFE OF BYRON. By Hon. RODEN NOEL.
LIFE OF HAWTHORNE. By MONCURE D. CONWAY.
LIFE OF SCHOPENHAUER. By Professor WALLACE.
LIFE OF SHERIDAN. By LLOYD SANDERS.
LIFE OF THACKERAY. By HERMAN MERIVALE and FRANK T. MARZIALS.
LIFE OF CERVANTES. By H. E. WATTS.
LIFE OF VOLTAIRE. By FRANCIS ESPINASSE.
LIFE OF LEIGH HUNT. By COSMO MONKHOUSE.
LIFE OF WHITTIER. By W. J. LINTON.
LIFE OF RENAN. By FRANCIS ESPINASSE.
LIFE OF THOREAU. By H. S. SALT.

LIBRARY EDITION OF 'GREAT WRITERS,' Demy 8vo, 2s. 6d.

LONDON: WALTER SCOTT, LTD., Paternoster Square.

BOOKS OF FAIRY TALES.

Crown 8vo, Cloth Elegant, Price 3/6 per Vol.

ENGLISH FAIRY AND OTHER FOLK TALES.

Selected and Edited, with an Introduction,

By EDWIN SIDNEY HARTLAND.

With Twelve Full-Page Illustrations by CHARLES E. BROCK.

SCOTTISH FAIRY AND FOLK TALES.

Selected and Edited, with an Introduction,

By SIR GEORGE DOUGLAS, BART.

With Twelve Full-Page Illustrations by JAMES TORRANCE.

IRISH FAIRY AND FOLK TALES.

Selected and Edited, with an Introduction,

By W. B. YEATS.

With Twelve Full-Page Illustrations by JAMES TORRANCE.

London : WALTER SCOTT, LIMITED, Paternoster Square.

NEW ENGLAND LIBRARY.

GRAVURE EDITION.

PRINTED ON ANTIQUE PAPER. 2s. 6d. PER VOL

Each Volume with a Frontispiece in Photogravure.

By NATHANIEL HAWTHORNE.

THE SCARLET LETTER.
THE HOUSE OF THE SEVEN GABLES.
THE BLITHEDALE ROMANCE.
TANGLEWOOD TALES.
TWICE-TOLD TALES.
A WONDER-BOOK FOR GIRLS AND BOYS.
OUR OLD HOME.
MOSSES FROM AN OLD MANSE.
THE SNOW IMAGE.
TRUE STORIES FROM HISTORY AND BIOGRAPHY.
THE NEW ADAM AND EVE.
LEGENDS OF THE PROVINCE HOUSE.

By OLIVER WENDELL HOLMES.

THE AUTOCRAT OF THE BREAKFAST-TABLE.
THE PROFESSOR AT THE BREAKFAST-TABLE.
THE POET AT THE BREAKFAST-TABLE.
ELSIE VENNER.

By HENRY THOREAU.

ESSAYS AND OTHER WRITINGS.
WALDEN; OR, LIFE IN THE WOODS.
A WEEK ON THE CONCORD.

London: WALTER SCOTT, LIMITED, Paternoster Square.

Count Tolstoy's Works.

The following Volumes are already issued—

A RUSSIAN PROPRIETOR.

THE COSSACKS.

IVAN ILYITCH, AND OTHER STORIES.

MY RELIGION.

LIFE.

MY CONFESSION.

CHILDHOOD, BOYHOOD, YOUTH.

THE PHYSIOLOGY OF WAR.

ANNA KARÉNINA. 3/6.

WHAT TO DO?

WAR AND PEACE. (4 vols.)

THE LONG EXILE, ETC.

SEVASTOPOL.

THE KREUTZER SONATA, AND FAMILY HAPPINESS.

THE KINGDOM OF GOD IS WITHIN YOU.

WORK WHILE YE HAVE THE LIGHT.

THE GOSPEL IN BRIEF.

Uniform with the above—

IMPRESSIONS OF RUSSIA. By Dr. GEORG BRANDES.

Post 4to, Cloth, Price 1s.

PATRIOTISM AND CHRISTIANITY.

To which is appended a Reply to Criticisms of the Work.
By COUNT TOLSTOY.

1/- Booklets by Count Tolstoy.

Bound in White Grained Boards, with Gilt Lettering.

WHERE LOVE IS, THERE GOD IS ALSO.

THE TWO PILGRIMS.

WHAT MEN LIVE BY.

THE GODSON.

IF YOU NEGLECT THE FIRE, YOU DON'T PUT IT OUT.

WHAT SHALL IT PROFIT A MAN?

2/- Booklets by Count Tolstoy.

NEW EDITIONS, REVISED.

Small 12mo, Cloth, with Embossed Design on Cover, each containing
Two Stories by Count Tolstoy, and Two Drawings by
H. R. Millar. In Box, Price 2s. each.

Volume I. contains—

WHERE LOVE IS, THERE GOD IS ALSO.

THE GODSON.

Volume II. contains—

WHAT MEN LIVE BY.

WHAT SHALL IT PROFIT A MAN?

Volume III. contains—

THE TWO PILGRIMS.

IF YOU NEGLECT THE FIRE, YOU DON'T PUT IT OUT.

Volume IV. contains—

MASTER AND MAN.

Volume V. contains—

TOLSTOY'S PARABLES.

London: WALTER SCOTT, LIMITED, Paternoster Square.

EVERY-DAY HELP SERIES
OF USEFUL HAND-BOOKS. Price 6d. each,
OR IN ROAN BINDING, PRICE 1s.

Contributors—J. LANGDON DOWN, M.D., F.R.C.P.; HENRY POWER, M.B., F.R.C.S.; J. MORTIMER-GRANVILLE, M.D.; J. CRICHTON BROWNE, M.D., LL.D.; ROBERT FARQUHARSON, M.D. Edin.; W. S. GREENFIELD, M.D., F.R.C.P.; and others.

The Secret of a Clear Head.
Common Mind Troubles.
The Secret of a Good Memory.
Sleep and Sleeplessness.
The Heart and Its Function.
Personal Appearances in Health and Disease.
The House and Its Surroundings.
Alcohol: Its Use and Abuse.
Exercise and Training.
Baths and Bathing.
Health in Schools.
The Skin and Its Troubles.
How to make the Best of Life.
Nerves and Nerve-Troubles.
The Sight, and How to Preserve It.
Premature Death: Its Promotion and Prevention.
The Nervous System.
Change, as a Mental Restorative.
Youth: Its Care and Culture.
The Gentle Art of Nursing the Sick.
The Care of Infants and Young Children.
Invalid Feeding, with Hints on Diet.
Every-day Ailments, and How to Treat Them.
How to do Business. A Guide to Success in Life.
How to Behave. Manual of Etiquette and Personal Habits.
How to Write. A Manual of Composition and Letter Writing.
How to Debate. With Hints on Public Speaking.
Don't: Directions for avoiding Common Errors of Speech.
The Parental Don't: Warnings to Parents.
Why Smoke and Drink. By James Parton.
Elocution. By T. R. W. Pearson, M.A., of St. Catharine's College, Cambridge, and F. W. Waithman, Lecturers on Elocution.

London: WALTER SCOTT, LIMITED, Paternoster Square.

Crown 8vo, Cloth. Price 6s.

AN EXCEPTIONAL NOVEL.

By the Author of " The Woman Who Didn't."

PAULA:

A SKETCH FROM LIFE.

By VICTORIA CROSS.

The theme of this story presents a study of the conflict of Art and
Life. Paula Heywood, the daughter of a country parson, comes up to
London with her brother on the death of her father, who has endowed
his children with a brilliant education, but who leaves them without
means. Young Heywood manages to find pupils to whom he gives
music-lessons, while Paula becomes an unimportant "super" at a
theatre; they thus eke out a precarious living. Paula's ambitions,
however, are great. She is a girl of singular beauty, as well as of
singular powers, in which latter she has the vast belief of inexperience,
and she is bitterly discontent with their lot. She has written a play,
which she has tried in vain to get accepted. Through the medium of
Vincent Halham, a young Australian capitalist who is taking a rest
from work in London, she obtains an introduction to Reeves, the
manager of a West-end theatre. A strong attachment has meanwhile
sprung up between Halham and Paula; Reeves, however, finding how
much luck has thrown in his way, not only in the gifts and person of
the girl, but also in her play, will consent to produce it (Halham at the
time being unable to do so) only on the condition that Paula marries
him. Passionately absorbed for the time being in the assertion of her
individual powers and in devotion to her art, Paula renounces Halham
and consents to an anomalous marriage, to the realities of which she is
not long in awaking. She reaches the extreme heights of her artistic
ambition without having found happiness as a woman, and the woman
in her before long asserts itself. To sketch this dramatic and tragic
story further would only tend to spoil the reader's interest in it. While
intently realistic in detail, it is one which yet possesses all the movement
and interest of romance.

London : WALTER SCOTT, LIMITED, Paternoster Square.

THE SCOTT LIBRARY.

Cloth, Uncut Edges, Gilt Top.   Price 1s. 6d. per Volume.

VOLUMES ALREADY ISSUED—

May be had in the following Bindings :—Cloth, uncut edges, gilt top, 1s. 6d. ; Half-Morocco, gilt top, antique ; Red Roan, gilt edges, etc.

London : WALTER SCOTT, LIMITED, Paternoster Square.

The World's Great Novels.

Large Crown 8vo, Illustrated, 3s. 6d. each.

(Uniform with the New Edition of "Anna Karénina.")

A series of acknowledged masterpieces by the most eminent writers of fiction. Paper, type, and binding will all be of the most satisfactory description, and such as to make these volumes suitable either for presentation or for a permanent place in the library. Three volumes are now included; to these others will be added from time to time. The greatest pains has been taken over the new translations of Dumas' two most famous works to render them both faithful and idiomatic.

THE COUNT OF MONTE-CRISTO.

BY ALEXANDRE DUMAS.

With Sixteen Full-page Illustrations drawn by FRANK T. MERRILL, and over 1100 pages of letterpress, set in large clear type.

THE THREE MUSKETEERS.

BY ALEXANDRE DUMAS.

With Twelve Full-page Illustrations drawn by T. EYRE MACKLIN, a Photogravure Frontispiece Portrait of the Author, and over 600 pages of letterpress, printed from large clear type.

JANE EYRE.

BY CHARLOTTE BRONTË.

With Sixteen Full-page Illustrations, and Thirty-two Illustrations in the Text, by EDMUND H. GARRETT, and Photogravure Portrait of Charlotte Brontë. Printed in large clear type; 660 pages of letterpress.

Tolstoy's Great Masterpiece. New Edition of Anna Karénina.

ANNA KARÉNINA.

A NOVEL. BY COUNT TOLSTOY.

With Ten Illustrations drawn by PAUL FRÉNZENY, and a Frontispiece Portrait of Count Tolstoy in Photogravure.

"Other novels one can afford to leave unread, but *Anna Karénina* never; it stands eternally one of the peaks of all fiction."—*Review of Reviews.*

LONDON: WALTER SCOTT, LTD., PATERNOSTER SQUARE.

THE CANTERBURY POETS.

EDITED BY WILLIAM SHARP. Cloth, Cut and Uncut Edges, 1s.; Red Roan,
Gilt Edges, 2s. 6d.; Pad. Morocco, Gilt Edges, 5s.

A Superior Edition Bound in Art Linen, with Photogravure Frontispiece, 2s.

London : WALTER SCOTT, LIMITED, Paternoster Square.

16

*9 7 8 3 7 4 2 8 8 2 4 9 3 *